CLINICAL NEGLIGE
A PRACTITIONER'S HAN

CLINICAL NEGLIGENCE: A PRACTITIONER'S HANDBOOK

CECILY CAMERON
Solicitor, Partner, Henmans LLP

ELIZABETH-ANNE GUMBEL QC
Barrister, One Crown Office Row

OXFORD
UNIVERSITY PRESS

OXFORD
UNIVERSITY PRESS

Great Clarendon Street, Oxford OX2 6DP

Oxford University Press is a department of the University of Oxford.
It furthers the University's objective of excellence in research, scholarship,
and education by publishing worldwide in

Oxford New York

Auckland Cape Town Dar es Salaam Hong Kong Karachi
Kuala Lumpur Madrid Melbourne Mexico City Nairobi
New Delhi Shanghai Taipei Toronto

With offices in

Argentina Austria Brazil Chile Czech Republic France Greece
Guatemala Hungary Italy Japan Poland Portugal Singapore
South Korea Switzerland Thailand Turkey Ukraine Vietnam

Oxford is a registered trade mark of Oxford University Press
in the UK and in certain other countries

Published in the United States
by Oxford University Press Inc., New York

British Library Cataloguing in Publication Data
Data available

Library of Congress Cataloging in Publication Data
Cameron, Cecily
Clinical negligence: a practitioner's handbook / Cecily Cameron, Elizabeth-
Anne Gumbel.
p. cm.
Includes bibliographical references and index.
ISBN-13: 978-0-19-929964-5 (alk. paper) 1. Physicians—Malpractice—
Great Britain. 2. Medical personnel—Malpractice—Great Britain.
3. Actions and defenses—Great Britain. I. Gumbel, Elizabeth-Anne. II. Title.
KD2960.M55C36 2007
344.4104'11—dc22
                                                        2007036172

Typeset by Cepha Imaging Private Ltd., Bangalore, India
Printed in Great Britain
on acid-free paper by
Biddles Ltd., King's Lynn, Norfolk

ISBN 978-0-19-929964-5

1 3 5 7 9 10 8 6 4 2

ACKNOWLEDGEMENTS

We are grateful to all those who provided encouragement and support. In particular we wish to thank Henry Witcomb for his contribution to 'Public Provision', Susan Booker for 'Costs and Cash Flow', Kirsten Wall for the List of Websites, and not least Ellen Hughes for her invaluable help with the typescript. Any errors or omissions are our own.

CC

EAG

SUMMARY OF CONTENTS

CONTENTS

TABLE OF CASES

TABLE OF STATUTES

TABLE OF STATUTORY INSTRUMENTS

TABLE OF EUROPEAN LEGISLATION

INTRODUCTION

This book is intended to be a guide for personal injury practitioners conducting clinical negligence cases. It includes basic and practical advice for those with little experience of clinical negligence cases, as well as more detailed analysis of the law in this area. The authors hope this book will be helpful to those beginning to undertake clinical cases as well as to those whose main area of practice is clinical negligence. The book does not purport to cover standard personal injury topics such as assessment of quantum, which are more appropriately dealt with in specialist textbooks on that topic.

The authors have approached the work from their different areas of expertise as solicitor and counsel. Their respective contributions reflect the difference in approach and style of solicitors and counsel. We hope that the book will be of value to both professions. Although both authors' own practices are primarily claimant work, they intend the book to be of interest and practical use to both claimant and defendant lawyers and to experts involved in litigation.

It is axiomatic that the authors have described their own working practices and experience. This is not intended to be prescriptive but offers ideas for consideration. There is usually more than one way of doing things. The practice and procedure described should either be a starting point for the new practitioner to develop their own style or a benchmark for the experienced practitioner to compare with their own practice. The advice in this book has been tried and tested.

The book is arranged so as to mirror the life of a case. It begins with the basic legal principles that the practitioner must have in mind when assessing any new clinical negligence case. It then sets out the steps that the practitioner will need to take in litigating a claim and finishes with some precedents, further sources of information, and reading material. It reflects our understanding of law and procedure as at April 2007.

Cecily Cameron
Elizabeth-Anne Gumbel
April 2007

1

1

BREACH OF DUTY

A. Direct Liability and Vicarious Liability

Every individual clinician owes a duty of care to his patient and his patient **1.01** may sue him for breach of duty. In the case of private treatment and in the case of treatment by a general practitioner the claim is brought against the individual clinician. In the case of National Health Service (NHS) treatment in a hospital the claim is brought against the Health Authority or NHS Trust ('the NHS Authority') who was responsible for that hospital at the time the treatment was given. In some cases a different NHS Authority will have taken over responsibility by the time the claim is brought and the identity of the correct defendant should always be checked with the potential defendant before proceedings are issued.

The NHS Authority is vicariously liable for the acts of all its servants or agents **1.02** so that if any doctor, nurse, midwife, radiographer, cytologist, or other employee is found negligent the NHS Authority itself will be found liable. This principle was first established in the cases of *Gold v Essex County Council* [1942] 2 KB 293 and *Cassidy v Ministry of Health* [1951] 2 KB 343. Prior to these cases it had been held that the hospital's obligation only extended to selecting competent doctors and nurses and that they could only be liable if they failed to do that. In the case of *Hillyer v St Bartholomew's Hospital* [1909] 2 KB 820, Kennedy LJ found that a hospital was responsible for due care in the selection of staff but not for the actions of the staff when exercising their professional skill and judgment. The modern position is that an NHS Authority will be vicariously liable for the actions of all of its staff that are carried out in the course of their employment or closely connected to their employment. Such vicarious liability now extends even to criminal activities including a sexual or violent assault of a patient. See *L v Hesley Hall Ltd* [2001] 2 WLR 1311, and Chapter 23.

1.03 There is a further situation in which a patient may sue an NHS Authority and that is where the NHS Authority itself is alleged to be directly liable for its failure to provide the necessary facilities for competent treatment of the patient. Whilst liability is still in respect of the actions of servants or agents of the NHS Authority (who can only act through their servants or agents) the concept of direct liability is different, it applies to the errors of the organisation itself rather than individual clinicians' errors. An example of an NHS Authority being directly liable to a patient is the case of *Bull v Devon Area Health Authority* [1993] 4 Med LR 117. In that case the NHS Authority was found liable when an obstetrician took 68 minutes to attend to deliver a second twin and the baby suffered brain damage. Delay occurred as the hospital operated on two sites and the obstetrician was required to travel from one site to the other to attend to the patient. The Court of Appeal in dismissing the Health Authority's appeal confirmed at page 142 that:

> The system should have been set up so as to produce a registrar or consultant on the spot within 20 minutes, subject to some unforeseeable contingency . . . there was an interval of about an hour . . . this interval was much too long. Either there was a failure in the operation of the system, or it was too sensitive to hitches which fell short of the kind of major breakdown against which no system could be invulnerable.

1.04 In the case of *Jac Richards (a child suing by his mother and litigation friend Mrs Joanne Richards) v Swansea NHS Trust* [2007] EWHC 487, Mr Justice Field found at paragraphs 31 and 32:

> In the absence of any evidence from the defendant that there were logistical constraints on those attending Mrs Richards that prevented *Jac* being delivered within 45 minutes of 1.10pm I infer that there were no such constraints and I find that the claimant has established on the balance of probabilities that those attending Mrs Richards negligently failed to deliver *Jac* as fast as possible and that had they not been so negligent, *Jac* would have been born before 1.55pm and intact.

1.05 A similar approach was taken in *Bull v Devon Area Health Authority* [1993] 4 Med LR 117:

> The defendant contended that it had an adequate system for the provision of appropriate care and that the fact that it could not now say why no registrar was present did not mean that it was at fault. The trial judge decided the onus was on the

defendant to show that the situation arose without fault on its part and that it had failed to do so. His decision was upheld by the Court of Appeal.

B. Situations in which Clinical Negligence may be Alleged

There are a number of different situations in which a patient who has suffered **1.06** personal injury may seek to bring a claim for clinical negligence against an individual clinician or those vicariously liable for the clinician. The first task is to establish a relationship between the patient and the clinician which gives rise to a duty of care. The second task is to identify why the clinician is said to be in breach of that duty. The following list illustrates the broad range of circumstances in which a clinical negligence claim may be brought:

(i) failing to arrange to see a patient when requested to do so and when urgent assessment is required;

(ii) when seeing a patient (in a hospital/clinic or at home), failing to examine the patient competently or at all;

(iii) after examining a patient failing to diagnose the patient's condition competently within the expertise of the clinician;

(iv) if a diagnosis cannot be made confidently by the initial clinician, failing to refer the patient to an appropriate specialist doctor, hospital/clinic for further investigation including failing to arrange for the patient's immediate admission to hospital where that is required;

(v) after examining a patient failing to give the patient competent advice as to his/her condition and the appropriate options for treatment;

(vi) failing to prescribe the correct and/or any treatment for the patient when treatment is required;

(vii) prescribing the wrong treatment for a patient so as to further injure the patient;

(viii) failing to carry out treatment by way of surgical operation or other procedure competently so that the result is to cause additional injury to the patient rather than any benefit;

(ix) failing to advise on the options for treatment and the relative risks of different methods of treatment;

(x) failing to interpret the results of tests correctly so as to give advice on the need for further treatment or investigation;

(xi) failing to monitor a patient whilst in hospital before, during or after treatment;

(xii) failing to follow up the patient after examination or treatment when follow-up is necessary.

C. The Identity of the Defendant

1.07   The patient with a potential claim will first need to ascertain the correct identity of the defendant/defendants who are to be alleged to be responsible for the injury.

1.08   If the treatment is carried out in an NHS Hospital under the provisions of the NHS this will be the Health Authority or NHS Trust responsible for running the hospital at the relevant time. This may be the NHS Authority who was in place at the time or may be a different NHS Authority who has taken over responsibility from a former NHS Authority. The relevant authority will be responsible for all the staff in the hospital whether doctors, nurses, radiologists, or other staff. In these cases it will not be necessary to identify a particular individual as responsible for negligent treatment, it may be that the responsibility is with the whole team, for example, where a mother has not been adequately monitored in labour, this may be the joint responsibility of the consultant, the registrar, and the midwives.

1.09   Where treatment is paid for privately or through private health insurance the position is more complicated. In the case of private surgery it will be necessary to sue the surgeon individually. If there is an issue in respect of the care of the patient before or after the surgery it may also be necessary to sue the anaesthetist individually. Other members of the team including the nurses, physiotherapists, radiologists, etc may have been privately paid or may be employed by the hospital. If the hospital is a private hospital they will need to be a defendant. On the other hand, if the private surgery is carried out in an NHS Hospital the NHS Authority may be responsible for all of the staff other than the surgeon and anaesthetist. The position will always need to be carefully checked prior to the issue of proceedings.

1.10   Where allegations are made in respect of a general practitioner, the general practitioner will need to be identified and sued personally. Even within the same general practice doctors may be insured by different medical protection insurers. General practitioner notes usually do not identify individual practitioners and it is sensible when requesting general practitioner notes to ask the practice to identify which doctor has made each entry during the relevant period. Where a locum has been working in the practice or an on-call service used it will be necessary to identify the individual doctor who was concerned with the treatment of the patient.

1.11   Nurses and midwives working in general practitioner surgeries may be employed by the NHS or may be employed directly by the general practitioner surgery, the position again needs to be checked in every individual case.

If there is an issue in respect of the prompt attendance of an ambulance it may **1.12** also be necessary to sue the ambulance service. The ambulance authority will be vicariously liable for the actions of individual ambulance drivers. See *Kent v Griffiths and London Ambulance Service* [1999] Lloyd's Med Rep 58, CA.

D. Duty of Care and Standard of Care

The test that needs to be satisfied in law to establish negligence in respect of medi- **1.13** cal treatment is the same whether it arises from negligent advice, failure to warn, negligent technique in carrying out surgery, development or treatment of subsequent complications, or any other complaint. The test is set out in *Bolam v Friern Barnet Hospital Management Committee* [1957] 1 WLR 582:

> The test is the standard of the ordinary skilled man exercising and professing to have that special skill. A man need not possess the highest expert skill; it is well established law that it is sufficient if he exercises the ordinary skill of an ordinary competent man exercising that particular art . . . there may be one or more perfectly proper standards, and if he conforms with one of those proper standards then he is not negligent . . . a mere personal belief that a particular technique is best is no defence unless that belief is based on reasonable grounds.

The House of Lords followed and applied the *Bolam* test in *Maynard v West* **1.14** *Midlands Regional Health Authority* [1984] 1 WLR 634 but pointed out that:

> It is not enough to show that subsequent events show that there is a body of competent professional opinion which considers there was a wrong decision, if there also exists a body of professional opinion equally competent, which supports the decision as reasonable in the circumstances . . . a doctor who professes to exercise a special skill must exercise the ordinary skill of his speciality. Differences of opinion and practice exist, and will always exist, in the medical as in other professions. There is seldom any one answer exclusive of all others to problems of professional judgment. A court may prefer one body of opinion to another: but that is no basis for a conclusion of negligence.

In the case of *Sidaway v Board of Governors of the Bethlem Royal Hospital and the* **1.15** *Maudsley Hospital* [1985] 1 AC 871 the House of Lords approved the *Bolam* test as being: 'A rule that a doctor is not negligent if he acts in accordance with a practice accepted at the time as proper by an acceptable body of medical opinion even though other doctors adopt a different practice.'

It was stressed in the *Sidaway* case that the *Bolam* test clearly requires a differ- **1.16** ent degree of skill from a specialist in his own special field than from a general practitioner. The qualifications of the doctor carrying out the treatment will therefore be relevant. First, it is necessary to investigate whether the doctor was suitably qualified and experienced at all to carry out the surgery he undertook. Secondly, if he was so qualified it is necessary to investigate whether the standard of the treatment was below that of a competent doctor in the same field. In the case of *Shakoor (Administratrix of the Estate of Abdul Shakoor decd) v Kang Situ (Trading as Eternal Health Co)* [2001] 1 WLR 410, Bernard Livesey QC, sitting as a deputy High Court Judge, considered the standard of care required of a practitioner of alternative medicine. He stated that:

> When a court has to adjudicate on the standard of care given by an alternative medical practitioner it will, pace Bolitho, often (perhaps invariably) not be enough to judge him by the standard of the ordinary practitioner 'skilled in that particular art'; it will often be to have regard to the fact that the practitioner is practicing his art alongside orthodox medicine, the court will need to consider whether the standard of care adopted by the alternative practitioner has taken account of the implications of this fact. The implications may vary depending upon the area of expertise and specific act or omission which is under scrutiny in the individual case.

1.17 In *Whitehouse v Jordon* [1981] 1 WLR 246 the House of Lords considered the standard of care of an obstetrician attempting to deliver a baby by forceps. The allegation on behalf the claimant was that he had been damaged during the trial of forceps delivery by the force that had been applied. It was alleged that the obstetrician had pulled too long and too strongly on the claimant's head during the attempt to deliver. Further, it was alleged that the obstetrician had continued traction with the forceps after the obstruction of the ischial spines had been encountered so that the claimant's head had become stuck. In the House of Lords, Lord Edmund Davies described how the principal questions calling for decision were:

> (i) In what manner did Mr Jordan use the forceps?; and
> (ii) Was the manner consistent with the degree of skill which a member of his profession is required to exercise?

1.18 Lord Edmund Davies pointed out that it was unacceptable to ask whether Mr Jordan had committed an error of judgment. He stated:

> To say that a surgeon committed an error of clinical judgment is wholly ambiguous, for while some such errors may be completely consistent with the due exercise of professional skill, other acts or omissions in the course of exercising clinical judgment may be so glaringly below proper standards as to make a finding of negligence inevitable ... 'The test is the standard of the ordinary skilled man exercising and professing to have that special skill'. If a surgeon fails to measure up to that standard in any respect ('clinical judgment' or otherwise), he has been negligent and should be so adjudged.

1.19 In *Loveday v Renton and Wellcome Foundation Ltd* [1990] 1 MLR 117, Stuart-Smith LJ emphasised that in applying the *Bolam* test: 'The court is not concerned to decide the merits of one practice as opposed to others but only to determine if a respectable and responsible body of medical practitioners would have acted as the defendant acted.'

In any case where a claimant seeks to establish that they have been damaged by **1.20** the negligence of a medical practitioner, the burden of proof is on the claimant, it is for the claimant to prove that:

- on the balance of probabilities the medical practitioner was negligent in that his treatment fell below the proper standard expected of a practitioner at his level in his field of expertise carrying out the treatment at a specific date; and

- the damage alleged was caused by the particular treatment or lack of it that is alleged to be negligent.

In the case of *Lillywhite v University College London Hospitals' NHS Trust* **1.21** [2006] Lloyd's Rep Med 268, the Court of Appeal considered a case in which a Professor of Obstetrics had failed to identify a serious brain abnormality on an *in utero* ultrasound scan. Although the defendant could give no explanation for having failed to detect the abnormality, the judge concluded that the claimant had not established negligence. By a majority the Court of Appeal reversed the decision of the Judge and held the defendant had been negligent. The Court accepted that the claimant could not rely on the maxim of *res ipsa loquitur* but explained where the claimant has established that the defendant has missed an abnormality which must have been present then the defendant must give an explanation for doing so and cannot simply rely on the claimant not having proved negligence. Lord Justice Latham considered the case of *Ratcliffe v Plymouth and Torbay Health Authority* [1998] Lloyd's Rep Med 162 and stated:

> But inherent in all these passages is, it seems to me, the fact that in some cases the evidence produced by a claimant may be such as to require the court to focus with some care on the explanation given by a defendant to displace that which would otherwise be the inevitable inference from the claimant's case that negligence has been established. A good example which has many echos in the present case, is *Pithers v Leeds Teaching Hospitals NHS Trust* [2004] EWHC (QB) 1392. In that case . . . [the Judge] noted that the duty of care owed at the Leeds General Infirmary demanded a high standard of care and skill because the scan was, as he put it 'a scan with a focus'. He concluded that 'there is a heavy burden on Leeds when seeking to reconcile its incorrect visualizations with the exercise of all reasonable care and skill'. He held the claimant had established her case.

The Court of Appeal found that the claimant in the *Lillywhite* case should also **1.22** have been held to have established her case. Lord Justice Buxton stated:

> That the examination had in mechanical terms, been carried out with scrupulous care was a necessary condition of the examination not having been negligent, but it was not sufficient for that purpose . . . A professional man is required, in the law of negligence as well as in the law of contract, to display not just care, but care and skill.

1.23 In this case Lord Justice Buxton found:

> The reading of ultrasound images requires not just care, but also skill and judgement. The complaint in this case is that the requisite level of skill and judgement simply could not have been exercised, given that the results produced were so disastrously wrong; and given that an earlier reader, in the person of Mrs Wright, had not made the same errors. As [Lord Justice Latham] says this is not a case of res ipsa loquitur. But it is a case in which the outcome that Dr Rodeck attributed to his reading calls for an explanation.

> To say that an explanation is required is not to reverse the burden of proof, any more than the doctrine of res ipsa loquitur, when it applies (being a rule of evidence and not a rule of law) reverses the burden: see on that point the judgment of Hobhouse LJ in *Radcliffe* cited by Latham LJ in his para 26 and the treatment in Clerk & Lindsell (18th edition). The claimant retains the burden of persuasion; but given the need for an explanation that at least goes far enough to raise questions about the initial assumption of negligence.

1.24 Lord Justice Buxton concluded that in the *Lillywhite* case the explanations advanced by the defence were neither possible nor plausible and did not discharge the inference of negligence which was properly made from what the claimant could prove had occurred.

E. Application of the *Bolam* Test to Advice

1.25 The advice given, or not given, prior to surgery is a frequent cause of complaint and potential litigation. The House of Lords considered in the case of *Sidaway* the application of the *Bolam* test to advice given prior to treatment (in that case spinal surgery). Lord Diplock at page 893D stated:

> In English jurisprudence the doctor's relationship with his patient which gives rise to the normal duty of care to exercise his skill and judgment to improve the patient's health in any particular respect in which the patient has sought his aid, has hitherto been treated as a single comprehensive duty covering all the ways in which a doctor is called upon to exercise his skill and judgment in the improvement of the physical or mental condition of the patient for which his services either as a general practitioner or specialist have been engaged. The general duty is not subject to dissection into a number of component parts to which different criteria of what satisfy the duty of care apply, such as diagnosis, treatment, advice (including warning of any risks of something going wrong) however skilfully the treatment advised is carried out. The *Bolam* case itself embraced failure to advise the patient of the risk involved in electric shock treatment as one of the allegations of negligence against the surgeon as well as negligence in the actual carrying out of the treatment in which that risk did result in injury to the patient. In modern medicine and surgery such dissection of the various things a doctor had to do in the exercise of his whole duty of care owed to his patient is neither legally meaningful nor medically practicable.

The usual test for establishing negligence applies whatever the purpose for **1.26** which advice was given. In *Gold v Haringey Health Authority* [1988] QB 481, the Court of Appeal (in the context of contraceptive advice) reversed the finding of the trial judge who had held that a different test applied to advice given in a non-therapeutic context to that given in a therapeutic context. Stephen Brown LJ summarised the position:

> In my judgment the test laid down in *Bolam v Friern Hospital Management Committee* as further considered and explained by Lord Diplock in *Sidaway v Board of Governors of Bethlem Royal Hospital* should be applied to the facts of this case. The judge appears to have been persuaded to find a distinction between advice given in a 'therapeutic' and a 'non-therapeutic' context. Such a distinction is wholly unwarranted and artificial.

The extent to which advice in respect of risks needs to be given was further **1.27** explored in the Court of Appeal in the case of *Pearce v United Bristol Healthcare NHS Trust* [1999] PIQR P53. In that case the claimant who suffered a stillbirth complained she had not been properly advised of the respective risks of induction of labour, Caesarean section, and additional delay through total lack of intervention. The Court of Appeal stated:

> Obviously the doctor, in determining what to tell a patient, has to take into account all the relevant considerations, which include the ability of the patient to comprehend what he has to say to him or her and the state of the patient at the particular time, both from the physical point of view and the emotional point of view. There can often be situations where a course different from the normal has to be employed. However, where there is what can realistically be called a 'significant risk', in the ordinary event, as I have already indicated, the patient is entitled to be informed of the risk.

The extent to which there is an obligation to advise patients of the risks of the **1.28** treatment they are recommended may be affected by the implementation of the Human Rights Act 1998. A case in Strasbourg suggests that there may be a breach of Article 8 of the European Convention on Human Rights if an authority fails to provide an individual with the necessary information to make proper decisions about his/her well-being, health, and home. In *Guerra v Italy* (1998) 26 EHRR 357, the court found a violation of Article 8 where the applicants were not provided with sufficient information about the risks to their health from pollution from a nearby factory. Similar principles could in certain circumstances apply in respect of information about medical treatment given after the Human Rights Act 1998 came into force.

F. The Exceptional Treatment of Failure to Warn Cases

In *Chester v Afshar* [2005] 1 AC 134, the House of Lords considered the posi- **1.29** tion where a surgeon had failed to give adequate warnings about the outcome of spinal surgery. The surgery carried a 1–2 per cent chance of cauda equine syndrome. The claimant would not have undergone the particular operation on the day she did if she had been properly warned. She could not, however, state that she would not have undergone the operation on a different day. The risk of cauda equine syndrome remained the same whenever the claimant had the operation. Unfortunately, the risk in fact materialised on the date the claimant had the operation.

1.30 In these circumstances the only connection between the failure to warn and the claimant sustaining injury was that the risk of non-negligent injury occurred on a day that the claimant would not in fact have undergone surgery had she been adequately warned.

1.31 Had the evidence entitled the Judge to conclude that the claimant, if warned, would never have had the surgery she would on conventional principles have been entitled to recover damages. The difficulty the case presents is how to achieve a result which recognises that the negligent failure to give advice has led to a different outcome, yet the outcome if the warning had been given cannot be ascertained with any certainty.

1.32 Lord Bingham in a dissenting speech stated that:

> If failure to warn and the occurrence of injury which should have been the subject of the warning are, without more, enough to found a successful claim then the claimant would presumably succeed even in a case like *Smith v Barking, Havering and Brentwood Health Authority* [1994] 5 Med LR 285 where it is found on the balance of probabilities that the claimant would have consented to the operation even if properly advised.

1.33 In the case of *Smith v Barking, Havering and Brentwood Health Authority* [1994] 5 Med LR 285, the situation was that the risk would have materialised in any event, as the judge found the claimant would have had the operation in any event. In the case of *Smith* the claimant was awarded £3,000 for the shock of becoming tetraplegic without having been warned. It was agreed if she had succeeded in showing she would not have undergone the operation the total damages would have been £12,500 to include a sum for the accelerated onset of tetraplegia.

1.34 In the *Chester* case, because the claimant would not have had the operation on the same day, she recovered damages in full even though the risks on another day would have been the same. The risk was not increased by the negligent failure to warn. However, on the balance of probabilities because the risk was only 1–2 per cent it would not have materialised on a different day and the damage would have been avoided. The House of Lords acknowledged that they were creating a new exception to the general principles of tort law in finding that the claimant should recover because the failure to warn had deprived the claimant of a choice and on policy grounds the test of causation was satisfied.

The *Chester v Afshar* case is therefore another example of an exception to the gen- **1.35**
eral principles of tort law being created by the House of Lords. The case of
McFarlane v Tayside Health Board [2000] 2 AC 59, was an exception to the normal rules for recovery based on placing the claimant in the position she would
have been in if the negligence had not occurred. That is, if negligence in failing to
sterilise a woman caused the birth of a healthy child and the claimant cannot
recover for the financial consequences of looking after a healthy child then the
claimant is not put in the position she would have been in but for the negligence.
In the case of *Parkinson v St James and Seacroft University Hospital NHS Trust*
[2002] QB 266, Lady Justice Hale (as she then was) described how:

> The true analysis is that this is a limitation on the damages which would otherwise
> be recoverable on normal principles. There is therefore no need to take that limita-
> tion any further than it was taken in *McFarlane*.

In the case of *Fairchild v Glenhaven Funeral Services Ltd* [2003] 1 AC 32, the **1.36**
claimant suffered mesothelioma after exposure to asbestos dust while employed
by a series of different employers. The claimants could not prove that on the balance of probabilities the onset of the disease was due to any particular employer
or that it was due to cumulative exposure. The House of Lords held that in these
exceptional circumstances it was not necessary to prove which employer caused
the disease. In that case Lord Nicholls explained how:

> The present appeals are another example of such circumstances where good policy
> reasons exist for departing from the usual threshold 'but for' test of causation . . .
> A former employee's liability to identify which particular period of wrongful expo-
> sure brought about the onset of the disease ought not in all justice to preclude recov-
> ery of compensation . . . I would not use the phraseology of legal inference the
> phraseology tends to obscure the fact that when applying the principle described
> above the court is not, by a process of inference concluding that the ordinary 'but for'
> standard of causation is satisfied. Instead the court is applying a different and less
> stringent test. It were best if this were recognized openly.

Chester v Afshar can therefore be viewed as a new exception to the general applica- **1.37**
tion of the law of tort and it may be said as it was by Lady Justice Hale in *Parkinson*
that there is no need to take the limitation further than it was taken in the case of
Chester itself. This appears already to have been the position adopted by the Court
in the cases of *Beary v Pall Mall Investments* [2005] EWCA Civ 415 and *Benedict
White v Paul Davidson & Taylor* [2003] EWCA Civ 1511.

In the *Beary* case, in the Court of Appeal, Lord Justice Dyson pointed out that in **1.38**
Chester v Afshar:

> It was accepted by the majority that their decision amounted to a departure from
> established principles of causation which was not justified except for good reasons:
> see per Lord Steyn at [20] and at [24] where he said that the claimant's 'right of
> autonomy and dignity can and ought to be vindicated by a narrow and modest

departure from traditional causation principles'. Lord Hope said at [85] that in the unusual circumstances of that case, justice required the normal approach on causation to be modified. He concluded at [87] that to leave the patient who would find the decision difficult without a remedy would render the doctor's duty to inform useless in cases where it might be needed most. On policy grounds, therefore, he held that the test of causation was satisfied in that case. Lord Walker essentially adopted the same reasoning as Lord Steyn and Lord Hope.

1.39   In the case of *Benedict White v Paul Davidson & Taylor,* the Court of Appeal also refused to apply the reasoning in *Chester v Afshar* to a claim involving negligent handling of litigation by a solicitor. In that case Lady Justice Arden stated at paragraphs 40 and 42:

> In my judgment [the case of *Chester*] does not establish a new general rule in causation. It is an application of the principle established in *Fairchild v Glenhaven Funeral Services Ltd* [2003] 1 AC 32 that in exceptional circumstances, rules as to causation may be modified on policy grounds . . . None of the long-established authorities on causation was over-ruled by the House of Lords in *Chester v Afshar*. For these reasons it would not, in my judgment, be right for this court to apply *Chester v Afshar* in preference to those traditional principles already summarized by Ward LJ. The basic rule remains that a tortfeasor is not liable for harm when his wrongful conduct did not cause that harm.

1.40   In the case of *Gregg v Scott* [2005] 2 AC 176, Lady Hale also emphasised the exceptional aspect of the decision in *Chester v Afshar* and stated:

> Well settled principles may be developed or modified to meet new situations and new problems: the decisions in *Fairchild v Glenhaven Funeral Services Ltd* [2003] 1 AC 32 and *Chester v Afshar* [2005] 1 AC 134 are good examples. But those two cases were dealing with particular problems which could not be remedied without altering the principles applicable to the great majority of personal injury cases which give rise to no real injustice or practical problem.

1.41   The message from cases following *Chester v Afshar* is clearly that it represents an exception to the general principles of causation. It is likely to be confined to similar cases rather than being of general application. The fact that the House of Lords have recently been prepared to make such exceptions in three personal injury cases opens the door to possible further exceptions in cases where the merits clearly call for such an application of policy. Identifying where the Court will be prepared to do this is of course enormously difficult. The prospect of exceptions increases the difficulty for practitioners representing both claimants and defendants in giving confident advice on the merits of a clinical negligence claim.

G. Examples of the Application of the *Bolam* Test by the Courts

1.42   In the case of *Bolitho v City and Hackney Health Authority* [1998] Lloyd's Rep Med 26 the House of Lords considered the implications of the *Bolam* test.

Lord Browne-Wilkinson considered the argument put on behalf of the claimant: 'that the Judge had wrongly treated the *Bolam* test as requiring him to accept the views of one truthful body of expert professional advice even though he was un-persuaded of its logical force.'

It was argued that if this were the position whenever a defendant could call a **1.43** truthful witness to say the practice adopted by the treating doctor was in accordance with a body of sound medical opinion the defendant would succeed in dismissing the claim. This would mean that even if the treatment defied logic it would not be negligent if other doctors also adopted it. Lord Browne-Wilkinson explained the position as follows:

> In my view, the court is not bound to hold that a defendant doctor escapes liability for negligent treatment or diagnosis just because he leads evidence from a number of medical experts who are genuinely of the opinion that the defendant's treatment or diagnosis accorded with sound medical practice. In the *Bolam* case itself, McNair J stated that the defendant had to have acted in accordance with the practice accepted by a 'responsible body of medical men'. Later at p.588 he referred to 'a standard of practice recognized as proper by a competent reasonable body of opinion' . . . in *Maynard's* case Lord Scarman refers to a 'respectable' body of professional opinion. The use of these adjectives—responsible, reasonable and respectable—all show that the court has to be satisfied that the exponents of the body of opinion relied upon can demonstrate that such opinion has a logical basis. In particular in cases involving the weighing of risks against benefits, the judge before accepting a body of opinion as being responsible, reasonable or respectable, will need to be satisfied that in forming their views, the experts have directed their minds to the question of comparative risks and benefits and reached a defensible conclusion on the matter.

Lord Browne-Wilkinson went on to accept in terms that if a professional opinion **1.44** is not capable of withstanding logical analysis, the judge is entitled to hold that the opinion is not reasonable or logical. That is, ultimately it is the Judge not the expert who determines whether a medical procedure or practice is acceptable as conforming to the standards expected of a particular type of medical practitioner at a given date. Considerable help will of course always be required from the expert evidence for the Judge to determine the question of acceptability. Lord Browne-Wilkinson considered it was likely to be rare that a judge would reject a genuinely held medical opinion as unreasonable. Nevertheless there may be cases where this argument succeeds. The fact that the defendant can call evidence supporting the practice adopted is not therefore conclusive to the outcome of the case.

It is clearly important that the judge should be provided with literature and other **1.45** evidence supporting the procedure adopted by the treating doctor in order for him to understand the logical basis of adopting that procedure.

A further respect in which the role of the Judge is to adjudicate on the opposing **1.46** medical experts' views and reach a conclusion of his own was considered in the case of *Penney, Palmer and Cannon v East Kent Health Authority* [2000] Lloyd's Rep Med 41. This case involved claims by three women whose cervical smears had been reported as negative. Each of the three women went on to develop invasive adenocarcinoma of the cervix which required radical and invasive treatment including hysterectomy. The trial was on the issue of liability only. Both causation and quantum were reserved. The issue for the Judge was whether the primary screeners had been negligent in reading each of the smears as negative, thereby terminating the investigation of those smears. A finding that the smear was 'borderline' or 'inadequate' would have led to it being repeated.

1.47 Despite the trial focusing on liability, none of the screeners who had read the smears gave evidence and there was no direct evidence as to the training and management of the screeners. The evidence called on each side was expert evidence from pathologists and a total of five pathologists gave evidence.

1.48 The defendant called expert evidence to support the proposition that:

> The abnormalities to be seen on the slides would not have been recognized as such by a reasonably competent cytoscreener at the time. In those circumstances the classification of the slides as 'negative' could properly have been made by a reasonably competent cytoscreener.

1.49 The defendant argued that that evidence was a complete defence within the *Bolam* test. In the Court of Appeal the defendant argued that the Judge had been wrong in failing to apply the *Bolam* test to the issues in the case.

1.50 The Court of Appeal analysed the position as follows:

> The *Bolam* test has no application where what the Judge is required to do is to make findings of fact. This is so even when those findings of fact are the subject of conflicting expert evidence. Thus in this case there were three questions which the Judge had to answer:
> (i) What was to be seen in the slides?
> (ii) At the relevant time could a screener exercising reasonable care fail to see what was on the slide?
> (iii) Could a reasonably competent screener, aware of what a screener exercising reasonable care would observe on the slide, treat the slide as negative?

1.51 As far as the issue of what was on the slides was concerned the Judge could not be expected to determine this without the help of expert evidence; however once he had heard the conflicting evidence in this respect it was ultimately a matter for him to determine as a question of fact what the slides showed. Once the Judge had resolved this issue he then needed to answer the second and third questions applying the *Bolam* test. The Court of Appeal described how at that stage:

> Whether the screener was in breach of duty would depend on the training and the amount of knowledge a screener should have had in order to properly perform his or her task at that time and how easy it was to discern what the Judge had found was

on the slide. These issues involved both questions of opinion as to the standards of care which the screeners should have exercised.

H. Summary

The factual situation in a clinical negligence case is frequently complex and it **1.52** may need a number of experts in different areas of specialism to address the standard of care that the claimant has received and the reasons for the poor outcome. The task of the lawyers should be to give clear instructions to the experts so that they can address the issues on liability and causation that the court will need to determine. Whilst the answers to the relevant questions may involve difficult medical analysis the questions should be relatively easy to state once the factual situation has been correctly analysed by the lawyers. In each case the questions need to be tailored to the particular facts but should be directed at eliciting:

- What happened to the claimant which left him with the injury of which he complains?
- Was any clinician who treated or failed to treat the claimant failing to act competently within the *Bolam* test?
- Would competent treatment on the balance of probabilities have avoided some injury?
- What would have been the claimant's condition and prognosis with competent treatment?

2

CAUSATION

A. The Problem

In essence, to succeed in a claim for clinical negligence the claimant must first **2.01** prove that the defendant owed him/her a duty of care. Secondly, the claimant must prove that the standard of clinical care provided was below a competent level. Thirdly, he must show that the lack of competent care caused the injury complained of. Proving causation can be the most difficult aspect of the claim.

One obvious problem in a clinical negligence case is that the claimant usually has **2.02** a clinical problem before any treatment commenced. It is necessary for the claimant to prove that it was the alleged treatment, or lack of it, which caused the injury and the loss and damage complained of rather than the natural progression of the underlying problem.

There are three situations in clinical negligence cases that give rise to different **2.03** causation issues:

- the issue of what would have happened if different treatment had actually been given;
- the issue of what would have happened if different treatment had been offered to the claimant;
- the issue of what difference competent treatment would have made to the claimant's condition and prognosis.

B. The Balance of Probabilities Test

2.04 If the issue is what would have happened if different treatment had been given, then the claimant needs to prove that if he/she had received competent treatment a particular result would have followed. This is the situation where what the claimant needs to prove is a matter of historical fact. The claimant must prove on a balance of probabilities that the result alleged would have resulted after competent treatment.

2.05 For example, a child injured through mismanagement of the mother's labour and the child's delivery must prove on the balance of probabilities that with competent care he would have been delivered as a healthy undamaged baby. If the claimant can prove it is 51 per cent likely that competent care would have led to safe delivery the claimant will recover damages assessed on the basis of 100 per cent compensation.

2.06 In the case of *Hotson v East Berkshire Health Authority* [1987] AC 750, the claimant suffered a hip injury that the defendant negligently failed to diagnose. There was an identifiable negligent act on the part of the defendant. However, even with competent diagnosis the claimant would only have had a 25 per cent chance of recovery. That is, on the balance of probabilities, the claimant would have been no better off with competent care. The House of Lords stated that unless the claimant could show that on the balance of probabilities he would have been better off he could not recover at all.

2.07 In a different situation, in the case of *Wilsher v Essex Area Health Authority* [1988] 1 AC 1074, the claimant suffered blindness following treatment in the special care baby unit. It was accepted that there had been negligence in that a junior doctor had inserted a catheter in the claimant's umbilical vein instead of the umbilical artery. There were a number of different factors identified that could have led to his injury, one of which was the administration of excess oxygen. The House of Lords confirmed that it was for the claimant to prove on the balance of probabilities that the administration of excess oxygen had caused his injury and that he had failed to do so.

2.08 As Lord Reid explained in *Davies v Taylor* [1974] AC 207:

> When the question is whether a certain thing is or is not true—whether a certain event did or did not happen—then the Court must decide one way or the other. There is no question of chance or probability. Either it did or did not happen. But the standard of civil proof is the balance of probabilities. If the evidence shows a balance in favour of it having happened, then it is proved that it did in fact happen.

The same test applies when the question is: what would have happened with **2.09** competent treatment? If on the balance of probabilities the claimant would have recovered then his recovery is treated as a certainty. If on the balance of probabilities he would not have recovered then that failure is also treated as a certainty.

A further complication arises when the alleged negligence involves an omission. **2.10** In this situation there is a two-stage test as explained by the House of Lords in *Bolitho v City and Hackney Health Authority* [1998] Lloyd's Rep Med 26. Lord Browne-Wilkinson described how:

> Where as in the present case, a breach of a duty of care is proved or admitted, the burden still lies on the [Claimant] to prove that such breach caused the injury suffered . . . In all cases the primary question is one of fact: did the wrongful act cause the injury? But in cases where the breach of duty consists of an omission to do an act which ought to be done (eg, the failure by a doctor to attend) that factual inquiry, is by definition, in the realms of hypothesis. The question is what would have happened if an event, which by definition did not occur, had occurred.

In dealing with the issue of causation in respect of omissions the claimant has two **2.11** possible ways of proving that the negligence caused his injury. Where (as in *Bolitho*) the allegation is that a senior doctor ought to have been called then the claimant may prove on the balance of probabilities, *either*:

- that had the senior doctor been summonsed then that particular doctor would have administered such treatment as would have saved the claimant from injury.

  In this situation, causation is proved even if failure by the senior doctor to administer the treatment would not have been negligent within the *Bolam* test;

  or:

- that had the senior doctor been summonsed then if he had failed to administer the treatment he would have been negligent within the *Bolam* test.

  In practical terms, if evidence is available from the senior doctor who would have been called and he states he would have given the treatment, then the claimant has proved causation. If on the other hand the doctor states he would not have given the treatment then enquiry is necessary as to whether such failure would have been negligent within the *Bolam* test. If it would be negligent the claimant proves causation, if it would not, he fails to prove causation.

C. Absence of Choice

Secondly, there is the situation where the claimant has, through the defendant's **2.12** negligence, missed the opportunity to undergo treatment or to avoid a situation or risk. Again in this situation the claimant must prove on a balance of probabilities that he would have done something different in the absence of negligence. In this situation it is necessary for the Judge to answer the hypothetical question: what would the claimant have done if the defendant had given competent advice?

2.13 An example of this situation is the case of *Newell and Newell v Goldenberg* [1995] 6 Med LR 371. In that case the issue was what the claimants would have done had they been properly advised of the risks of failure of a vasectomy operation. The claimants needed to prove that on the balance of probabilities they would have taken other additional contraceptive measures. The Judge found that had they been given competent advice they would have been content to take the risk of relying on the husband's vasectomy. The Judge found that Mrs Newell would not have undergone a sterilisation operation, which would in any event have been contraindicated. The claimants having proved breach of duty received only £500 damages to compensate them for the anxiety and distress of finding Mrs Newell was pregnant. They failed in respect of all other heads of damage as they could not prove on the balance of probabilities the outcome would have been different. That is they could not prove on the balance of probabilities that the claimants would have instigated sufficient additional contraception to avoid a pregnancy.

2.14 A similar situation arises in cases where the claimant has not been warned of all the risks of surgery but would have made the same choice even with a fuller account of the risks. In these cases it cannot be shown on the balance of probabilities that the outcome would have been different with competent advice and warnings. An example of this is the case of *Smith v Barking, Havering and Brentwood Health Authority* [1994] 5 Med LR 285.

D. Loss of a Chance

2.15 In the third situation the future outcome of the defendant's negligent act depends on the hypothetical action of a third party. In this situation the claimant only needs to prove that he/she has lost the chance of achieving a particular result. This chance may be significantly less than 50 per cent but the claimant will only recover damages assessed in the proportion of the lost chance.

2.16 In *Anderson v Davis* [1993] PIQR Q87, the claimant recovered two-thirds of his alleged loss of earnings as a lecturer on the basis that he had had a two-thirds chance of obtaining promotion to this job. In *Doyle v Wallace* [1998] PIQR Q146 the claimant recovered damages on the basis that she had a 50 per cent chance of becoming a teacher which was lost as a result of her injury. In *Langford v Hebran* [2001] EWCA Civ 361 the Court of Appeal approved an award of damages for future loss of earnings based on the claimant's percentage chance of reaching various levels of achievement as a professional kick-boxer.

As discussed above in the case of *Chester v Afshar,* the Court did not award dam- **2.17**
ages on the basis of conventional causation principles but made a specific exception in respect of a failure to warn case.

E. Foreseeability

The claimant must show on a balance of probabilities that the defendant caused **2.18**
the injury. The claimant must also show it was foreseeable if the clinician was
negligent the claimant would suffer injury of the type in fact suffered. In the case
of *Brown v Lewisham and North Southwark Health Authority* [1999] Lloyd's Med
Rep 110, Lord Justice Beldam set out the position:

> A doctor is obliged to exercise the care and skill of a competent doctor. He must take
> care in the examination, diagnosis and treatment of his patient's condition to pre-
> vent injury to his health from risks which a competent practitioner would foresee as
> likely to result from his failure to do so. He is not a clairvoyant nor if he tells his
> patient that he can find nothing wrong is he liable if his patient has a condition
> which was not discoverable by competent examination. The public policy of limit-
> ing liability of tortfeasors by the control mechanism of foreseeability seems to me to
> be as necessary in cases of medical as in any other type of negligence. I do not see on
> what policy ground it would be fair or just to hold a doctor to be in breach of duty
> who failed to diagnose an asymptomatic and undetectable illness merely because he
> was at fault in the management of a correctly diagnosed but unrelated condition. In
> short it must be shown that the injury suffered by the patient was within the risk
> from which it was the doctor's duty to protect him.

The test is based on that applied by Lord Bridge in *Caparo Industries plc v Dickman* **2.19**
[1990] 2 AC 605, where he pointed out: 'It is never sufficient to ask simply
whether A owes B a duty of care. It is always necessary to determine the scope of
the duty by reference to the kind of damage from which A must take care to save
B harmless.'

In the case of *Rahman v Arearose Ltd and University College London NHS Trust* **2.20**
[2001] QB 251, the claimant lost the sight in one eye and suffered psychiatric
injury after an assault followed by negligent medical treatment. Complex issues
of causation arose in respect of the responsibility of the respective defendants for
the psychiatric injury. Laws LJ explained that:

> in all these cases the real question is, what is the damage for which the defendant
> under consideration should be held responsible . . . [the question] in truth can only
> be understood, in light of the answer to the question, from what kind of harm was it
> the defendant's duty to guard the claimant. Novus actus interveniens, the eggshell
> skull, and (in the case of multiple torts) the concept of multiple tortfeasors are all no
> more and no less than tools or mechanisms which the law has developed to articulate
> in practice the extent of any liable defendant's responsibility for the loss and damage
> which the claimant has suffered.

2.21 In the case of *Jolley v London Borough of Sutton* [2000] 1 WLR 1082, the House of Lords examined the general position in respect of foreseeability of injury in personal injury cases and Lord Hoffmann summarised the position as follows:

> It is also agreed that the plaintiff must show that the injury which he suffered fell within the scope of the council's duty and that in cases of physical injury, the scope of the duty is determined by whether or not the injury fell within a description which could be said to have been reasonably foreseeable. *Donoghue v Stevenson* [1932] AC 562 of course established the general principle that reasonable foreseeability of physical injury to another generates a duty of care. The further proposition that reasonable foreseeability also governs the question of whether the injury comes within the scope of that duty had to wait until *Overseas Tankship (UK) Ltd v Morts Dock and Engineering Co Ltd (The Wagon Mound)* [1961] A.C. 388 ('*The Wagon Mound No 1*') for authoritative recognition. Until then, there was a view that the determination of liability involved a two-stage process. The existence of a duty depended upon whether injury of some kind was foreseeable. Once such a duty had been established, the defendant was liable for any injury which had been 'directly caused' by an act in breach of that duty, whether such injury was reasonably foreseeable or not. But the present law is that unless the injury is of a description which was reasonably foreseeable, it is (according to taste) 'outside the scope of the duty' or 'too remote'.
>
> It is also agreed that what must have been foreseen is not the precise injury which occurred but injury of a given description. The foreseeability is not as to the particulars but the genus. And the description is formulated by reference to the nature of the risk which ought to have been foreseen. So, in *Hughes v Lord Advocate* [1963] AC 837 the foreseeable risk was that a child would be injured by falling in the hole or being burned by a lamp or by a combination of both. The House of Lords decided that the injury which actually materialized fell within this description, notwithstanding that it involved an unanticipated explosion of the lamp and consequent injuries of unexpected severity. Like my noble and learned friend Lord Steyn, I can see no inconsistency between anything said in *The Wagon Mound No 1* and the speech of Lord Reid in *Hughes v Lord Advocate*. The 2 cases were dealing with altogether different questions. In the former, it was agreed that damage by burning was not damage of a description which could reasonably be said to have been foreseeable. The plaintiffs argued that they were nevertheless entitled to recover by the two-stage process I have described. It was this argument which was rejected. *Hughes v Lord Advocate* starts from the principle accepted in *The Wagon Mound No 1* and is concerned with whether the injury which happened was of a description which was reasonably foreseeable.

2.22 In a clinical negligence case it is therefore not necessary that a negligent clinician should have been able to foresee the precise mechanism of the injury that might occur in the absence of competent treatment. As described by Lord Hoffmann in the *Jolley* case: 'what must have been foreseen is not the precise injury which occurred but injury of a given description. The foreseeability is not as to the particulars but the genus.' A good example of this is found in the case of *Wisniewski v Central Manchester Health Authority* [1998] Lloyd's Rep Med 223. This was a cerebral palsy case in which the cause of injury was strangulation as the umbilical cord was looped around the baby's neck and tightened as he travelled down the birth canal. The Court of Appeal confirmed the Judge's finding that although the precise mechanism of this injury was not foreseeable it was harm of the type that the defendant was required to take steps to address and that the defendant should have delivered the claimant by Caesarean section at an earlier time thereby avoiding the injury that in fact occurred.

F. *Gregg v Scott*

The case of *Gregg v Scott* [2005] 2 AC 176 concerned the negligent delay follow- **2.23** ing a failure by a general practitioner to refer a patient with a lump under the left arm who had non-Hodgkin's lymphoma. The assessment of the difference in outcome between competent prompt diagnosis and negligence delayed diagnosis is on any view difficult from both a medical and a legal point of view.

The arguments in the House of Lords in this case focused on whether a claimant **2.24** whose diagnosis of cancer had been negligently delayed could recover for the loss of the chance to be 'cured' when that chance was inevitably and unavoidably less than 50 per cent. That is, whether a man who, on the balance of probabilities, even with competent care would not have recovered can be said to have lost something by his chance of recovery being reduced even further below 50 per cent.

The House of Lords pointed out that if the delayed diagnosis (on the balance of **2.25** probabilities), caused the claimant some loss such as increased pain and suffering, distress, requirement for more care, or even loss of expectation of life then these items could be claimed for and recovered (the conventional damages claim). This type of approach was seen as uncontroversial (although not claimed or recovered in this case). The controversial issue was that the claimant sought to recover a percentage of the loss he would have recovered if he could have shown prompt diagnosis would have avoided the cancer altogether or led to a cure (the loss of a chance claim).

The difference in approach of the majority and the minority of the House of **2.26** Lords was described and explained by the House of Lords as a difference in legal analysis. The central question being whether it is necessary for the claimant to show that on a balance of probabilities he would have recovered without negligence or whether the reduced chance of recovery is in itself the loss of something of value.

As Lord Hoffmann described: 'To say the claimant can therefore obtain damages **2.27** for the reduction of his chances of survival assumes in his favour that a reduction in the chance of survival is a recoverable head of damage.'

2.28 Lord Hoffmann (in the majority) considered to allow Mr Gregg to recover would require departure from both *Hotson* and *Wilsher*.

2.29 Lord Nicholls and Lord Hope (in the minority) considered the correct approach should be to assess the claimant's lost opportunity, that is to treat the case like that of *Kitchen v Royal Air Force, Chaplin v Hicks,* and *Allied Maples v Simmons and Simmons.* However, the minority recognised that loss of a chance in clinical negligence cases is very difficult to evaluate and even more difficult in cancer cases.

2.30 Lord Nicholls' solution would have been simply that: 'A patient should have an appropriate remedy where he loses the very thing it was the doctor's duty to protect.' He considered that where the claimant suffers a 'diminution of his prospects of recovery by reason of medical negligence whether of diagnosis or treatment that diminution constitutes actionable damage'.

2.31 The division of view as described by Lord Nicholls was a difference in perception as to what constitutes injustice. Lord Nicholls stated: 'Some believe a remedy is essential and that a principled ground for providing an appropriate remedy can be found. Others are not persuaded.'

2.32 The conclusion of the majority as expressed by Lord Hoffmann was that:

> A wholesale adoption of possible rather than probable causation as the criterion of liability would be so radical a change in our law as to amount to a legislative act. It would have enormous consequences for insurance companies and the National Health Service . . . I think any such change should be left to Parliament.

2.33 Lord Nicholls and Lord Hope recognised recovery for the claimant would require progression and development of the existing law and Lord Nicholls stated:

> The law must strive to achieve a result which is fair to both parties in present day conditions. The common law's ability to develop in this way is its proudest boast. But the present state of the law on this aspect of medical negligence, far from meeting present day requirements of fairness, generates continuing instinctive judicial unease.

2.34 As discussed in paragraph 1.39 above Lady Hale recognised that both *Fairchild v Glenhaven Funeral Services Ltd* [2003] 1 AC 32 and *Chester v Afshar* were examples of the law developing to meet new situations or new problems.

2.35 In simple terms it could be said the split in this decision appears ultimately to turn on whether development of the law should be achieved by the courts or left to parliament. However, in the course of the analysis the speeches of the House of Lords reveal that analysis of the issues could have led to either result. The case illustrates the wider difficulties in analysing causation in clinical negligence cases and the way in which a different analysis of causation can lead to a different outcome.

Lord Nicholls considered the distinction between the test in respect of past **2.36**
events—the balance of probabilities test as applied in *Hotson v East Berkshire*
Health Authority and the test as to future imponderables as applied in *Davies v*
Taylor and *Doyle v Wallace*. He described the position as follows:

> What would have happened in the past but for something which happened in the
> past is, at least generally, a question decided by the courts on an all or nothing
> basis of the balance of probability. In contrast, what would have happened in the
> future but for something which happened in the past calls for the assessment of
> likelihood.

Lord Phillips, however, analysed the case in terms of the different heads of loss for **2.37**
which the claimant might have a claim including principally loss of expectation
of life. He focused on considering the practical consequences of a change in the
law to allow recovery for loss of a chance of a better outcome in these circumstances and showed the very real difficulties of doing so in this case. Lord Phillips
pointed to the difficulty and inconsistency that would arise if dependants under
the Fatal Accidents Act 1976 could claim only if they could establish that on the
balance of probabilities death resulted from negligent treatment but the claimant
could recover for lost years on a chances basis. Lord Phillips pointed out that
Mr Gregg could have advanced a lost years claim on a conventional basis by
calculating by how much his life expectancy has in fact been reduced. Instead he
sought to claim a proportion of lost earnings up to age 65 on the basis he had a
reduced chance of earning to that age as a result of the negligence.

Lady Hale emphasised that there are advantages to both claimant and defendant **2.38**
in a system which assesses causation on a balance of probabilities test. Otherwise
claimants who could show there was a 60 per cent probability they would not
have lost a leg in the absence of negligent treatment would recover only 60 per cent
of their damages. Likewise a cerebral palsy child who could prove a 60 per cent
chance that earlier delivery would have avoided hypoxic damage would recover
only 60 per cent of full liability damages. Lady Hale pointed out that when the
claim in *Gregg v Scott* was pleaded what was claimed was 100 per cent of the
damages that would have been recovered if the claimant had established on a
balance of probabilities that with competent diagnosis he would have been cured.
It was pointed out that if the claimant has succeeded on this basis of showing a
greater than 50 per cent chance of cure nobody (including the defendant) would
have suggested a reduction for the (less than 50 per cent) chance that he would
not have been cured. Lady Hale described the position as being that:

> Doctors do not cause the presenting disease. If they negligently fail to diagnose and
> treat it, it is not enough to show that a claimant's disease has got worse during the
> period of delay. It has to be shown that treating it earlier would have prevented that
> happening, at least for the time being.

2.39 Lady Hale pointed out that almost any claim for loss of an outcome could be redefined as a loss of a chance. If as the claimant argued there should be alternatives open to the claimant to claim either total loss on a balance of probabilities or loss of a chance in the alternative then the claimant would be in a 'heads you lose everything, tails I win something situation'. In almost every case where a doctor is negligent the claimant's chances can be said to be affected in one way or another.

2.40 On the facts of *Gregg v Scott* Lady Hale suggested that her analysis would not necessarily have meant the claimant got nothing. On conventional principles the defendant would have been liable for any additional pain and suffering, financial loss such as additional care that could be established on a balance of probabilities including 'the anguish of knowing that his disease could have been detected earlier'. Further lost years could be calculated by comparison of how long he is now likely to live compared to how long he would have been likely to live if treated promptly. However, Lady Hale pointed out that none of this was argued before the Judge. What was argued was that the claimant would on the balance of probabilities have been cured completely and what the claimant sought by way of appeal was proportionate damages for the less than 50 per cent chance of a complete cure.

2.41 By a majority of three to two the House of Lords have confirmed that the existing principles of causation and consequent calculation of damages in personal injury cases should continue to apply, even in failed diagnosis cases. The claimant must show that on the balance of probabilities the negligent treatment has resulted in a particular loss. If he does so he can then recover 100 per cent of that loss. What the claimant cannot do is calculate the damages he would have recovered had he been able to show on a balance of probabilities the outcome would have been cure or recovery from the illness and then claim that he had a 20 per cent chance of this cure and should recover 20 per cent of the total damages.

2.42 The exercise in cancer and other failed diagnosis cases has to continue to be to assess (applying a balance of probabilities test) what would have happened if the defendant had not been negligent. Then to assume this is what would inevitably have been the position and to compare it with the claimant's actual position following negligence. Comparison between the two situations provides the measure of damages recoverable as assessed at 100 per cent.

2.43 The House of Lords appear to have given very serious consideration to a change in the law. Ultimately, in trying to assess the consequences of such a change, by a majority they have ruled that such a change would over complicate the assessment of damages. Lord Phillips and Lady Hale demonstrated that a system of percentage recovery on a chances basis for all personal injury damages would have advantages and disadvantages for both claimants and defendants.

3

LIMITATION

A. Introduction

3.01 A clinical negligence case will almost always be a personal injury claim with a primary limitation period pursuant to sections 11 and 14 of the Limitation Act 1980. The Court will have a discretion to extend the limitation period pursuant to section 33 of the Limitation Act 1980. The exception is a claim which includes a deliberate assault when the limitation period is six years pursuant to section 2 of the Limitation Act 1980 and there is no discretion to extend this period in accordance with the House of Lords decision in *Stubbings v Webb* [1993] AC 498.

3.02 If the claimant is a child or a patient within the meaning of the Mental Health Act 1983 and Civil Procedure Rules 21.1 then the limitation period does not apply whilst the claimant continues under a disability and the provisions of section 28 of the Limitation Act 1980 apply.

3.03 The circumstances in which a claimant has a date of knowledge after the date on which the negligent treatment or advice were given are very varied and disputes as to limitation have given rise to a huge body of case law. The following cases summarise some of the principles involved but the position has to be carefully considered on a case-by-case basis. Clearly, as a matter of practicality, the assumption should be that any possible limitation date should not be missed and proceedings should always be issued to protect the limitation period unless agreement for a particular date can be reached with the defendant to avoid early issue of proceedings.

B. The Statutory Provisions

3.04   Pursuant to section 11 of the Limitation Act 1980 the period applicable is three years from:

(i)   the date on which the cause of action accrued; or

(ii)   the date of knowledge (if later) of the person injured.

3.05   Pursuant to section 14 the claimant's date of knowledge is the date on which he first had knowledge of the following facts:

(i)   that the injury in question was significant; and

(ii)   that the injury was attributable in whole or in part to the act or omission which is alleged to constitute negligence, nuisance, or breach of duty; and

(iii)   the identity of the defendant; and

(iv)   if it is alleged that the act or omission was that of a person other than the defendant, the identity of that person and the additional facts supporting the bringing of an action against the defendant; and knowledge that any acts or omissions did not, as a matter of law, involve negligence, nuisance, or breach of duty is irrelevant.

3.06   Section 33 of the Limitation Act 1980 allows the Court to disapply the provisions of section 11 but in doing so the Court must consider the degree of prejudice to both the claimant and the defendant and the matters listed in section 33(3).

3.07   Pursuant to section 33(3) the Court shall have regard to all the circumstances of the case and in particular to:

(i)   the length of and reasons for the delay on the part of the claimant;

(ii)   the extent to which, having regard to the delay, the evidence adduced or likely to be adduced by the claimant or the defendant is or is likely to be less cogent than if the action had been brought within the time allowed by section 11;

(iii)   the conduct of the defendant after the cause of action arose including the extent (if any) to which he responded to requests reasonably made by the claimant for information or inspection for the purpose of ascertaining facts which were or might be relevant to the claimant's cause of action against the defendant;

(iv)   the duration of any disability of the claimant arising after the date of the accrual of the cause of action;

(v)   the extent to which the claimant acted promptly and reasonably once he knew whether or not the act or omission of the defendant, to which the injury was attributable, might be capable at that time of giving rise to an action for damages;

(vi) the steps, if any, taken by the claimant to obtain medical, legal, or other expert advice and the nature of any such advice he may have received.

C. The Court of Appeal and House of Lords Decisions

The following Court of Appeal and House of Lords cases give guidance in the application of these principles, each is summarised below: **3.08**

   (i) *Walkley v Precision Forgings Ltd* [1979] 1 WLR 606, HL;

  (ii) *Nash v Eli Lilly & Co* [1993] 1 WLR 782;

 (iii) *Dobbie v Medway Health Authority* [1994] 1 WLR 1234;

 (iv) *Hallam-Eames v Merrett Syndicates Ltd* [1995] 7 Med LR 122;

  (v) *Forbes v Wandsworth Health Authority* [1997] QB 402;

 (vi) *North Essex District Health Authority v Spargo* [1997] 8 Med LR 125;

(vii) *Coad v Cornwall v Isles of Scilly Health Authority* [1997] 1 WLR 189;

(viii) *Farthing v North East Essex Health Authority* [1998] Lloyd's Rep Med 37;

 (ix) *Smith v Leicester Health Authority* [1998] Lloyd's Rep Med 77;

  (x) *Das v Ganju* [1999] PIQR P260;

 (xi) *Rowbottom v Royal Masonic Hospital* [2002] Lloyd's Rep Med 173;

(xii) *Adams v Bracknell Forest Borough Council* [2005] 1 AC 76;

(xiii) *Cressey v Timm* [2005] EWCA Civ 763;

(xiv) *Horton v Sadler* [2006] UKHL 27, [2006] 2 WLR 1346;

 (xv) *McCoubrey v Ministry of Defence* [2007] EWCA Civ 17.

Walkley v Precision Forgings Ltd   **3.09**

House of Lords Judges: Lord Wilberforce, Viscount Dilhorne, Lord Diplock, Lord Edmund-Davies, and Lord Keith

Court of Appeal Judges: Lord Justice Megaw, Lord Justice Shaw, and Lord Justice Waller

Appeal from: Master Lubbock and Swanick J

Length of time outside primary period: Four years three months

Result: Master Lubbock struck out the action, the Judge allowed the appeal and permitted the action to proceed, the Court of Appeal (by a majority) dismissed the defendant's appeal, the House of Lords allowed the defendant's appeal and re-instated the order of the Master.

The House of Lords held the Court could not exercise its discretion pursuant to section 33 of the Limitation Act 1980 (then section 2D of the Limitation Act 1939 as amended) to allow a claim to proceed where a claim had already been issued and then discontinued. The provisions for the exercise of discretion to extend the limitation period only applied where the claimant was prejudiced by the primary limitation period under the Act. In circumstances where the first writ had been issued in time the claimant was not prejudiced by the terms of the Act but by his own failure to pursue the first proceedings.

This decision has now been overruled by the House of Lords in the case of Horton v Sadler *[2006] 2 WLR 1346.*

Background facts:

1966	Claimant employed by the defendant as a dry grinder.
November 1969	Claimant became aware that he was suffering from Raynaud's Phenomenon, when it was diagnosed by his doctor. He also understood it was caused by his work.
December 1969	Claimant consulted trade union shop steward, the union's legal department advised he had no case.
October 1971	Writ issued against the defendant claiming damages for personal injury. No further action taken by solicitors issuing the writ after receipt of counsel's advice.
November 1972	Primary limitation period expired.
6 December 1976	Second writ issued.
23 February 1977	Second writ served.
1 June 1977	Master Lubbock struck out the claim.
20 April 1978	Swanwick J allowed the claimant's appeal against the strike out.
20 June 1978	The Court of Appeal dismissed the defendant's appeal.
17 May 1979	House of Lords allowed the defendant's appeal.

Court's analysis: Lord Diplock summarised the position as follows:

> In my opinion, once a plaintiff has stated an action (the first action) within the primary limitation period it is only in the most exceptional circumstances that he would be able to bring himself within section 2D [now section 33] in respect of a second action brought to enforce the same course of action. If the first action is still in existence, as it was in the instant case when the matter was before the Master and the Judge, cadit quaestio he had not been prevented from starting his action by section 2A or 2B [now 11 and 14] at all so the provisions of those sections cannot have caused him any prejudice. Does it make any difference if the first action is no longer in existence at the time of the application under section 2D either because it has been struck out for want of prosecution or because it has been discontinued by the plaintiff of his own volition? In my view it does not. These are self-inflicted wounds. The provisions of section 2A caused him no prejudice at all; he was able to start his action. The only cause of prejudice to him in the case of dismissal for want of prosecution is dilatoriness which took place after the action was started whether on his own part or on the part of his legal advisers. In the case of discontinuance the only cause of the prejudice is his own act.

The only exception I have been able to think of where it might be proper to give a direction under 2D, despite the fact that the claimant has previously started an action within the primary limitation period but had subsequently discontinued it, would be a case in which the plaintiff had been induced to discontinue by a misrepresentation or other improper conduct by the defendant, but there is no suggestion of this in the instant case.

Where a claim has been started and struck out on a procedural basis or discontinued the claimant cannot start the same action again and rely on the court exercising its discretion to allow the action to proceed using the balance of prejudice provisions in section 33 of the Limitation Act 1980.

However, the fact that an action has been started and discontinued does not prevent a claimant beginning a second action in the following circumstances:

(i) If the primary limitation period has still not expired.

Where a claimant has issued proceedings within the primary limitation period and for any reason needs to start the claim again he can do so within the primary limitation period. In *Birkett v James* [1978] AC 297, the House of Lords confirmed that there was no point in striking out a claim for failure of the claimant to proceed when the claimant could simply exercise his right to commence fresh proceedings.

(ii) If the claimant is still under a disability by reason of age or Mental Health Act 1983 status.

(iii) If the claimant has a date of knowledge pursuant to sections 11 and 14 of the Limitation Act 1980 that is less than three years before the issue of the second proceedings.

(iv) Where the second proceedings are brought against a different defendant.

In *Shapland v Palmer* [1999] 1 WLR 2068 the first proceedings were against the employer who was vicariously liable for the employee, the second proceedings were against the employee himself.

Simon Brown LJ pointed out that as the *Walkley* case depended upon a narrow and technical construction of section 33 and it was reasonable that the claimant could also escape the sanction of *Walkely* on a narrow and technical construction.

(v) Where it can be shown the first proceedings were not properly constituted.

In *Piggott v Aulton* [2003] RTR 540, the first proceedings were against the estate of the deceased but no personal representative had been appointed. In *White v Glass* (CA 18 Feburary 1989) the first proceedings were issued against a company which had been struck off and were therefore ineffective until its restoration to the register.

(vi) If there are exceptional circumstances such a misrepresentation by the defendant leading to the withdrawal of the first proceedings.

This was the ground on which Cox J found the claimant entitled to proceed in *Clay v Chamberlain* [2002] EWHC 2529, although in the *Piggott* case the Court of Appeal found that the *Clay* case could also have proceeded because the first claim against the estate of the deceased was not properly constituted.

3.10   *Nash v Eli Lilly & Co*

Court of Appeal Judges: Lord Justice Purchas, Lord Justice Ralph Gibson, and Lord Justice Mann

Appeal from: Hidden J

Length of time outside primary period: Varied for different claimants in the group

Result: Appeals of three claimants in the group allowed to proceed, appeals of others refused

Background facts: In this group action concerning a claim against a drug company arising out of damage alleged to be caused by an anti-arthritic drug, Opren, limitation was heard as a preliminary issue. The Court of Appeal allowed the appeal of three claimants by applying a wider test than the Judge for date of knowledge pursuant to section 11 and 14 and a wider discretion under section 33 of the Limitation Act 1980

Court's analysis: The Court considered the proper interpretation of section 11 and Lord Justice Purchas explained that, in respect of the difference between knowledge and belief:

> Whether a claimant has knowledge depends upon both the information he has received and upon what he makes of it. If it appears that a claimant whilst believing that his injury is attributable to the act or omission of the defendant, realises that his belief requires expert confirmation before he acquires such a degree of certainty of belief as amounts to knowledge then, he will not have knowledge until that confirmation is obtained. Frequently as it seems to us it will be safe to proceed upon the basis that a claimant did realise that he required confirmation if he acted in a manner consistent with that state of mind even if he is, as he may frequently be, unable to recall with any degree of precision what his state of mind was. Conclusions as to a claimant's state of mind will, we think, usually be more securely based upon inference from conduct in the known circumstances than from a claimant's later assertion as to how he now recalls his then state of mind as between, for example, belief or knowledge.

In respect of attributability: The Court of Appeal approved the analysis of Hidden J and his citation from *Guidera v NEI Projects (India) Ltd* (CA, 30 January 1990) that: 'the stark strength of the word "knowledge" does not stand alone. It is knowledge that attribution is merely possible, a real possibility and not a fanciful one, a possible cause as opposed to a probable cause of the injury.'

And that the cases indicate: 'There must be a degree of specificity and not a mere global or catch-all character about the act or omission which is alleged to constitute negligence.'

Purchas LJ concluded: 'It was not the intention of Parliament to require for the purposes of section 11 and section 14 of the Act proof of knowledge of the terms in which it will be alleged that the act or omission of the defendants constituted negligence or breach of duty. What is required is knowledge of the essence of the act or omission to which the injury is attributable.'

In respect of constructive knowledge: Section 14(3), which deals with 'constructive knowledge' applies generally not only to the nature of the injury under subparagraph (a) but also to attributability, to the knowledge of the nature of the cause of action in (b) and the question of identification of the defendant in (c).

The proper approach is to determine what the plaintiff should have observed or ascertained while asking no more of him than is reasonable. The standard of reasonableness in connection with the observations and/or the effort to ascertain are therefore finally objective but must be qualified to take into consideration the position and circumstances and character of the plaintiff. In considering whether or not the inquiry is not reasonable, the situation, character, and intelligence of the plaintiff must be relevant.

However, in *Adams v Bracknell Forest Borough Council* [2005] 1 AC 76, the House of Lords stated that they preferred the reasoning of Stuart-Smith LJ and Evans LJ in *Forbes v Wandsworth Health Authority* [1997] QB 402 in respect of the test for constructive knowledge and Lord Scott stated that:

> Personal characteristics such as shyness and embarrassment, which may have inhibited the claimant from seeking advice about his illiteracy problems but which would not have been expected to have inhibited others with a like disability, should be left out of the equation. It is the norms of behaviour of persons in the situation of the claimant that should be the test.

In respect of section 33 discretion, it was pointed out that the issue of discretion never arises unless the claimant is outside the primary limitation period and has failed to establish a date of knowledge sufficiently postponed to less than three years before the issue of proceedings.

The test under section 33 was summarised as follows:

> The primary exercise of balancing the degree to which either party is prejudiced by the decision made under section 33, as provided for in subsection 1(a) and (b), has been considered in a number of recent cases. These establish that the consideration under section 33 must be broadly based; and that the primary purpose of the limitation period is to protect the defendant against the injustice of having to face a stale

claim (not relevant in this case). Moreover it is established that once a plaintiff has allowed the permitted time to elapse, the defendant is no longer subject to the disability of accepting without protest the limitation period itself. In such a situation the court is directed to consider all the circumstances of the case including conduct before the expiry of the limitation period and to balance the prejudice to the parties: see *Donovan v Gwentoys Ltd* [1990] 1 WLR 472.

The Court of Appeal further considered the cases of:

(i) *Hartley v Birmingham City, District Council* [1992] 1 WLR 968; and the earlier cases of

(ii) *Firman v Ellis* [1978] QB 886; and *Thompson v Brown* [1981] 1 WLR 744.

The point on which the Court of Appeal criticised the Judge was that in considering how the delay affected the cogency of the evidence under section 33(1)(a) and (b) the Judge took into account the point made by the defendant that lack of cogency of evidence might be used to the advantage of the claimant by covering up or explaining away omissions or contradictions in the claimant's case. The Court of Appeal found this argument was not sustainable and stated:

> Generally under section 33, when deciding whether it would be equitable to allow the action to proceed having regard to the balance of prejudice to the respective parties under section 33(1)(a) and (b) 'cogency' within section 33(3)(b) is in our judgment, directed to the degree to which either party is prejudiced in the presentation of the claim or defence because the evidence is either no longer available or has adversely been affected by the passage of time. There is no room in the provisions of this subsection for the concept, apparently accepted by the judge from the submissions of Mr Playford, that lack of cogency in the case of a plaintiff could inure to benefit of that plaintiff's and thereby prejudice the defendant. While we understand what the judge had in mind, we regret to have to say that in our view that is logically unsustainable. It depends upon an assumption that the trial judge will not be able properly to assess the evidence led on behalf of the plaintiff.

The Court of Appeal did, however, agree with the Judge that the overall weakness of a claimant's case was a factor that could be taken into account in assessing the balance of prejudice.

This case sets out in the context of a group action general principles in respect of the application of the test for date of knowledge under section 11 and 14 and the test for the exercise of discretion under section 33. It also reviews the authorities up to 1993.

3.11 *Dobbie v Medway Health Authority*

Court of Appeal Judges: Sir Thomas Bingham MR, Lord Justice Beldam, and Lord Justice Steyn

Appeal from: Otton J

Length of time outside primary period: 13 years

Result: Court of Appeal found the claimant knew within a short time of the operation that she had been injured in that her breast had been removed and knew this act was attributable to the defendant surgeon, her date of knowledge was not postponed until she also knew it had been negligent to remove her breast without first carrying out a biopsy. The length of delay after the claimant had such knowledge being over 13 years was too long for the court to exercise its discretion under section 33 of the Limitation Act 1980.

Background facts:

27 April 1973	Claimant admitted to hospital for excision of a lump from her breast, the surgeon considered the lump looked cancerous and without carrying out microscopic examination removed the claimant's breast. After removal of the breast the lump was sent for analysis.
April 1973	Analysis of the lump revealed it was benign, claimant informed.
1976	Primary period of limitation expired.
1988	The claimant became aware that her breast need not have been removed prior to pathological examination when she watched a television programme about a similar case. The claimant consulted solicitors shortly thereafter.
5 May 1989	The claimant issued proceedings.
20 October 1990	Statement of claim served.
14 February 1992	Otton J held the claim was time barred and gave judgment for the defendant.
11 May 1994	Court of Appeal dismissed the claimant's appeal.

Court's analysis: Sir Thomas Bingham MR (as he then was) described the history of the provisions under sections 11 and 14. He explained that the provisions had been introduced primarily to meet the unfairness in industrial disease cases when a claimant did not know his illness was caused by his working conditions. Sir Thomas Bingham MR described the test under sections 11 and 14 as follows:

> Time starts to run against the claimant when he knows that the personal injury on which he founds his claim is capable of being attributed to something done or not done by the defendant whom he wishes to sue. This condition is not satisfied where a man knows that he has a disabling cough or shortness of breath but does not know that his injured condition has anything to do with his working conditions. It is satisfied when he knows that his injured condition is capable of being attributed to his working conditions, even though he has no inkling that his employer may have been at fault.

Sir Thomas Bingham MR summarised the findings of Otton J from which
the Judge concluded the claimant had the requisite knowledge shortly after the
operation, as follows:

> On her evidence [the Judge] was entitled to conclude that the plaintiff knew within
> three years of the operation (i) that she had been admitted for excision of a lump only;
> (ii) that her left breast had been removed; (iii) that the lump when removed had not
> been malignant but benign; (iv) that the decision to remove the breast had been taken
> before any microscopic test had been carried out; (v) that there had been no facilities
> for microscopic examination at Sheppey General Hospital; (vi) that she had not given
> her consent to the removal of her breast; (vii) that the removal of her breast had caused
> her acute and prolonged anger, distress and psychological as well as physical damage.

With these facts being known Sir Thomas Bingham MR agreed with Otton J that
the claimant had actual knowledge soon after the surgery. It is clearly significant
that the claimant knew that the lump was benign and not malignant: (iii) above;
and that she knew the decision to remove the breast had been taken before the
tests were carried out: (iv) above. It is these two facts effectively which would have
constituted the allegations of negligence in the claim. It would clearly not have
been sufficient if all that had occurred was that the claimant had awoken after the
operation and found her breast had been removed when she was expecting only
the lump to be removed. If the claimant had not been told that the lump had
turned out to be benign or that it had not been tested before removal then it
seems inevitable that in these circumstances her date of knowledge would have
been postponed until she found out that the lump was benign and found out that
it had not been tested before removal.

Sir Thomas Bingham MR concluded:

> The personal injury on which the plaintiff seeks to found her claim is the removal of
> her breast and the psychological and physical harm which followed. She knew of this
> injury within hours days or months of the operation and she at all times reasonably
> considered it to be significant. She knew from the beginning that the personal injury
> was capable of being attributed to, or more bluntly was the clear and direct result of
> an act or omission of the health authority. What she did not appreciate until later was
> that the health authority's act or omission was (arguably) negligent or blameworthy.
> But her want of that knowledge did not stop time beginning to run.

This passage is sometimes quoted in isolation to suggest that the claimant simply
needed to know that her breast had been removed to have the requisite knowledge. It has to be read in the context of the passage above setting out the findings
of Otton J and the significance of the claimant also knowing that the lump was in
fact benign and had not been tested has to be stressed. These factors are also
emphasised by Beldam LJ when he stated:

> The injury in respect of which the claimant claims damages is the loss of her left
> breast and the severe psychological symptoms which followed. The act or omission

of the defendant on which she relies is the act of the surgeon in removing the breast and the omission to carry out a test before doing so which would have indicated that the removal of her breast was unnecessary. Thus the plaintiff had actual knowledge within a few days of the operation being performed.

This can be seen as a particularly harsh decision on limitation as far as this particular claimant was concerned. The difficulty is not in the analysis of the legal principles nor how they were applied. It is in the fact that this particular claimant clearly did not appreciate until she saw the television programme about another case that it was wrong of the doctor to remove her breast when the lump was a benign lump. This is all the more understandable in circumstances where she was apparently reassured how fortunate she was after being told of the result. The test for date of knowledge however is objective and depends on what a claimant with a similar condition could be expected to understand.

The Judge refused to exercise his discretion to allow the claim to proceed under section 33 because of the overall length of the period of delay and the Court of Appeal agreed with this decision, although Beldam LJ added:

> However I cannot agree with the judge that it is appropriate to take into account the factor which he took from the judgment of Lord Denning MR in *Biss v Lambeth, Southwark and Lewisham Health Authority (Teaching)* [1978] 1 WLR 382 that there had been prejudice because the action had been hanging over the head of the attendant doctor for so many years. I do not see how such a consideration can apply to a doctor who does not know that any action is contemplated against him.

The fact that the Court will only in very exceptional circumstances allow a discretionary extension of time under section 33 of over ten years has recently been confirmed by the Court of Appeal in the context of sexual abuse claims in two cases discussed in Chapter 23: *T v Girls and Boys Welfare Society* [2004] EWCA Civ 1747 and *KR v Bryn Alyn Community (Holdings) Ltd and Royal and Sun Alliance plc* [2003] QB 1441.

Hallam-Eames v Merrett Syndicates Ltd   3.12

Court of Appeal Judges: Sir Thomas Bingham MR, Lord Justice Hoffmann, and Lord Justice Saville

Appeal from: Gatehouse J

Length of time outside primary period (the primary period in this case was six years as it was not a personal injury case): At least two years outside the six-year period

Result: The Court of Appeal reversed the decision of the Judge and found the claimant's date of knowledge was less than three years before the issue of proceedings.

Background facts: This was part of the Lloyd's names litigation and involved the following dates:

1978–1983	Run-off policies written by which certain Lloyd's syndicates reinsured other Lloyd's syndicates.
1979–1985	Reinsurance to close contract closed.
1985–1991	Six-year primary period of limitation expired.
January 1993	First proceedings issued.
1994	Gatehouse J struck the claims as limitation barred.
13 January 1995	Court of Appeal allowed the appeal against the striking out.

Court's analysis: The Court of Appeal in this case examined the application of section 14A which applies to non-personal injury claims but is in similar terms to section 14. The Court examined the date of knowledge issues by reference to personal injury cases in particular: *Broadley v Guy Clapham & Co* [1993] 4 Med LR 328 and *Dobbie v Medway Health Authority* [1994] 5 Med LR 160. In the judgment of the court given by Hoffmann LJ (as he then was) it was stated:

> If all that was necessary was that the plaintiff should have known that the damage was attributable to an act or omission of the defendant, the statute would have said so. Instead it speaks of the damage being attributable to 'the act or omission which is alleged to constitute negligence'. In other words the act or omission of which the plaintiff must have knowledge must be that which is causally relevant for the purposes of an allegation of negligence . . . It is this idea of causal relevance which various judges of this court have tried to express by saying the plaintiff must know 'the essence of the act or omission to which the injury is attributable' . . . Or 'the essential thrust of the case' . . . or that one should 'look at the way the plaintiff puts his case, distil what he is complaining about and ask whether he had in broad terms knowledge of the fact on which that complaint is based'.

Hoffman LJ further explains in the *Hallam-Eames* case the reasoning in *Dobbie v Medway Health Authority* [1994] 1 WLR 1234:

> If one asks on common sense principles what Mrs Dobbie was complaining about, the answer is that the surgeon had removed a healthy breast. It would in our view be a seriously incomplete statement of her case to say that it was simply that the surgeon had removed her breast . . . If one asks what is the principle of common sense on which one would identify Mrs Dobbie's complaint as a removal of the healthy breast rather than simply removal of a breast, it is that the additional fact is necessary to make the act something of which she would prima facie be entitled to complain . . . as Hoffman LJ said in *Broadley*, the words 'which is alleged to constitute negligence' serve to identify the facts of which the plaintiff must have knowledge. He must have known the facts which can fairly be described as constituting the negligence of which he complains.

Section 33 did not apply as this was not a personal injury case. The analysis of the *Dobbie* case and *Broadley* case emphasises that the facts that the claimant needs to be aware of are those facts that underpin the allegations of negligence when they are eventually made. The starting point is to examine the allegations of negligence pleaded in the particulars of the claim and to ascertain what facts the claimant would have needed to know in order to inquire with the help of solicitors and experts as to whether those facts taken together constituted negligence. In the *Dobbie* case the relevant facts were the fact that the claimant's breast had been removed together with the fact that the breast had been healthy when removed and the fact that no tests had been carried out to ascertain whether it was healthy or not.

Forbes v Wandsworth Health Authority   3.13

Court of Appeal Judges: Lord Justice Stuart Smith, Lord Justice Evans, and Lord Justice Roch

Appeal from: Judge Peter Baker QC sitting as a judge of the Queen's Bench Division

Length of time outside primary period: Seven years outside the primary period of limitation

Result: The Court of Appeal reversed the finding of the Judge and found the claimant had the requisite constructive knowledge more than three years before the issue of proceedings so that the claim was limitation barred.

Background facts:

24 October 1982	Claimant admitted to hospital and underwent bypass procedure.
25 October 1982	Claimant underwent second procedure.
5 November 1982	Claimant underwent operation to amputate his leg, he was advised this was necessary to prevent gangrene and to save his life.
November 1985	Primary limitation period expired.
26 June 1991	Claimant consulted solicitors.
October 1992	Expert report obtained
December 1992	Writ issued.
11 August 1994	Judge Peter Baker QC ruled the claim was not limitation barred.
14 March 1996	Court of Appeal reversed the decision of the Judge and found the claim limitation barred.

Court's analysis: The Court of Appeal were unanimous in finding that the claimant did not have actual knowledge which enabled him to commence proceedings until he obtained supportive medical evidence in 1992. However, in respect of constructive knowledge the decision was a majority decision.

Lord Justice Stuart-Smith in considering when it was reasonable for the claimant to take advice stated:

> In my judgment a reasonable man in the position of the deceased, who knew the operation had been unsuccessful, that he had suffered a major injury which would seriously affect his enjoyment of life in the future, would affect his employability on the labour market, if he had any, and would impose substantial burdens on his wife and family in looking after him, if he was minded to make a claim at any time, should and would take advice reasonably promptly.

Stuart-Smith J concluded:

> I have come to the conclusion, therefore that in the circumstances of this case the deceased did have constructive knowledge. That knowledge could not be attributed to him immediately he came out of hospital; clearly he would have to have time to overcome the shock, take stock of his grave disability and its consequences, and seek advice. That would take about 12–18 months.

The extent to which, in cases where a claimant does not have actual knowledge, there can be said to be an additional period of 12–18 months before the claimant has constructive knowledge is unclear but there seems no reason why these comments should not apply at least in every case of severe injury where it is effectively necessary to obtain expert evidence in order to identify an act or omission that might constitute negligence.

Lord Justice Evans came to the same conclusion as Lord Justice Stuart-Smith on the issue of constructive knowledge and found the test was an objective test and it was reasonable of the claimant to have taken further advice soon after the surgery.

Lord Justice Roch in a dissenting judgment agreed with the Judge and found it had not been shown that the Judge was clearly wrong in his conclusion.

On the issue of section 33 Lord Justice Stuart-Smith and Lord Justice Evans agreed that the Court should not exercise its discretion to allow the claim to proceed. Lord Justice Roch did not give judgment on this point. Lord Justice Evans particularly took into account that on the evidence before the Court on the preliminary limitation point it appeared that the claimant had only a very limited, almost negligible chance of success. Lord Justice Stuart-Smith described the claimant's prospects of success as modest.

There is a particular problem for both claimants and defendants when limitation is tried as a preliminary issue in placing before the Judge evidence that gives a fair assessment of the strength of the case. In the exercise of discretion under section 33 the Court has to consider all the circumstances including the strength or weakness of the claimant's case and this may in many cases be a reason for asking the Court to hear limitation together with issues of liability and causation rather than as a preliminary issue. This issue is discussed further in Chapter 23 with reference to sexual assaults.

North Essex District Health Authority v Spargo   **3.14**

Court of Appeal Judges: Lord Justice Nourse, Lord Justice Brooke, and Lord Justice Waller

Appeal from: Collins J

Length of time outside primary period: 15 years outside the primary period. Four years outside the period of postponed date of knowledge as found by the Court of Appeal

Result: The Court of Appeal reversed the finding of the Judge and found the claimant had the requisite knowledge more than three years before the issue of proceedings so that the claim was limitation barred.

Background facts:

1975	Claimant admitted as a compulsory patient to mental hospital. Allegation that misdiagnosis in 1975 led to wrong treatment, failure to cure, and detention for longer than necessary in hospital.
1981	Claimant released from hospital.
10 January 1986	The claimant obtained an expert report which stated the claimant was not suffering from brain damage.
October 1986	Claimant consulted solicitors. This was the date of knowledge found by the Court of Appeal. At this date when the claimant consulted solicitors she knew there had been a wrong diagnosis and that that the wrong diagnosis was connected to her treatment and detention in hospital. Those facts were sufficient for her to have the requisite knowledge.
30 January 1987	Application for legal aid.
23 March 1987	Legal aid granted.
15 July 1988	Letter before action and request for medical records.
August 1988	General practitioner and hospital records received.
21 February 1989	Negative expert report received.
6 December 1989	Counsel advises against the issue of proceedings.
20 March 1990	Legal aid granted for a second opinion.
4 December 1990	Instructions sent to Dr Trimble.
22 July1991	Supportive report of Dr Trimble received—claimant's alleged date of knowledge.
14 December 1993	Writ issued.
1996	Collins J allowed the action to proceed on the basis that the claimant's date of knowledge was the date of Dr Trimble's report.
13 March 1997	Court of Appeal allowed the defendant's appeal and found the date of knowledge was the date the claimant instructed solicitors.

Court's analysis: Lord Justice Brooke analysed the position in respect of sections 11 and 14 as follows:

> This branch of the law is already so grossly overloaded with reported cases, a great many of which have been shown to us or cited by counsel, that I see no reason to add to the overload by citation from earlier decisions. I have considered the judgments of this court in *Halford v Brooks* [1991] 1 WLR 443; *Nash v Eli Lilly & Co* [1993] 1 WLR 782; *Broadley v Guy Clapham* [1993] 4 All ER 439; *Dobbie v Medway Health Authority* [1994] 1 WLR 1234; *Smith v Lancashire Health Authority* [1995] PIQR 514; and *Forbes v Wandsworth Health Authority* [1996] 7 Med LR 175. From these decisions I draw the following principles:
>
> (i) The knowledge required to satisfy sect 14(1)(b) is a broad knowledge of the essence of the causally relevant act or omission to which the injury is attributable;
>
> (ii) 'Attributable' in this context means 'capable of being attributed to', in the sense of being a real possibility;
>
> (iii) A plaintiff has the requisite knowledge when she knows enough to make it reasonable for her to begin to investigate whether or not she has a case against the defendant. Another way of putting this is to say that she will have such knowledge if she so firmly believes that her condition is capable of being attributed to an act or omission which she can identify (in broad terms) that she goes to a solicitor to seek advice about claiming compensation;
>
> (iv) On the other hand she will not have the requisite knowledge if she thinks she knows the acts or omissions she should investigate but in fact is barking up the wrong tree; or if her knowledge of what the defendant did or did not do is so vague or general that she cannot fairly be expected to know what she should investigate; or if her state of mind is such that she thinks her condition is capable of being attributed to the act or omission alleged to constitute negligence, but she is not sure about this, and would need to check with an expert before she could be properly said to know that it was.

This summary gives a good basis of examining a claimant's date of knowledge. In most cases the date that the claimant consults a solicitor will be the latest date that a claimant can rely upon. This provides a three-year period for investigation and fits with the test adopted by the Court of Appeal in the *Bryn Alyn* cases discussed in Chapter 23. In those cases the court asked the question: when was it reasonable for a claimant damaged by abuse in childhood suffering from the shame and embarrassment of having been abused to turn his mind to litigation? Once the claimant does find himself able to go to solicitors, almost inevitably time will then begin to run. It may be many years outside the primary period of limitation when a claimant first instructs solicitors but once he does so commencement of proceedings become urgent.

It is logical that in most cases once a claimant has been able to consult a solicitor about a claim and give instruction about the claim the claimant has the requisite knowledge to start the three-year time limit running. In the *Spargo* case Lord Justice Brooke accepted this might not always be the case as the claimant might be 'barking up the wrong tree' at that stage. This allows for a claim to be brought later where the investigation of a claim concentrates on a line of inquiry mistakenly believed by the claimant to be the cause of his injury but the first line of inquiry reveals a completely different line of inquiry then needs to be followed. In the *Spargo* case this argument failed on the facts and timings in that case but it succeeded in the later case of *Rowbottom v Royal Masonic Hospital*.

Coad v Cornwall v Isles of Scilly Health Authority   **3.15**

Court of Appeal Judges: Rose LJ, Ward LJ, and Judge LJ

Appeal from: Judge Anthony Thompson QC sitting as Judge of the QB Division

Length of time outside primary period: Six years six months.

Result: The Judge found the claimant's date of knowledge was August 1983 and the primary limitation period expired in August 1986. The Judge exercised his discretion to allow the claim to proceed pursuant to section 33 and the Court of Appeal dismissed the defendant's appeal.

Background facts:

August 1983	Claimant suffered a back injury in the course of her employment as a nurse.
August 1986	Primary limitation period expired.
1990	A CT scan revealed bulging of the disc and the claimant realised she would never work again.
January 1991	Claimant discovered she could sue her employers after contacting the Royal College of Nursing.
February 1991	Claimant consulted solicitors.
July 1991	Claimant notified to defendant by letter.
January 1993	Proceedings issued.
May 1995	The judge allowed the claim to proceed pursuant to section 33.
July 1996	Court of Appeal dismissed the appeal.

Court's analysis: The Judge accepted that the claimant simply did not know she had a cause of action until she contacted the Royal College of Nursing, she thought she could not sue her employers whilst she had not lost her job. The Court of Appeal pointed out that the test in section 33(3)(a) was a subjective one (in contrast to the date of knowledge test under section 11 and 14, the test under section 33 was not a test based on 'reasonableness'). As Rose LJ pointed out at page 198:

> The concept of reasonableness was clearly well known to the draftsman of this legislation. It appears with mantra-like frequency in section 14(2) and (3) and section 14A(7) and (10) as well as in section 33(3)(e). The omission of that concept from section 33(3)(a) is therefore striking and in my mind significant. Its omission is accordingly fatal for the reasons given by Ward LJ. To Mr Edis's submissions on the construction of the statute.

Ward LJ described how the test in section 33(3)(a) of the Limitation Act 1980 requires the court to conduct an inquiry into two factual situations. The first is the length of the delay; the second is the reason for the delay on the part of the claimant. To add 'on the part of the claimant' indicates that it is a subjective inquiry in which the Court is there engaged. Having found what the reason is, the Court must decide whether it is a good or bad reason or, in the language of Russell LJ in *Halford v Brookes* [1991] 1 WLR 428, whether the claimant is culpable or not.

Each of the three Judges in the Court of Appeal observed that they might have reached a different decision if deciding the case at first instance, but that was not a relevant consideration to the appeal.

3.16 *Farthing v North East Essex Health Authority*

Court of Appeal Judges: Lord Justice Simon Brown, and Mrs Justice Hale (as she then was)

Length of time outside primary period: 11 years

Result: Date of knowledge was found to be shortly after the operation in 1981 but the Judge exercised his discretion to allow the claim to proceed, the Court of Appeal dismissed the appeal from the Judge's exercise of discretion.

Background facts:

28 July 1981	Claimant underwent total abdominal hysterectomy, during the operation the right ureter was damaged leading to a triple fistula involving the ureter, the bladder, and the vagina.
7 August 1981	Claimant discharged home, the surgeon wrote to the claimant's general practitioner stating she had made a satisfactory recovery. In fact the claimant suffered substantially from incontinence of urine.
9 September 1981	Diagnosis of triple fistula made when the claimant underwent cystoscopy.
December 1981	Claimant underwent surgery which cured the incontinence.
1986	Claimant developed an abscess on the site of the incision for the corrective surgery procedure in December 1981.

1987	Abscess resolved spontaneously.
February 1989	Claimant admitted to hospital for emergency surgery as a stone had formed in the stump of the ureter as a result of the various procedures.
August 1993	Claimant's general practitioner told her all her problems were attributable to the hysterectomy operation which in his opinion was negligently performed.
September 1993	Claimant consulted solicitors.
November 1993	Defendant asked to provide medical records and did so.
April 1994	First three expert reports obtained for the claimant were unsupportive.
September 1994	Claimant obtained first supportive expert report.
January 1995	Claimant obtained second supportive expert report.
24 August 1995	Proceedings issued.
2 January 1997	Judge Bradbury found the claimant's date of knowledge was late 1981 but that the claim should proceed pursuant to section 33.
3 December 1997	Court of Appeal dismissed the defendant's appeal.

Court's analysis: In looking at the exercise of discretion pursuant to section 33 the Court considered the fact that the issues would be determined largely by the medical records. Simon-Brown LJ pointed out that:

> Here, by contrast (with the case of *Shtun v Zalejska* [1996] 1 WLR 1270) the case must inevitably turn not upon the recollection of witnesses like these doctors as to precisely what they did or observed when variously they saw the plaintiff (and in the case of Dr Yashlaha and Mr Hunt, operated on her) but rather upon what is stated in the contemporaneous material in the way of hospital records, notes and correspondence . . . Their findings recorded there seem to me the all-important parts of the contemporary evidence. The experts will then give their opinions as to whether negligence is properly to be inferred from it.

And stated that:

> Even had this case been tried, as at the earliest it could have been, some 4 or 5 years after 1981, the contribution that Dr Yashlaha could have made by way of recollection and oral evidence to the court's ability to resolve the issues arising would not have been significantly greater than it would were the matter to be tried now. Of course there must be some degree of prejudice to defendants in such a situation but that was plainly not lost upon the judge below.

The Court would not interfere with the Judge's discretion unless as described in *Nash v Eli Lilly* the Judge took into account factors he should not have, failed to take into account factors he should have taken into account, or was plainly wrong. In this case the defendant could not meet these criteria for upsetting the exercise of discretion. Simon-Brown LJ observed that he might have reached a different decision if deciding the case at first instance but that was irrelevant to the appeal.

3.17 *Smith v Leicester Health Authority*

Court of Appeal Judges: Lord Justice Roch, Lord Justice Mantell, and Sir Patrick Russell

Appeal from: May J (as he then was)

Length of time outside primary period: The primary period ran from the claimant reaching 21 years in 1964, the claim was issued 25 years after this.

Result: The Court of Appeal allowed the claimant's appeal from the decision of the Judge that the claim was statute barred. As the Judge had found negligence and causation proved the claimant succeeded in recovering damages at the age of 54 years in respect of a breach of duty that occurred 43 years earlier.

Background facts:

1943	Claimant born.
1950	Claimant developed weakness in her right leg.
1952	An orthopaedic surgeon diagnosed the claimant suffered from spina bifida.
November 1953	Claimant underwent an operation at Leicester Hospital to her right knee which did not improve her condition.
August 1954	Neurogenic bladder dysfunction diagnosed.
December 1954	Claimant underwent a further operation at Leicester Hospital to excise the neck of the bladder, after the operation her incontinence increased.
1954 and 1955	X-rays at Leicester Hospital showed enlargement of the spinal canal, the enlargement was not reported by the radiologist, if it had been reported a myelogram would have been carried out. This would have revealed a mass which would have been removed with little risk of subsequent paralysis occurring.
9 May 1957	Claimant underwent an operation at London Hospital by way of exploratory laminectomy which revealed a cyst in the spinal cord, the cyst was benign but had been the cause of the claimant's bladder and leg problems. In the course of removal of the cyst the claimant became tetraplegic. The claimant was then 14 years of age.
1964	Claimant became 21 years of age and primary limitation started to run. (The age of majority was not reduced to 18 until the implementation of the Family law Reform Act 1969 on 1 January 1970.)
December 1983	The claimant heard a doctor at the National Hospital for Nervous Diseases say that somebody had made a mistake in her case.
1984	The claimant was advised by the Spinal Injuries Association that the limitation period for bringing a claim relating to her surgery in 1957 had long since expired.
1987	Claimant became resident at Wakerly Lodge Young Disabled Home.

1988	Claimant met a solicitor who was visiting another resident at Wakerly Lodge. He advised the claimant it was worth investigating possible claim, the solicitor applied for legal aid for the claimant.
March 1989	Legal aid certificate granted in respect of possible claim against the London Hospital in respect of surgery in 1957.
November 1990	Claimant obtained an expert report stating that the surgery in 1957 had no choice but to operate and there was no negligence at that date, however the clinicians at Leicestershire Hospital had failed 'to get to grips with the true nature and import of her deteriorating neurological condition'. Date of actual knowledge found by May J.
February 1991	Legal aid certificate amended to show Leicester Health Authority as a potential defendant.
13 August 1991	Leicester disclosed hospital records.
22 May 1992	Writ issued.
1995	X-rays from 1954 and 1955 disclosed to the claimant's solicitor.
14 September 1995	Liability, causation, and limitation ordered to be heard together but quantum separately.
17 May 1996	May J gave judgment for the defendant on the basis that negligence was established against the defendant in respect of the failure of the radiologist to report on the 1954 and 1955 X-rays, the negligence was causative of the claimant's tetraplegia. The claimant did not have actual knowledge until November 1990 but had constructive knowledge and that the claimant should have sought medical advice some time in the 1970s at the latest, the defendant was prejudiced by the delay so that the action should not be permitted to proceed.
18 December 1997	Court of Appeal allowed the claimant's appeal and held the claim was not limitation barred.

Court's analysis: The claimant had become tetraplegic after an operation at the London Hospital in 1957. Liability for this catastrophic injury lay not with the doctors at the London Hospital but with the doctors at Leicester Hospital who had failed to report an X-ray showing a cyst two years earlier. Prompt treatment of the cyst would have avoided the need for surgery in 1957 and then inevitable consequences of that surgery. The claimant's evidence, which was accepted by the Judge, was that it never occurred to the claimant until she saw the report of Mr Wilson, consultant neurosurgeon, in November 1990, that her injury was caused by the doctors at Leicester Hospital rather than the London Hospital.

The Judge had found that the claimant did not have actual knowledge in respect of the claim against Leicester Health Authority until she received the expert report in 1990 as until then she been 'barking up the wrong tree' and did not know in the sense described in *Halford v Brookes* [1991] 1 WLR 428 that her injury was capable of being attributed to Leicester Health Authority.

The Judge then considered constructive knowledge and applying *Forbes v Wandsworth Health Authority* [1997] QB 402 found that the claimant could have acquired the relevant knowledge earlier. The Judge and the Court of Appeal accepted that *Nash v Eli Lilly* and *Forbes v Wandsworth Health Authority* were conflicting authorities in respect of the constructive knowledge test and that pursuant to *Young v Bristol Aeroplane Co Ltd* [1946] 1 KB 718 they could follow either authority. The Court preferred the reasoning in the *Forbes* case to the reasoning in the *Nash* case. Subsequently the House of Lords in the *Adams* case confirmed that the *Forbes* case was to be preferred to the *Nash* case in respect of constructive knowledge.

Effectively, the Judge found the course of events that was set in train when the claimant spoke to a solicitor in 1988 could have been put in train some time in the preceding 20 years and at the latest during the 1970s after the claimant had reached her majority. The Judge did not consider he should exercise his discretion to allow the case to proceed pursuant to section 33 as he found the defendant was prejudiced in not being able to call doctors involved in the claimant's treatment in the 1950s. The Judge stated there had been 'enormous delay' and the prejudice to the defendant outweighed the factors in the claimant's favour.

The Court of Appeal reversed the Judge's findings both on the constructive knowledge point and section 33 and stated that the Judge rather than referring to 'enormous delay' should have referred to the long interval of time, as delay already implied fault on the part of the claimant.

In respect of constructive knowledge the Court of Appeal accepted for the purposes of that appeal that the test was: 'what would the reasonable person have done placed in the situation of the plaintiff?'. For this test the individual characteristics of the claimant should be disregarded and described the position as follows:

> At no time did it ever occur to her that the treatment she had had at Leicester had played any part in her becoming tetraplegic or that the doctors at Leicester might have treated her in a different fashion from the way in which they had treated her.
>
> Would these things have occurred to a reasonable person in the plaintiff's position? We do not believe that the defendants can establish or that the defendants did establish that these matters would have occurred to a reasonable person or that a reasonable person would have sought medical expert advice, particularly not in relation to the plaintiff's treatment at Leicester.

Roch LJ explained that:

> In our judgment there was no basis on which the judge could accept the defendant's submission that some time in the 1970s at the latest, the plaintiff should have

taken advice . . . What the plaintiff has to know in cases of omissions such as the present is, as Evans LJ pointed out in *Forbes* at page 420G, that there was a lost opportunity to prevent the injury, her tetraplegia which she later suffered because the presence of the dermoid cyst could have been diagnosed in 1954 or 1955. That knowledge could only be gained by the plaintiff seeking expert medical advice. This case is different from Forbes . . . In our judgment it was an error to equate the situation of Miss Smith following the 1957 operation with that of Mr Forbes. Miss Smith did not know the 1957 operation had been unsuccessful. On the contrary she had been told and believed that it had been successful in saving her life. There is no evidence that she was told at the London Hospital or at Stoke Mandeville that her tetraplegia was due to the operation itself as opposed to being caused by the pressure which had been exerted by the dermoid cyst on her spinal cord.

In the case of *Smith* she had first been alerted to the possibility of negligence by a consultant at the National Hospital for Nervous Diseases in 1983. Thereafter she had consulted the Spinal Injuries Association and been advised that any claim relating to the way the surgery was performed in 1957 would now be limitation barred. The case is unusual because it could not be said as it was in the case of *Forbes* that if the claimant had taken expert medical advice in 1984 she could have taken the same steps she later took in 1992. The success of this case depended on the discovery of the X-rays from 1954 and 1955 and the only point on which the Judge made findings of breach of duty was the fact that the X-rays were not properly reported. This could not have been ascertained even with expert medical help until the X-rays were discovered and that was not until 1995.

In respect of section 33, the Court of Appeal reversed the Judge's finding and held that this was a case where on the basis of the Judge's finding they were unable to identify any evidence on the identification of the cyst on the X-rays that the defendant could have adduced that would have assisted them on that issue. Further, there was no evidence before the court as to the availability (or lack of availability) of the radiologist concerned.

Das v Ganju   3.18

Court of Appeal Judges: Lord Justice Nourse, Lord Justice Buxton, and Sir Christopher Staughton

Appeal from: Garland J

Length of time outside primary period: 15 years outside the primary period. Five years outside the agreed latest date of knowledge

Result: Court of Appeal upheld the Judge's exercise of discretion to allow the action to proceed pursuant to section 33 of the Limitation Act 1980.

Background facts:

24 October 1978	Claimant's daughter born with congenital rubella syndrome suffering from blindness, deafness, and other severe disabilities. The claimant had consulted her general practitioner during her pregnancy with a rash and he had failed to consider whether this was rubella.
June 1987	Claimant first consulted a solicitor. Before the Court of Appeal this was agreed as the earliest date of knowledge.
21 August 1987	Letter before action to defendant.
May 1988	Counsel incorrectly advised the claim was not a personal injury claim and was already barred by a six-year time limit although he also advised the limitation obstacle could be overcome. Counsel correctly advised that the child could not have a claim (*McKay v Essex Health Authority* [1982] QB 1166).
October 1988	Supportive expert report obtained. Before the Court of Appeal this was agreed as the latest date of knowledge.
April 1989	Claimant advised by solicitors she would need to make a substantial legal aid contribution but that her disabled daughter would be entitled to legal aid on attaining 16 years. This was incorrect advice and contrary to counsel's advice based on *McKay v Essex HA*.
July 1993	Claimant instructed different solicitors.
17 September 1996	Proceedings issued against the defendant.
1998	Judge held action should proceed pursuant to section 33.
31 March 1999	Defendant's appeal dismissed by the Court of Appeal.

Court's analysis: In dismissing the appeal the Court of Appeal found that the fault of the claimant's previous solicitors should not be relied upon against her but distinguished *Whitfield v North Durham Health Authority* [1995] 6 Med LR 32. In that case a concession had been made that the party's action or inaction could not be divorced from that of his solicitor. Instead the Court relied on the case of *Thompson v Brown* [1981] 1 WLR 744 and *Halford v Brooks* [1991] 1 WLR 428 and also pointed out that the claimant would not necessarily have a clear-cut case against her former solicitors. The Court further pointed out that even if the case had been issued within the agreed period of postponement for date of knowledge to 1988 it would not have been heard for at least ten years after the events that occurred and the defendant would have had to deal with it on that basis.

The proposition that failings on the part of a claimant's solicitor which occurred without fault on the part of the claimant should not as a matter of law be attributed to the claimant was followed and applied by the Court of Appeal in the subsequent case of *Corbin v Penfold Metallising Company Ltd* [2000] Lloyd's Rep Med 247.

Rowbottom v Royal Masonic Hospital   **3.19**

Court of Appeal Judges: Peter Gibson LJ, Mantell LJ, and Wall J

Appeal from: Master Murray

Length of time outside primary period: Two years three months

Result: Claim allowed to proceed on the basis of the claimant's date of knowledge being less than three years before the issue of the second writ. Prior to that the claimant was 'barking up the wrong tree'. The claimant could not rely on section 33 because of the decision in *Walkley v Precision Forgings Ltd* [1979] 1 WLR 606.

Background facts:

9 February 1991	Hip replacement followed by wound infection and amputation; claimant believed the complication was failure to insert drain.
June 1991	Claimant consulted solicitors.
9 February 1993	Expert report found failure to insert drain was not negligent, however if antibiotics were not used that was negligent.
12 May 1993	Counsel's advice raising questions for the expert re giving antibiotics.
18 May 1993	Claimant saw expert report and counsel's advice. Date of knowledge found by Master Murray.
22 July 1993	Expert advised if antibiotics had been given leg would have been saved. Date of knowledge found by the Court of Appeal.
3 December 1993	Writ issued.
7 November 1995	Proceedings discontinued.
12 July 1996	Second writ issued.

Court's analysis: The Court found that the relevant issue was when the claimant knew of the omission which he relied on in the pleaded claim as constituting negligence. On the facts of this case the relevant omission was the failure to administer a course of antibiotics. The claimant did not have the relevant knowledge of this fact until he received the expert advice on this point on 22 July 1993. Until that date this claimant was barking up the wrong tree in the sense described by Brooke LJ in the *Spargo* case. The date of knowledge was therefore July 1993 and the proceedings were issued within three years of that date. If the claimant failed to establish a date of knowledge he could not have relied on section 33 because he had discontinued earlier proceedings and was barred by the *Walkley* case from any exercise of discretion.

3.20   *Young v Western Power Distribution (South West) plc*

Court of Appeal Judges: Simon Brown LJ, Mummery LJ, and Laws LJ

Appeal from: HH Judge Mackay

Length of time outside primary period: Two months outside the primary period of three years from the deceased's death

Result: The Court of Appeal allowed the defendant's appeal against the Judge's exercise of discretion pursuant to section 33. The Court applied the *Walkley* principle to the claim brought by the widow under the Fatal Accidents Act 1976 and the Law Reform (Miscellaneous Provisions) Act 1934 to find that there was a complete bar to her relying on section 33 even for a two-month extension because the deceased had brought and then discontinued a claim.

Background facts:

December 1993	The deceased diagnosed as suffering asbestos-related mesothelioma.
1995	The deceased brought a claim against his employer claiming damages for personal injury as a result of his exposure to asbestos.
December 1996	The deceased's primary period of limitation expired as his date of knowledge was December 1993.
1997	The deceased discontinued the proceedings on the basis the diagnosis of mesothelioma was at that date said to be doubtful.
March 1999	The deceased died from asbestos-related malignant mesothelioma and the post-mortem report confirmed the diagnosis.
May 2002	Fatal Accidents Act 1976 and Law Reform (Miscellaneous Provisions) Act 1934 claims brought by the widow.
2002	HH Judge Mackay allowed the claim to proceed pursuant to section 33 of the Limitation Act 1980.
July 2003	Court of Appeal allowed the defendant's appeal.

Court's analysis: The Court of Appeal held that at the date the deceased died there was no cause of action vested in him as he had discontinued his claim. The widow could not be placed in a better position and the discontinuance of the claim was a bar to her relying on section 33 in respect of the Fatal Accidents Act claim or the Law Reform (Miscellaneous Provisions) Act claim.

3.21   *Adams v Bracknell Forest Borough Council*

House of Lords Judges: Lord Hoffmann, Lord Phillips, Lord Scott, Lord Walker, and Baroness Hale

Court of Appeal Judges: LJ Peter Gibson, LJ Tuckey, and LJ Keene

Appeal from: HH Judge Vincent

Length of time outside primary period: Nine years

Result: The Judge and the Court of Appeal found the claimant's date of knowledge was less than three years before the issue of proceedings, the House of Lords allowed the defendant's appeal and held the claim was statute barred.

Background facts:

13 March 1972	Claimant born.
1981–1988	Claimant attended the defendant's school where his dyslexia was not diagnosed.
13 March 1990	Claimant attained 18 years.
November 1999	The claimant met an educational psychologist at a salsa dancing class and she suggested to him he might be suffering from dyslexia.
12 January 2000	Claimant first consulted a solicitor.
25 June 2002	Claimant issued proceedings.
2002	Judge found the claimant's date of knowledge was November 1999 and less than three years before the issue of proceedings.
2003	Court of Appeal upheld the Judge's decision.
2004	House of Lords allowed the defendant's appeal.

Court's analysis: The Court considered the limitation period in respect of a claim arising out of the failure to diagnose dyslexia. Both the Judge and the Court of Appeal allowed the case to proceed under sections 11 and 14 of the Limitation Act 1980 but the House of Lords overturned the decision of the Court of Appeal and held the claim statute barred. The facts were summarised as follows by Lord Hoffmann:

> The plaintiff Mr Adams issued proceedings on 25 June 2002 against the *Bracknell Forest Borough Council* claiming damages for negligence in failing to provide him with a suitable education. The claim is based upon the alleged neglect of the council properly to assess the educational difficulties he was experiencing at its schools which he attended between 1981 and 1988 and to provide him with appropriate treatment. He alleges that an assessment would have revealed that he suffered from dyslexia and the treatment would have ameliorated the consequences of that condition. As it is, his literacy skills are less than they should have been and he has been disadvantaged in the employment market. He also suffers from disabling psychological syndromes such as depression, panic and lack of self-esteem.

As far as the limitation position was concerned Lord Hoffmann applied the test in section 14 as follows:

> The judge held that Mr Adams acted reasonably in making no inquiry into the reasons for his literacy problems. I do not think that he based this finding upon matters of character or intelligence which were peculiar to Mr Adams. If the judge had been

relying upon his personal characteristics, he might have been hard put to explain why someone who was willing to confide in a lady he met at a dancing party was unable to confide in his doctor. But the judge appears to have thought that extreme reticence about his problems was the standard behaviour which ought to be expected from anyone suffering from untreated dyslexia and that the conversation with Ms Harding was an aberration. In principle, I think that the judge was right in applying the standard of reasonable behaviour to a person assumed to be suffering from untreated dyslexia. If the injury itself would reasonably inhibit him from seeking advice, then that is a factor which must be taken into account. My difficulty is with the basis for the finding that such a person could not reasonably be expected to reveal the source of his difficulties to his medical adviser. In the absence of some special inhibiting factor, I should have thought that Mr Adams could reasonably have been expected to seek expert advice years ago. The congeries of symptoms which he described to Dr Gardner, which he said had been making his life miserable for years, which he knew to be rooted in his inability to read and write and about which he had sought medical advice, would have made it almost irrational not to disclose what he felt to be the root cause. If he had done so, he would no doubt have been referred to someone with expertise in dyslexia and would have discovered that it was something which might have been treated earlier.

The judge's finding as to the generally inhibiting effect of untreated dyslexia appears to have been based upon judicial notice. There was certainly no basis for such a finding in Dr Gardner's report, which was the only expert evidence before him. What the report did establish was that dyslexics are characteristically normal intelligent people and that Mr Adams was such a person. Although one can easily understand someone wanting to avoid the social embarrassment of revealing his difficulties about reading and writing to colleagues at work and other acquaintances, I think that it would need some evidential foundation before one could assume that such a person was likely to be unable to speak about the matter to his doctor. Such evidence was entirely lacking.

In my opinion, there is no reason why the normal expectation that a person suffering from a significant injury will be curious about its origins should not also apply to dyslexics. In the absence of such an expectation, there is no reason why the limitation period should not be prevented from running for an indefinite period until some contrary impulse leads to the discovery which brings it to an end. For the reasons given by Stuart-Smith LJ in *Forbes* case, this could face a defendant with a claim so stale as to be virtually impossible to defend. It also means that although Tuckey LJ said, at para 26, that the decision of the judge and Court of Appeal did not mean that 'such a conclusion would be reached in every case where, by chance, sometimes many years later, a claimant discovers that he is or may be dyslexic', I do not find it easy to see why not. For these reasons the date of constructive knowledge was in my opinion well before three years before the issue of the writ.

The other Judges in the House of Lords also found that the test of constructive knowledge was an objective test based on the reasonable actions of a claimant with a similar disability but disregarding specific characteristics of that claimant. The House of Lords followed the reasoning of Lord Justice Stuart-Smith and Lord Justice Evans in *Forbes v Wandsworth Health Authority* on this point.

Lady Hale analysed the position slightly differently in respect of the date of knowledge test and reviewed the Law Commission Reports on Limitation of Actions. However on the facts of this case Lady Hale stated as follows:

> In cases of educational failure (like the present) or child care failure (as in *Barrett v Enfield London Borough Council* [2001] 2 AC 550), there may be no dramatic trigger such as an amputation. But there will often be enough in what the claimant does know to make it reasonable for that claimant to make further enquiries. This case is a good example. Mr Adams knew that he was experiencing serious problems in his life as a result of his difficulties with reading and writing. He felt himself to be of normal intelligence. He knew that his education had not equipped him with reading and writing skills commensurate with his intelligence. He was consulting his doctor about his problems, yet he did not tell his doctor about his difficulties with reading and writing. He clearly had good reason to seek such advice yet he failed to do so: he 'did not want to go there'. On the test proposed by the Law Commission section 14(3) would have applied to him.
>
> In my view all the cases to which we have been referred are explicable on the basis that the law expects people to make such inquiries or seek such professional advice as they reasonably can when they have good reason to do so. Their motive for not doing so will generally be irrelevant. But I would not want to rule out that their personal characteristics may be relevant to what knowledge can be imputed to them under section 14(3).

All of the members of the Committee of the House of Lords allowed the defendant's appeal on the basis that the claimant in that case had constructive knowledge that his inability to read and write was attributable to the failures of his education and he could have sought expert advice earlier. In assessing the date of knowledge the House of Lords adopted the reasoning of the Court of Appeal in both *Forbes* and *Smith* and described the test as the objective test for a person with the claimant's disability but without taking into account particular characteristics of that claimant which distinguished him from other claimants with a similar disability.

The House of Lords failed to exercise discretion under section 33 to allow the action to proceed.

Cressey v Timm & Son Ltd and E Timm & Son Holdings Ltd　　　　　**3.22**

Court of Appeal Judges: Lord Justice May, Lord Justice Rix, and Lord Justice Jonathan Parker

Appeal from: DJ Robinson and HH Judge Cracknell

Length of time outside primary period: Three months

Result: The date of knowledge was the date the claimant knew the correct identity of the defendant employer was *E Timm and Son Holdings Ltd* which was not until April 2001, five months after the accident.

Background facts:

2 December 2000	Claimant injured at work when in the course of using a forklift truck a pallet collapsed causing another pallet to strike and break his leg. The claimant then consulted solicitors through his trade union.
30 March 2001	Solicitors wrote a protocol letter to E Timm & Son Ltd who were thought to be the claimant's employers.
30 April 2001	The claimant's solicitors received a response to the protocol letter through the insurers Zurich, the insurers' client was identified as 'E Timm & Son Holdings & Subsidiary Companies'.
9 October 2001	Zurich wrote to the claimant's solicitors admitting liability subject to contributory negligence.
7 March 2002	Zurich and the claimant's solicitors agreed contributory negligence as 25 per cent.
18 November 2003	Claimant's solicitors wrote to Zurich stating in the absence of proposals for settlement they would issue proceedings and asked for the name of the correct defendant.
20 November 2003	Zurich confirmed the correct defendant was E Timm & Son Holdings.
27 November 2003	Claim form issued against both E Timm & Son Ltd and Holdings. The claimant's solicitors failed to serve this claim form within four months.
20 December 2003	Primary limitation period expired.
30 March 2003	Second claim form issued and served.
15 July 2004	District Judge Robinson held the claimant's date of knowledge was 30 April 2001 when he first knew his employer was E Timm & Son Holdings Ltd.
8 November 2004	HH Judge Cracknell dismissed the defendant's appeal.
24 June 2005	Court of Appeal dismissed the defendant's appeal.

Court's analysis: In this case the claim was issued only four months outside the primary limitation period and liability was already agreed at 75 per cent. Because the claimant had issued a claim form and failed to serve it in time the claimant was precluded by the *Walkley* principle from relying on section 33. The claim was allowed to proceed because at the date of injury the defendant did not know the identity of the company employing him and he did not discover this until a response was received to a protocol letter written by his solicitors. The Court applied *Simpson v Norwest Holst Southern Ltd* [1980] 1 WLR 968. It was pointed out that the claimant could not know enough to pursue the claim until they could identify a name to place on the claim form. If the name the claimant identified was merely a misnomer then he might already have the requisite knowledge but in this case the claimant had not identified the correct company until notified by the defendant's insurers in April 1991.

Horton v Sadler   **3.23**

House of Lords Judges: Lord Bingham, Lord Hoffmann, Lord Rodger, Lord Carswell, and Lord Brown

Court of Appeal Judges: Jonathan Parker LJ, and Scott Baker LJ, the Court of Appeal dismissed the appeal by consent as the House of Lords had granted permission to appeal

Appeal from: HH Judge Roger Cooke

Length of time outside primary period: Five months

Result: The Court would exercise its discretion pursuant to section 33 of the Limitation Act 1980 to allow the action to proceed even though proceedings had first been issued just inside the limitation period and then withdrawn. The decision in *Walkley v Precision Forgings Ltd* was expressly overruled.

Background facts:

12 April 1998	Claimant injured in a road traffic accident which was entirely the fault of the defendant uninsured driver. The MIB nominated insurers to act as agents in the proceedings.
October 2000	MIB made an interim payment.
10 April 2001	The claimant's solicitors issued proceedings two days before expiry of the primary limitation period. The solicitors failed to notify the MIB of the issue of proceedings. The MIB served a defence relying on the failure to comply with the notice provisions.
September 2001	Claimant's solicitors issued fresh proceedings after complying with the notice provisions.
7 May 2003	HH Judge Cooke held that the claim was limitation barred because of the decision in *Walkley*, in the absence of that decision the Judge would have exercised his discretion to allow the claim to proceed.
28 June 2004	Court of Appeal dismissed the claimant's appeal.

Court's analysis: In this case the claim was issued only five months outside the primary limitation period and liability had already effectively been admitted. Because the claimant had issued a claim form and failed to notify the MIB the claimant was required to issue a second claim form with proper notification. The Judge found the claimant was precluded by the *Walkley* principle from relying on section 33, he would otherwise have exercised his discretion to allow the claim to proceed. The House of Lords drew attention to the unsatisfactory result of the *Walkley* decision and the number of cases in which the Court of Appeal had made artificial distinctions in order to circumvent the *Walkley* decision. The House of Lords interpreted section 33 as giving a wide discretion to first instance Judges and accepted the basis on which HH Judge Cooke would have exercised his discretion as a reasonable one. The restraint provided by the *Walkley* decision was effectively found to be inconsistent with the wide ambit of section 33 and was overruled. Lord Brown described how:

> The curious but plain fact is that in *Walkley* Homer nodded: an impossible and illogical construction was put on the section. The House's mistaken approach appears clearly from the passage in Lord Diplock's speech cited by Lord Bingham at paragraph 16 above. In stating there that a plaintiff who had already brought a first action in time 'has not been prevented from starting his action by section 11 . . . he was able to start his action'... Lord Diplock appears to have confused or conflated the two separate sets of proceedings: it is not the first action in which the plaintiff is prejudiced by the time bar but the second; and it is the second action for which the plaintiff seeks the favourable exercise of the court's section 33 discretion to allow the action to proceed having regard to the degree to which . . . the provisions of section 11 . . . prejudice him.

> It is for that very reason that the *Walkley* ruling is so lacking in logic and intrinsically productive of anomalies that the courts have found such difficulty in its subsequent application. There is simply no coherent principle by which to judge its true scope and how in any particular case which raises the smallest factual distinction it should apply. Small wonder that it has given rise to so much unsatisfactory jurisprudence.

3.24 *Jason McCoubrey v Ministry of Defence*

Court of Appeal Judges: Lord Justice Ward, Lord Justice Neuberger, and Mr Justice Tugendhat

Appeal from: HH Judge Cox

Length of time outside primary period: Eight years

Result: The date of knowledge was the date that a reasonable person in the claimant's position would have considered the injury sufficiently serious to institute proceedings. The claimant knew he had symptoms from the injury shortly after it occurred in 1993 and was aware of the medical diagnosis from 1994. Date of knowledge ran from 1994, not from 2001 when the injury first detrimentally affected his career in the army.

Background facts:

July 1975	The claimant is born.
1991	The claimant joined the army.
15 October 1993	The claimant was injured when on a training exercise on Salisbury Plain a non-commissioned officer threw a thunderflash into his trench, it exploded a metre away causing injury to his ears. Within a day or two the claimant noticed the hearing in his left ear had deteriorated.

March 1994	The claimant was examined by an ENT consultant who reported marked sensorineural hearing loss.
15 October 1996	Three year primary limitation period expired.
August 2001	The claimant's status in the army was downgraded because of his hearing defect and he was no longer entitled to travel in a helicopter or to fire a rifle.
January 2003	The claimant was formally downgraded because of his hearing defect and not allowed to serve in Iraq.
April 2003	The claimant first consulted solicitors.
21 July 2004	Proceedings issued.
10 January 2005	Defence served raising limitation issues.
17 March 2006	HH Judge Cox gave judgment on the preliminary issue of limitation to find that the claim had been brought within the claimant's requisite date of knowledge for section 11(4)(b).
24 January 2007	Court of Appeal reversed the judge's decision and found the claimant's date of knowledge for the purposes of section 11 was March 1994. The case was remitted to HH Judge Cox to decide whether to exercise her discretion pursuant to section 33.

Court's analysis: The Court of Appeal stated that the decisions in the cases of *Adams v Bracknell Forrest Borough Council* [2005] 1 AC 76 and *Catholic Care (Diocese of Leeds) v Young* [2006] EWCA Civ 1534 mean that the law as it had been previously understood and applied had changed. The test under section 14(2) is substantially objective. Further the question whether an injury is 'significant' within section 14(10)(a), as expanded in section 14(2) must be decided by reference to the seriousness of the injury, and not by reference to its effect, on the claimant's private life or career. Lord Justice Neuberger concluded:

> The question the Judge should have asked herself was whether a reasonable person in the claimant's position, and with his knowledge of the injury, would on the hypothesis postulated by section 14(2), have considered the injury sufficiently serious to justify the institution of proceedings by February 1994 at the latest. Had the Judge asked herself that question it could, in my opinion, only have admitted of one answer, namely that the claimant could not bring himself within section 14(2). First, he was plainly aware, from his own personal experience, of the nature and extent of the damage to his hearing within a day or 2 of the injury occurring. Secondly, thanks to the 3 medical assessments which he had had in late 1993 and the one assessment in early 1994, he was, within 6 months of the injury at the absolute outside, aware of the medical diagnosis, loss of hearing, tinnitus and pain, all of which confirmed his own experience. Thirdly, ever since he had suffered the injury, it had not got any worse. In other words, in terms of the cause, nature, and extent of the injury, the claimant had been as aware and as well informed by early 1994 (at the latest) as he was at all times thereafter.

> In my judgment, that is really the beginning and end of this appeal, subject to the section 33 issue.

Lord Justice Neuberger pointed out that the Judge had been wrong to take into account the fact that the injury caused in 1993 did not result in any setback in the claimant's career until 2001. He concluded the claimant had all the information he needed about the injury by February 1994 at the latest.

D. Summary of Questions in Respect of Limitation

3.25 In considering the limitation period in respect of a clinical negligence claim the following questions need to be addressed:

(i) *Is the claimant still a child?*
     If the claimant is a child under 18 years there are no limitation problems even if the injury occurred many years earlier. Section 28 Limitation Act 1980 applies and the limitation period does not start to run until the claimant ceases to be a child.
     It is necessary to identify a suitable litigation friend, this may need to be the Official Solicitor if there is no suitable relative. The claimant's 18th birthday needs to be identified and a claim issued within three years of that date for limitation purposes. Whether a claim needs to be issued earlier for evidential or other reasons will need separate consideration.

(ii) *Is the claimant over 18 years but under 21 years of age?*
     If the claimant is still under 21 there are no limitation problems but a claim will need to be issued urgently before the claimant reaches 21. Section 28 allows the claim to be brought within three years of the claimant ceasing to be under a disability.
     The only alternative is to negotiate an agreement with the defendant that limitation ceases to run from a specified date.

(iii) *Is the claimant now a patient within Part 21 of the CPR, section 1 of the Mental Health Act 1983?*
     In many catastrophic brain damage cases it will be obvious that the claimant is a patient and requires a litigation friend. In cases where it is not obvious but the claimant has a head injury or serious psychiatric damage then it is possible the claimant is a patient. If it is not entirely clear it is necessary to obtain a psychiatric report on this issue applying the test in *Masterman-Lister v Brutton & Co* [2003] 1 WLR 1511. If the claimant is now a patient it is then necessary to identify a suitable litigation friend, however question (iv) below has to be addressed before the limitation position is secure.

(iv) *If the claimant is now a patient, can it be established that the claimant has been a patient for the entire period since the injury?*
     If the claimant was a patient from the date of injury then no problem of limitation arises unless the claimant improves and then ceases to become

a patient. Section 28 of the Limitation Act 1980 applies and the claimant will have three years to bring a claim from any date on which he ceases to be a patient.

(v) *If the claimant became a patient after the injury, was the claimant an adult at the date he became a patient?*

In some cases the claimant suffers an injury as a result of negligence but would not qualify as a patient for the purposes of the Mental Health Act 1983 immediately. The claimant's primary limitation period will start to run from the date of this injury (subject to any arguments as to date of knowledge). The claimant may subsequently suffer a further injury or a deterioration in his condition so that he becomes a patient and requires a litigation friend. This deterioration does not stop the limitation period running although it is a factor for the court to take into consideration in the exercise of discretion under section 33(3)(d) of the Limitation Act 1980. Proceedings should therefore be issued within three years of the original injury or three years of the claimant reaching 18 years of age.

(vi) *Was the claim limitation barred before August 1980?*

The Limitation Act 1980 did not come into force until 1 May 1981. Under paragraph 9 of Schedule 2 to the Limitation Act 1980 it is provided that: 'Nothing in any provision of this act shall enable any action to be brought which was barred by this act or (as the case may be) the Limitation Act 1939 before the relevant date (being 1 August 1980).'

It is therefore necessary to consider whether the claimant's claim was barred by the Limitation Act 1939 on 1 August 1980. Causes of action which accrued prior to June 1954 have been held to be limitation barred and unextendable:

See: *Arnold v Central Electricity Generating Board* [1988] AC 288, *McDonnell v Congregation of Christian Brothers Trustees* [2003] 1 AC 1101.

Whilst it may be unusual it is not impossible to have claims relating to birth damage or damage in childhood which date from prior to 1954. Had the X-rays in the case of *Smith v Leicester Health Authority* which were taken in September 1954 and June 1955 been taken a few months earlier the claim would have been limitation barred on this basis as neither the date of knowledge nor discretion arguments apply to claims arising from a breach of duty prior to June 1954.

(vii) *If the injury occurred more than three years ago has the claimant got a later date of actual knowledge?*

The actual date of knowledge pursuant to sections 11 and 14 of the Limitation Act 1980 will depend on when the claimant knew of the facts that he/she will need to rely on to bring a claim. In some cases this will be immediately after the injury occurs in others it will not be until the claimant has a medical expert report explaining what occurred. The following are examples of cases involving actual knowledge:

(a) The claimant is admitted to hospital for a procedure and the hospital carry out a different procedure causing injury. The allegation is the wrong procedure was carried out and this can be pleaded even without medical evidence. For example, the hospital removes the right breast instead of the left. The date of knowledge will be the date the claimant discovers the wrong breast was removed.

(b) The claimant is admitted to hospital for removal of a breast lump and the doctor removes the claimant's breast. The claimant is told on returning to hospital six months later that the lump was benign and the breast should not have been removed. The allegation is removing a non-malignant breast, the date of knowledge is the date the claimant is told the lump was benign.

(c) The claimant is admitted to hospital for a hip replacement, the claimant has significant complaint about the operation afterwards and complains but is reassured his condition will settle down and his problems are the normal result of surgery. The claimant two years later goes to a different doctor who X-rays the hip and finds the femur has been inserted at the wrong angle. The claimant's date of knowledge is when he is told about the X-ray by the treating doctor.

(d) The claimant is admitted to hospital for a simple operation. After the operation he suffers a respiratory arrest and brain damage but is not a patient. The claimant is told the collapse occurred because he had an unusual reaction to a drug he was given. The claimant consults solicitors who obtain an expert report which advises that the claimant did not suffer a reaction to a drug but suffered internal bleeding which should have been identified with proper monitoring. The claimant's date of knowledge is when he receives the expert report as the allegation that he suffered bleeding cannot be made until he receives the report.

(e) If there are good arguments that the claimant did not have actual knowledge until less than three years ago then constructive knowledge needs to be considered.

(f) If the claimant clearly had actual knowledge more than three years ago then section 33 needs to be considered.

(g) In any case where the primary period of limitation has expired it is sensible either to negotiate a suspension of limitation from a specified date with the defendant or to issue and serve proceedings immediately and apply on notice to the defendant for an extension of time to serve particulars of claim.

(viii) *If the injury occurred more than three years ago has the claimant got a later date of constructive knowledge?*

If the claimant did not have actual knowledge of the facts he will need to plead in respect of the allegations of negligence it is necessary to consider the date of constructive knowledge. That is the date on which it would have been reasonable for the claimant with his particular injury (but not taking into account other personal characteristics or character traits) to seek legal and medical advice. If the claimant has a very serious injury which was not the anticipated result of the surgery it is reasonable for him to wait some period of months before consulting solicitors.

The date of constructive knowledge will depend on when the claimant could reasonably consider that something had gone wrong with the treatment he received. If the result is one that the claimant has been warned may occur he is more likely to be acting reasonably if he does not immediately enquire whether there has been negligence. If on the other hand the result is entirely unexpected then the claimant may reasonably be expected to enquire why the result occurred within a few months of the injury occurring.

As with actual knowledge where there is an issue as to when the claimant had constructive knowledge, the safest course is always to negotiate a limitation suspension date or to issue protective proceedings immediately.

(ix) *If the claimant had actual or constructive knowledge more than three years ago will the Court exercise its discretion to allow the action to proceed?*

Where it is necessary to rely on the Court's discretion it is essential to ensure that proceedings are issued as soon as possible or a limitation suspension is negotiated with the defendant. Further delay after a claimant instructs a solicitor will always weaken the case for the Court exercising its discretion. Where the claimant's date of knowledge is more than ten years before the issue of proceedings it will be very unusual for the court to exercise its discretion to allow the action to proceed.

Careful thought must be given to whether limitation should be heard as a preliminary issue; the more the Court knows about the circumstances of the case the easier it is to balance the prejudice. In many cases it will be unfair to hear limitation separately as the Court will not get a full account of the strength of the case or a full understanding of the significance or lack of significance of the absence of witnesses or documents.

In the case of *Smith v Leicester Health Authority* limitation was heard together with liability and causation (at the defendant's request) and the Judge made findings on the allegations of negligence in respect of the radiologist without any difficulty through the delay. Without being able to review the strength of the case and the lack of difficulty from the absence of witnesses once the X-rays had materialised it would have been difficult for the Court of Appeal properly to review the limitation issues.

4

FUNDING

The clinical negligence practitioner needs to be aware both of the professional **4.01** rules governing the solicitor–client retainer and of the evolving case law relating to insurance and conditional fee agreements. A detailed discussion of these is outside the scope of this work. pThis chapter outlines the different methods of funding available for clinical negligence litigation, describes the relationship between the different methods of funding, and discusses problem areas. Later chapters cover funding considerations that arise during each stage of the litigation.

A. Initial Considerations

Careful consideration should be given to the funding of the claim at the outset, **4.02** on the basis that the case will proceed to trial. This analysis will reveal those cases where proportionality issues will arise, and other cases where the immediate funding available will be insufficient to pursue the matter to a final hearing. It may be perfectly possible to investigate and attempt settlement of a claim that it would be difficult to fund to trial but the identification at an early stage of the point at which funding problems will arise ensures that both practitioner and client have realistic expectations, and enables them to agree a strategy for managing the claim within these constraints and to set regular review stages. Overall, whatever the funding method to be applied, careful case planning at the outset will encourage a sensible assessment of risk when accepting instructions and enable realistic cost assessments to be given to the client as well as reducing to a minimum the amount of time spent working for no remuneration.

B. Before-the-Event Insurance

4.03 Before any other funding is explored, meaningful enquiries should be made as to whether the client has the benefit of legal expenses insurance. The enquiries and the client's response should be carefully recorded on the file.

4.04 *David Myatt v National Coal Board* [2007] All ER (D) 301 (Mar) established that failure to make sufficient enquiries into the existence of before-the-event legal expenses insurance will render a conditional fee agreement unenforceable whether or not such legal expenses insurance was in fact in place. The extent of the enquiries to be made was considered. In effect, the position is that a client must be asked whether he has any home, credit card, or motor insurance, whether he has any legal expenses insurance in force and if the insurance would extend to the claim in contemplation. This last question is one that should be investigated by the practitioner unless the client can confidently be assumed to be capable of establishing the fact for himself.

4.05 An application for a substantive certificate of public funding must be accompanied by copies of building, contents, or motor insurance policies and the application form asks whether or not legal expenses insurance attaches to any policy and requires confirmation that these have been inspected by the applicant's solicitor.

4.06 The most sensible approach is for a letter to be sent confirming the initial appointment, with a request that the client bring with them copies of any policies and schedules for any insurance cover they have in place, including buildings, contents, motor, and credit card cover. As cover will not be retrospective, it should be made clear that the policies and schedules provided for inspection should relate to insurance in place at the time of the alleged negligence, whether or not they are in force at the time of the interview.

4.07 Although not an absolute requirement in all cases, personal inspection of the insurance documentation, duly recorded on the file, is the most certain method of establishing that proper enquiries have been made.

4.08 A surprising number of clients do have legal expenses insurance but are unaware of the fact, or unaware that it may cover clinical negligence litigation. Where legal expenses insurance exists, it is a substantial benefit to the client and will enable a thorough investigation into the merits without financial risk. The client must be advised to notify the insurer of a potential claim without delay; this should be done regardless of whether or not the insured has decided to instigate a claim. Before-the-event insurance policies require potential claims to be notified within a specified time period following the occurrence giving rise to the claim—the limit is normally six months. The time limits tend to be strictly applied.

The policy schedule and policy booklet should be examined to establish the following points.   **4.09**

Are Clinical Negligence Claims excluded from Cover?

Claims arising from medical treatment may be specifically excluded but this should be carefully checked in the policy wording. The representations of the insurance broker or the insurance company's helpline representative should not be accepted as definitive, as frequently incorrect advice is given on this point.   **4.10**

Does the Cover Extend to the Potential Claimant?

If the potential claimant is not the policyholder, the relationship of the claimant to the policyholder at the time in question needs to be established. Adult children living away from home may well not be covered under a family policy and again the details need to be checked carefully.   **4.11**

Was the Policy in Force at the Relevant Time?

Where there is a single identifiable date of negligence, establishing this point does not present a difficulty. However, where there has been a long course of treatment and it is not clear when the earliest date of negligence may be, difficulties can arise in securing cover under the policy, particularly if it was not in place from the onset of the illness.   **4.12**

Has any Time Limit for Notification of a Potential Claim been Exceeded?

The practitioner should advise the client to report a potential claim to their legal expenses insurer without delay, even if they have not decided whether they intend to take any further steps. As indicated above, most, if not all, policies require potential claims to be notified within a specified period of the alleged negligence, normally six months. These time limits tend to be strictly applied.   **4.13**

Insurers may refuse to accept a claim against a policy, if the date of knowledge is more than six months after the date of alleged negligence. The insurer's argument is that the policy provides that the time period for notification of a claim   **4.14** runs from the date on which the injury occurred and not from a later date of knowledge.

4.15 Some insurers will guide—or attempt to propel—the policyholder to one of their own nominated panel of solicitors. This is not something they should insist upon when a clinical negligence claim is in contemplation. The Financial Ombudsman's Service has considered the question of choice of solicitor and stated: '… we expect insurers to agree the appointment of the policyholder's preferred solicitors in cases that involved large personal injury claims, or that are necessarily complex (such as those involving allegations of medical negligence).' (*Ombudsman's News*, March 2003, issue 26, at: <http://www.financial-ombudsman. org.uk> (accessed 2 April 2007)).

4.16 Insurers vary as to their practice in this regard, but despite the clarity of the Ombudsman's view, the argument may have to be pursued vigorously in order to obtain the authority to act under the policy.

4.17 The substantive content of the claim form should be drafted by the practitioner on the client's behalf. This will ensure that the legal expenses insurer is provided with sufficient information to reach a prompt decision to accept the claim. A thorough and competently drafted claim form should assist in securing authority to act under the terms of the policy. The claim form should include the following information:

   (i)   a brief summary of the facts and the identity of the parties including all relevant dates;
   (ii) the allegations of negligence under the separate heading of breach of duty and causation;
   (iii) initial assessment of quantum;
   (iv) comment on any limitation issues or confirmation that there is no limitation problem;
   (v)   outline steps required for an initial investigation of the merits;
   (vi) comments on likely costs and proportionality and assessment of the overall merits;
   (vii) who is likely to be handling the case, their qualifications, experience, and hourly rates;
   (viii) the application should be checked and signed by the policyholder;
   (ix) if the policyholder is not the potential claimant, it would be good practice for the potential claimant to sign the form as well;
   (x)   the claim form should be sent with a covering letter asking the insurer to confirm authority to act for the claimant under the terms of the policy. This will be subject to agreeing to their terms and conditions.

The time spent establishing funding will not be recovered in costs as before-the- **4.18**
event legal expenses insurance policies exclude any legal costs incurred before the
insurer has accepted the claim, confirmed the authority under the indemnity, and
terms and conditions have been agreed. However, the information required to
complete the claim form should be readily available as it is essentially the same
as the information required to complete the initial risk assessment.

The insurer's terms and conditions should be carefully noted. If the insurer's **4.19**
hourly rate is unacceptable, it may be possible to arrive at an agreement for the
fee earner's standard hourly rate, on the basis that the insurer will only indemnify
the insured at the lower rate if a claim is made against the policy. The fee earners
standard rate should be quoted in the initial client care letter which should enable
that rate to be recovered inter partes at the successful conclusion of the claim.
It is open to the fee earner to waive their entitlement to recover the shortfall
from the claimant if the claim is unsuccessful.

The insurer's reporting requirements should also be carefully noted together **4.20**
with those steps which require prior authority, which usually include instructing
experts and counsel. It is helpful to ascertain at this stage the insurer's preference
for requesting increases in the financial authority. Some prefer a brief written
request, others require a detailed written report, yet others prefer to discuss the
request by telephone.

Generally insurers will adhere strictly to financial limits and will rarely grant **4.21**
authority retrospectively. Where it is impossible to be precise about likely expenditure, for example where a conference with counsel and experts may run over the
anticipated time, this possibility should be flagged up when applying for the
authority.

It is essential to keep a close eye on the overall costs in relation to the extent of **4.22**
the client's indemnity. This may be as little as £25,000 but is now commonly
£50,000 or £75,000. If the initial case plan suggests that funds are likely to be
sufficient to take the action beyond the service of proceedings, it must be kept in
mind that from that point on, calculations on the balance of the indemnity need
to allow for the claimant's potential liability for the defendant's costs.

It is important to give consideration at this stage as to how the claim will be **4.23**
funded once the insurance indemnity has been exhausted. This should be discussed with the client, even if only to point out that there may well be a need to
review the funding arrangements in the future if the claim does not settle before
the insurance is exhausted. Some before-the-event insurers will offer top-up
insurance to pursue the claim to a conclusion. Alternatively, it may be possible to
proceed under a conditional fee agreement with after-the-event insurance, or
public funding may be available (for example, for a child claimant).

C. Membership Benefits

4.24 All clients should be asked, and where appropriate requested, to make full checks as to whether they may have the benefit of assistance with legal expenses through a trade union or other professional membership. If such assistance is available, the general approach should be as set out above for before-the-event insurance.

D. Public Funding

4.25 Public funding may be available where there is no legal expenses insurance policy on which the client can rely, no alternative membership benefit on which they can draw and where there is no other party to the action who might reasonably be expected to bring the action. The regulations can be found in the *Legal Services Commission Manual (Volume 3) Part A Section 5*. Public funding in clinical negligence cases may only be granted through a firm that has the specialist expertise recognised by the Legal Services Commission by grant of a Specialist Quality Mark and a contract to undertake clinical negligence work for the Commission.

Where there is No Contract in Place

4.26 A solicitor has a professional duty to advise a client on the availability of legal aid where the client might be entitled to assistance. Guidance as to that duty is contained in *The Law Society's Regulations and Professional Conduct Guide 5.01* and may be found at <http://www.lawsociety.org.uk> (accessed 27 March 2007). It is important in this context to consider whether the client may be eligible for public funding when any other preliminary source of funding has been exhausted, for example when personal savings have been expended or when the limits of indemnity have been reached under before-the-event insurance.

4.27 To be eligible for public funding the claimant's case must meet the funding code criteria which can be found in the *Legal Services Commission Manual (Volume 3)*, which is available on their website at <http://www.legalservices.gov.uk> (accessed 2 April 2007). The applicant must be financially eligible and the claim must pass the relevant Community Legal Services tests of merits and costs benefits. An initial assessment of financial eligibility can be made by using the eligibility calculator on the Community Legal Service website. A definitive assessment of eligibility can only be made by the Community Legal Service itself. This will be based on the information supplied by the client through the formal application process, by a solicitor working in a firm with a clinical negligence contract.

It follows that a practitioner in a firm without a Specialist Quality Mark (SQM) **4.28**
and clinical negligence contract must advise a client whom it appears may be
eligible for assistance about the availability of public funding through another
firm. The benefits to the eligible claimant of a certificate of funding are very
considerable and the client should be encouraged to consult a firm that will be
able to make the application.

A conditional fee agreement will be unenforceable if the client is not fully **4.29**
advised regarding the availability of public funding, see *Tracey Hughes v Newham
London Borough Council; Karin Opoku-Donker v Newham London Borough
Council; Valerie Thornton v Newham London Borough (2005) Supreme Court Costs
Office* (Master O'Hare) (28 July 2005).

Where there is a Contract in Place

A firm with an SQM and clinical negligence contract will have in place in-house **4.30**
procedures for managing the funding of these claims and will be familiar with the
SQM transaction criteria and these will not be set out in detail in this work but
can be found on the Legal Services Commission website. Some general observations on points that may be overlooked by less experienced practitioners are
discussed below.

As mentioned above, the Community Legal Services' section of the Legal Services **4.31**
Commission website includes an up-to-date eligibility calculator which will
provide an indication of whether the client is financially eligible for public funding. It is important to be aware that a final assessment of financial eligibility
can only be made by the Community Legal Service, and an application should
be submitted for any client whose claim has legal merits, if their financial eligibility appears to be borderline or where their financial circumstances are unusual.

There is no appeal against refusal of public funding on the grounds of financial **4.32**
ineligibility, but the Legal Services Commission do provide the figures forming
their calculation when they send notification of refusal of funding. These figures
and calculations should be checked. The applicant is entitled to ask for the figures
to be reviewed if the figures or the calculation appear to be erroneous.

Legal Help

Some firms have ceased to offer Legal Help in clinical negligence claims because **4.33**
of the limitations on what can be achieved within the extremely limited funding
available and the complexities involved in recouping costs from the Legal Services
Commission. For those who do offer Legal Help, it may be of particular assistance to fund the cost of obtaining and perusing the records, particularly where
the medical records are likely to contain factual information that will be critical

to establishing prima facie evidence of negligence in support of an application for legal representation.

4.34 Financial eligibility criteria for Legal Help are more stringent than for legal representation. An important difference is that child claimants are assessed on their parents' means rather than their own as they would be under Legal Representation.

4.35 In view of the circumscribed nature of Legal Help it is very important to define within appropriately narrow limits what can be achieved and what should be attempted under this funding regime before making an application for a substantive certificate for Investigative Help. It is only too easy to overlook the financial limits and spend time on the records and on research which cannot be recouped.

Problem Areas for Public Funding

Fatal injuries—inquests

4.36 Advice on inquests may be given under the Legal Help scheme.

4.37 Representation at inquests is outside the scope of public funding but there are special arrangements for 'exceptional funding' for representation at inquests under Section 6(8)(b) of the Access to Justice Act. Applications must be made in accordance with the Lord Chancellor's Guidance. These provisions can be found in the *Legal Services Commission Manual (Volume 3)* Section 27.1; the application procedure is at Section 27.6. The Lord Chancellor's Guidance is at Section 27.2 and Volume 1, Part C.

4.38 The financial criteria for representation at an inquest are those applied to the Legal Help scheme. Furthermore, the Legal Services Commission will enquire into the financial circumstances of family members, beyond the parents and immediate family, to establish whether there is any interested party who might reasonably bear the cost of representation.

4.39 Applications for exceptional funding should be made to the Legal Services Commission's Special Cases Unit in London and should be accompanied by a completed CLSAPP1 form and the appropriate Community Legal Service financial information form. The application should address the issues set out in the Lord Chancellor's Guidance. If funding is refused, an application must be made within 14 days for the decision to be reconsidered. If the decision is confirmed this can be appealed. The time limit for submitting representations to the appeal panel will be notified by letter. The Commission's final decision is subject to Judicial Review.

4.40 If an application for Investigative Help is submitted in a claim where an inquest is pending, the Legal Services Commission may refuse to grant a certificate until the inquest has been concluded, on the grounds that it is appropriate to wait until further information is known to enable the merits of a civil claim to be evaluated. Unless the inquest is fixed for a very early date and matters will not be delayed, a refusal on these grounds should be contested as:

(i) the inquest may be delayed and delay is prejudicial to all parties to a civil claim;

(ii) the outcome of an inquest is not determinant of the merits of a civil claim for negligence;

(iii) prospects of early settlement are jeopardised by delay.

Fatal injuries—child claimants

There are particular difficulties associated with applications for funding **4.41** for dependent children in fatal claims. The Legal Services Commission regulations provide that funding should not be granted where there is another person who could reasonably bring the claim. The position is set out in Community Legal Service Funding Code (Section 5.4.2). There is at least arguably scope for interpretation and discretion, but the Commission's general position is that certificates will be refused to financially eligible children who may have a claim for loss of dependency, if the surviving parent is financially ineligible for public funding. This position is adopted on the basis that the surviving parent has an interest in the claim and is 'another person who could reasonably bring the claim'. This stance should not be regarded as immutable as there may be circumstances in which it could be challenged. However, in most circumstances, applications for funding should be made in accordance with the principles set out below.

The executor or administrator of the estate is the proper person to bring a claim **4.42** on behalf of the estate under the Law Reform (Miscellaneous Provisions) Act 1934 and on behalf of the dependants under the Fatal Accidents Act 1976 (section 192). The executor is likely to be the surviving spouse, but that may not be the case and the situation needs to be clarified at the first interview.

When applying for a certificate of funding, if the executor has no beneficial inter- **4.43** est in the residual estate and no dependency claim, a CLSAPP1 form should be submitted for each of the dependants together with the appropriate assessment form. As the claimant in the action, the executor will also require a certificate of funding; a CLSAPP1 should be submitted on behalf of the executor. This should be accompanied by a MEANS1 form completed with details of the assets of the estate and the terms of the will, including a copy of the will. The assessment of financial eligibility will be made on the basis of what funds are available in the estate that could be applied to support litigation, together with the dependants' own financial means. The executor's personal finances are not relevant to this assessment.

4.44   Where the executor is a residuary beneficiary or has a potential claim for loss of dependency, a CLSAPP1 will reflect this dual status and should be accompanied by the appropriate means assessment form setting out the executor's personal financial means. The executor should be ready to provide such information about the assets in the estate as requested by the Community Legal Service.

Fatal injuries—no surviving spouse and no dependants

4.45   If there has been a relatively short period of pain and suffering attributable to the negligent treatment and no significant loss or expense, quantum is unlikely to reach five figures. Such a claim is not likely to satisfy the Legal Services Commission's Funding Code criteria. Careful analysis of the facts may yield sufficient information to allow an application to be made in certain circumstances. For example, elderly parents may have had real expectations of future financial support from their deceased child. The cost-benefits test may be less strictly applied in cases of overwhelming importance to the client as this is a criterion to be taken into account, as provided for in the Regulations at Volume 3, Part 1, Section 5.7.2; accordingly, an application for funding should stress the overwhelming importance that the claim has for the surviving relatives. Consideration should also be given as to whether it could be argued that the case genuinely has wider public importance or Human Rights Act elements as these aspects, if accepted, may influence the Commission's decision.

4.46   A claim arising from a stillbirth or death of a child may not meet the Legal Services Commission's Funding Code criteria because of its low value in damages but it is likely to be accepted that such a claim is a matter of overwhelming importance to the client. The possibility of additional claims for psychiatric injury to the parents should be explored.

E. Private Funding

4.47   If no other source of funding is available, the client needs frank advice as to the costs and implications of funding an investigation from their own resources. The feasibility and appropriateness of such a commitment will naturally vary from client to client. If the practitioner goes into a client interview without a predetermined scale of charges for private funding, there is a risk that this will result in an offer to carry out the investigation at an unfeasibly low figure and it may be unclear to both parties what the agreement was intended to cover. For these reasons it is of great assistance to have a predetermined scale of fees to put to the client, with a clear description of what steps the fee would cover, for example whether the agreement covers one expert report or two, or one expert report and a conference with counsel. The client should be advised that a positive outcome to the investigation would ideally result in an offer to proceed under a conditional fee agreement, but that when it comes to obtaining after-the-event insurance, the insurers may want more information about the defendant's stance, further expert comments, or counsel's opinion, at the client's expense, before cover will be offered.

The majority of clients who can afford to do so will willingly enter into such **4.48** an arrangement when it is made at a reasonable cost with 'a view to' a conditional fee agreement, as this is seen as an equitable risk sharing exercise. The arrangement should include a clear agreement about how much is to be paid up front and the arrangements for interim billing. This is not only good business practice, it is much easier for the client to pay in this manner and there is nothing more likely to embitter a client whose investigation has been negative than being presented with a bill for the whole investigation at the unsuccessful conclusion.

Difficulties can arise with applying for after-the-event insurance, particularly **4.49** when the expert report is ambiguous or only partly supportive. The potential insurers may require counsel's opinion before making a decision. Counsel invited to act under a Conditional Fee Agreement would normally read the papers and advise in conference on an initial limited Conditional Fee Agreement, but any fees for experts' attendance will have to be met by the client. The possibility of these additional costs arising before a final decision can be made as to whether the claim can proceed must be explained to the client at the outset.

From time to time it may seem like a good idea to help a client in these circum- **4.50** stances by asking an expert to provide an opinion in a letter rather than a report. This may be useful in establishing whether the premise underlying the analysis of the case is one that is worthy of investigation, but beyond that, such an approach is of doubtful value. If the expert is encouraging, the report will need to be commissioned and paid for and yet may not support the claim on the facts of the particular case. If the expert is negative, the practitioner may not feel fully confident in relying on that opinion and in any event the client may well be dissatisfied. That is not to dismiss such an approach out of hand; sometimes needs must, and in these circumstances the expert approached should be one in whom the practitioner has thorough confidence.

An expert should be asked to telephone to discuss the position before embarking **4.51** on a report, if the case that has been put to them is an obvious non-runner. A decision can then be taken with the client as to whether to pay for a full report.

4.52 There are some cases where it is possible to offer a Conditional Fee Agreement at the outset. It should be made clear to the client that the Conditional Fee Agreement is limited to the investigation and will be reviewed in the light of the merits of the case. The extent to which this facility can be offered naturally will depend upon each firm's attitude to risk.

4.53 Although many fee earners feel uncomfortable talking to clients about fees and billing, most clients are very concerned about the cost implications. The more clarity there is on the subject, the more confidence the client will have in the practitioner and the firm overall.

5

THE DEFENDANT

A. Introduction

This chapter outlines the broad structure of the NHS, points to sources of detailed information, describes the organisational arrangements that commonly apply in public and private health care, and discusses problematic areas and how to resolve them. It is necessary to understand the organisation of health care in the UK to appreciate the indemnity or insurance arrangements that will apply to any specific claim. **5.01**

Fortunately, despite the size and complexity of the NHS structure and the variations in the health care arrangements in different geographical areas, in the majority of clinical negligence cases, identifying the defendant does not present a problem. More often than not, the allegedly negligent treatment will have been provided by a clinician employed at a hospital or clinic administered by an NHS **5.02**

Trust, or by an individual clinician in a private practice. Nevertheless, there are some circumstances in which establishing the identity of the correct defendant is less straightforward.

5.03 To avoid over-elaboration, throughout this work the arrangements in force are taken to be those that apply in England; readers interested in the arrangements in other countries may find the sources of information mentioned below useful starting points.

B. National Health Service

5.04 The NHS covers the whole of the UK but the organisational structure of health care provision differs between the several countries that make up the UK.

5.05 The States of Guernsey, the States of Jersey, and the Isle of Man each have independent health services. Information about these can be found at <http://www.gov.gg> (accessed 2 April 2007), <http://www.gov.je/HealthWell> (accessed 2 April 2007), and <http://www.gov.im/dhss/health> (accessed 2 April 2007).

Wales

5.06 The National Assembly is the strategic authority responsible for the NHS in Wales. The NHS in Wales is composed of 15 NHS Trusts. Claims are handled by the Welsh Risk Pool, a mutual self-insurance arrangement. The Welsh Risk Pool is also responsible for risk management and audit. Further information about the NHS in Wales can be found at <http://www.wales.nhs.uk> (accessed 2 April 2007).

Scotland

5.07 Delivery of National Health Services in Scotland is the responsibility of the NHS National Services Scotland. Further information about the NHS in Scotland can be found at <http://www.show.scot.nhs.uk> (accessed 2 April 2007).

Northern Ireland

5.08 The Department of Health, Social Services and Public Safety is responsible for NHS services in Northern Ireland. Further information can be found at <http://www.dhsspsni.gov.uk> (accessed 2 April 2007).

England

5.09 Responsibility for administering NHS services in England belongs to the Department of Health, which is also responsible for Social Services.

Arrangements for handling clinical negligence claims in England are described in   **5.10**
detail in the National Audit Office, *Handling Clinical Negligence Claims in England*
(HC 403, 2000–2001), 3 May 2001. The function of the Department of Health
(and equivalent bodies in other UK countries) is overall control of NHS services,
standards, and working practices dealing with strategy, quality standards, funding, and integration in support services. A wealth of information is available at
<http://www.nhs.uk/england> (accessed 2 April 2007).

Strategic Health Authorities

The next administrative tier down consists of the Strategic Health Authorities.   **5.11**
There are ten Strategic Health Authorities in England, which are responsible for
planning services and monitoring performance for their own geographical area.
Within each Strategic Health Authority, responsibility for services will be divided
among different Trusts.

Special Health Authorities

The Special Health Authorities provide specific services to the whole of   **5.12**
England. The NHS Blood and Transplant Authority and the National Institute
for Health and Clinical Excellence (NICE) are Special Health Authorities, as
are the National Patient Safety Agency and the National Health Service Litigation Authority. NHS Direct, originally a Special Health Authority, became a
Trust on 1 April 2007. A full list of Special Health Authorities can be found on
the NHS website.

Trusts

There are five different kinds of NHS Trusts responsible for different aspects   **5.13**
of NHS service provision in their geographical area: Primary Care Trusts, Acute
Trusts, Ambulance Trusts, Care Trusts, and Mental Health Trusts. A relatively
recent development is the Foundation Trust, a more independent form of NHS
Trust established under the Health and Social Care (Community Health Standards) Act 2005. Existing Trusts may apply to become Foundation Trusts, which
have a different constitution from and more financial and operational freedom
than the NHS Trust but will nevertheless remain accountable within the NHS
framework for the services provided.

Primary Care Trusts

Primary Care Trusts control a very large proportion of the NHS budget. The   **5.14**
Trusts are charged with commissioning and monitoring all local NHS services.
It is the role of the Primary Care Trust to organise the integration of the social

care systems, that is, the overlap between local authority provision and local NHS care. Doctors, dentists, NHS opticians, and pharmacists will be contracted by the local Primary Care Trust to provide services in that area.

Acute Trusts

5.15 Acute Trusts are responsible for the management and administration of acute services hospitals. Acute Trusts are also responsible for the strategic development and performance of local acute services. The Acute Trust is the employer of the NHS workforce employed in acute services hospitals.

Mental Health Trusts

5.16 Mental Health Trusts are broadly analogous to Acute Trusts and provide mental health services including specialist services such as clinic-based psychological therapy and inpatient treatment for acute mental illness.

Ambulance Trusts

5.17 There are 13 Ambulance Trusts providing emergency access to care across England; each Ambulance Trust therefore covers a much larger geographical area than the Acute and Primary Care Trusts. Some Ambulance Trusts also organise services for patients requiring transport for non-urgent treatment.

Care Trusts

5.18 Care Trusts may be created when the Strategic Health Authority perceives a need for closer relationships between health and social (local authority) care. Care Trusts will provide services which include social care, mental health, and primary care. Alternatively, the services may be provided variously by the Acute and Primary Care Trusts and local Social Services without the organisation of a Care Trust.

C. Identifying the Defendant

5.19 When allegations of negligence arise from NHS treatment, the identity of the defendant is dependent upon the employment or contractual arrangement between the allegedly negligent health care professional and the NHS organisation providing the service.

NHS Hospitals

5.20 Where the client is concerned about NHS treatment given in an NHS Hospital by a hospital employee, the Trust responsible for the hospital will be the correct defendant, as the employer is vicariously liable for the torts of their employees.

Special Health Authorities

If the treatment complained of relates to a service provided by a Special Health **5.21** Authority, for example NHS Direct, the Health Authority will be the legal defendant.

Primary Care

Where the NHS treatment complained of was given in the primary care setting, **5.22** some investigation will be required. If the treatment was given by a general practitioner or a general practitioner dentist under the NHS, the practitioner in question will be an independent contractor and not an employee of the Primary Care Trust. General practitioners and dentists generally practise in partnerships. The current partnership will have arrangements in place to meet the liabilities of deceased or departed partners and all current partners will be jointly and severally liable in respect of any claims against individuals. The individual doctor or dentist is the correct defendant; each doctor or dentist is responsible for arranging their own professional indemnity cover.

Where the treatment was given by an optician or a pharmacist, they are likely to be **5.23** independent practitioners with a contractual agreement to undertake NHS work. In those circumstances, the optician or pharmacist will have professional indemnity arrangements in place, possibly through their professional organisation and commonly backed by one of the major insurers. The solicitor should request details of the indemnity arrangement when first writing to give notice of the claim.

A chiropractor or physiotherapist providing NHS treatment may be employed **5.24** as an independent contractor but it is more likely that they are employed by the Primary Care Trust, possibly on a sessional basis; in which case the Primary Care Trust is the correct defendant.

NHS Treatment in the Private Sector

Where NHS treatment was given in a private hospital under arrangements made **5.25** by the NHS, the picture is a little more complex. Private hospitals or clinics which have entered into these arrangements with the NHS are known as 'Independent Sector Treatment Centres' and are contracted to provide services to the NHS. If the care provider is a 'designated' Independent Sector Treatment Centre, NHS indemnity is extended to cover treatment given by that provider. In those circumstances, the correct defendant would be the Trust under whose auspices the patient was referred to the Independent Sector Treatment Centre.

If the Independent Sector Treatment Centre is not 'designated', the indemnity **5.26** arrangements are a matter of contract between the NHS and the clinic; the contract will need to be reviewed to ascertain the arrangements in place. If the NHS has not extended indemnity under the contract, the legal defendant would be the hospital or clinic (or its parent body), or the individual practitioner, as discussed in the context of private medical treatment below. However, in these circumstances, the solicitor should ensure the commissioning Trust is kept informed of the claim as the NHS has an interest, and might wish to intervene in a way helpful to the claimant. If non-pecuniary remedies are important to the client, it is likely that these will be a matter for the Trust.

Older Claims

5.27 It is important to remember that the current NHS structure has only existed since 1998, although changes to achieve its current structure were implemented from 1988. The evolving nature of the NHS structure has meant that organisations have undergone several changes in name and function over this period. This can create a difficulty in identifying the legal defendant in older cases. Particular care is required for those now obviously rare claims where the cause of action pre-dates 1988. The National Health Service Litigation Authority is the legal defendant in cases brought against the old Regional Health Authorities, in all other cases the legal defendant is the relevant NHS body. Between 1991 and 1995 all local health services became organised into NHS Trusts, which replaced the District Health Authorities. Pre-Trust liabilities are likely to lie with the Strategic Health Authority that covers the relevant health population. The successor Trust's legal department or the National Health Service Litigation Authority will be able to advise on the correct defendant if there is uncertainty.

5.28 Where there has been a change in Trust identity after 1 April 1995, it is likely that the new Trust has adopted the liabilities of the predecessor Trust and the current Trust should be cited as defendant. Again, the claimant practitioner can expect the Trust's legal services department to be helpful in clarifying the position where there is doubt.

National Health Service Litigation Authority

5.29 All claims against the NHS are managed by the National Health Services Litigation Authority; there are several schemes, each of which covers a different liability.

Existing Liabilities Scheme

5.30 The Existing Liabilities Scheme provides cover for all the NHS, in respect of claims arising from clinical incidents which occurred before 1 April 1995.

Clinical Negligence Scheme for Trusts

The Clinical Negligence Scheme for Trusts is a risk-pooling scheme for NHS **5.31** Trusts which provides cover for member Trusts for claims arising from clinical incidents which occurred on or after 1 April 1995. Membership of the Scheme requires that the National Health Service Litigation Authority handles all these claims, whatever their value. Lower value claims are no longer managed at local level.

Liability to Third Parties and Property Expenses Schemes

Collectively known as the 'Risk-Pooling Scheme for Trusts', these schemes provide **5.32** cover for claims arising from accidents that occurred on or after 1 April 1999. From the claimant practitioner's point of view, this would include claims made on the basis of the NHS's public liability, employer's liability, and occupier's liability—including for example slips, trips, food poisoning, injuries from defective products, and assaults.

When instructed in a claim that may come under this Scheme, it is important for **5.33** the claimant to establish how the defendant intends to treat the case, and to argue for a different interpretation if necessary. A tripping injury that may be expensive to investigate and difficult to win if treated as a claim for nursing negligence may have better prospects of success if it is pursued as a claim in occupier's liability. It is likely to be difficult to resolve the matter and to recover investigative costs in full, if the claimant and defendant have not agreed the basis on which the claim is to be advanced.

Redress Scheme

This long-promised scheme does not have a start date at the time of writing. **5.34** The current prediction is 'not before 2008'. Such information as there is, and doubtless further information as it becomes available, can be found on <http://www.dh.gov.uk> (accessed 26 March 2007). It should be noted that this information is couched in terms of intention and that there may be changes before the Scheme is in force.

It is intended that the Redress Scheme will compensate patients who have **5.35** been injured as a result of clinical negligence arising from hospital treatment, where the claim has a specified maximum monetary value, currently suggested as £20,000, on a basis broadly equivalent to common law principles. Claims arising from treatment given as primary care are excluded, even where primary care has been delivered from a hospital site, such as a walk-in centre for out-of-hours GP services.

5.36   The information currently available indicates that the Scheme members (that is, NHS Trusts) will review adverse incidents and identify where patients have been injured as a result of clinical negligence. The potential claim will then be reported to the 'Scheme Authority'. The Health Commissioner may also refer cases. If the case is deemed to fall within the scheme, the patient will be informed, offered an explanation or apology. Where it is considered appropriate to do so, compensation will be offered. Remedial treatment may be offered in addition to or instead of monetary compensation. Compensation payments will be subject to recoupment by the Compensation Recovery Unit in the usual way and the compensation will not be disregarded in the calculation of means tested state benefits—a personal injury trust would be required to protect entitlement to these benefits.

5.37   A claim may be made to the Scheme by a patient, a patient's authorised representative, or representative for a patient who is under a disability, or by a dependant who might have a claim under the Law Reform (Miscellaneous Provisions) Act 1934 or the Fatal Accident Act 1976.

5.38   Time limits for applications are still undecided but it is envisaged that the limitation period for litigation will not start to run until the patient has decided whether or not to accept the Scheme's decision or offer. The settlement agreement under the Scheme will include a waiver of the right to pursue litigation for the same injury. It is intended that the patient will be able to have an independent evaluation of the offer by a solicitor to whom the Scheme will pay a 'flat fee'. The patient will be able to choose a solicitor from a list kept by the Legal Services Commission. Any settlement for a person under a disability would require court approval in the usual way.

D. Private Treatment

5.39   When instructed by a client who has concerns about hospital treatment provided on a private paying basis, the solicitor must establish whether the hospital (or its parent body) is the potential defendant or whether the claim will lie against an individual clinician. The organisation will be the appropriate defendant if the claim arises from inadequate systems or services, or by its vicarious liability for the negligence of its employees. The individual clinician will be personally liable (and the organisation will escape liability) if, as is commonly the case, he is not an employee of the organisation, but instead is a clinician with a contractual right to use the hospital or clinic facilities, as a self-employed private practitioner. A consultant with such 'admitting rights' will use the hospital facilities to see and treat patients who have been referred to the consultant by their GP. Therapists may also agree facilities for sessional work referred by the admitting consultants but they may equally be employed by the organisation direct. Nursing staff are generally employed by the organisation.

In most circumstances the treating doctor's status is quite clear as it will be easy   **5.40**
to establish when the doctor is an NHS consultant, often employed by a local
Trust, who is entitled to undertake a number of sessions in private practice on a
self-employed basis.

In other circumstances, the status of the treating doctor is less clear. This situation   **5.41**
arises most commonly in clinics providing exclusively, or almost exclusively, cosmetic or laser surgery services. These organisations do frequently employ medical
staff who work for them on a regular basis and do not have any NHS commitment. To determine the identity of the defendant, it is necessary to establish
whether they are employees or self-employed contractors.

Where there is any uncertainty as to the status of the health care professional, the   **5.42**
clinic or the corporate body behind the clinic will need to be asked to confirm
whether or not they regard themselves as the employer of the person in question.
If they accept that they are the employer and by implication vicariously liable, it
is safe to proceed on the basis that the clinic or its corporate parent is the appropriate defendant.

Where the health care organisation claims not to be the employer of the allegedly   **5.43**
negligent professional, the practitioner must be alert to the fact that a dispute
may arise on this point, initiated either by the doctor who claims to be an
employee, or between the doctor's medical defence organisation and the organisation's insurer, one of whom will ultimately be liable for paying any damages.
Fortunately both insurers will have an incentive to come to an agreement about
this, possibly agreeing an apportionment behind the scenes, which need not concern the claimant.

The important point here is to keep the issue at the forefront of one's mind until   **5.44**
a safe solution is arrived at. The claimant must keep both of the potential defendants in the frame until this question is formally resolved, as bringing the claim
against the incorrect defendant is likely to result in adverse costs consequences or
create a limitation problem, if it is too late to bring a claim once the identity of
the defendant is known.

E. Indemnity and Insurance Arrangements in the Private Sector

Individual health care professionals, notably doctors and dentists but also phar-   **5.45**
macists, opticians, and physiotherapists, can be expected to be covered by professional liability insurance or to be members of an indemnity scheme. Claimants'
solicitors will most commonly encounter the Medical Protection Society, the
Medical Defence Union, and the Medical and Dental Defence Union of Scotland.

There are also several other insurers offering professional liability insurance to individual practitioners and health care organisations. While the lawyers employed by the main defence organisations are well used to handling their clinical negligence claims, the claimant's solicitor may well find that other less specialist or less experienced insurers are less at home in the clinical negligence protocol.

5.46 There is a potential gap in insurance or indemnity cover where a clinician has committed a negligent or otherwise tortious act or omission that takes them outside the terms of their indemnity cover, for example, a physical or sexual assault on a patient. Where there is no employer to be held vicariously liable, the insurance or indemnifier may refuse to extend cover for the incident in question. If that is the case, the claimant will need to consider whether the defendant will have sufficient personal financial resources to satisfy a claim for damages and costs. Naturally this will depend on what can be established or reasonably deduced about the potential defendant's current and future personal and professional circumstances.

6

THE CLAIMANT AND ALTERNATIVE REMEDIES

Clinical negligence practice requires a particular combination of compassion, empathy, sensitivity, and tough-mindedness. A client who requests advice on a clinical negligence matter has suffered a distressing experience, either personally or because they have witnessed the suffering, or even death, of someone close to them. The belief that medical treatment has been inadequate is peculiarly disturbing, in that it may add loss of confidence and a sense of powerlessness to pre-existing worries about a health problem. Furthermore, a patient usually feels out of their depth when attempting to discuss these concerns with the health care professionals. This loss of confidence has very frequently been exacerbated and even turned to anger by what the client perceives as an inadequate or dishonest response to those concerns on the part of the treating professionals or the organisation to which they belong. Unfortunately, all too often, the complaint correspondence suggests that this perception is justified. In these circumstances, the patient may turn to a solicitor as much to regain a sense of equality of arms as

6.01

because they have a fully formed wish to obtain a legal remedy. Inevitably, work in this area of law will involve meeting many clients who have suffered and who continue to suffer severe health problems, with all the financial, social, and emotional consequences that follow. Compassion, a non-judgmental approach, and ensuring the client is fully included in the claims process will help to restore to the patient a sense of respect and dignity.

6.02 The first interview is a very important opportunity to explore what the client wishes to achieve and to explain the alternative courses of action. This process is described as one of the good practice commitments in the Pre-action Protocol for Resolution of Clinical Disputes at 3.5(ii), where patients and their advisers are expected to:

> Consider the full range of options available following an adverse outcome of which the patient is dissatisfied, including a request for an explanation, a meeting, a complaint, and other appropriate dispute resolution methods (including mediation) and negotiation, not only litigation. (<http://www.dca.gov.uk> (accessed 26 March 2007))

A. Complaints about Treatment in NHS Trusts

6.03 Complaints about NHS treatment are now managed as part of the clinical governance, clinical audit, and risk management process. The complaint system consists of three tiers: local resolution, review by the Healthcare Commissioner, and finally review by the Healthcare Ombudsman. The relevant statutory provision is in the NHS (Complaints) Regulations 2004, SI 2004/1768 and NHS (Complaints) Regulations amended September 2006, SI 2006/2084 and the Health Service Commissioners Act 1993.

Patient Advice and Liaison Service

6.04 When an initial enquiry relates to dissatisfaction about current NHS medical or dental treatment, the client should be advised to try and resolve the matter with his treating consultant or general practitioner. If this is ineffective or inappropriate, he should be advised to ask to speak with the Patient Advice and Liaison Service (PALS). This service is intended to provide confidential advice and support to families and their carers, guidance on NHS services and health-related matters, assistance in resolving problems and concerns, explanations of complaints procedures, and how to get in touch with someone who can help. There is a PALS at every NHS Hospital, and in each Primary Care Trust, Ambulance Trust, Care Trust, and Mental Health Trust.

6.05 Information about local services should be advertised within the NHS organisation and be available on the Trust's website.

Formal Complaint

Local resolution

In a situation where the client's concerns are not amenable to informal resolution, **6.06** the client should consider making a formal complaint. Details of the complaint procedure should be provided by the hospital or surgery. This first stage is known as 'local resolution'. A complaint may be made either verbally or in writing; this should be acknowledged within ten days and the CEO of the Trust should respond within 25 days. If the written response does not satisfy the complainant, a local resolution meeting will be offered. Mediation may be available.

A formal complaint should normally be brought within six months from the date **6.07** of the incident that gave rise to the complaint, or date of knowledge of the grounds for complaint, although there is discretion to extend time.

Information about the complaints procedure should be advertised within the **6.08** NHS organisation and be available on the Trust's website.

Second stage

If local resolution fails, or is not completed within six months, the complainant **6.09** may ask the Healthcare Commissioner to review the complaint. The Healthcare Commissioner may appoint an Independent Adviser to report on clinical aspects of the complaint. After the review, the Commissioner may refer the complaint back to the Trust for resolution or the Commissioner may put forward proposals for resolution.

The time limit for bringing a claim to the Healthcare Commissioner is six months **6.10** from the completion of the local resolution process or 12 months from the date of the incident that gave rise to the complaint, with discretion for time to be extended.

More information about the Healthcare Commissioner's service can be found at **6.11** <http://www.healthcarecommission.org.uk> (accessed 2 April 2007).

The Ombudsman

If the Commissioner's response does not satisfy the complainant, the complain- **6.12** ant may ask the Health Service Ombudsman to consider the complaint. The Ombudsman will review whether there has been maladministration which has resulted in injustice and can recommend (but not enforce) a range of remedies including an apology, a policy review, compensation for injustice (usually a modest sum), or more significant compensation if the injustice to the complain- ant has resulted in financial losses. Remedies are normally agreed with the body whose actions are being reviewed.

6.13   The time limit for bringing a claim to the Ombudsman is six months from the completion of the local resolution process or 12 months from the date of the incident that gave rise to the complaint, with discretion for time to be extended.

6.14   More information about the Health Service Ombudsman can be found at <http://www.ombudsman.org.uk> (accessed 2 April 2007).

Assistance with the NHS Complaints Procedure

6.15   Regulation 8 provides that: 'at the local resolution stage the complainant is entitled to be represented by a friend or advocate but may not be represented by a legal representative *acting as such*' (emphasis added).

6.16   Section 18 of the Health Service Commissioners Act makes the same provision for cases reviewed at the second stage.

6.17   Under Section 11(3)(b) of the Health and Social Care Act the Ombudsman may determine whether a person may be represented by counsel or solicitor or otherwise.

Independent Complaints Advocacy Service

6.18   The Independent Complaints Advocacy Service (ICAS) can provide information, support and, in some cases, assistance to patients wishing to make a formal complaint during each stage of the procedure. Although the complaint procedure is relatively straightforward on paper, in practice it tends to be protracted and often unsatisfactory. The client may have to do a considerable amount of letter writing and chasing up meeting dates. A meeting between clinicians and managers on the one hand and a patient on the other is not a level playing field and it is not surprising that badly handled complaints tend to lead patients to consider litigation. ICAS have limited resources to assist in person, but can provide an information pack and general advice and will assist with letter writing or representation insofar as their resources allow. Contact details and maps for ICAS areas are at <http://www.dh.gov.uk> (accessed 2 April 2007).

NHS Complaints and Litigation

6.19   A patient is free to litigate a claim at any point, irrespective of whether a complaint is under investigation or has been brought to a conclusion. However, the complaint process will be stayed once the complainant decides to take legal steps, unless the complaint concerns a distinct and different aspect of treatment. The client must be warned of the length of time a complaint may take to come to a conclusion, even if it stops at local resolution level. If the complaint is referred to the Health Commissioner rather than resolved locally, a significant proportion of the three-year limitation period for bringing a claim will have expired by the time the Commissioner's findings are given. Even at the local level, it frequently takes more than a year before all issues are examined, meetings convened, and minutes approved. It is sensible to agree a maximum six-month time limit to be expended on the complaint before the client makes a decision as to whether or not to pursue a claim. Clients commonly believe that they are obliged to pursue a complaint to its conclusion before they are entitled to litigate or apply for public funding, or, most dangerous of all, that the limitation period will not start to run while they are actively pursuing a complaint. Clear advice on these points must be given to the client who decides to make a complaint before taking legal steps.

6.20 A client who has legal expenses insurance in place must notify the insurer of a possible claim immediately or at least within the time limit laid down in the policy of insurance; if notification is delayed until the complaint has run its course there is a real risk that a claim will not be covered.

6.21 Some clients may wish to pursue litigation from the outset. There may be many reasons for this, ranging from scepticism about the complaints procedure to a pressing need for financial compensation due to the severity of the injury. Nevertheless, in all but the most severe cases, the Legal Services Commission is likely to require the applicant to pursue a complaint before a certificate of public funding is granted. The client should be advised to return in six months' time, even if the relevant body has not responded adequately, or at all, by that point. If the client is still of the same mind, an application for public funding should be submitted without further delay.

B. Complaints about Treatment in the Private Sector

6.22 The Private and Voluntary Healthcare (England) Regulations 2001 came into force on 1 April 2002. Under regulation 23 independent hospitals must establish a complaints procedure, investigate complaints fully, and supply a written copy of the complaints procedure to every patient. No particular form of complaints procedure is laid down. A substantial majority of private health care providers are members of the Independent Sector Complaints Adjudication Service. This service encompasses a complaint handling procedure which in structure closely mirrors the NHS complaints system. This would be an appropriate procedure to invoke if the treatment complained of related to private hospital services or treatment by clinical staff employed by the private facility or its parent organisation. The code does not cover and the scheme will also investigate complaints against independent clinicians (usually medical staff) who treated the patient on the private organisation's premises. Further information is available at <http://www.independenthealthcare.org.uk> (accessed 2 April 2007).

6.23 Concerns about standards of care in private invasive cosmetic surgery or laser services may be referred to the Healthcare Commissioner (see 6.09 above).

6.24 There is no provision for complaints about treatment provided by independent doctors outside private hospital services—for example, in the doctor's private consulting rooms or in NHS facilities.

6.25 Complaints against dentists working independently in the private sector will be considered by the Dental Complaints Service of the Dental General Council whose details can be found at <http://www.dentalcomplaints.org.uk> (accessed 2 April 2007).

6.26 Under the Registered Homes Act 1984, independent hospitals and clinics must register with the Local Health Authority. A complaint that is relevant to the registration of the clinic may be reported to the Health Authority but the Health Authority will not investigate clinical complaints unrelated to registration roles.

C. Regulation of the Professions

6.27 A client may wish to consider reporting an individual health care practitioner to the disciplinary arm of the profession's regulatory body. This can be done irrespective of any other decision that is made regarding litigation or NHS complaint. There is considerable change underway in the regulation of health care professions. What follows is a guide to the provisions in force at the time of writing.

Doctors

6.28 The medical profession in the UK is regulated by the General Medical Council. Complaints investigated relate to fitness to practise and generally arise from misconduct, incompetence, criminal behaviour, and physical or mental health issues. Further information can be found at <http://www.gmc-uk.org> (accessed 2 April 2007).

Dentists

6.29 The dental profession in the UK is regulated by the General Dental Council. A complaint relating to fitness to practise will follow a similar course to that for doctors (at 6.28 above). Further information is available at <http://www.gdc-uk.org> (accessed 2 April 2007).

Nurses and Midwives

Nurses and midwives are regulated by the Nursing and Midwifery Council. **6.30** There is no time limit to reporting a complaint or concern. The Council's Fitness to Practise directorate will investigate, among other matters, reports concerning a registrant's misconduct, lack of competence, and physical or mental ill health. More information can be found at <http://www.nmc-uk.org> (accessed 27 March 2007).

Other Professions

The Health Professions Council regulates 13 other health care professionals, **6.31** including chiropodists and podiatrists, paramedics, physiotherapists, radiographers, and speech and language therapists. It is intended that more professions will come to be regulated by the Council in the near future. As is the case for nurses, the matters that will be considered by the Fitness to Practise unit include misconduct, lack of competence, and physical or mental ill health. Further details are available at <http://www.hpc-uk.org.com> (accessed 2 April 2007).

A client who is considering making a complaint to a regulatory body will want **6.32** some information about what will be involved. All the organisations mentioned above have information leaflets directed to the general public which can be downloaded from the Internet. In general terms, the investigation of a complaint will follow a similar course in each organisation. A complaint will be subject to an initial screening process. If the complaint meets the criteria for investigation, it will be adopted and pursued by the regulatory organisation. The complainant should be advised that he or she is a witness to the investigation and may be required to appear as well as provide a sworn statement. Generally, the complainant will not require separate legal representation. Naturally, he or she might require support and guidance through the process; this should be provided through the regulatory body.

There is no stay of the disciplinary investigation when litigation is underway; **6.33** and the processes are independent of each other. If the client is intending to consider litigation at a later date, it is a good idea to ask them to keep you informed as the complaint progresses so that the limitation period can be kept under active review by both solicitor and client.

National Patient Safety Agency

The National Patient Safety Agency is a Special Trust set up to collect information **6.34** about adverse incidents and 'near misses' occurring in NHS treatment and coordinate and develop patient safety initiatives. Information will be stored anonymously. Information provided by patients will be confidential. The Agency's website states: 'patients and carers will be encouraged to report any unexpected suffering or harm that they have experienced resulting from contact with NHS services for the benefit of helping others' <http://www.npsa.nhs.uk> (accessed 2 April 2007).

D. Charities

Action *against* Medical Accidents (AvMA)

6.35 AvMA is an independent charity which, among other services, provides free and confidential advice to individuals who have suffered or been affected by a medical accident. Most if not all clinical negligence practitioners will be aware of AvMA's work. Clients unsure about whether there are grounds to litigate, particularly those whose means are modest but who are nevertheless ineligible for public funding, may find it helpful to discuss their case with AvMA before deciding how to proceed. AvMA's website is at <http://www.avma.org.uk> (accessed 2 April 2007).

The Patient's Association

6.36 The Patient's Association is an independent charity which works to improve health care for NHS patients. It offers a 'Help and Advice' service, including advice on complaints about treatment. More information can be found on their website at <http://www.patients-association.org.uk> (accessed 2 April 2007).

Other Medical Charities

6.37 Some clients very much appreciate being told of reputable charities that offer advice and information about specific medical conditions; this is often particularly useful when the claimant is a child. Information about medical charities proliferates on the Internet; the usual caution applies in respect of establishing an organisation's bona fides before making contact.

7

THE FIRST INTERVIEW

A pre-interview telephone conversation will make the best use of the practitioner's **7.01** and enquirer's time. Ideally, the telephone discussion should be conducted by a practitioner with sufficient experience to establish that the case merits an interview and to weed out those cases that are hopelessly statute barred, where there is little or no financial value, or where there is no meaningful reason to believe that there has been a breach of duty. Most enquirers are looking for information in the first instance and are grateful to be given an explanation for reasons advising that there is no basis to take things further. Otherwise, the enquirer is entitled to be advised how to go about obtaining a second legal opinion if they wish to do so.

If there are categories of cases which the firm does not take on, it is good risk **7.02** management to formalise the position, for example by including the policy in the departmental manual. The same consideration applies to a policy directing certain types of cases to specific fee earners. This will minimise the risk of fee earners taking on bad risk cases on an ad hoc basis, or taking on cases themselves which are beyond their expertise or more suited to another fee earner.

A. The First Interview

The first interview is demanding both emotionally and intellectually. Each prac- **7.03** titioner must develop their own style, to enable the client to tell their story with dignity and to absorb a considerable amount of new information, some very complex, in a short space of time. What the client has to say will be deeply personal, often very intimate, and not infrequently very sad. The practitioner's task is to reflect the experience described by acknowledging the events and their impact and then to take the client through the legal tests and the legal processes and choices available to them. It is essential to explain how the facts of the client's case and the client's experience and understanding of events fits into this legal framework. The client needs to feel their adviser is trustworthy, unpatronising, and capable of representing their interests against what they may perceive as the monolithic strength of the NHS. The skills required in this situation cannot be taught but may be developed over time. A great deal can be absorbed by sitting in with an experienced colleague as often as possible.

Preparing for the Interview

7.04 If the practitioner is not familiar with the medical background of the case to be considered, some preparatory research will pay dividends. While still keeping an eye on cost effectiveness and profitability, it is possible to spend a useful half an hour or so reading up in medical textbooks or the Internet before seeing the client. Further research should wait until instructions are confirmed and funding is in place.

7.05 In general, time spent reading any advance papers provided by the client should be kept to a minimum at this stage. It is easy to spend two hours or so reading voluminous papers, but this is time lost before a retainer is established and generally adds little useful information that cannot be derived directly from the client. An exception to this rule would be a claim that has been investigated by a previous solicitor or a history that suggests that documentary evidence is essential to forming a view on limitation.

7.06 The first interview is the first and last occasion on which the claimant will have the opportunity to relate the history of their concerns unmediated by the requirements of the legal process. At the same time, a systematic approach to information gathering will, in most cases, enable an effective risk assessment and meaningful case planning following on from the interview.

7.07 It is important to be clear who the client will be. It is quite common to receive enquiries on behalf of—or about—third parties. This preliminary telephone discussion may not be particularly helpful, except as a possible introduction to a potential client. It can be difficult to know whether to agree to an interview to discuss this further and indeed the answer must depend on the circumstances. Clearly, it would be more proper to do so if, for example, the potential client is seriously ill and the family member wants initial advice. It would not be appropriate if the caller cannot give a reasonable explanation for the potential client's inability to attend. The discussion could only be very limited and the client will need to be seen in any event if the matter is to progress. It is a better use of time to have a comprehensive telephone discussion with the relative and then arrange to see the potential client when they are ready.

When an enquiry is initiated by a third party on behalf of a competent (albeit **7.08** possibly incapacitated) adult, before taking any further steps it is essential to make reasonable enquiries to establish whether the prospective client is willing and able to give instructions and that they have a real prospect of benefiting from the damages or are able to express a wish that a claim should be investigated with a view to benefiting their estate. This is a matter for the family to agree amongst themselves but where a terminally ill or very elderly person is not a legal patient very careful discussion needs to be had with the family members as to the appropriate course of action taking into account prospects of success and likely quantum. It is perfectly acceptable to act for a client with capacity who prefers to be represented by a friend or family member in day-to-day aspects of the claim, although with the proviso that the client must follow the progress of the claim, give instructions, attend conferences, and understand the nature of the documents to be signed.

If the client represents a child or an adult under a disability, an arrangement for **7.09** visiting the claimant should be agreed at the first interview. It is very important to meet the claimant before much time has passed. This is not only in order to verify the information that has been provided but also to see the claimant in their daily setting, which will form the background of the claim. The first reasonable opportunity for this visit may be when proofing family members for the first witness statements.

Previous Investigations

It will need to be determined whether the potential client has already pursued an **7.10** investigation into their claim with other solicitors and if so, how far that investigation went. While most clients will volunteer this information, others will not, either because they do not perceive the relevance or because they fear that the next solicitor will not approach their case with an open mind if they are aware that it has already been investigated. Where there has been a previous investigation, it is sensible to ask for the papers and read them before the first interview. The fact that the client is seeking a second opinion suggests that at some level the explanation they were given by their first solicitor was not understood, or not accepted, and the client is unlikely to be able to give a proper account of it themselves in a telephone call. When considering the merits of the case it should be borne in mind that if the claim will be advanced as a claim for damages for professional negligence, the claimant will only need to establish a loss of a chance of succeeding in the underlying clinical negligence claim in order to recover damages.

It is perfectly possible to turn a case around, even when it has run into the ground in other hands. The client should be reassured that the case will be approached afresh but that the results of any previous investigation will need to be taken into account. Reading the papers before the first interview will establish whether the client has been unable to accept the negative outcome of a previous investigation that was thorough and competent or whether the claim has some prospects of being revived.

B. The Interview

7.11 After the usual introductions the client should be given a brief summary of what it is intended to cover and achieve in the meeting. This will include the history of the client's concerns in the client's own words, followed by an explanation of the legal elements of clinical negligence, how the claim would be investigated, how the client's concerns relate to the legal aspects of the case, possible funding arrangements, and a review of the alternative courses of action open to the client. Many clients find it reassuring to be reminded that there is no charge for this interview and that there is no obligation to take things further on either side but that the firm and the client will have the opportunity to consider what they wish to do next.

7.12 It is recommended that the client be invited to tell their story after this very brief introduction. They are likely to have been rehearsing in their mind what they intend to say and will not be able to concentrate on any advice or other issues until they have unburdened themselves. The client should be given enough time to tell the whole story as they understand it, as this is generally their first and last opportunity to do so. Clarification of factual matters such as dates, the order of events, the names and other details of personnel involved, and so on should be sought as necessary so that subsequent paperwork can be completed accurately.

7.13 The subsequent discussion can be taken in any order. The meeting should include a discussion about what the client hopes may be achieved by the legal process. The discussion that follows from this will naturally vary from case to case but should include an exploration of the possibility of making a formal complaint, together with the other possible courses of action discussed elsewhere in this work, as appropriate to the circumstances. The roles of ICAS, AvMA, or other agencies in the area who may be able to help should also be outlined. It should be established whether the client is more concerned about disciplinary issues or training improvements than taking legal action. How important is an apology at this stage? It is often the case that by the time of seeking legal advice, clients have gone beyond the stage where an apology would be enough, for other clients this remains an important matter which should be kept in sight.

The client must be given an explanation of the elements of negligence and the **7.14** other legal hurdles that must be overcome. Breach of duty, causation, extent of injury, and proportionality need to be defined and the explanation should demonstrate how these relate to the facts of the client's case, insofar as it is possible to determine that at this early stage. A preliminary view should be given as to whether or not the case merits investigation on the basis of these four factors.

There should be a discussion of the steps that are involved in investigating and **7.15** litigating and an explanation of the client's role. The client needs an explanation of what can and what cannot be achieved by litigation. It is important to remember that most clients will have no idea at all about what is involved and will tend either to expect a settlement in a few days or envisage a trial in ten years. It is therefore important to explain the different ways and different stages at which the matter might be resolved.

Almost all clients are very concerned about funding and it is helpful if sufficient **7.16** enquiries are made at this first interview to establish whether or not the client is likely to be eligible for public funding. An eligibility calculation can be carried out later on the Legal Services Commission website although it should be stressed that this is only a guide. More information about funding considerations can be found elsewhere in this work.

Consideration should be given to whether the client might be assisted by **7.17** welfare benefit advice. If so, an offer should be made for referral to an appropriate adviser. It is extremely helpful for some clients for that appointment to be made for them.

The practitioner should next explain the alternative courses of action open to the **7.18** client. Is this a case where a quick and cheap resolution would be appropriate and achievable? The practitioner should consider and discuss whether this is a case where the Trust could be approached immediately with a view to resolving matters early. By way of example, in a case which will be largely or entirely restricted to general damages, it may be appropriate to suggest a course of action designed to achieve a combination of non-pecuniary and pecuniary remedies, with a prospect of an early negotiated settlement. Where there is any likelihood of a large claim with a significant claim for loss of earnings or cost of care, litigation is likely to be the most appropriate means of meeting the client's need for a substantial sum of damages. The advice on this point will depend partly on the policy and practice of the Trust in question and partly on whether it is possible to form a view on whether or not liability is likely to be defensible, and finally on quantum.

It goes without saying that an open and shut case of low financial value is likely to settle easily where either a more complex case or one of higher value will be defended.

7.19   Early resolution without investigation is unlikely to be an appropriate route where the client is under a disability, except in a very low quantum case and, in that situation, the client must be advised that court approval will be required for any settlement.

7.20   The client needs to know what the case might bring in damages at full valuation in order to be able to make a properly informed choice as to how to proceed. However, particularly in lower value cases, early settlement may be a strongly preferred option, even at undervalue, particularly if non-pecuniary remedies are important and are put forward as part of the settlement package. In this way, the client may be able to obtain an apology, a meeting with relevant staff to discuss outstanding concerns, agreement about remedial treatment, or confirmation that treatment will not be compromised by the fact that a claim has been brought. The client needs to understand that they will not be provided with information relating to disciplinary proceedings or other action against an individual health care practitioner.

7.21   At the conclusion of the meeting, it is important to agree with the client what is to happen next. The client should be offered the opportunity to go away and think about what they want to do. It is helpful if the agreement on next steps is briefly summarised, reminding the client what further information on documents needs to be provided if they decide to proceed. The client should be advised that a letter will follow which will summarise the meeting, set out the advice given in the interview, and confirm whether or not the firm will take the case on. A detailed follow-up letter, while perhaps burdensome to compose, is very helpful in providing an opportunity for any misunderstandings to be corrected. It will also minimise the risk of any disagreement or uncertainty about the client's initial instructions, as can sometimes occur when factual aspects of the claim are challenged later in the case.

8

RISK ANALYSIS

Unsuccessful cases are unprofitable for the business; uncertainty over the likely **8.01** timescale to conclude cases and receive costs means that it is extremely difficult to make accurate costs projections. Clinical negligence practitioners become used to—or perhaps resigned to—working with these uncertainties, but that should not lead to the benefits of risk analysis procedures being overlooked.

It is an accepted fact of life that in the great majority of clinical negligence cases **8.02** it is difficult to assess the prospects of success with any degree of accuracy in the very early stages. This is both because the factors which will determine the merits of the case tend to be case specific and because the analysis of those factors is heavily dependent upon expert advice. It is also difficult to predict the length of time it will take to bring a case to a conclusion, as this will be influenced by numerous factors such as expert waiting times, the order in which evidence must be obtained, and whether there is a credible defence or an opportunity for early settlement. When a case is won, there are often lengthy procedures to be completed before the costs are received.

The rationale for developing a risk assessment process is that inevitably there **8.03** must be some claims which the firm would be ill-advised to take on, and that of those cases that are taken on, there is a decision to be made as to which fee earner should be responsible for it. The reality is that these decisions are often made in an ad hoc manner and without systematic consideration.

8.04   It is not suggested that the presence of particular risk factors, or indeed a high level of risk should preclude accepting instructions. Rather, it is suggested that identifying the risks as accurately as possible is an essential service to the client, a duty owed to the funding body, and a tool for building a profitable practice based on well-directed, focused, and expeditious claims management.

8.05   The advantages of systematising the decision-making process are a reduction of risk and an increase in information and knowledge. To achieve both these benefits, a decision as to whether or not to take on a case should made by the team, even if the team consists simply of the fee earner and supervisor, as it is important to have a genuine opportunity to canvass the issues that arise in each case. The assessment should be recorded centrally. In due course, the final outcome of the claim and the profitability figure (which can be produced by the accounts system) should be recorded. There should be an opportunity to discuss the actual outcome as against the initial assessment and any observations recorded—for example, whether enough time was recovered at enhanced rates to justify the senior fee-earner's involvement. Over time, there will be an accumulation of experience which will be available to inform future decisions on what cases are taken on, how cases are handled, and how long it will be before costs are received.

8.06   It should be noted that this risk assessment is for the benefit of the practice and is not the same exercise as that which must be carried out for a funding body, for example when reporting to a legal expenses insurer, or for the Legal Services Commission, when reporting on the costs/benefits ratio in support of an application for a certificate of funding. Those assessments are concerned with prospects of success as against likely costs, whereas the risk assessment procedure described here goes considerably wider to address issues of capacity, quality, and profitability.

8.07   The starting point for the risk assessment process is the fact that the merits of each case will depend upon a unique set of circumstances which is made up of the client's own characteristics, the nature of the medical condition, the course of the clinical events, the particular circumstances surrounding the allegedly negligent treatment, and the severity of the alleged injury. The initial risk assessment depends upon assessment of the apparent facts and a careful analysis of the steps that would be required to elucidate the strengths and weaknesses of the case.

8.08   The merits and demerits of any new case need to be considered in the light of both financial and professional risks. The process described below may seem over-formalised but in practice it is neither formal nor cumbersome, rather it is essentially a codification of thought processes that are probably undertaken by every practitioner whenever a new case is considered. The benefit of turning an intuitive procedure into a system is that the exercise can be shared, due diligence can be demonstrated, and expertise developed.

It is important to bear in mind that while risk factors—that is, the ratio of **8.09** probable costs to probable benefits, the legal merits, and overall prospects of success—must be regularly reviewed during the course of the case, it is only at the outset that a high risk threshold can be applied. Once instructions have been accepted, the only justification for abandoning a case will be if the conditions applied by the funding body are no longer met or the client considers that the risks no longer justify proceeding.

A. Financial Risk

The financial risk to be evaluated when considering accepting instructions **8.10** encompasses the risk not only of taking on a case that will be lost at trial, but also a case that is discontinued following investigation or during the course of proceedings, or in which the claimant may be penalised on costs for reasons of proportionality.

Whatever the funding method, if a case does not settle, or loses at trial, a signif- **8.11** icant financial risk has materialised. While it is easy to feel there is more security in a full caseload, the reality is that taking on cases unselectively is likely to reduce profitability overall.

In the event of discontinuance or of losing at trial, instead of inter partes costs, **8.12** the firm will of course recover nothing for work under a Conditional Fee Agreement, but on publicly funded cases costs recovered will be at Legal Services Commission rates (and limited to the amount authorised). Even where there is a before-the-event legal expenses insurer, the rate recoverable from the insurer is generally less than the firm's standard charging rate. Where a claim is discontinued after an initial investigation with private funding, the costs recoverable will often be limited to a fixed or capped fee agreed with the client and this will almost inevitably be less than the work-in-progress figures.

Despite the difficulty of assessing the medico-legal merits before expert opinion **8.13** has been obtained, some high risk cases can be identified very early, for example a case in which it is apparent from the outset that quantum is likely to be contentious, perhaps where the client has recently become self-employed or where a loss of earnings is alleged but there is no stable employment history, or a case which is logically capable of proceeding on an analysis of its legal merits but has a high risk of failing at trial—ie where breach of duty turns on lay evidence alone or where the case theory relies on a single *Bolitho* point. The obvious evidential or technical risks should not be overlooked in the process of considering the medico-legal issues.

B. Professional Risk

8.14 Careful decisions about what cases should be accepted will substantially reduce the risk of providing a service that falls below the standard that the client is entitled to expect, which is likely to result if fee earners have too large a workload or are conducting cases which are beyond their competence without adequate support and supervision. Poor client care is of course unacceptable in any circumstances but is particularly damaging to a client with a potential clinical negligence claim who already perceives that they have been injured by shortcomings on the part of their health care professional. At the very least the client will tell anyone who asks that they have been let down, but it is likely that the fee earner will be faced with a complaint and a damaged relationship with the client that may hinder the progress of the case. At worst, a lapse in the standard of care that prejudices the client's interest may amount to a claim for professional negligence, a devastating outcome for the client, not to mention the impact this will have on the fee earner and the reputation of the practice.

C. Risk Assessment in Practice

8.15 There are various ways in which risk assessment may be carried out. It may be possible to expand upon a process already in place within the team or it may be necessary to devise a new procedure. Whatever the system adopted, it will involve setting a series of questions to be answered when considering each new case as accurately as current knowledge of the facts allows. The answers should be evaluated as objectively as possible to arrive at a risk profile. While it is possible to carry out a risk assessment alone, it is this objective evaluation which benefits from input from other colleagues. It is all too easy to be swayed by sympathy for the client, the challenge of a difficult case, interest in the particular subject matter or simply the fear of turning away work. The assessment should focus on the overall needs of the practice and the resources available to accomplish the work.

8.16 As mentioned above, a record should be made of the facts of the case, the risk factors identified, the decision made with reasons. The outcome of the claim and the profitability rating will be noted at the conclusion of the matter. This will develop into a useful database which will assist in future decision making.

D. The Process

A summary of the salient facts should be prepared by the fee earner who **8.17** attended the client at the first interview. This is best done immediately following the interview as the client will need to know as soon as possible whether or not the firm will be taking the case on. The work involved in preparing a summary will be minimal if it is done at the same time as the attendance note is drafted.

The summary should include: **8.18**

- Facts of the case in brief with key dates.
- The client's allegation(s) of breach of duty crystallised into one sentence.
- Observations on breach of duty; for example is there prima facie evidence?
- Where should the investigation focus in order to establish breach of duty?
- The client's view of causation.
- Observations on causation. For example, is the client's view plausible? Has this accounted for the pre-existing condition and expected outcome of treatment? What reports are likely to be required?
- The limitation date—is it certain? Does it need to be checked against the medical records?
- The names of personnel and institutions involved, if these are known. Is there a possible conflict of interest? Does the claim involve a doctor who is an important medico-legal expert in the firm's personal injury practice?
- Initial assessment of quantum and any factors that might take quantum significantly above or below that initial assessment.
- Likely costs to carry out initial investigation.
- Likely source of funding.

An outline case plan should be drawn up, estimated dates for achieving each **8.19** step, covering in stages at least the initial investigation and the full investigation, up to the service of proceedings. Later stages of the case generally cannot be planned at this point but even a sketch outline of steps to trial will assist the risk assessment meeting to arrive at a realistic view of what would be involved in taking on the case in terms of costs and time. The summary and case plan should be discussed in the light of the questions set out below. When used as a checklist, this can be undertaken more rapidly than the length of the list suggests. Those risks identified may then be discussed as a whole.

E. Internal Issues

8.20 *Should the fee earner presenting the case take on this matter within their existing workload? If not, is there another member of the team who could competently run the case?*

8.21 *Is this case potentially much larger or more complex than previous cases handled by the proposed fee earner or the team as a whole?*

8.22 *Is there anyone available who can supervise the proposed fee earner to the level required?*

8.23 *Is there a team structure to enable delegation of the less specialised work to a more junior fee earner?*

8.24 *Is the fee earner who is to handle the case likely to recover their hourly rate for all their time, or sufficient time to run the case profitably?*

8.25 *Is it assumed that the firm will seek to recover any shortfall in profit costs from the client? If so, is this fair and reasonable and is it clear that this will be allowable within the terms of the proposed funding arrangements?*

8.26 *Will the fee earner be able to carry out the necessary work to investigate and pursue the claim within the funding constraints that are likely to apply? If not, what further funding arrangement is envisaged?*

F. Medico-legal Issues

8.27 *Does the proposed fee earner or another member of the team have any experience in a clinical negligence claim of this type?*

Some consideration of the similarities and differences will enable the focus of the investigation to be correctly decided and may assist in terms of a choice of expert.

8.28 *Was the outcome of any previous similar case based on the facts unique to that case and do those facts correlate well with this one?*

8.29 *If the condition or treatment that gave rise to the alleged negligence is entirely new to the team, would it be helpful to carry out some further research into the medical issues and review how the investigation should be directed before deciding that the case should or should not be taken on?*

8.30 *Where there is no in-house experience, would it be helpful to carry out a brief search on reported cases as this may show up areas of difficulty or strengthen the case for investigation?*

Is the allegation of breach of duty credible?　　　　　　　　　　　　　　　**8.31**

Even a markedly unsatisfactory outcome of treatment is not indicative of negligence, though it may reasonably arouse suspicion in the client. If the course of treatment and the client's complaints and concerns are complex, time spent defining the allegations of substandard care will clear the picture.

Are there multiple allegations of breach of duty?　　　　　　　　　　　　**8.32**

When a client complains of several breaches of duty involving different aspects of care, careful consideration needs to be given to how convincing this picture may sound and how causation may be thought to flow from the alleged breaches. Such a case will be problematic to investigate and may well have poor prospects of success.

Do the allegations of breach of duty involve more than one clinician? Are these related　**8.33**
or unrelated incidents?

It would be reasonable to be more optimistic about a case where there was an initial error in treatment or diagnosis, which other doctors subsequently followed without correcting the error, than one would about a case where several doctors allegedly each made the same negligent error, or where several doctors each made an unrelated negligent error. If a client is alleging a long series of medical events each or all of which fell below the reasonable standard of care, the client's anxiety is likely to be the result of a loss of confidence on the part of the client in the treating doctors. Such severe anxieties not infrequently take patients to solicitors, but they much more commonly arise from communication difficulties or unreasonable expectations than from overt failures in medical treatment. Such a scenario should not be dismissed out of hand but, to have a realistic prospect of success, the presenting picture demonstrate a coherent and credible sequence of events, which should be capable of being analysed into the essential components of breach of duty and causation. It should be possible to determine what medical experts would be required to report, what specific concerns about the standard of care would be put to the expert, and what can reasonably at this stage be deduced as to causation. If the picture is less clear than this, either more information should be obtained, or a decision should be taken to decline instructions on the grounds that the case does not have reasonable prospects of success.

Does the timeframe suggest causation may be difficult to establish?　　　　**8.34**

Thought needs to be given as to whether the outcome of the alleged negligence could reasonably have followed within the timescale put forward. This will depend entirely on the facts of the case. For example, generally one might assume that a relatively short delay referring somebody acutely ill is more likely to have caused an injury than a longer delay might have done in referring somebody with a chronic condition for a consultant opinion, but the reverse would be true if the first patient was too ill to benefit from treatment and the second patient was on the verge of moving from a chronic condition into acute deterioration. At this stage, one is only looking to put forward a case that holds together on preliminary analysis and that can be put to an expert for serious consideration. Where the practitioner is unfamiliar with the condition or treatment in question, common sense and general experience will need to be brought into play but this will need to be supplemented with some research into the condition.

8.35 *Is the clinical picture so uncertain that it is too soon to determine the likely extent of causation? Will any procedural steps need to be taken before a full investigation has been completed in order to preserve the position while causation is being investigated or established?*

There is a clear tension in this situation between commencing on an investigation promptly, but possibly prematurely with respect to either investigating the extent of causation, and the possible limitation difficulties that may arise from deferring an investigation for an indefinite period. Where it is clear that there will be some causation attributable to the alleged breach of duty, it is reasonable to start the ball rolling. A course of action and timetable which takes into account planned treatment and investigations should be agreed with the client.

8.36 *Does either the pre-existing condition or the known non-negligent complications of the treatment suggest causation may be difficult to establish?*

Research or previous experience will reveal various known complications of treatment which may be very serious but are rarely the result of negligence. For example, where bowel surgery has taken place, it is not uncommon for there to be a breakdown of the bowel at the point of repair which will cause serious illness within a very short space of time. The bowel may be injured during gynaecological or abdominal surgery, or the uterus may be perforated in the course of a termination. None of these injuries necessarily arise as the result of negligent surgical technique but they may be followed by significant morbidity. The central question to be considered here is whether there was a delay in diagnosis and treatment of the injury. In the absence of such delay it is doubtful whether a claim could be made out, although the medical records may assist.

8.37 In brief, when considering potential cases that present these sorts of difficulties the assessment process should consider whether it is possible to identify the core issues for the investigative stage and how many experts will be likely to be required in order to determine the merits and settle a meaningful letter of claim each will address. This is a further step that helps to bring proportionality into a sharp focus in a case where the clinical issues are unclear. Some claims have to be regarded as unmeritorious because it is evident on analysis that they cannot be properly investigated without expense that is disproportionate to quantum.

G. Legal Issues

On considering the outline case plan, are there any significant limitation problems? **8.38**

It is very important to establish that the overall plan of investigation is realistic within these constraints.

Is it feasible to carry out the investigation that is required without the need to issue **8.39** *protective proceedings?*

The need to issue protective proceedings must be factored into the timetable and must be tied into the plans for funding—not least, the client will have to be clear who is to pay the issue fee, which is now a considerable outlay. If this has to be undertaken before the client can be advised as to whether the claim should proceed, the costs and therefore the risks to the client or funding body are significantly increased. Limitation problems will create considerable pressure on a fee earner unless they have the capacity in their workload.

The risks to the firm are increased by the issue of protective proceedings, not **8.40** only because one potentially fatal headline has been substituted for another, but because the deadline for service may well not be incorporated in a case management systems and the due date with warnings will need to be inserted manually, increasing the risk of human error.

Is the timetable set out in the case plan realistic and manageable? **8.41**

This is a very important consideration in a complex case requiring several experts.

Is this a case where a date of knowledge argument will be relied upon? **8.42**

Wherever possible, in all but the most unambiguous date of knowledge cases, a claim should be issued within the primary limitation period. If that date has passed, the claim should be progressed expeditiously as it may be that the claimant will need to ask the court to exercise section 33 discretion. The case plan must provide time to review the time line once the medical records have been collated. The records may contain entries that damage or destroy the client's case on date of knowledge or that at the very least require careful consideration by counsel based on the client's detailed proof of evidence. It may be necessary to reproof the client before the experts are instructed or alternatively it may be that the issue of limitation should be heard as a preliminary issue.

8.43 *Is the client's factual evidence crucial to this case and is it likely that this factual evidence will be disputed?*

8.44 *Are there other important witnesses, for example, did a partner attend appointments with the claimant or witness the delivery? Has the practitioner met those witnesses?*

It is helpful if first impressions are that the client and witnesses will be able to provide coherent, truthful, and consistent statements. If the client's or their witnesses' factual evidence will be crucial to the case, the credibility of the witnesses is key and it is important that early proofing and possible reproofing of witnesses is included in the planning of the investigation.

8.45 *Does the cause of action arise many years ago?*

There will be significant risks in running older cases when lay factual evidence is key unless there is likely to be corroborative contemporaneous documentary evidence and this should be inquired into—for instance, did the client keep a diary and is it still in existence?

8.46 *Is it a low quantum case? Do the medical facts suggest that it will be straightforward to investigate?*

It is very useful to have a mix of cases but low quantum clinical negligence cases do need careful handling because of the proportionality issues and the fact that in most cases the defendant's position on liability cannot be confidently predicted, except where the breach of duty is entirely indefensible.

8.47 *Has the potential defendant been found to be particularly difficult, or reluctant to compromise, or unwilling to consider early settlement in other cases?*

It may only be feasible to take on a very low value claim if it can be settled speedily; this partly relies on the particular defendant's approach.

8.48 *Can the case be fully quantified with relative ease?*

Cost-effective early settlement is more likely to be achieved if all the facts and documents necessary to prove the claim and support the schedule of loss can be assembled promptly. This will enable the defendant to be presented at the earliest point with everything that is necessary for a decision on a settlement offer.

H. The Client

8.49 *What would be the costs and benefits to the client in bringing this claim?*

The client must receive advice about the financial costs, as discussed in previous chapters, but the client should also have an opportunity to consider the investment of time and emotion as against what may be achieved and the risks of failing. In order to make that decision, the client must be given clear and honest advice based on a 'best estimate' of the merits, likely quantum, and the probable timescale involved in the client care letter.

Are the client's expectations unrealistic?   **8.50**

If so, the client care letter must set out very clearly what cannot be attempted as well as what it is hoped to achieve.

Would the client really prefer non-pecuniary remedies or would an alternative to **8.51** *litigation in fact be more appropriate in the circumstances?*

If the client is to attempt this course with a view to litigation, will that leave enough time before the limitation period expires? The client must have very clear advice on this point.

Where the initial meeting was with the third party on behalf of the potential client, is **8.52** *the potential client too elderly or too severely ill to benefit personally from the claim for damages?*

This difficult matter has to be grasped; the potential claimant must be seen in order to be advised and to give instructions, unless under a disability.

If the claimant is unlikely to survive to benefit from a claim, is it likely that there could **8.53** *be a subsequent claim under the Law Reform (Miscellaneous Provisions) Act 1934 and Fatal Accidents Act 1976 for the estate and dependants?*

Advice should be given on this point in the client care letter. Although it may **8.54** seem difficult to raise the issue of the client's death, the client is in fact seeking this information.

Is the client in the position or state of mind to make a reasonably prompt decision on whether or not to proceed?

If not, a view should be taken on how much time is required to take the necessary steps before issuing proceedings. The client should be given a long stop date for returning to confirm instructions and that date should be noted in the case management system so that a letter is sent with a repeat of the limitation advice once that date is reached.

I. History

Has the claim been in the hands of previous solicitors?   **8.55**

Clients often have unrealistic expectations of what a change of solicitor can achieve.

8.56 *Is the previous solicitor's file available?*

Clients are often unwilling or unable to give a clear account of what work has been done to date, particularly when the advice has been negative. A further risk analysis should be carried out once the previous solicitor's file has been read.

8.57 *Is this likely to be a professional negligence case—for example, is it statute barred or struck out, or have steps been taken which have prejudiced the client's interests?*

If so, the case must be run as a professional negligence claim and not as a conventional clinical negligence matter.

8.58 *Has the previous solicitor's investigation covered a lot of ground?*

Whether the case has been well or badly investigated to date, the source of funding may be nearly exhausted. It may be necessary to work with some unsatisfactory experts, with very tight purse strings, with the statutory charge and other liabilities looming for the client and a defendant who has lost patience with the claimant. When applying for authority for further funding, a clear, comprehensive, and cost-effective case plan will need to be devised, focusing on the core issues that are still to be resolved. In competent hands and with careful management very difficult cases of this kind can be turned around and produce very good outcomes.

J. Funding

8.59 Funding is discussed in detail elsewhere in this work. The points below are issues to be considered in outline during the risk assessment.

8.60 *Does the client have legal expenses insurance?*

The claim form should be completed and submitted on the client's behalf to avoid the claim being forwarded automatically to the insurer's panel solicitors.

8.61 *Is the level of indemnity sufficient to cover the client's potential liabilities to the conclusion of the case?*

8.62 *Is the client likely to be financially eligible for public funding, now or after utilising legal expenses insurance cover?*

If so, unless the firm is able to undertake publicly funded work, the potential client must be fully advised about the availability of public funding through other firms.

8.63 *Is the case to be privately funded at least to the investigative stage?*

What will be the likely realised hourly rate under the proposed fixed/capped fee **8.64**
agreement?

What is to be the arrangement for meeting the cost of disbursements? **8.65**

In the worst case scenario, how many expert reports will be required before the client **8.66**
will be offered a Conditional Fee Agreement with realistic prospects of obtaining legal
expenses insurance?

K. Summary

It should be emphasised that very few of the factors set out above should in them-   **8.67**
selves preclude the case being taken on, unless the process exposes risk or risk that
cannot be managed. The risk analysis process is equally concerned with ensuring
measures are taken to manage the risk in a way that provides a high-quality service
at reasonably profitable rates.

L. Retrospective Risk Assessment: Counsel's View

When a case needs to be discontinued before trial, there should be an investi-   **8.68**
gation as to why the case was ever started. There are a number of reasons why a
case that had been assessed as having reasonable prospects of success at the outset
needs to be discontinued. The most common reasons are discussed below.

A situation that not uncommonly arises is that one of the key experts can no   **8.69**
longer support the case after seeing the defendant's witness statement. This may
be because the medical records and the defence had failed to give an adequate
account of the procedure or the advice given. The case was therefore brought
in ignorance of the defendant's justification. If the defendant has not disclosed
the basis of the treating doctor's defence until exchange of witness statements,
there are good arguments that the defendant should not recover its costs when
the claimant withdraws the claim and there are also grounds for arguing that the
claimant should be able to recover some costs from the defendant.

It may be that one of the key experts can no longer support the claim after seeing   **8.70**
the defendant's expert evidence. This will usually be the expert's responsibility, in
that they failed to apply the *Bolam* test correctly, or they failed to research the relevant literature sufficiently carefully. It is vital that experts are reminded in the
solicitor's letter of instruction that they should carry out a thorough search of the
relevant literature and they should provide the claimant's solicitors with full copies of all the relevant literature before the first conference. The practitioner can

expect counsel to consider the literature carefully before a first conference and to discuss it with the expert at the first conference. If the expert is ultimately unable to support the case, it is essential to ascertain this at the outset rather than after exchange of expert evidence. The first conference is critically important in testing and challenging the claimant's own experts' views, particularly where the case is difficult and has borderline prospects of succeeding.

8.71 There are some cases where it is found the claimant's own account of events cannot be correct in the light of further evidence. Most clinical negligence cases do not depend on the credibility of the claimant's factual evidence. Usually the case will depend on the interpretation of the medical records and proving that what the defendants recorded themselves constitutes a breach of duty. Sometimes, however, the case is based on the claimant's account of events. This is particularly so in cases of lack of consent, for example, in failure to offer a termination. Testing the client's own credibility is always a sensitive matter and requires careful handling. It is an area where the use of counsel at an early stage can be helpful, particularly where the case itself may not be of particularly high value, as counsel will be forced to make an independent assessment of the credibility of the claimant and to advise on the prospects of success in the light of that assessment.

8.72 The cost of litigation may become disproportionate to the value of the claim. For publicly funded cases this can be a major problem. In theory, to write off costs already expended with no hope of recovering them from the defendant by withdrawing the claim seems illogical. It is often argued that a privately paying client would probably rather spend a bit more in order to try and recoup the costs already spent. The public funding criteria however require that the Legal Services Commission (LSC) withdraw funding when the cost has become disproportionate. This is something that in theory should be predictable, but in practice can be difficult to manage.

8.73 Careful case management as advocated throughout this book can be of great assistance but clinical negligence litigation is inherently complex and can be unpredictable. The discontinuance of a case either before or after proceedings should be examined for the lessons that can be learnt for future case management and risk analysis but is not in itself an indication of poor decision making.

9

CASE MANAGEMENT

The concept of case management advocated in this work does not relate to any **9.01** one particular scheme or process. Rather, 'case management' is used as a general term which is intended to cover a process or system that has been devised and applied with the aim of ensuring that clinical negligence cases are correctly focused, appropriately supervised, regularly reviewed, and driven forward as expeditiously as possible. It is a process which contributes to professional development when it is applied across a team of several fee earners but has many benefits even if the 'team' consists only of one fee earner and a supervisor.

The choice of system will depend on many factors, including the overall size of **9.02** the clinical negligence workload and whether or not there are any existing systems or processes that can be adapted or refined to work effectively for clinical negligence litigation. An effective case management system might be a commercial software program or alternatively a paper-based process developed in-house. The important issue is not what technology is employed but that the system for case management should be tailored to the life history of clinical negligence claims rather than more or less awkwardly adapted from a personal injury litigation tool, as this will inevitably be circumvented by busy fee earners. To be fully effective, a case management system should include two essential tools: a case list for each fee earner, and a case plan for each case. The place of these documents in case management is described below.

9.03 The clinical negligence team manager must ensure that the system is in fact fit for purpose and that it is complied with by all fee earners with conduct of clinical negligence matters.

9.04 The implementation of an effective case management system will not only warn of key dates and deliver prompts for regular interim billing, it will also make supervision easier, reduce the opportunity for a complex claim to slide into long periods of inactivity or investigative cul-de-sacs. The case discussions that arise when regular reviews are undertaken help to raise the quality of the work of less experienced fee earners to level of the experts in the team. All the steps advocated as good practice below, and in later chapters, are capable of being incorporated into a case management system and are directed at ensuring work is carried out to a high standard as cost effectively as possible. The overall benefits of implementing systematic case management will include improving standards of service, minimising delay in recovering costs, and maximising profitability.

A. Good Practice

9.05 It is easy for the less experienced fee earner to overlook the need to keep pre-retainer work to a minimum. Before funding is in place, the work undertaken should normally be restricted to the following:

- taking initial instructions and drafting note;
- enquiries to clarify key dates and identities;
- brief research on the medical issues;
- compiling case summary for funding application and risk analysis;
- draft outline case plan;
- risk analysis discussion;
- settle funding application.

9.06 The processes listed above have been considered in detail in previous chapters.

9.07 The next step required is to establish the retainer with the client care letter. It is assumed that every firm will have centralised pro-forma documentation setting out terms of business and providing general information on funding, costs, and client care. It is also helpful to provide generic information relevant to clients with clinical negligence matters. This can be included in the body of the client care letter but is perhaps more accessible if enclosed as a leaflet. There is a considerable amount that has to be conveyed in the client care letter, in order to put the client in possession of the relevant facts to enable the client to decide whether or not to proceed, and to understand what will be involved once that decision is taken. This is the opportunity to provide key information that will help a client follow the progress of their claim. The time taken producing precedents and ensuring that these are included in the case management system is well worthwhile. Suggested topics for information sheets are:

- *The elements of clinical negligence*—an explanation of limitation rules, breach of duty, causation of injury;
- *The process of litigation*—an outline of how clinical negligence cases are investigated and litigated, with an indication of likely timescales that might apply;
- *Funding*—the different rules and constraints governing the various funding methods and the client's and solicitor's responsibilities and obligations;
- *Damages*—how damages are calculated, the need to prove a loss, the importance of documentation;
- *Offers and settlements*—how settlement may be achieved, the implications of Part 36 offers, judicial awards;
- *Handling damages monies*—wills, court funds office, personal injury trusts, tax, and inheritance planning.

There are also leaflets available free from external sources that may be helpful, **9.08** for example the Legal Services Commission's *Medical Accidents* (LPC014E) or *Paying for your Legal Aid* (LSC1L4E).

B. Client Care Letter

Use of a precedent client care letter will ensure that all the mandatory advice **9.09** and information is given at the opening of each file. The client care letter should also include a considerable amount of detail about the client's individual matter. It is not enough to give generic advice along the lines that the claim is worth investigating further. It is more helpful and more respectful of the client to give advice, for example, to point out any particular difficulty that seems apparent at this stage. An example of this might be that while breach of duty is unlikely to be defended, causation may be difficult to establish. This will ensure that solicitor and client fully understand the basis on which the claim will go forward.

The letter should cover the points set out below. **9.10**

Identities

The identity of the claimant should be confirmed, and the role of any other **9.11** individual involved should be defined, for example, the litigation friend, or a family member who is to be copied into correspondence.

9.12   The identity of the defendant should be confirmed; any uncertainty as to the identity of the likely defendant should be explained.

Instructions

9.13   The claim should be summarised succinctly, preferably in one sentence—as in 'I would be happy to act for you in your claim for damages for injuries you sustained as a result of clinical negligence against Blank NHS Trust as a result of treatment you received during the period 1–10 January 2007'.

9.14   The instructions given at the first interview should be summarised in the form of a précis of the client's story that includes enough detail to enable the client to correct any errors or inaccuracies.

Advice

9.15   The advice given at the initial interview should be summarised and, if necessary, expanded upon. Any further or different advice shown to be required as a result of the risk analysis discussion should be given.

Quantum

9.16   The client should be provided with an estimate of quantum, or a range in which quantum is likely to lie, an indication of what factors would affect that assessment, and at what point it will be possible to give a firmer view. The client should be advised of the importance of retaining documents and receipts and keeping a journal or other documentary record of difficulties encountered and expenses or losses incurred as a result of the alleged negligence.

Costs

9.17   The Law Society's Solicitors Practice Rule 15 (costs information and client care) provides that the solicitor must discuss with a client the estimated costs of legal services at the outset and as the matter progresses. The Code of Practice that will come into force in July 2007 sets out in more detail the information to be given to the client; see <http://www.sra.org.uk> (accessed 11 April 2007). The client must be given the best information possible about the likely overall cost of the matter both at the outset and as the matter progresses. In particular, advice must be given on the basis and terms of the solicitor's charges, whether charging rates are to be increased and likely disbursements. There must be a discussion with the client about how they will pay, whether the client is eligible for public funding or whether the client's own costs are covered by insurance or may be paid by an employer or trade union; the client must be told that there may be circumstances where you may be entitled to exercise a lien for unpaid costs. The client must have explained to them their potential liability for any other party's costs and it should be established whether their potential liability for another party's costs may be covered by existing insurance or whether after-the-event insurance may be available. The client and solicitor must discuss whether the potential outcome of a legal case will justify the expense or risk involved, including the risk of having to pay the opponent's costs. The advice on costs must be clear and confirmed in writing.

It is very difficult to estimate overall costs at the outset of a clinical negligence **9.18** case. Wherever possible, realistic figures that relate to the client's particular matter should be provided. The work done on the case plan and in risk analysis will be of great assistance in arriving at a figure that can be justified in retrospect. However, if the costs to trial are very speculative, it is reasonable to provide an estimate of the costs of investigation, together with generic information about the levels of costs to trial in clinical negligence cases generally.

Cost-benefits Advice

Rule 15 and the Code of Conduct provide that the solicitor must discuss with a **9.19** client whether the likely outcome in a matter will justify the expense or risk involved, including, if relevant, the risk of having to bear an opponent's costs. The letter therefore should give the solicitor's view on the likely benefits set against the likely overall costs and the risks of failing to recover the client's own costs and incurring a liability for the defendant's costs. As in most clinical negligence cases it will be impossible to quantify this with any real accuracy, it is reasonable to advise on the costs-benefits for the initial stage, explaining that the client will receive further advice at appropriate stages in the future.

Next Steps and Action Plan

The letter should set out what the client needs to do next (and any time limits **9.20** that apply), for example, completing and returning a funding application, returning the signed forms of authority and terms of business, or sending in outstanding documentation. If any further steps were agreed at the meeting these should be described, for example the client may have indicated that they wish to speak with their doctor personally before the practitioner notifies them of an investigation.

The letter should conclude with confirmation of which fee earner is working on **9.21** the case and the identity of any other members of their team. If the case is to be run by a more junior fee earner with partner supervision, it is proper to make that clear in the letter, rather than to claim the partner would be running the case personally when that is not in fact intended.

C. The Investigation: Limited Scope and Limited Costs

9.22 It is very easy for the practitioner to do more work than they are authorised to do under the funding regime during the investigative stages of the claim, with the risk of failing to recover the costs or worse, disbursements incurred. This problem should be entirely avoidable if there is an agreed case plan on the file.

9.23 It is probably not possible to avoid spending time in excess of what the costs authorisation will cover, given the restricted funding that usually applies to the initial investigation. It is very difficult—one might say impossible—to properly investigate a clinical negligence claim without the time spent on the work exceeding the financial limits that are imposed by the Legal Services Commission. In the same way, the costs ceiling in a private funding agreement is very unlikely to allow the work to be done at anywhere close to standard charging rates. The situation can be almost as difficult, particularly in the larger cases, where a before-the-event legal expenses insurer funds the investigation.

9.24 Although the indemnity principle is disapplied in a publicly funded case and in a successful case any time reasonably spent is potentially recoverable at inter partes rates, the unsuccessful publicly funded cases are generally run at a loss. Where the case is funded under any other arrangement, the indemnity principle will limit costs recovered to the authority given.

9.25 In order to bring these matters under control, the funding limit, the steps that have been authorised, and the funding body's reporting requirements should be recorded in a prominent place on the file and should be entered in the case management system as alerts. Some accounts systems can be set up to produce email alerts when a financial limit is reached.

Case Planning the Investigation

9.26 The medical records should be sent for as soon as the client has responded to the client care letter with signed forms of authority and terms of business. While waiting for them to arrive, the next step is for the outline case plan to be reviewed and extended to cover in as much detail as possible the likely course of the action from the start to the conclusion of the case, with target dates for each step. While this may not seem to be an easy exercise, the difficulty is more psychological than real and the exercise becomes easier with practice. Naturally, the case plan will need to change over time but that is at the heart of case management.

This version of the case plan, which will be sent to the client with the letter   **9.27**
confirming that funding is in place and that records have been requested, serves
several purposes:

- it enforces realistic budgeting of time and costs as far ahead as possible;

- target times can be set for each stage and this reduces the likelihood of a case
  being allowed to drift;

- it leads to a realistic overall timetable, which helps the practitioner and the
  client;

- the target times should be transferred to the client list and this in turn will
  form the basis for a task list at monthly file reviews (see 9.29 below). This is
  a simple technique which has remarkable effect on progressing cases;

- the focused thinking required to produce the case plan maximises the prospect of anticipating where problems may crop up and how these may impact
  upon the overall timescale and limitation date or alternatively how they can be
  overcome;

- the case plan can form the basis for reports to funding bodies, including a high
  cost case plan, saving time and improving the quality of those reports;

- planning well ahead means that experts can be identified and their commitment secured as soon as the medical records are to hand. In some instances
  this will mean it will be possible to obtain the services of the very best expert
  before they are asked to advise the defendant;

- the case plan creates an opportunity to consider choice of counsel at an early
  stage. Once that decision has been made, it is possible to work effectively as a
  team from the outset, for example, by having discussions with counsel about
  the experts to be instructed;

- a detailed case plan improves longer term case planning, and case management.
  For example, the case plan can identify the earliest possible date to make
  arrangements for the first conference, for a date as soon as possible after the
  expert reports are due. The fixing of this date will give the experts a deadline
  to work to that even the least organised is likely to observe. This is likely to
  move the case forward by weeks or months compared with waiting for the
  reports before organising the conference. The conference can always be cancelled or rearranged if this proves necessary;

- a detailed case plan reduces the chances that the case will be afflicted with
  serious slippage in the later stages of the case. If the defendant asks for more
  time, if the claimant's preferred expert has a longer than usual waiting list, or if
  delay will result from any other decision, it is a simple matter to review the

impact this will have on the case plan and calculate the effect it will have on the overall timetable. The client can be advised accordingly and involved in the decision as to how to proceed;

- case planning enables matters to be run proactively. For example, it will be clear what directions the claimant wants well before receiving the Allocation Questionnaire and these can be drafted and put to the other side for agreement, in advance;

- the production of detailed case plans across the board allows the practitioner or the team to develop a feel for the overall workload for the coming months and enables planning to include provision for the times ahead that may be very busy. For example, if three cases are to be issued in the same month, is it likely that all the agendas will need to be prepared at the same time? Is this avoidable by adjusting the case planning or by re-allocating cases?

- although case planning allows the practitioner to more effectively control cases and workload, one of the most important benefits is that the client will have a better idea of what is to be done on their behalf, which should restore some sense of control rather more effectively than simply receiving intermittent correspondence as the case develops;

- tasks can be allocated to the appropriate fee earner where there is the opportunity to delegate cost effectively;

- cost projections can be based on planned steps rather than guesswork and past experience.

The Case List

9.28 The case list is a very useful adjunct to the case plan described above. Although either tool could be used independently, using them together enables case management across the caseload.

9.29 The case list is a regularly updated chart that contains key facts about every open file. Each fee earner should maintain the case list of all his or her cases by updating it on a monthly basis. New cases should be added to the case list as part of the process of opening a new file and should be removed as part of the process of file closure. Although each fee earner has their own list, it may also be helpful for those lists to be merged into a team or departmental list for the supervisor.

9.30 Key elements to be included on the chart are:

- name of the client/file;

- fee earner(s) reference, for example fee earner, junior fee earner, supervisor;

- matter number/reference;

- brief description, eg 'erbs palsy';
- limitation date;
- funding source;
- value of case in damages—coded bands may be useful for departmental statistics;
- source of work;
- reference to any link files (for example, an inquest);
- other key dates;
- box for comments, to include status quo and target dates.

The client list can be further expanded in many ways, depending on what data **9.31** may be considered useful, for example, it could include initial estimates of prospects of success or of costs on completion, but it should not become so complex or unwieldy that it is a burden rather than a useful tool.

The objective of the monthly case list review is to ensure that all cases are pro- **9.32** gressed by picking up on any slippage or problem areas. The review can be carried out on an individual basis but if it is incorporated into a monthly team meeting it provides an invaluable forum for discussion and supervision.

The aim of the review is to consider each case in the light of any key dates and the **9.33** comments in the final column, to consider what step needs to be taken next, and to amend the list for discussion at the next monthly review. If the target dates have slipped, the list should be annotated to include rescheduled target dates and a note to update the detailed case plan on the file in question. Where significant changes have to be made, the client should receive a copy of the amended case plan (and at least every six months in any event).

Help and Support

Planning a case far ahead implies a good understanding of how clinical negli- **9.34** gence cases work and the complications that may arise. Gaining that experience can be difficult, but if the practitioner has a real interest in this area of work but is without experienced supervision at hand, much can be gained by way of support from AvMA's website, lawyers service, and lawyers support group meetings and training courses, and from APIL Special Interest Group meetings, website, and courses. Both organisations produce useful publications and provide networking opportunities.

Choice of counsel is important; a less experienced practitioner in particular **9.35** will find specialist counsel an invaluable source of advice. That is not to suggest that counsel should be expected to provide unremunerated advice at every opportunity, but most counsel involved in clinical negligence cases wish to work as a team and are happy to give some informal input on appropriate issues in the early stages, particularly, for example, on choice of experts. Once the first conference has taken place, the best counsel will be pleased to be kept informed of progress from time to time, and in particular will wish to be informed of major developments, as well as being formally instructed at appropriate points. There is more discussion about working with counsel in Chapters 14 and 20.

The Physical File

9.36 Physical file management is important. Those clinical negligence matters that proceed beyond initial investigation become large files very rapidly. Even with the best of case planning, clinical negligence cases tend to run for a long time. These facts of life are imperatives for systematic and meticulous management of the physical file. Almost the most important rule of all is that there should be no loose papers.

9.37 A file management system should be implemented; the system should comply or aspire to comply with one of the recognised standards, such as the Legal Services Commission's Specialist Quality Mark, Lexcel, or ISO 9000. Management of the physical file should be an element of quarterly supervision.

9.38 Dedicated storage for X-ray films is helpful, as most films are still not supplied on disc, although that is likely to change. Where imaging is provided on disc, this is rarely, if ever, accompanied with a list of contents and may not contain all the imaging that it claims to from the defendant's covering letter. Someone therefore must be delegated the task of checking the disc and compiling an index of what is on it.

9.39 Medical records are often extensive. The master file should always be kept in the office and not sent to experts or counsel. The master file of medical records will be handled frequently during the life of the case as records are added and copy sets are made. Copy sets in lever arch files will be sent backwards and forwards to counsel and experts. It is worthwhile paying slightly more for lever arch files whose mechanism will not be distorted in transit.

Case Reports

9.40 It is to the benefit of all that cases should be reported, and the case does not need to be very unusual for a report to be accepted. It is all too easy to overlook this possibility until a considerable amount of time has passed in dealing with costs, by which time the case may have been archived. Ideally, the possibility of reporting the case should be integrated into the case planning, perhaps to be raised after the damages have been paid. Timing is a matter of sensitivity and difficulties can arise in asking for and or obtaining a client's agreement. This is often due to the personal and sensitive nature of the clinical issues, but the client may agree if the case is reported using initials instead of names. In other cases, the request is probably made too late, when the client has either become wearied waiting for the balance of their damages, or has moved on and is getting on with their life. Many claimants would wish to help other potential claimants and the usefulness of case reporting in this connection should be stressed or it is liable to be seen as simply an invasion of privacy.

10

MEDICAL RECORDS

A. Conduct

The conduct of the parties in the pre-action period is the subject of the guidance **10.01**
and 'Good Practice' commitments set out in the CPR Protocol for Resolution
of Clinical Disputes, which can be found at <http://www.dca.gov.uk> (accessed
2 April 2007). The steps set out in the Protocol are intended to encourage greater
openness between the parties, encourage parties to find the most appropriate way
of resolving the particular dispute, reduce delay and costs, and reduce the need
for litigation (1.6). Under CPR rule 44.3(5) the conduct of the parties in the
pre-action period may be taken into account when the question of costs is
considered.

The specific objectives of the Protocol are openness, timeliness, and awareness **10.02**
of options (2.2). When the claimant has considered his or her alternative courses
of action and decided to pursue a claim for damages, there is an obligation to
explore the merits of the claim as fully as possible before litigation is commenced.
The question of alternative courses of action may re-emerge with the defendant's

letter of response. In the meantime, while it is inevitable that the claimant's ability to fully comply may from time to time be restricted by short time limits, restricted funding, or the defendant's own conduct, in most circumstances all the steps laid down in the Protocol should be followed before proceedings are commenced. The protocol steps are discussed below.

10.03 The first stage in the investigation is to obtain, organise, and review the medical records. A patient's right to disclosure of their medical records is provided for in the Data Protection Act 1998. Disclosure of the health care records of a patient who is deceased is governed by the Access to Healthcare Records Act 1990; it is usually necessary to submit a copy of the Grant of Probate or Letters of Administration with the application for disclosure.

10.04 The recommended protocol and other guidance for the parties applying for disclosure and responding to applications are set out in Protocol Annex B3.7–3.13.

Which Records?

10.05 The general rule is that medical records should be obtained from all organisations and individuals who have treated the claimant at any time, as the claimant's previous medical history may be relevant to all elements of the claim. Although the claimant may feel the older records are irrelevant, they need to be seen by each expert instructed on liability issues. The expert advising on breach of duty must consider, among other matters, whether there was a negligent failure to take an existing condition into account when deciding on or administering treatment. The expert who is to advise on causation must consider whether there is any pre-existing condition that may be partly or wholly responsible for the claimant's alleged injury. The report on condition and prognosis must comment on all the claimant's current health problems and the prognosis overall, in particular if there is a pre-existing unrelated condition which is likely to impact upon the client's future health or life expectancy.

10.06 Accepting the general rule, some common sense should be applied when sending for records; for instance, it is unlikely to be necessary to obtain records relating to a hospital admission in childhood in a case involving obstetric injury. On the other hand, in all cases of obstetric injury or birth damage, the records relating to any previous pregnancy and delivery should be obtained. These will enable the medical expert to consider whether any factors arising in a previous pregnancy or delivery are relevant to the issues the expert has been asked to consider.

10.07 The initial request should include a request for copies of medical imaging (which includes X-rays, MRI scans, CT scans, hard copies of ultrasounds, and photographs). An additional charge may be made for the cost of copying the imaging. To save both parties unnecessary costs, the radiology should not be copied automatically, unless only one or two images are held. Normally the Trust will compile a list of the radiology held, from which the relevant studies may be selected for reproduction.

If it is decided that certain records are not to be requested, the nature and loca- **10.08** tion of these records should be recorded on the case plan for future reference. It should also be recorded that if additional records are obtained for one of the experts at a later date, copy sets should be sent to all the experts. It is very important that all the medical experts are asked to acknowledge receipt of the additional records, review them and provide additional comments if the expert considers that the records contain information relevant to the issues in their report.

Careful case planning and file management will ensure that there is a clear note **10.09** of what records exist, which records have been requested, and which received, and that those records that are outstanding are chased up promptly.

B. Records Held by NHS Trusts

Records should be requested on the Law Society application form which can **10.10** be found at Annex B of the CPR Pre-Action Protocol for Resolution of Clinical Disputes which can be found at <http://www.dca.gov.uk> (accessed 10 April 2007). The application should be completed as fully as possible. The more accurate and complete the information the more easily the records can be located. Of particular importance is the claimant's address at the time of the treatment, the date of treatment given (even approximate dates will assist), and the department in which the treatment was provided.

Although a completed form may contain sufficient information in itself, it will **10.11** frequently be necessary or helpful to deal with the request in more detail in a covering letter, particularly when writing to a Trust that is the proposed defendant.

The Protocol expects records to be provided within 40 days, in compliance with **10.12** provisions of the Data Protection Act 1998; a prompt explanation should be provided in those 'rare circumstances' where this is not possible (3.10). A reasonable explanation might be that the claimant is having frequent appointments for ongoing treatment; some delay may be unavoidable in this situation, in order to ensure that the records are available to the clinicians who are due to see the client and it may be that copying will need to wait until there is a suitable gap in time between appointments.

10.13 If the records are not forthcoming after 40 days and no reasonable explanation has been given, it is often helpful to telephone the officer who is dealing with disclosure, in the medical records or legal services department, to discuss the situation. Personal communication is often effective in resolving the problem but in the absence of any convincing reason for delay, notice should be given that the claimant intends to issue an application for disclosure (see below).

C. General Practitioner Records

10.14 The Law Society form is not designed for requesting general practitioner records. Instead, a letter should be sent to the GP enclosing the client's signed form of authority. The amount of information given will depend upon whether or not the GP is the proposed defendant. The letter should include the following information:

- the name of the potential defendant;
- a brief indication of the treatment complained of with dates;
- a request for disclosure of all the records in the GP's possession, specifying that these should include all computer printouts, clinical records including any handwritten notes, all correspondence, reports, and investigations;
- if ancillary staff are relevant to the investigation, a request for clarification of the employment status;
- if neither the general practitioner nor any member of the practice staff is the likely defendant, confirmation of this fact;
- if the general practitioner is the likely defendant, a summary of the allegations and request for medical defence membership details.

D. Other Record Holders

10.15 The procedure described for seeking disclosure from the GP is suitable for obtaining health care records from other sources, including private practitioners, although if convenient, the Law Society request form may be used for obtaining records from private hospitals.

Private Hospital Records

10.16 When requesting records relating to private hospital treatment, the treating consultant will hold the clinical notes and that may include the anaesthetic records if the treating consultant is a surgeon. The nursing notes, drug charts, theatre notes, and so on will be held by the hospital. The patient will often have been given the medical imaging to look after. The hospital in question will not coordinate a request for disclosure, request for different types of records will usually be made to each record holder.

E. Formats and Media

It is important to have some regard to the different formats and media in which records may exist. The record holder should be asked to provide copies of imaging in the original format if this is technically possible. A copy produced in a different medium is unlikely to be satisfactory for the purposes of the experts in preparing their reports. Even copies in the same medium may be less than satisfactory. When that is the case, in due course arrangements will need to be made for the expert to access the original image. Some situations that may be encountered from time to time are discussed below. **10.17**

Ultrasound Scans

Ultrasound scans are not always available as films; sometimes the scans may have been viewed by the ultrasonographer in real time, in which case the only record is the ultrasonographer's report. Some scans may have been printed onto paper subject to rapid deterioration; these may be beyond recovery. It is difficult to be sure that any of these is the correct explanation for the absence of films that may simply have been lost. The relevant medical expert should be able to advise whether the explanation given is a plausible one in the circumstances of the case. Where films do exist, they may be photocopied for disclosure and this may not be adequate for the expert's purpose. **10.18**

Digital Storage

Fortunately, medical imaging is now increasingly created in digital format. This has the advantage that first generation copies can be recreated quickly and easily at little expense. Older medical imaging is sometimes stored digitally. If the record holder claims that radiology is lost, it may well be productive to enquire whether it was digitally created or stored; the officer dealing with disclosure may not have investigated this possibility. **10.19**

Imaging provided on disc is likely to be unlabelled and without an index. The disc should be opened and checked; an index of the contents should be made and checked against the imaging requested. **10.20**

Patient-held Records

10.21 Maternity patients often have their own notes of their GP and midwifery care in pregnancy and postnatal period, often known as the 'cooperation card' or 'red book'. This tends to remain in the mother's possession; it is often a very important record of information that is not found elsewhere and should not be sent by post or any other insecure means, it should either be collected in person or the client should be asked to bring it into the office.

Colour Copies

10.22 Colour copies of records may be requested if the medical notes appear to have been corrected or overwritten or where the original records are colour coded, which is sometimes the case with charts. This is not always a substitute for examination and inspection of the original records, but may suffice to resolve problems of interpretation, at least at the initial investigation stage.

Paper Sizes

10.23 Certain medical documentation is created on paper of less common dimensions. Charts may be on A5; various physiological investigations may be recorded on continuous paper of varying sizes. Such records will normally be disclosed on A4, either reduced to fit or copied in sections. When it is clear that the experts need to see these records in the original format, copies in that format should be requested from the record holder. If the service cannot be provided by the Trust, there are commercial services available.

10.24 In cases involving injuries to a child in the antenatal period or at the time of delivery, the Trust should be asked to provide the CTG traces in continuous copy format. Unless this is specified, they will normally be provided as A4 page sections, joined with sticky tape. This is never satisfactory as it is impossible to be sure that every part of the trace is there and the trace itself will be distorted at the joins. A sufficient number of copies should be requested, as the cost of additional copies is insignificant in relation to the inconvenience of having a single copy on file. It is sensible to obtain one copy for the master file of records, one to send to the obstetric expert, one for the neonatology expert, and one for Counsel's bundle. It is more cost effective to do this at the outset of the claim than later and avoids delay.

Specimens

10.25 Consideration should be given as to whether pathology material is likely to be relevant to the case; if so, it will need to be examined by the expert. For example, in a case involving delayed diagnosis of cancer, the claimant and defendant histopathology experts will need to access the pathology material to advise on causation. Any organisation holding pathology material should be asked to confirm in writing that their pathology department has located and retains any specimens until the conclusion of any proceedings. When the claimant's pathology expert is instructed, arrangements should be made with the Trust for the material to be transported from the hospital to the expert and back by courier.

10.26 Many general practices hold computer and handwritten records and the practitioner must ensure that both are disclosed. If the GP records are key to the client's allegations, the practice should be asked to disclose at the time of disclosing the records the software used by the practice. This will enable the expert to understand the way the records are organised and what one could expect to find in them.

F. Incomplete or Delayed Disclosure

10.27 It will be necessary to make an application to the court for an Order for disclosure if there has been unacceptable delay with no reasonable explanation. Any explanation given should be critically examined. If records are said to be 'lost', further efforts are likely to result in them being found. If records are genuinely lost, a full explanation is likely to specify the circumstances, for example reference will be made to the guidelines under which they were destroyed or to the date of the flood or fire that beset the building in which they were housed.

10.28 An application may be made against the proposed defendant (3.12) and, as the Protocol makes clear, against a third party, as third-party health care providers are expected to cooperate with pre-action disclosure (3.13). The claimant should ask for the costs of the application.

10.29 Commonly enough, the records will be disclosed once an application has been listed for a hearing. Alternatively, a full explanation will be served by way of a witness statement, describing the difficulty in locating the records. If the claimant is satisfied that disclosure is complete, or that the explanation must be accepted, the respondent should be asked to agree to meet the claimant's costs, to enable the hearing to be vacated.

G. Organising the Records

10.30 The Suggested Model Directions, version 3 (11 March 2005) for Clinical Negligence Cases before Master Onley and Master Yoxsall provide for maintenance of records as follows:

> Legible copies of the medical records of the claimant/deceased/claimant's mother are to be placed in a separate paginated bundle at the earliest opportunity by the

claimant's solicitors and kept up to date. All references to medical notes in any report are to be made by reference to the pages in that bundle.

10.31 The Master's Model Directions can be found at <http://www.hmcourts-service. gov.uk> (accessed 10 April 2007).

10.32 The records must be organised in a format that is logical and internally consistent. Any missing or unreadable records need to be identified, and better copies requested. Double-sided or incorrectly aligned records must be recopied. The records must be sorted, paginated, and indexed.

10.33 A chronology of the claimant's treatment should be drawn up. This should briefly summarise the claimant's previous medical history, highlighting any aspects that may be relevant to the issues in the claim. Medical events that occurred in the particular period under consideration in the claim should be set out in detail in the chronology, and each should appear in the index, so that all involved in the claim may easily refer to the relevant entries in the notes.

10.34 It is a matter of choice whether this work is undertaken by the practitioner or whether it is sent out to a commercial collation service. There is much in favour of having the records organised professionally. There are many collation services available, from large organisations to freelance individuals, usually with nursing or medical backgrounds. The quality of the work is variable but once the practitioner has found a satisfactory service, the advantages are numerous:

- The expertise of the collator can be matched to the treatment in question. It is essential to have a midwife, or a doctor with obstetric experience to collate the records in an obstetric or birth injury case. A nurse with intensive care experience will be invaluable when treatment in ITU is in question, and so on.

- A good collator will be able to comment on to what extent the client's allegations are supported or contradicted by the notes. This is not to be relied on as an expert opinion, but it can be very helpful information when instructing the expert and proofing the client.

- Professional collators are well placed to identify missing records and advise as to their importance to the issues under consideration. This is especially true when they have an expertise in the clinical area in question. This can prevent considerable delay, as otherwise these gaps may not come to light until the medical expert cannot find the record when trying to write his or her report.

- Professional collation is an effective use of time. Sorting, collating, paginating, and indexing the records is a very time consuming task, even in experienced hands. During the month or so that the records are with the collator, time can be spent instead on identifying and inviting the medical experts, in readiness for formally instructing them.

- Professional collation is cost-effective. Collators' hourly rates are relatively low even compared with paralegal rates, and much lower than solicitors' rates. The overall disbursement is relatively modest and unlikely to be challenged at assessment, in contrast there may be a difficulty in recovering the cost of a fee earner's time collating the records.

H. Other Relevant Documents

Clinical Governance

There may be documentation arising from the claimant's injury that is not rou- **10.35** tinely disclosed but that is relevant to investigating liability. The Protocol CND Annex B states: 'Reports on an "adverse incident" and reports on the patient made for risk management and audit purposes may form part of the records and be disclosable: the exception will be any specific record or report made solely or mainly in connection with an actual or potential claim.'

Disclosure of all documents of this nature should be requested; disclosure should **10.36** not be restricted to the complaints file.

National Policy and Guidance and Local Protocols

National policy and guidance on health care topics are promulgated by the **10.37** Department of Health. The Royal Colleges and other specialist medical organisations also produce guidance and recommendations on clinical standards and procedures.

Protocols are guidelines created and implemented at a local level. They are often **10.38** adapted from national guidance, in order to take account of local health care organisations and resources. They are guidelines for hospital staff relating to specific clinical situations, setting out what should happen, when it should happen, and who should be involved in the process.

If research suggests there should be a local protocol reflecting proper practice in **10.39** an area relevant to the issues in a case, the defendant should be asked to provide a copy. The protocol should of course be contemporaneous with the treatment in question but superseded protocols can usually be tracked down. The expert should be asked to comment upon whether clinical processes described in the local protocol provide reasonable standard of care, in the *Bolam* sense. Any national guidance would make a useful comparator. The expert should also comment on whether the protocol—reasonable or not—was complied with in the particular case. It is not uncommon for the protocol in place to have been out of date compared with the accepted professional standards at the time of the alleged negligence, particularly in older cases.

10.40 The possible existence of additional relevant documents needs to be reviewed on a case-by-case basis. Disclosure of these documents will not be given routinely and the practitioner may need to persist to obtain them.

10.41 There is an enormous amount of useful background information on the Department of Health website dealing with national guidelines, performance, waiting times, and the freedom of information issues, among many others, which can be found at <http://www.dh.gov.uk> (accessed 10 April 2007).

I. Understanding the Records

10.42 An effective clinical negligence litigator must become familiar with and develop some understanding of medical records. Professional collation of the records is an aid to reading and understanding, not a substitute. A degree of skill in interpreting the records accumulates only by long exposure. The process is assisted if the firm adopts a house style for the organisation of records, to be followed in every case by the collator.

10.43 When they are returned from the collator, the collator's comments on salient points should be followed in the chronology and cross-referenced with the notes. When reading the expert's report, references in the report should be correlated to the entry in the medical records. In this way, the practitioner will acquire an invaluable familiarity with the detail of the case.

J. Medical Vocabulary

10.44 There are various dictionaries and medical abbreviations published and available on the Internet, some of which are listed at the end of this work. Although there are many standard medical abbreviations, abbreviations in clinical notes are often non-standard and sometimes quite idiosyncratic and even medical experts sometimes struggle to interpret them. If it is a matter of significance, the record holder should be asked to provide an explanation. Anatomical terms, medical conditions, and clinical procedures may be researched on the Internet, as well as in textbooks.

Medical Personnel

10.45 It can be useful to compile a 'cast list' of the staff attending or responsible for the claimant at relevant points. If the information is incomplete, the practitioner should be able to fill in the gaps from various sources. Most (but not all) doctors have individual entries in the Medical Directory. Old issues of the Medical Directory can be useful for historical searches. Whether or not the doctor has an individual entry in the Medical Directory, a consultant will be listed in their specialty sections under the names of the Trust or the hospital in the 'Organisations' section. Consultants are also generally easy to identify and locate through surfing the Internet or using a website such as <http://www.specialistinfo.com> (accessed 2 April 2007). Junior doctors can be more difficult to identify. An enquiry of the potential defendant may produce the information.

The medical expert should be asked to check whether any junior member staff **10.46** involved in the allegedly negligent treatment appeared to be suitably experienced and qualified for the work undertaken. The expert will be able to consult membership lists of specialist organisations.

K. Reviewing the Records

The records should be read with a view to establishing whether they support or **10.47** weaken the client's case, particularly on the factual points such as dates, timings, and the identity of persons present on salient occasions. The client may believe that the nursing staff failed to notify medical staff of a problem, whereas the notes may establish that they did do so, but that the doctor failed to respond. The client may believe that there was no attendance by medical staff because they have forgotten or been unaware through drowsiness or the effect of medication. Information of this kind should be used to ensure the investigation is directed to the real issues.

Disparity between the client's account and the medical facts may be insignificant. **10.48** On the other hand, if the client's factual evidence is at the heart of the case, any disparity will have to be carefully considered and investigated. Witnesses such as family members may need to be proofed. The discrepancy should be discussed with the client and the difference between the client's recollection and the evidence in the medical records will need to be addressed in the client's proof of evidence.

It is probably rare but certainly not unknown for records to be tampered with. **10.49** Records may be amended or overwritten, or there may be retrospective entries that are not credible or that are at least self-serving. If there seems to be reason to doubt the genuineness of a record, the first step is to ask for a colour copy (which may show up different coloured inks that appear the same in black and white). The original records should be inspected where there remains any doubt. If the notes are suspicious, the best way of dealing with this should be discussed with counsel.

10.50 The claimant may be concerned that there are retrospective notes in the records, but this is not in itself sinister. Notes do have to be written up after the event when events move swiftly. If the timing shows they were entered after the adverse outcome became known, the expert should consider them critically. The defendant should be asked to explain, if there is any significant lapse of time between the event and the note, particularly if there is a discrepancy between other contemporaneous notes and the later notes. Case planning should ensure that this point is revisited when instructing counsel.

L. Updating the Records

10.51 The medical records will need updating during the course of litigation, possibly more than once. This requirement should be incorporated into the case plan, as it is easily overlooked until an expert, or the defendant, makes a request for updated records, a situation that often causes delay. A bundle of paginated up-to-date notes with an amended index should be sent to all experts and counsel as they are received, so that everyone is working from the same up-to-date bundle.

11

WITNESS EVIDENCE

A. The Importance of the Statement

The first draft of a claimant's witness statement may be put together hurriedly, **11.01** often for the purposes of supporting an application for funding. The statement may then lie on the file without further review until the first conference with counsel, when it may be found to need considerable expansion and amendment before it can be served. By this time, all the experts will have referred to the first draft statement in their reports.

Detailed proofing of witnesses and drafting of statements tends to be an unpopu- **11.08** lar job that is often delegated to very junior fee earners or trainees. This approach belies the importance of the witness statement to the claimant's case.

It is important to bear in mind the specific purpose of the statement. The rules **11.03** relating to witness evidence are in CPR Part 32. The rules state that a witness statement should:

- contain the evidence which the witness would be allowed to give orally (32.4(1));
- stand as the witness's evidence-in-chief unless the Court orders otherwise (32.5(2));

- the Court may give the witness permission to amplify his statement or to give evidence in relation to new matters that have arisen since the witness statement was served (32.5(3));

- but the Court will do so only if it considers there is good reason not to confine the evidence of the witness to the contents of his witness statement (32.5(4)).

11.04 It follows from this that a witness statement should be carefully drafted to ensure that it touches upon all the factual issues in the case of which the witness has personal knowledge; it should explain as far as possible in the claimant's own words the effect of the negligent treatment on his or her physical, emotional, and financial well-being, and its impact on family life.

11.05 If the witness's evidence on the facts of the case is key to the success of the case, it is particularly desirable that the conducting solicitor undertakes the proofing and drafting. If recollection of detail is important, it may be productive to proof the client using cognitive interviewing techniques. The principles of this well-established method of interviewing can be learnt in a day, although the results achieved will improve with practice. Training courses are available through the usual legal training organisations; attending a course should pay dividends in the practitioner's increased understanding of the importance of careful and purposeful witness proofing.

B. Liability and Quantum Statements

11.06 In smaller cases, particularly those where special damages are low or relate only to past loss, it is sensible for the claimant to provide one statement that covers both liability and quantum issues. In larger cases, while it will be necessary to proof the claimant on both liability and quantum issues, it is generally better that the claimant's evidence be separated into two statements. The first step will be to finalise an early statement dealing with the claimant's evidence on the liability issues, which will touch on quantum issues only to indicate the nature of the losses and expenses in fairly general terms. A detailed statement on quantum issues will be prepared later in the case, before the quantum experts are instructed. This should be included at the appropriate point in the case plan timetable. Preparation of the quantum statement should be organised before the quantum experts are instructed; this may be before or after the commencement of proceedings, depending on funding considerations, the claimant's clinical condition, and so on.

11.07 The advantages of this approach are:

- the liability statement may be finalised, dated, and signed early in the case without needing to be updated as the quantum evidence develops;

- the liability statement may be updated, for example to comment on factual issues arising from the defence, without the need to update quantum issues prematurely;
- the quantum statement may take account of the expert evidence on causation and on prognosis;
- the quantum statement may be amended to address all the heads of damage claimed once the Schedule of Loss has been settled;
- the statements may be detailed without becoming unwieldy.

C. Selection of Witnesses

Liability

Consideration should be given to whether there are any witnesses other than the claimant and immediate family members who may be able to give helpful evidence on liability issues. Arrangements should be made to proof any such witness, who should be offered a home visit. **11.08**

As a general principle, where there are other witnesses who can give useful factual evidence, the practitioner should ensure that these witnesses are proofed and signed up to their statements as soon as practicable. This is a safeguard against contingencies such as death, departure, or disaffection. It is impossible to predict every issue that may need to be addressed in the course of a case, but if the witnesses have set down their recollections of events, this will assist their memories if further questions need to be put at a later date. **11.09**

In a case that involves an allegation of delay in effecting a transfer or referral between facilities administered by different Trusts, it may emerge during the first conference that it may be necessary to obtain a witness statement from the clinician responsible for the relevant service of the non-defendant Trust, in order to establish the probable course of events had the transfer or referral taken place. The position should be reviewed with counsel after the defence has been served. **11.10**

Quantum

There is a tendency for potential witnesses on quantum issues to proliferate, as people with significant health problems and limited resources are generally obliged to make ad hoc arrangements for care and support among a variety of people drawn from family, friends, and formal care agencies. For reasons of proportionality and convenience, the number of witnesses should be kept to a reasonable minimum consistent with providing evidence of all of the claimant's losses. The defendant will share some responsibility for this later in the case, **11.11** when there is an opportunity to concede reasonable or non-contentious items in the claimant's schedule.

11.12 If there is documentary evidence to support a loss, it is unlikely that witness evidence will be required to substantiate it. Otherwise, the best principle is that where there is a witness who can give supportive evidence on a factual point, the witness should be asked to give a statement. The witness should be included in the list on the allocation questionnaire. A decision can be made in due course as to whether or not they should be called.

D. Content

11.13 For the CPR requirements that apply to the form and content of witness statements the reader is referred to Practice Direction 32, paragraphs 17–22; the rules governing exhibits are set out at paragraphs 11–14.

Liability

11.14 The body of the statement should set out, as far as practicable in the claimant's own words:

- the claimant's current personal circumstances;
- a chronological account of the relevant events from the claimant's point of view;
- a description of the physical and psychological effects of the injury from the date of the incident;
- a description of the effect of the injury on the activities of daily living;
- the impact of the injury on the claimant's employment and employment plans;
- past and future losses and expense; itemised in detail if no quantum statement is to be served, otherwise sufficient detail should be included to support a preliminary schedule of loss and to give a reasonable indication of the likely nature and value of the claim;
- any other relevant matters.

E. Interviewing the Witness

11.15 It is desirable to have a detailed signed statement early on in the case and clearly this is of critical importance if the claimant is unlikely to survive the litigation. The claimant should be proofed in detail once the medical records have been collated and reviewed. The initial attendance note will provide the basic frame-work for the interview; and there may have been factual gaps in the instructions that were identified in the risk analysis procedure. The medical records may have revealed additional information or entries that contradict the client's recollection of events. These are all matters that the claimant should comment upon. If the records do not tally with the claimant's recollection of events and the claimant remains of the view that the records are wrong or misleading, the claimant's statement should refer to the disputed records and set out his or her alternative account. If this is likely to be an issue in the case, thought should be given to whether any other witnesses may be able to give evidence on the point or whether there is documentary evidence in the claimant's possession that may support the claimant's account, such as a diary, appointment calendar, or journal record. If so, this should be exhibited to the statement.

In general, but particularly in cases that rely in whole or in part on the claim- **11.16**
ant's factual account, it is desirable that there should be a detailed signed state-ment that pre-dates receipt of the medical reports and conference with counsel. If issues do arise later in the investigation that need to be addressed by the claim-ant before exchange of witness evidence, consideration should be given to whether it is preferable to amend the statement, which will then bear a later date, or to prepare a supplementary statement dealing with the late issues that have arisen. If an amended statement is served, the superseded statement should be kept on file, so that it may be produced should there be any suggestion that the claimant's evidence was influenced by the medico-legal evidence.

Some Cases Requiring Particular Care

Failure of Response

Additional lay witness evidence will be very important where complaints or **11.17**
requests were allegedly ignored by those responsible for treatment. It is fairly common for a claim to be based partly on the claimant's assertion that their concerns, or the concerns of their relatives, were not attended to. Unfortunately, it is in the nature of this situation that complaints or requests are not recorded in the notes. A witness's supportive statement, given early in the case, in as much detail as possible, is of great assistance in these circumstances.

Neglect or Abuse

The same considerations of supportive, timely witness evidence of concerned **11.18**
relatives would apply in a case where the allegation concerns abuse or neglect of a vulnerable claimant. If the claimant is unable to give their own account of events, the records are unlikely to help but instead may present a conflicting or confused picture as to what treatment was or was not given. The witness evidence

of a concerned relative, with as much accuracy in dates and times as can be achieved, is essential in these circumstances.

Lack of Consent

11.19 An early signed witness statement is of great importance when the claimant alleges they were given inadequate advice on risks and benefits of treatment. In a case that hinges on lack of consent, the medical notes of the key consultation tend to be markedly scant. The claimant's recollection of what he or she was told and what he or she understood is central to the allegations. A good witness statement will play an important part in rebutting the defendant's case that the clinician would have followed his 'usual practice'.

11.20 As soon as the medical records have been collated the claimant should be taken through the chronology and the medical records. The questioning should be directed at eliciting answers to the following questions:

- What was the claimant told and what did he understand about the risks and benefits of the proposed treatment?

- If it is the claimant's case that there was no discussion of any risks, what was his own perception of the risk and, had there been a discussion of risks and benefits, would he have done anything differently?

- If the claimant had been told of the particular risk that in fact materialised, what, if anything, would he have done differently?

11.21 This can be a difficult process for the claimant as it involves a degree of detachment that does not come easily in the circumstances. It is only too easy for anyone to believe that one would not willingly have incurred a risk that has in fact materialised. Nevertheless, the claimant should be asked to give full attention to these questions very early on in the case. This will enable the strengths of the claim to be assessed as soon as possible and will ensure that the claimant's evidence will be as robust as it can be, as it will have been crystallised before the claimant was exposed to expert advice on what the risks were and what advice should have been given. If necessary, the statement may be amended to include the claimant's further evidence of issues raised by the expert. The first statement should be retained on the file.

CPR Part 22

11.22 Under CPR PD 20.1A witness statements must be verified by a statement of truth. All witnesses should be advised in writing of the possible consequences of making a false statement, which are set out in CPR 32.14.

12

EXPERT EVIDENCE

The selection and instruction of medical experts is at the heart of clinical **12.01** negligence practice. It is critically important that the expert is prepared get to grips with the minutia of the medical records, understands the particular issues that must be addressed in the report and how these interface with the legal tests in negligence. The expert must be impartial and should be familiar with his or her obligations under CPR Part 35 and PD35, in particular the overriding duty to the court.

A. Finding an Expert

The best means to select an expert is through personal experience or personal **12.02** recommendation. The majority of practitioners will have access to a list of approved experts maintained by the firm but an expert recommended for instruction in a personal injury case may be unwilling or unsuitable for instruction in a clinical negligence matter. Such a list is unlikely to contain suitable experts in every specialty; for these reasons it is frequently the case that an expert previously untried by the practitioner will need to be identified and instructed. There is a plethora of websites and agencies which may assist in identifying medical experts who undertake medico-legal reporting; there are directories that may be consulted, and some individual experts send out advertising flyers.

Advice and Research

12.03 If the practitioner is at a loss as to the appropriate expert, counsel may be able to provide some recommendations (and, just as importantly, some warnings). AvMA may be able to advise on possible experts through their Lawyers Service at <http://www.avma.org.uk> (accessed 3 April 2007) but are not able to help on all occasions. The APIL website at <http://www.apil.com> (accessed 3 April 2007) has some information about experts but does not provide much detail. There are subscription services available, such as <http://www.specialistinfo.com> (accessed 3 April 2007) which holds information on doctors' clinical and medico-legal interests or free sites such as <http://www.expertsearch.co.uk> (accessed 2 April 2007).

Conflict of Interest

12.04 It should not be difficult to avoid inviting an expert who has an obvious conflict of interest. Clearly, the practitioner may not instruct another consultant on the staff of the defendant Trust but previous employees should also be excluded—if a CV is not available on file or online, the expert's Medical Directory entry may show the past employment history. A short period of employment at the defendant Trust which occurred many years previously may not be grounds for exclusion, in principle, depending upon the expert's own views and the client's preferences.

Locality

12.05 An expert who practises in a hospital close to the defendant Trust area may feel unable to assist if he or she has had personal or professional contact with the doctor criticised. Some geographical distance from the defendant is therefore desirable. However, the expert must be reasonably convenient for seeing the claimant if there is to be an examination, and the expense associated with the expert travelling to conference and trial will need to be taken into account when considering funding and proportionality.

Medico-legal Experience

12.06 It is a very great advantage if the expert has had previous experience of advising in clinical negligence cases. Many doctors enjoy personal injury reporting and are interested in becoming involved in clinical negligence litigation. It must be borne in mind that the requirements of an expert in a clinical negligence case are much more onerous, extend over a longer period of time, and require an objectivity and level of intellectualisation that are different from that required in a personal injury case. If it is not clear from the information to hand whether the expert has been instructed in clinical negligence cases previously, the question should be asked. Experts have to gain experience somewhere of course, but unless the practitioner is reasonably experienced, an inexperienced expert should not be instructed if this can be avoided. If a less experienced expert is to be instructed, this should be in the first instance on the less contentious area, which in many cases will be current condition and prognosis.

B. Choosing an Expert

Breach of Duty

Specialism

The expert who is asked to advise on whether there was a breach of duty of care **12.07** should be a practitioner in the same specialty (and sub-specialty) as the allegedly negligent practitioner. The expert should be of consultant standing (or equivalent), as the expert's opinion on the standard of care must be authoritative.

It is necessary to understand how clinical services are organised in general, **12.08** although this will vary in detail from Trust to Trust. As with most professions, medicine is becoming ever more specialised; although the most highly specialised units are found in the larger university teaching Trusts, district hospitals may provide quite a considerable degree of specialisation within departments. In a teaching hospital it is likely that more specialists will have titles that reflect their particular expertise, such as 'Consultant in Renal Medicine', whereas in a district hospital the nomenclature may be less specific, with large departments of 'general surgery' or 'general medicine'. A consultant seen in the diabetic clinic may be variously called a Consultant Physician with an interest in diabetes, a Consultant in General Medicine, a Consultant in Endocrinology, or a Consultant in Diabetes. The title used will give an indication of the extent to which a specialist service is provided by the hospital and the extent to which the individual holder of the title confines their practice to that particular area.

When looking to identify an expert to advise on breach of duty, some research on **12.09** the organisation of the work of the defendant Trust will be of assistance. A considerable amount of information can be gleamed from the Trust's own website and other websites such as <http://www.specialistinfo.com> (accessed 2 April 2007).

Contemporaneousness

The expert must have been in practice at consultant level in the relevant specialty **12.10** at, or very close to, the time of the allegedly negligent treatment. This is essential to ensure that the expert can speak with authority on the standard of care that would have been considered reasonable at the time in question. It would be unwise to instruct an expert who had retired from practice more than two years or so after the index events.

Comparability

12.11 The expert should be currently practising, or have had very recent experience of practising in a clinical unit broadly similar to the one in which the doctor who is criticised treated the claimant. A professorial consultant in a specialist unit in a university teaching hospital would not be in a position to say with authority what standard of care could reasonably be expected in a district general hospital; the expert would be vulnerable to the argument that he or she was applying too high a standard of care. In the same way, a consultant in a district hospital should not be invited to advise on the standard of care to be expected in a university teaching hospital. Not only is it likely that the doctor will feel unable to comment upon the standards to be applied in a more specialist unit, but also the defendant's expert is likely to be drawn from a specialist unit and hence will be considered more authoritative.

Causation

Specialism

12.12 The causation issues must be carefully analysed to enable the relevant expert to be identified. It may be that only one expert is required to report on breach of duty, causation, and current condition and prognosis, for example, in a case involving failure to diagnose a fracture in an orthopaedic clinic. On the other hand, in a case in which there was failure to diagnose or investigate a fracture in the accident and emergency department and the patient was sent home without follow-up, an accident and emergency expert would be required to report on breach of duty and an orthopaedic surgeon would be required to report on causation and current condition and prognosis. In a case where there was bladder damage during a Caesarean section, an obstetric report will be required dealing with the primary breach of duty, a urologist report on the standard of the subsequent diagnosis and management and a psychiatrist's report may be require on psychiatric damage and prognosis. These may be relatively straightforward examples; in more complex cases or in areas of medicine not commonly encountered, the breach of duty expert will be able to help identify the specialties that should be covered if the case analysis is put to him or her.

Expertise

12.13 The expert who is to advise on causation should be chosen on the basis that he or she is the best available expert in terms of authority and expertise to advise on the medical condition in question. The considerations of comparability and contemporaneousness do not apply to the elucidation of the causation issues. Proportionality issues are relevant, of course; it might be difficult to justify the fee of a third-tier specialist if causation could reasonably and properly be dealt with by the breach of duty expert.

Current Condition and Prognosis

Specialism

It is likely in many cases that either the breach of duty or the causation expert **12.14** may be able to advise on current condition and prognosis, but in some situations, one or more experts from other specialties are required. For example, in a case involving abdominal surgery, a plastic surgeon may be required to comment on the scarring.

Expertise

As for the causation expert, the expert on current condition and prognosis **12.15** chosen should be chosen on the basis that he or she is the best available expert in terms of authority and expertise to advise on the medical condition in question. If the claimant has developed psychiatric symptoms, the psychiatrist will be instructed to advise on the attribution of those symptoms as well as the current condition and prognosis. It is sometimes overlooked that psychiatrists may have special expertise in certain areas; there are psychiatrists who specialise in many different areas, such as psychiatric conditions arising during the perinatal period or in cancer patients.

C. Inviting the Experts

Thought should be given to the order in which experts are to be instructed on **12.16** a case-by-case basis. It should not be assumed that the legally logical order of breach of duty followed by causation is necessarily the most appropriate in any given case. Sequential reports may be appropriate in some cases, for example where it is evident that the timing of breach of duty has to be established before the causation expert can usefully advise, but in other cases a different approach will be more effective.

There may not be a choice—if funding is short for the investigative stage, it **12.17** may be necessary to obtain reports sequentially in any event, but otherwise consideration must be given to how long the investigation will take if that approach is adopted. The best plan may be to commission both reports at the outset, on the basis that they will be reviewed and amended after the first confer-ence with counsel.

12.18 In other cases, it may be useful to first obtain a report that will underpin the primary liability opinions, if this will help direct the investigation. An example of when this might be the best approach is a brain damage case, where the timing of the injury is unclear and the prima facie evidence of breach of duty is weak. In those circumstances, a neuroradiology report will help to clarify both these points.

12.19 Once a shortlist of experts has been drawn up and the sequence of reports has been decided upon, the first step is to invite the expert to accept instructions. It is not appropriate to instruct an expert without first determining their willingness and medical records should certainly not be sent with a letter of invitation. This will be inconvenient and annoying if the expert is unable to accept instructions.

12.20 It is important that the expert be provided with enough information in the invitation to act, but not too much. It is possible the expert has already been approached by the defendant or may know the doctor involved and therefore the letter of invitation should not give more detail than necessary about the claimant's analysis of the case. Additionally, the expert is likely to be irritated if there is an enormous amount of detail to read through.

12.21 The letter of invitation must name the claimant and litigation friend, the defendant, the consultant in charge of the patient, and the doctors or other personnel criticised (if they are known). The letter should give a brief summary of the background to the case and summarise the allegations. The summary should not extend to more than one or two short paragraphs but should be sufficient to make it clear to the proposed expert what is the nature of the case. The expert will need to be satisfied that he or she will be acting within their area of expertise and also the summary should be sufficiently informative to allow the expert to establish whether it is a case that is of interest to them and indeed whether it has, on the face of it, any plausibility.

12.22 Finally, the letter of invitation must request that if the expert wishes to accept the invitation, he or she must:

- confirm that there is no conflict of interest;
- confirm that he or she will not delegate any parts of the report writing without the instructing solicitor's agreement;
- confirm what proportion of their clinical negligence experience has been on instruction by the claimants, how much for the defendant, and how much on joint instruction;
- supply a full CV with the letter of acceptance.

12.23 The expert's reply should be critically evaluated on receipt.

The full CV may reveal points which need discussion, for example if their special- **12.24** ist area of interest has recently changed, or points of particular concern, for example the fact that the expert has spent much of their career advising the defence.

The terms of business may need to be renegotiated. It may be possible to choose **12.25** between two or more experts who are prepared to act. One of the factors to consider in addition to all the matters mentioned above is the expert's charging rate, and how that compares with the amount allocated by the funding body and the amount charged across the board, both in general and in that specialty. Charging rates are very variable but as a rule of thumb, the doctors in super-specialties can reasonably charge more than the less rare specialists. Legal expenses insurers generally insist on approving in advance the fees to be incurred in instructing experts.

Every client should have the opportunity to consider the CV and likely fees of **12.26** an expert it is proposed to instruct. It is one of the Legal Services Commission Specialist Quality Mark transaction criteria that the client be asked to approve the instruction of each expert. The client must be advised whether the fee is reasonable (that is, within the normal range or otherwise justifiable) or whether there is a risk that it will not be recovered in full. Where there is good reason to instruct an expert who has an unusually high hourly rate, or who estimates an unusually high overall charge, it would be prudent to seek prior authority on a publicly funded case. Although the fee will still need to be met within the overall financial limits available, this is protection against the fee itself being assessed down if the case is unsuccessful.

D. Instructing the Expert

Once approval has been gained from client and funding bodies, the expert can **12.27** be instructed. Each expert should be supplied with their own bundle of records. The master file should always remain in the solicitor's keeping and should never be sent off to the expert. The expert should be asked to retain the records until the matter is concluded.

The letter of instruction to the expert is the place to set out the facts of the case **12.28** as far as they are known, the claimant's particular concerns, and the issues that the expert is being invited to consider. The letter should also briefly mention what other reports are to be obtained and explain what the position is with regard to any procedural steps that have been taken or that are imminent. The letter should enclose:

• a complete bundle of medical records;
• medical imaging if required;

- chronology of treatment;
- claimant and witness statements;
- complaint correspondence;
- a clear instruction to the expert to carry out a full review of all the relevant literature and to provide copies with their report.

12.29 It is suggested that at this point the expert should not be supplied with any other reports that have been obtained. There are exceptions to this rule, for example, a neuroradiological report, if available, would be of great assistance to the neonatologist or paediatrician considering current condition and prognosis or causation. However, in most cases, any disclosure should be deferred until the experts are preparing for the first conference with counsel. In the first instance, experts often prefer to arrive at their opinion independently, without being consciously or unconsciously influenced by the views of their fellow experts. The extent to which they agree or disagree with each other should be explored in conference with counsel, a topic that is discussed further in Chapter 14. Secondly, the expert must list in their report any documents they have relied upon in coming to their conclusions. Complications arise if an expert has read and listed a report of another expert, if that report is subsequently amended, as this will risk creating the undesirable effect of making the preliminary report disclosable.

12.30 The letter of instruction should include a series of specific questions the expert is to consider, as well as a general invitation to comment or can simply guide the expert to the area in more general terms. This is a matter of the practitioner's personal preference and experience of the expert.

12.31 The letter of instruction should confirm the nature of the client's funding arrangements and confirm the agreed timescale within which the report is expected.

E. The Client

12.32 Most experts who undertake medico-legal work are well organised and the date at which the report is expected can be relied upon with reasonable confidence. Other experts unfortunately are less predictable and need to be chased repeatedly. It is important to keep in touch with the claimant while the report is being waited for. It is very easy to overlook the extent to which the claimant may lose confidence in the whole procedure when weeks and months go by with little result. Claimants are aware that the expert reports are the most critical stage of the claim and are often anxious that the doctors will be closing ranks; any delay in receiving the report may be seen as confirming these anxieties. In the circumstances, a minor courtesy such as dropping the claimant a brief letter to acknowledge that the report is due and has been chased can make a significant difference to the client's confidence.

F. Evaluating the Report

When the expert report is received, the case plan should be revisited as a reminder **12.33** of the issues that were to be addressed. The narrative of the report should be followed in conjunction with the medical records and the chronology. This will not only increase the practitioner's familiarity with all the medical data but will demonstrate how the expert's train of thought leads to the conclusion. The report needs to be critically evaluated; it should be checked for factual errors; it should be internally coherent, should have addressed all the questions in the letter of instruction, should demonstrate an understanding and correct application of the legal tests, and the conclusion should follow logically from the commentary and should be expressed in terms of the legal tests applied. If the report falls short of these requirements, clarification or amendment should be requested immediately.

It is essential that the expert has reviewed all the relevant literature; if copies **12.34** have not been included with the report, the expert must be asked to provide them. The expert's conclusions should be supported by the literature or, where not so supported, the expert should explain why his or her opinion should prevail. Failure to carry out this exercise creates a risk that weaknesses in the case are not evident until much later in the litigation.

The expert advising on breach of duty should have referred to the relevant **12.35** edition of each of the major textbooks on the subject on which the medical staff may have relied and should also refer to any contemporaneous published guidelines. If the textbooks differ in the management advocated, the expert should say why one textbook should be preferred over another.

The expert advising on causation should have reviewed all the relevant journal **12.36** and research literature to date and the report should state which of the papers support the expert's conclusions, which do not, and should explain why any particular study may be more relevant to the issues in question than another.

The expert report with any additional expert comments should be sent to the **12.37** client with a brief summary of the findings and an invitation to discuss it in detail with the practitioner. It will be obvious in some situations that this should be preceded by a telephone call.

If the expert medical opinion does not support the case, the claimant should be **12.38** invited to make an appointment to discuss the position and discuss whether any further steps may be taken. Although some will prefer not to do so, other clients find it helpful to meet, in order to ensure that they understand the experts' reasoning and the implications for the legal argument. This is almost certainly the client's only opportunity for redress; there should be no omission to probe the expert opinion or to explore whether there are any doors left open for further investigation, for example, if there are missing records that may be relevant and may change the picture. The claimant should be given the opportunity to put any outstanding questions to the expert. A decision should be made as to whether it will be useful and justifiable to go to counsel for an opinion or a conference with the experts, in other words whether there is any prospect that one of the experts will change their mind in discussion.

12.39 When finally advising the client that the case cannot proceed, it is essential that they are given limitation advice again at this point and that they are advised to take further steps immediately if they wish to consult other solicitors for a second opinion.

12.40 Where experts' reports are supportive or partially supportive, once the breach of duty and causation evidence is to hand, the next step, in all but the smallest cases, is likely to be a conference with counsel.

G. Managing the Expert

12.41 There are some simple steps that can be taken which will contribute to the expert's confidence that there is a properly constituted well-managed team pursuing a claim which does not lose momentum. The expert should be kept informed of relevant developments. Not least, this should include informing the expert when the case has settled, which is surprisingly often overlooked. Practice Direction 35 6A provides that where an order requires an act to be done by an expert, or otherwise affects an expert, the party instructing that expert must serve a copy of the order on the expert instructed by him.

12.42 In general, an expert will appreciate clear instructions, sensible and reasonably well-informed questions, efficient arrangements for conferences, joint meetings and trial, and prompt payment of fee notes. No expert should be instructed before proper arrangements are made for funds to be available to pay the costs of the report. It goes without saying that an expert should not be expected to defer his or her fees unless there is a specific agreement to do so.

12.43 The instructing solicitor must not hesitate to challenge the expert if they find that the expert's report is inconsistent or contains factual inaccuracies. Not infrequently, expert reports do not fully address the issues they were asked to consider, or do not apply the legal tests correctly; or less often, the report may contain factual inaccuracies. It will be a matter of concern if there are serious factual inaccuracies, but minor ones can be easily corrected and should simply be drawn to the expert's attention. If possible, corrections should be made before the client receives the report, as factual inaccuracies tend to undermine the client's confidence in the expert.

It is a matter of concern if a report is logically inconsistent; for example, an **12.44** expert may find that the treatment given was 'unacceptable' but conclude that there was no breach of duty. Although this problem may be resolved in correspondence or in conference, it may be indicative of an expert who is reluctant to commit to the claimant's case.

If the legal issues have not been fully addressed, this may be a question of the **12.45** expert failing to express the conclusion of the report in legal terms. It is a matter of concern if on the other hand there is some ambiguity about the expert's view or an unwillingness to commit to a firm view. Rather than deal with this sort of issue in correspondence, it may be more effective to flag up the concerns with both the expert and the client, and to defer discussion until the first conference with counsel. At conference the expert's opinion can be fully explored and at the same time his or her consistency and reliability can be assessed.

An expert who has given a positive report and later undergoes a change of mind **12.46** and goes back on their evidence should be asked to account for this volte-face. A very serious situation has arisen, in which possibly considerable costs have been thrown away. If new factual or medical evidence has come to light, the change of view may be quite proper or at least justifiable. On the other hand, if the expert has not done a proper job in the first instance or has collapsed in the face of a contrary opinion from the defendant's expert, he or she should not be used again.

In some circumstances, it may be possible to rescue the claim by instructing a **12.47** second expert, but clearly this is difficult to justify to the funding body unless it is possible to demonstrate that the case does not have a fatal weakness, but rather the problem lies with the expert who has not carried out the task adequately. Instructing a substitute expert is likely to be a realistic option. Once expert reports have been exchanged, and certainly after joint meetings have taken place, introducing a substitute expert is a desperate measure that might be undertaken in a very high value case but would otherwise be difficult to justify.

The issue of accreditation for expert witnesses is very much alive at the time of **12.48** writing. There are various organisations that provide expert witness training and own accreditation. In all circumstances one would expect an expert witness who was to be instructed on a clinical negligence matter to have undergone some level of training in the duties and responsibilities of the expert witness.

13

LETTER OF CLAIM AND RESPONSE

At the point that the claimant's investigation has been completed, it should be **13.01** borne in mind that in the majority of cases, the defendant will have no meaningful indication of the progress or direction of a potential claim beyond the small amount of information provided with the request for disclosure at the outset of the claimant's investigation.

Once the claimant's investigation has reached the stage when a decision may be **13.02** made on whether the claim will be pursued, the defendant should be notified if the claimant has decided against taking any further steps, or if the solicitor is no longer instructed, as provided in the Pre-Action Protocol for Resolution of Clinical Disputes (3.5(3)).

A. Letter of Claim

Timing

If the claim is to be pursued, paragraph 3.15 of the protocol states that the **13.03** claimant should serve a letter of claim 'as soon as practicable'. This is an important stage of the claim. The first question to be determined is whether the letter of claim should be served before the particulars of claim have been settled, which would usually mean before the first conference with counsel. This question raises tactical considerations, which include the relative complexity of the issues, the extent to which the experts have reached firm conclusions, and the likelihood of early settlement.

13.04 The timetable of the claim may be a factor in the decision. If it has been possible to fix the first conference for a date shortly after the expert reports are received, in all but the most straightforward cases the advantage will lie with deferring the letter of claim for a brief period, until it can be served with draft particulars of claim. On the other hand, if with the best of planning, the conference is more than three months ahead, there is much to be said for serving a letter of claim promptly in the expectation of having the response to consider in conference, where the case is otherwise suited to this approach.

13.05 A disadvantage of this course of action is that any subsequent amendment of the claimant's allegations may be perceived as revealing a weakness in the claimant's case or in the calibre of the claimant's expert evidence.

13.06 By contrast, it is a significant advantage to have the defendant's letter of response by the time the experts and counsel meet in conference as the claimant and experts may consider the defence and add to or amend their advice if appropriate to take into account the defendant's case before the particulars of claim are settled.

13.07 One of the aims of the protocol is to avoid litigation where possible. In a claim that is of relatively low value, and in which the issues are straightforward, it will be entirely appropriate for the letter of claim to be served without recourse to counsel. If the claim has been quantified a Part 36 offer to settle may accompany the letter.

13.08 It also may be advantageous to serve the letter of claim before the first conference even in a more complex or higher value claim, but this should only be undertaken if the expert opinions are clear, unambiguous, and in all important respects consistent with each other, otherwise it is unlikely that the allegations of negligence in the letter of claim will withstand critical analysis. Although it may be less likely that there will be an early settlement in a complex or higher value case, the defendant may make admissions in the letter of response. This may reduce the costs of litigation, if, for example, the admissions enable one of the claimant's liability experts to be discharged. An important admission would allow litigation risk to be reassessed in the claimant's favour; this should increase the settlement value of the claim, may secure funding for the next steps of the claim, and reduce insurance costs.

13.09 A letter of claim should not be sent before the particulars of claim are settled in cases of maximum severity, or in other substantial cases where the liability arguments involve a panel of experts from different specialties. The conference is an essential process in finalising the allegations and thoroughly exploring the expert's support for the various aspects of the claimant's case. In a claim of this sort, the opinions of the experts may change substantially in the course of the conference; the outcome of the conference may be to take the claim forward on a different footing. Neither party is likely to be assisted by a premature letter of claim in these circumstances.

The purpose of the letter of claim is to provide the defendant with sufficient **13.10** information to carry out such investigations as are required to enable the claim either to be settled, or to put the defendant in a position to respond to the allegations before litigation is underway. A letter of claim should not be sent until the claimant is able to provide enough information to make it meaningful. If the limitation period will expire before the end of the three months allowed for the defendant's response, it is best to be open with the defendant about the difficulty and to provide as much information as it is possible to disclose before the claimant's allegations are set out in full in the particulars of claim once proceedings are served. It may then be reasonable to agree an extension of time for the defence.

Content

Annex C1 to the protocol provides a template for the letter of claim; this lists **13.11** essential information, optional information, and possible enclosures. Essential information includes the usual identifying particulars, name, address, and relevant dates, together with a description of the circumstances that gave rise to the claim, the allegations of breach of duty and the case on causation, a description of the claimant's condition and prognosis. Quantum information should be given as far as possible, with at least the likely heads of claim. Optional information suggested includes an offer to settle without the expense of obtaining expert evidence or proposals for alternative dispute resolution, as well as information and proposals regarding expert evidence.

The information given should be drafted with care. The allegations of breach of **13.12** duty, causation, current condition, and prognosis should reflect the opinions stated in the expert reports. The heads of damage claimed and the past losses will largely be based on the client's instructions and for that reason if no other, before the letter is served, the client should approve it. A letter of claim which provides insufficient or inaccurate information may be justly criticised and may render the claimant vulnerable on costs if litigation could have been avoided or investigative costs saved had the claim been correctly stated.

The following documents can usefully be enclosed: **13.13**

- the chronology of treatment provided by the collator;
- draft particulars of claim if they are available;

- report on current condition and prognosis if this is in final form and ready for service with proceedings;
- preliminary or full schedule of loss;
- if an offer to settle is included, documentation supporting the schedule.

B. Letter of Response

13.14 The protocol at paragraph 3.25 stipulates that the defendant should respond within three months with a reasoned answer to the letter of claim. It should be clearly stated if there is a full or partial admission; there should be reasons given if any allegations are denied, it should be stated whether the chronology and factual account is disputed and if so, the defendant's chronology and account should be given; any documents relied on in refutation of the claim should be provided.

13.15 Annex C2 to the protocol provides a template for the letter of response; this lists essential information, optional matters, and possible enclosures. Essential components include dealing with any outstanding requests for medical records or further information required from third parties, proposals for next steps for settlement, further investigation, or alternative dispute resolution. Optional matters include an offer to settle or counter-offer, or copies of expert reports.

C. Admissions

Withdrawal of Admissions made up to 6 April 2007

13.16 Pre-action admissions made up to 6 April 2007 may be withdrawn. The case of *Stoke-on-Trent CC v Walley and Smith and Wall* [2006] EWCA Civ 1137, CA (Civ Div) established that CPR 14.1(5), which provides that the defendant must apply to the court for leave to withdraw an admission, did not apply to pre-action admissions. The defendant was at liberty to withdraw an admission made before proceedings. It is for the claimant to apply to strike out all or part of the defence denying liability, on the grounds that withdrawal of the admission amounted to an abuse of process, demonstrating that the defendant acted in bad faith or that the claimant would suffer some prejudice that would affect the fairness of the trial.

Withdrawal of Admissions made after 6 April 2007

13.17 CPR 14.1A has been inserted into CPR 14; this new rule applies to the pre-action protocol for resolution of clinical disputes, as well as to personal injury and disease pre-action protocols. Under CPR 14.1A, a party may make a 'pre-action admission' in writing, either in response to a letter of claim or by stating the admission is made under CPR 14. To withdraw a pre-action admission before the commencement of proceedings, the consent of the person to whom the admission was made is required. The court's permission is required to withdraw a pre-action admission once proceedings are underway.

Judgment on Admissions

Under CPR 14.1A(4), pre-action admissions are grounds for an application for judgment. The party who made the application may apply to withdraw it. **13.18**

D. Case Management Considerations

It should be apparent from the foregoing paragraphs that considerable delay may be incurred in the period following initial investigation before proceedings are started. If the case is conducted reactively, the expert reports will be received first and then arrangements will be made for the conference. Unless otherwise instructed, counsel will generally defer drafting the particulars of claim until after the conference. Unfortunately this may be weeks later. The experts will need to approve the wording of the allegations; and if there has been any delay, they will need to set aside time to read into the case again. In this way, six months may very easily be added to the course of the claim before proceedings have begun. **13.19**

This problem can best be avoided by planning well ahead to ensure that the first conference takes place as soon as possible after the liability and prognosis reports are available. Counsel should be instructed to draft particulars of claim before the conference, in order that they may be discussed in conference and the wording approved by the experts in person; the particulars may be settled there and then or immediately following the conference. **13.20**

Whether the letter of claim is sent before or after the first conference, the three months allowed for the defendant to respond can be used to progress matters: **13.21**

• witness statements can be finalised and any additional witnesses proofed;

• additional experts may be instructed and appointments with quantum experts may be put in place. Although funding may not be available to confirm instructions, it is generally possible to make appointments with quantum experts ahead of time. This can result in very significant time saving. If, for example, an expert needs to see a child during term time, the school holiday dates can be taken into account well in advance;

- outstanding documentary evidence of loss and expense may be obtained with a view to supporting the schedule of loss and settling the claimant's list of documents;

- the preliminary schedule of loss may be drafted or augmented.

E. The Defendant in the Pre-action Protocol Period

13.22 As discussed in Chapter 5, all claims notified since 1 April 2002 will be reported to the National Health Service Litigation Authority (NHSLA), who will manage the claim thereafter. During the pre-action protocol period, while the claimant is investigating the merits of the claim, there may or may not be significant activity on the part of the defendant Trust. The reporting procedure is set out in the *Clinical Negligence Reporting Guidelines*, which can be found at <http://www. nhsla.com> (accessed 2 April 2007). In accordance with those guidelines, claims must be reported within two months of notification; it is likely however that few of these claims will be sent out to solicitors before the claimant's letter of claim is served, other than those cases where there is a serious risk of liability being established or the claim is one where the injuries are of maximum severity. The NHSLA will have regard to the internal investigation at trust level; where this has suggested there is a significant risk of the claimant succeeding (for example, where there is criticism of the standard of care given), the risk will be reported to the NHSLA who may well decide to send the file to solicitors for preliminary action and advice. These are factors that are likely to influence the ability of the defendant to provide a response to the letter of claim within the time allowed.

14

INSTRUCTING COUNSEL

A. The First Conference: High Value Cases

Introduction

The first conference with counsel should be an important landmark in the life **14.01** of a clinical negligence claim. It is an expensive exercise. The cost is justified if the conference moves the case on significantly. Ideally the conference should be a pivot that moves a potential claim to the point where the claim is ready to issue. To achieve this it is vital that you, counsel, and the experts prepare thoroughly for the conference. The following summary sets out a suggested format to help you achieve as much as possible from the first conference in a high value complex case. A modified approach more suitable to smaller cases is set out in 14.51 below.

Who Should Attend?

The client/litigation friend

The client or litigation friend should be invited to every conference or round **14.02** table meeting. It is the client's case and to exclude the client without very good reason is simply unacceptable. Most clients or litigation friends will want to attend.

If the client cannot travel or does not want to travel then the conference, if at all possible, should be organised at a venue that suits the client. This may mean everybody else has to travel. Occasionally it may be necessary to include the client by video or telephone but this should be the exception rather than an easy compromise.

14.03 If the client wants to bring their spouse, a friend, or a social worker this person should be included in the arrangements as well. There may be problems about a witness attending the conference. If the client asks to bring a witness you should discuss the position with counsel ahead of the conference. It can cause embarrassment if the client has brought a companion, expecting them to attend the conference, and on arrival at the conference counsel excludes that person because they are a witness of fact who it would be inappropriate to allow to attend the conference.

14.04 If the client has a litigation friend careful consideration needs to be given as to whether the client should also attend the conference. If the client is a young child it will probably be inappropriate for them to attend. A separate conference should be arranged so that counsel can meet the client at home. There is no substitute for meeting the client in attempting to understand the consequences of the client's injuries. A video may be a useful tool to help the defendant and the judge understand the extent of the claimant's disabilities but for counsel it is always necessary to meet the client. An early visit to the client's home allows counsel to assess the priorities for the client; for example, the urgency of obtaining an interim payment.

14.05 If the client is an adult without capacity but will be able to understand the purpose of the conference and wants to attend then it may be appropriate for both the litigation friend and client to attend. If the client is a child close to 18 years and will become an adult of full capacity during the course of the case it will almost certainly be sensible for both the litigation friend and the client to attend.

The solicitor

14.06 The senior solicitor or partner with conduct of the case should always try to attend the first conference, rather than delegate this to a junior colleague or trainee.

14.07 This is important for a number of reasons. First, it underlines to the client, to the experts, and to counsel the significance of the conference. Secondly, it allows the conducting solicitor a vital overview of the case and identifies its strengths and weaknesses. Thirdly, it allows the conducting solicitor to deal with the client's anxieties after the conference. For example, the client may be unhappy with one of the experts or with counsel and the conducting solicitor will need to be in a position to evaluate such complaints.

If there is an assistant fee earner working on the case he/she should also attend. **14.08**
First, an accurate and detailed note of the conference is essential. This should be
circulated after the conference to counsel and the experts and signed by counsel.
It may avoid the need for advice in writing from counsel after the conference and
saves that expense. Secondly, the conference should discuss the further steps that
need to be taken in the case and the assistant fee earner should have the opportunity to discuss these with counsel, the client, and the experts. The opportunity to
plan ahead whilst everybody is in the same room needs to be maximised. It should
save expense rather than increase the expense to have the assistant fee earner
present at the conference. The assistant fee earner can then go straight back to the
office and get on with the tasks identified in the conference.

Counsel

The choice of counsel will be a matter for you and it is an important decision. **14.09**
Unless you have complete confidence in counsel you cannot be surprised if the
client is unhappy with the choice. The gender, age, and personality of counsel
may be significant to particular clients. If a client expresses preferences in respect
of the gender of counsel the client's wishes should be accommodated, as far as is
reasonably practical.

If a case will ultimately need leading and junior counsel there are considerable **14.10**
advantages in both counsel being instructed to attend the first conference.
Thereafter the work can then be appropriately split between them. The first conference is the opportunity for the client to meet counsel and for counsel to gain
the confidence of the client. This is important for the future management of the
case. There may be points in the case where difficult decisions have to be taken on
the advice of counsel. If the client has met both leading and junior counsel at the
outset they are more likely to accept difficult advice from either leading or junior
counsel further down the line. However, the Legal Services Commission will not
routinely allow the cost of both junior and leading counsel at the first conference.
If there is a difficulty in obtaining authority for two counsel at the conference,
leading counsel should be asked to write a short note setting out the advantages
and future cost savings in having both counsel at the first conference.

If leading counsel is ultimately to be instructed it is preferable they should attend **14.11**
the first conference. It is at this conference that vital decisions may need to be
taken about the way the case is pleaded and the experts that will be used. These
decisions are best made by the same counsel who will ultimately be expected to
conduct the case at trial. Setting the case off on the right track at the outset will
save costs in the end. Bringing leading counsel into a case only when it appears to
have developed complications is not ideal. It should be apparent from the outset
whether a case justifies leading counsel or not.

14.12 If the client has only met leading counsel they may not be happy with junior counsel attending interlocutory hearings. If junior counsel is to attend interlocutory hearings and draft agendas for expert meetings and the schedule of loss there is a huge advantage in having junior counsel attend the first conference. Whilst the initial cost for the conference may be increased by the attendance of two counsel this additional cost is justified if it enables savings to be made thereafter. If only leading counsel attends the first conference it will then be necessary to instruct leading counsel for all further steps involving counsel or to bring junior counsel into the case at a stage when they will need to spend a lot of time catching up. The reading in costs for junior counsel will be incurred at some stage so they might as well be incurred at the outset.

The experts

14.13 Normally any expert whose report will be disclosed should attend the first conference. You should discuss with counsel when planning the conference whether other experts will be required for the case. If counsel recommends further experts, it will be necessary to decide whether to postpone the conference until these further experts can attend. This will vary on a case-by-case basis, depending on a number of issues including whether a decision can be taken to proceed before the further expert is instructed and whether there are limitation issues. The objective whenever possible should always be to have everybody who is significant to the case in the same room at the first conference. This will allow a broad overview of the case as well as addressing the detail. Again if there are difficulties in obtaining legal services funding for all experts to attend the conference, counsel should be asked to write a short note confirming the need for this.

14.14 There are enormous advantages to having experts attending the conference in person rather than by telephone or video link. The examination of CT and MRI scans, X-rays, continuous CTG traces, or original documents may be important. Even without these, the face to face contact between experts and the discussion generated between experts of different disciplines, counsel, solicitors, and the client frequently allows the overlapping issues of breach of duty, causation, and damage to slot into place at a much earlier stage than they otherwise would. It is often a false economy to have some experts on the telephone or only to invite the lead experts to the conference.

14.15 To obtain the maximum value from the input of the experts it is necessary to instruct them fully. The experts should be provided with a complete and up to date bundle of medical records, with the client's statement, the witness statements, the reports from all the other experts, and with the draft particulars of claim, well in advance of the conference.

A thorough review of the medical literature is a vital part of the expert's task. The **14.16** importance of this cannot be over-emphasised. Each expert should specifically be told that they will be expected to provide, ahead of the conference, copies of all the relevant literature and guidelines. These should already have been referred to in the expert reports, but often the references themselves are not included in the first draft. Without having read all the research papers, counsel cannot be expected to advise on the significance of the literature. Far too often, vital medical research papers surface just before trial or even at trial itself. The first conference is the proper place to discuss these papers, and the significance of them. This may need to be revisited after exchange of expert evidence, but if the groundwork is prepared thoroughly at this stage, the literature produced by the defendant's experts should not come as an unpleasant surprise.

Timing

Almost always, the objective of the first conference should be to consider and **14.17** revise draft particulars of claim. A draft of the particulars of claim should always be available before the conference. If the counsel you instruct does not routinely provide a draft particulars of claim before the first conference they should specifically be instructed to do so. The draft particulars of claim provides the best working document for the conference, unless the claim can be pleaded the case will not be able to proceed. For counsel to draft the document after the conference often leads to considerable delay and duplication in work as the draft will then need to be circulated to the experts for comments and approval. At the end of the conference the draft should reflect the strongest case that can be made for the claimant. Only when everybody has an opportunity to consider the best case that can be pleaded can a decision properly be made as to whether the case should be issued, needs further investigation, or must be abandoned. At the end of the conference counsel should be asked to forward a corrected draft immediately. If leading and junior counsel attend the conference it may be that junior counsel has made the corrections on a laptop during the discussion. This is the ideal procedure as corrected drafts can then be printed and approved by the client and experts at the end of the conference. If counsel has been asked to confirm to the Legal Services Commission the need for two counsel at the first conference one valuable point to be made will be that this will enable finalisation of the particulars of claim at the conference and avoid the cost of subsequently instructing each of the experts to comment on the draft, an exercise which can be costly in itself.

In a complicated case the first conference should usually take place before the **14.18** letter of claim is sent to the defendant. After the particulars of claim have been revised to reflect the discussion in the conference this document can be sent with the letter of claim. This ensures that the case first put to the defendant is the claimant's best case and one that the claimant's experts and counsel can support. Whilst it is sometimes tempting to test the defendant's reaction by an early letter of claim the risk is that the allegations based on the initial expert reports may be significantly refined by the discussion in the first conference. In a complicated case the overlapping issues of breach of duty, causation, and damage need to be discussed between the experts and with the input of counsel before the strengths and weaknesses of the case can be identified. Once the particulars of claim have been discussed and approved in the conference the letter of claim can far more confidently present the case to the defendant.

14.19 In a relatively straightforward case or an obviously very strong case it may be that a letter of claim has already been written and a response received before the first conference. This allows the opportunity to discuss the merits of the defendant's case at the first conference. However, if this leads to a different case being pleaded the claimant's negotiating position may have been weakened by the change of position on behalf of the claimant.

14.20 All the experts on liability and causation that are likely to be required should have reported before the first conference. If there is any doubt as to whether other experts are needed you should discuss this with counsel before the arrangements for the conference are finalised. If another expert is needed, for example a midwife in an obstetric case when only an obstetrician has been instructed, then if possible the further expert should be instructed, have reported, and been invited to attend, before the first conference.

14.21 In cases where the claimant is neither a child nor a patient, the timing of the conference may be driven by limitation issues. If the client has instructed the solicitor close to the expiry of the limitation period then the defendant should be asked to agree to a limitation extension. If the defendant will not do so, it may have been necessary to issue proceedings to protect the position. If particulars of claim need to be served in four months this may dictate the timetable. In these cases every effort should still be made to ensure that all the experts who will need to provide reports are at the conference.

Preparation

The solicitor

14.22 Once the solicitor has the medical records and the expert reports, plans can be made for the first conference. Once suitable counsel has been identified, counsel should be consulted on the plans for the conference. The medical records and expert reports should be sent to counsel well ahead of the conference for consideration of:

- whether any further experts are required to report before the conference;
- whether any further medical records need to be obtained;

- whether any other documents should be requested, for example hospital protocols, inquiry reports, etc;

- whether any companion the client proposes to bring to the conference might
need to be excluded from the conference because they will be a witness of fact.

Where there is a possible claim against a general practitioner the Lloyd George **14.23**
card entries are likely to be unsigned. If the general practitioner practice has a
number of different general practitioners it will be vital to identify which general
practitioner saw the client on each attendance. The solicitor representing the
Medical Defence Union (MDU) or Medical Protection Society (MPS) should be
asked to provide details of who made each of the relevant entries in the Lloyd
George cards or any other relevant general practitioner records. Unless this is
done before the conference the identity of the defendant cannot be confirmed
and the particulars of claim may subsequently need substantial amendment.

If any of these further investigations are required it is much better they are **14.24**
identified before the first conference than during it. If there are outstanding
investigations to carry out after the first conference this will prevent particulars
of claim being finalised and prevent a final decision being made at the conference
as to whether proceedings can be issued. Whilst you may be confident that all
the necessary investigations have been carried out, confirmation of this from
counsel before the conference will not delay matters. If counsel does think of
a different line of inquiry it is preferable this is put into effect before the
conference.

Once the conference date has been fixed all those attending should be sent **14.25**
identical paginated bundles for the conference including:

- the relevant medical records;

- the client's statement;

- the expert reports;

- the hospital protocols;

- the medical literature;

- any inquiry report, inquest report, complaint investigation, etc;

- any essential correspondence with the defendant, for example an admission of
breach of duty, an apology in response to a client's complaint, but not other
correspondence.

At the outset of the case the medical records should have been separately pagin- **14.26**
ated in a way that can be used throughout the case. That is, the experts should
all have been sent identical paginated records and been asked to refer to records
in their reports with these page references. Counsel should be asked to use these

page references in the pleadings. It is now the practice of masters and district judges to order the defendant to disclose paginated medical records. If the records are disclosed early on by the defendant without an order the defendant should be asked to paginate them. If this has not been done the claimant's solicitors should paginate the records and notify the defendant of the pagination.

14.27 For the purposes of the conference it may be that only a core bundle of medical records are required and these should then be selected (keeping the original pagination) and included in the conference bundles with the expert reports and the client's statement.

14.28 Arrangements need to be made for the conference to be at a location that the client can attend. If the client needs wheelchair access, you will need to check the arrangements ahead of the conference. The client will often find the first conference with counsel an anxious time. Everything that can be done needs to be done to make it as easy as possible for the client and to save the client any embarrassment or difficulty. It can be a good idea to arrange for the client/litigation friend and any companion to arrive at the conference ahead of the experts to meet counsel and be put at ease before all the experts arrive. The conference time with a number of experts in attendance is expensive. If the client comes to the conference early counsel can complete introductions and explain to the client what will happen at the conference without keeping the experts waiting outside the door.

14.29 Whatever the funding arrangement for a case the cost of the conference will need to be calculated in advance. Counsel should be asked how long it will take, and how much of that time the experts need to attend for. The experts' hourly rates and travel costs will then need to be ascertained. It is important to check these ahead of the conference and if necessary cap the cost of any particular expert whose charges are out of line with others. Counsel's time for preparation will also need to be ascertained and if necessary capped.

Counsel

14.30 Counsel instructed for the first time in a case should be sent the papers well ahead of the conference and the instructions should make clear that you expect to discuss the planning of the conference with counsel ahead of the conference. If counsel is well known to you this may be done informally and you may rely on the past practice of counsel to do this. If not you should book a telephone conference with counsel formally into his or her diary to discuss the case. This will ensure that counsel looks at the papers ahead of the date of the telephone conference rather than just before the main conference. Counsel should be asked to consider ahead of the telephone conference any further experts that are required, further documents, further reports, or other investigations it would be helpful to carry out before the conference.

As discussed in 14.17 above counsel should always be asked specifically to draft **14.31** particulars of claim before the first conference. Simply discussing the strengths of the case with the experts and then drafting particulars of claim after the conference is much less satisfactory. The experts need to approve the particulars of negligence in the precise form in which they are pleaded. To circulate particulars of claim for comment some weeks or months after the conference is very much less satisfactory and less cost effective than discussing the draft particulars of claim in the conference and finalising the wording of the document with all the experts present. If these experts might ultimately need to give evidence in the case they should always have been asked to support the precise wording of the particulars of negligence. Further, in order to draft the particulars of claim properly, counsel will need to have gone through every medical note and set out the relevant notes. If this has been done ahead of the conference the experts can advise on any entries which are significant and ought to be added to the summary of the notes in the particulars of claim. The transposition of the clinical notes into the particulars of claim will involve interpretation of manuscript entries. Where there is difficulty reading an entry the combined expertise of the experts at the conference will usually resolve the problem. It may also reveal that the note has been read differently by different experts. If that is the case the defendant may need to be asked to confirm the entry.

The particulars of claim will usually be the main focus of the discussion at the **14.32** first conference. However, in addition to drafting particulars of claim, counsel may need to draft an agenda for the conference setting out other points that need to be discussed in addition to the draft particulars of claim. Further, counsel will usually need to draft a chronology and in an obstetric case a schedule of labour may also be helpful. Examples of these documents are shown below at Appendix 2 and 3. If these documents are available before the first conference they can be checked by the experts and once confirmed as accurate they will then be valuable documents to attach to a skeleton argument for an interlocutory application or for trial or to an advice on approval. These documents should represent an agreed summary of the factual backdrop to the case.

The experts

The draft particulars of claim, chronology, and summary of labour prepared by **14.33** counsel should be circulated to the experts ahead of the first conference. The experts should be asked to consider the documents and come to the conference with any comments. In addition it should be stressed that if they have not already provided full references and copies of all relevant medical literature they must do so by the date of the conference. It should be emphasised to the expert that attendance in person at the conference is considered an important part of the expert's contribution to the case. A last minute request to attend by telephone will not be satisfactory except in a genuine emergency.

Aims and Objectives

14.34 The aim of the first conference is to review the merits of the case at a point when all reasonable preliminary investigation has been completed. Counsel, the experts, and the client should be able to discuss together the strength of the case based on:

- the medical records;
- any report from an inquiry, complaint, or inquest;
- the client's statement and any other claimant witness statements;
- the hospital protocols;
- the expert opinions;
- counsel's opinion.

14.35 With this material the draft particulars of claim need to be considered. By the end of the conference counsel should be able to advise on the prospects of success. This advice can then be recorded in the conference note. The conference note can be signed by counsel and sent to the Legal Services Commission or insurer and the client.

14.36 If by the end of the conference the case cannot be pleaded in a way that the experts can support and counsel considers there are not reasonable prospects of success, then that conclusion will need to be recorded and discussed with the client. It may be that a further line of enquiry will justify some further investigation. However, the aim should always be to have carried out sufficient investigation before the conference that a final decision can be made by the end of the conference.

14.37 If the advice of counsel is that the claim has reasonable prospects of success then counsel will need to amend the particulars of claim in accordance with the discussion in the conference. The revised particulars can then be attached to a letter of claim to be sent to the defendant. Instead of writing a separate advice confirming the prospects of success for the Legal Services Commission counsel should be asked to sign a conference note in which the advice on the prospects of success has been recorded.

14.38 If the case has reasonable prospects of success but also significant risks on liability or causation it may be appropriate for the conference to discuss whether a percentage Part 36 offer should be made at the same time as the letter of claim. The input from the experts on this topic may be helpful. An offer of 95 per cent in a strong case may result in certainty for the client at an early stage. An offer of 75 per cent may start early negotiations and result in an early compromise. Clearly this is a point that needs careful consideration on a case-by-case basis. However, some consideration should be given at the first conference as to whether a Part 36 offer should be made and when.

At the end of the first conference it is often helpful to the client if there is a short **14.39** general discussion with counsel after the experts have left. This discussion can usefully cover the following topics in summary:

- the future timetable for the case;
- whether the claimant should ask for a split trial with liability and causation heard before quantum and the advantages and disadvantages of doing so;
- the instruction of quantum experts and what is expected of the client in respect of seeing both claimant and defendant experts;
- a very approximate estimate of the quantum of the case;
- the prospects of obtaining an interim payment and what will be involved in such an application;
- the concept of periodical payments and whether the case would be appropriate for periodical payments;
- the need to assess life expectation.

If the advice of counsel is that the case does not have reasonable prospects of **14.40** success and that there is no merit in further investigation, then this will need to be dealt with sensitively. Confirmation of this position may need to be obtained in the presence of the experts. Thereafter some additional time will be needed with the solicitor and counsel explaining the position to the client.

If, as sometimes happens however careful the planning, new avenues to explore **14.41** emerge at the conference then it may simply not yet be possible to make a decision as to whether the case can proceed. In this event the prospective time-table needs to be carefully explained to the client, so that they can understand exactly when and how a final decision on whether the case can proceed will be made.

Follow-up Work

Solicitor

After the conference the detailed conference note will need to be typed and **14.42** circulated to everybody who has attended the conference. It should record counsel's advice on the merits and be signed by counsel. In most cases this will avoid the need for written advice from counsel as well as the advice in conference.

14.43 If the advice of counsel at the conference is that the case has reasonable prospects of success then a letter of claim needs to be sent as soon as possible. Counsel should be asked to send the revised particulars of claim immediately after the conference and these can then be attached to the letter of claim.

14.44 The experts will not be required to finalise their reports for disclosure until after the defence is received and after exchange of witness statements of fact. However, if as a result of the conference any of the experts needs to make significant alterations to the preliminary report the expert should be asked to do so immediately after the conference. It is preferable for each of the experts' concluded views at the end of the conference to be reflected in the working copy of that expert's report. The alterations that each expert suggested they would make should be set out in the conference note. If the experts are sent the conference note they should then each be able to amend their reports to reflect those changes. When the witness statements are received and the experts need to finalise their reports this task will be much less protracted if an updated version of the reports has already been written and sent to the solicitor.

14.45 The expert who is to provide the condition and prognosis report for service with the particulars of claim will in any event need to provide a concluded report suitable for disclosure and should be asked to do so promptly after the conference.

14.46 A preliminary schedule of loss needs to be served with the particulars of claim. Thought needs to be given to whether expert evidence is required prior to service of the preliminary schedule. In most high value cases a care and occupational therapy report will cover a large proportion of the claim and if this is obtained the defendant will have some idea at least of the overall value of the claim. If no report is obtained and every item in the preliminary schedule is marked 'TBA' the defendant will have no clue as to the value of the claim and the claimant may be in difficulty in assessing an early Part 36 offer from the defendant. If at all possible a care report should be commissioned after the first conference and before service of the particulars of claim. In addition, the client should be asked to provide as much information as possible in respect of past losses.

14.47 A timetabled plan for the case needs to be constructed after the conference so that the client understands the timescales involved. A date should be set when proceedings will be issued in the absence of an admission of liability to the protocol letter.

14.48 The directions that will be sought at the first case management conference should be considered. This will include the issue of whether there should be a split trial. If there is not to be a split trial it will include consideration of which quantum experts to seek permission for and whether there are any specialisms in which joint experts can be instructed.

B. Conclusion in Respect of High Value Cases

The first conference is a vital stage in the case for all those involved. It is essential **14.49** that the importance is appreciated and that everybody asked to attend prepares sufficiently for the conference. It is also important that the client both understands the significance but is also placed at ease. The client should be reassured that the conference is arranged only for their benefit and that they should participate fully in it. The client should not be made to feel intimidated by the number of professionals assembled to discuss the case.

By the end of the conference it is to be hoped that the client will have confidence **14.50** in the entire team. If there are weak links in the team or the client is unhappy about part of the team this should be discussed fully with the client after the conference and every attempt made to resolve the problem at this early stage. By the end of the conference the client should be able to understand the timetable for the case and the future crucial steps that will need to be taken.

C. Modification for Smaller Cases

The basic procedure for instructing counsel will be the same whatever the size of **14.51** the case. However, the steps set out above which are appropriate for complex high value cases will need to be modified for smaller or more straightforward cases.

In some small cases or cases where liability is admitted in response to the protocol **14.52** letter it may not be necessary to instruct counsel at all. An appropriate settlement in many cases will be negotiated between solicitors at an early stage and if the client is not a patient or a child, will not need the approval of the Court. If the Court's approval is required then an advice from counsel may be sought simply for this final stage.

If a case is likely to be contested and counsel will need to be involved at the **14.53** trial stage then it will usually be sensible for you to instruct counsel to settle the particulars of claim. To do this counsel will always need:

- all of the client's up-to-date medical records including general practitioner records and including any X-rays, scans, etc;
- the expert reports including the report on condition and prognosis to serve with the particulars of claim;

- the client's witness statement and any other witness statements;
- the reports of any internal inquiry, any inquest, or any other investigation.

14.54 In almost every clinical negligence case counsel will need to meet the client to form an overall view of the merits of the case and the likely quantum of the case. Often assessment of the client and the client's likely impact as a witness is more important in a small case than a catastrophic injury case. In the latter cases there is usually little dispute as to the extent of the claimant's injury, it is breach of duty, causation, and life expectation that are controversial. In a smaller case there may be a great deal of dispute as to the level of pain, anxiety, and disability suffered by the claimant. Counsel will need to meet the client to assess the case properly. The client will want to meet counsel in order to have confidence in his ultimate view and advice. Therefore a conference with counsel at the point that particulars of claim are drafted is still the best course.

14.55 In a smaller case there may be only one expert. Even if there are other experts it may be that only one expert is necessary for drafting the particulars of negligence. It may not be cost effective to have all the experts at the conference as you would do in a high value case. The liability expert may need to attend the conference by telephone or video if the cost of his attending in person cannot be justified. However, the client may not have met the liability expert and it is preferable for the client to meet the expert face to face. Again, the client's confidence in the expert is important and the expert's assessment of the client may also be a relevant consideration. If the cost can be justified, and that will be a matter of your judgement, a conference should be arranged with counsel and at least the lead liability expert in order that the particulars of claim can be discussed and approved by the expert and client. It may well be necessary to place a time limit on the conference in advance in order to be able to restrict the cost. If the conference has a time limit of one and a half hours then counsel will need to ensure a tight agenda is drafted and that the particulars of claim are circulated to the expert in advance of the conference. This is particularly important if the expert is attending by telephone. The expert can then comment immediately on the particulars and alterations can be discussed within a specific time constraint.

14.56 Where a conference is held at the stage where particulars of claim are finalised then as much use as possible will need to be made of the conference, as it may be the only conference in the life of the case. At the conference the quantum of the case should be discussed with counsel and instructions taken from the client on a Part 36 offer. It is convenient for you to type in advance of the conference a draft letter from the client giving instructions in respect of a Part 36 offer so that the sum arrived at can be filled in during the conference and the letter signed before the client leaves.

In a smaller case the schedule of loss will probably not need to be drafted by **14.57** counsel. You will need to take instructions on special damages in advance of sending instructions to counsel for the conference. A draft schedule can then be provided to counsel with the instructions. This will enable counsel to advise on the overall value of the case and the client to agree to a suitable Part 36 offer being made immediately.

In a smaller case therefore the aim should be: **14.58**

- to achieve the maximum benefit from a single conference;
- to make the conference cost effective by restricting it to one and a half to two hours maximum;
- to use the conference as an opportunity for the client to meet both counsel and the liability expert and gain confidence in each;
- to instruct counsel to draft the particulars of claim ahead of the conference and in time to circulate them to the experts ahead of the conference;
- to instruct counsel to advise on quantum and to discuss a Part 36 offer with the client taking into account litigation risks;
- to provide counsel with a draft schedule or sufficient details of special damages for a proper assessment of the overall value of the case to be made at the conference;
- by the end of the conference (or shortly afterwards) to have particulars of claim ready for service and a Part 36 offer ready to send to the defendant.

15

CLAIM AND DEFENCE

A. Protective Proceedings

15.01

There are no procedural factors that distinguish the process of issuing protective proceedings in clinical negligence claims from those employed in personal injury litigation. However, the situation carries more risk because the steps required to complete the preparation of the claim for service tend to be more complex. Consequently, there may be logistic and funding problems that are difficult to overcome. The claimant is likely to be highly anxious in this period and the solicitor will have the stressful responsibility of ensuring the necessary steps are taken within the four months before proceedings must be served.

15.02

Careful case planning will ensure that the need to issue protectively rarely arises and that the contingencies that must be met as a result are kept to a minimum and that the contingencies that may arise are fully provided for.

Late Instructions from Client

15.03   If new client instructions are considered within 12 months or so of expiry of the limitation period, the possible need to issue protective proceedings should be factored into the risk assessment, when deciding whether to accept instructions, and in allocating the case to a particular fee earner. The proposals for managing the situation should be included in the case plan and form part of the representations to the funding body, not least because the court fee must be added to the costs of investigation. Case planning must take into account whether the additional period of four months will be sufficient to complete the preparation of the case. If this may not be so, an application to extend time for service should be included in the plan.

15.04   If instructions are accepted without detailed consideration of how the case is to be investigated against the time limits, the possible need to issue protective proceedings may be overlooked until close to the expiry of the limitation period. It is very easy to imagine that a year or so is more than sufficient time to complete an investigation; unfortunately this is rarely the case.

15.05   One of the very important benefits of case planning is that it should make it virtually impossible to commit to an unrealistic timetable; plans can be made to deal with most of the likely eventualities. For example, an appointment may be made in advance for a report on current condition and prognosis, which will be required if the investigation is positive and otherwise cancelled. Although the claimant may be unable to comply with the Pre-action Protocol in serving a letter of claim three months before proceedings, it may be possible to notify the defendants of the likely allegations of breach of duty and causation, even if the report on prognosis is not yet available. Without information on quantum, this will not constitute a letter of claim as provided for under the Protocol, but it will enable the defendant to begin enquiries and hence improve the claimant's position on costs if there is an early admission.

15.06   There are clients who will not accept that their claim cannot be pursued, no matter how well the investigation has been carried out. If that investigation has concluded close to the expiry of the limitation period, this will be little time to convince the client that there is no claim to be pursued. The client is likely to feel very distressed at having to make an unpalatable decision while time is running out. It is understandable that the client's emotions are likely to be heightened if the client has been paying privately, and is now facing the loss of the investigative costs. This is one of the most difficult situations to manage and the best course of action may be to issue protective proceedings, if funds are available to pay the court fee. The purpose of protective proceedings in this situation is simply to enable the client to take advice elsewhere if they so wish or to give client and solicitor further time to discuss the merits of the claim and, if appropriate, for counsel's advice to be obtained.

Limitation Period Wrongly Calculated

The need to issue protective proceedings may occur if too much reliance has been placed on the information given in the client's first interview when calculating the limitation date. In some circumstances, even where the limitation date is reconsidered on review of the medical records, the expiry date may be so much sooner than envisaged that protective proceedings cannot be avoided. In this situation, the case plan will need to be completely reviewed to shorten the timetable—for example, by finding an alternative expert with a shorter waiting time and booking in experts and counsel as far ahead as possible. **15.07**

Difficulties can arise in cases where the calculation of the limitation date is based on a date of knowledge, which has been taken from the client's instructions. Where the medical records or other evidence indicate that the date of knowledge was considerably earlier than was first thought, protective proceedings may be the only way out of the difficulty. Alternatively, and not uncommonly, on review of the medical records, it may prove difficult to be confident about when the claimant's date of knowledge arose. It is advisable in cases that depend upon a date of knowledge argument that counsel's advice should be sought as early as is reasonably practicable, after the medical records have been collated, the client has been proofed, and in cases where the primary limitation has long passed, if counsel advises that the date of knowledge argument will not succeed, the case can be discontinued before the expense of obtaining medical reports has been incurred. Where counsel advises that the date of knowledge argument is likely to succeed and the case should be appropriately investigated, the investigation can be undertaken in the normal way in reasonable confidence. It should be borne in mind that in cases where the date of knowledge or section 33 arguments are to be deployed, an expeditious investigation is particularly important (section 33(3)). **15.08**

Investigative Delays

Where the investigation of a claim has been bedevilled by experts who have delayed in providing reports well beyond their agreed timescales, or where counsel has been particularly slow in dealing with the paperwork, there is little to be done except to annotate the expert's and counsel's entries on the firm's recommended supplier list. This is an unfortunate situation, particularly so because the client may feel a loss of confidence, not only in the expert or counsel, but also in the solicitor who recommended them. The most important consideration here is to plan for contingencies as far as it is possible to do so, keep the client informed, and take all subsequent steps as promptly as possible. **15.09**

Settlement Negotiations Underway

15.10   Once the period of time for the defendant to respond to the letter of claim has elapsed, the claimant should not be deterred from serving proceedings simply because settlement negotiations are underway. The use of protective proceedings in these circumstances simply replaces the risk of exceeding the limitation period by the risk of failing to serve proceedings. Instead, proceedings should be issued and served and it should be left to the defendant to request agreement for an extension of time for service of the defence. This protects the client's position and also provides an incentive for the defendant to expedite settlement while the clock is ticking. Under CPR 15.5, the parties may agree up to 28 days' extension of time for service of the defence. The defendant therefore must apply to the court if a longer period of time is required.

Defendant's Delay

15.11   The defendant's failure to provide a formal response to the claimant's letter of claim within the three months allowed, or to deal with any other outstanding matters, should not deter the claimant from serving proceedings. If the claimant is ready, proceedings should be served, even if the defendant holds out the prospect of an imminent 'helpful response'. In this situation, it is in the claimant's interest to transfer the risk on time to the defendant.

Claimant's Delay

15.12   If the claimant's letter of claim was not served in time to allow the defendant three months to respond before the expiry of the limitation period, but the claimant is otherwise ready, proceedings should be served. This protects the claimant's position and would be difficult to criticise on costs even if the defendant indicates that a favourable response may be forthcoming. It is open to the claimant to agree an extension of up 28 days for service of the defence and to consent to a subsequent application on the part of the defendant, if appropriate.

Extending Time for Service of Proceedings

15.13   The claim form must be served within four months after the date of issue of the claim form, in accordance with CPR 7.5. If the claimant is not ready to commence proceedings before the due date for service, it will be necessary to apply for more time. CPR 7.6(1) provides that an application may be made for an extension of time, 7.6(2) states that an application should be made before the time for service has elapsed, other than in the specific circumstances defined in 7.6(3).

15.14   The need to extend time, possibly more than once, is likely to occur from time to time, for example if the defendant repeatedly fails to disclose important medical records and this is something the claimant cannot fully control. On the other hand, the situation should not be allowed to occur needlessly, as a result of lack of case planning, as it carries a significant risk. Although an application for an extension of time may be made without notice, it is not appropriate or safe to assume that the court will automatically find that the interests of justice require the order to be made, merely because the claimant needs more time. CPR PD 7.8.1 states that an application under CPR 7.6(1) must be supported by evidence, including all the circumstances relied on and a full explanation as to why the claim form has not been served.

B. Issue and Service

CPR 7 governs the commencement of proceedings. As all personal injury practi- **15.15** tioners will be aware, CPR PD 7.2.2 states that proceedings that include a claim for damages in respect of personal injury may not be started in the High Court unless the value of the claim is £50,000 or more. However, paragraph 2.4 of the Practice Direction is helpful to the claimant, as it states that a claim should be started in the High Court if the claimant believes that the claim ought to be dealt with by a High Court Judge because of the financial value of the claim and the amount in dispute and/or the complexity of the facts, legal issues, remedies, or procedures involved, and/or the importance of the outcome of the claim to the public in general.

The lowest value cases are probably unlikely to justify proceedings in the **15.16** High Court but relatively modest claims may reasonably do so, given the inherent complexity of the evidence in the majority of clinical negligence claims. An example of a case of this sort would be a fatal accident claim, with a small claim for the estate and limited loss of dependency; the claim might have a relatively low financial value but may be based on complex liability arguments. The choice of court will depend to some extent on local factors but the main consideration is the desirability of the case being heard before a High Court Judge.

The letter to the Court requesting proceedings to be issued and served should **15.17** enclose the Court fee and the documents listed below. Documents should be provided in triplicate plus one copy for each additional claimant or defendant.

Claim Form

There are no particular rules pertaining to clinical negligence with regards to **15.18** completion of the claim form (Practice Form N1), but it can be difficult to summarise the claim in more complex matters; some examples can be found at the end of this work.

Particulars of Claim

15.19 The particulars of claim must be provided in triplicate, plus one copy for each additional claimant and defendant. In clinical negligence cases, particulars of claim should be settled or approved by counsel and should also be approved by the experts whose evidence forms the basis for the allegations of breach of duty and causation. The Practice Direction to CPR 16 deals with the contents of the particulars of claim at paragraphs 4.1–4.4 in a personal injury case and paragraphs 5.1–5.3 in a fatal accident claim. These include a schedule of details of any past and future expenses and losses claimed and a report from a medical practitioner dealing with personal injuries alleged.

Medical Report

15.20 The current condition and prognosis report or reports should be annexed to the claim form. If psychiatric injury is alleged either as the sole or additional injury arising from the negligence, the psychiatric report must be appended. It is essential that the reports to be served with proceedings deal only with current condition and prognosis and psychiatric condition. It is not in the claimant's interest to disclose liability evidence at this stage. If the expert reports have not been vetted by this stage, as they should have been, they must be reviewed now so as to ensure that the current condition and prognosis reports are free of any opinion on the breach of duty or liability issues.

Schedule of Details of any Past and Future Expenses and Losses

15.21 It is frequently not feasible to fully quantify the claim and to provide a complete schedule of loss when proceedings are issued in clinical negligence claims. This may be for a number of reasons:

- instructions from the claimant or the funding body to apply for an order for a trial of liability;
- the initial investigation has been lengthy and it is appropriate and/or necessary to issue proceedings and quantify the case while liability issues are being resolved;
- the claimant's condition or financial circumstances are likely to change during the course of proceedings and a more accurate schedule can be served after liability issues have been dealt with.

15.22 Generally speaking, it should suffice to serve a schedule of loss that sets out all the likely heads of damages claimed, with as much information as is available at the time of service. The schedule should contain headings for all likely losses claimed in order that the defendant will obtain a reasonable indication of the likely quantum. Details of specific items of past expenditure or loss should be available and these should be itemised. Past losses that relate to matters that will be the subject of later expert reports, such as care costs, should be listed in the schedule as heads of loss, marked 'to be advised'. Future losses should be itemised and calculated insofar as they are known, otherwise listed as heads of loss 'to be advised'.

Certificate of Suitability

This is required where the claimant proceeds by litigation friend.   **15.23**

Notice of Issue of Legal Aid (Form LSC1)

The defendant is entitled to know the scope of the certificate, but not the limita-   **15.24**
tion placed upon it and this information should not be disclosed, just as one would not disclose the limits of a private client's instructions or financial authority.

Notice of Funding (Practice Form N251)

This form should be filed at court and served on each party; the Notice of   **15.25**
Funding confirms the existence of a Conditional Fee Agreement, and where appropriate the insurance details should be inserted. Care must be taken to serve a further Notice of Funding if there are changes in the funding or insurance arrangements.

C. The Defence

In clinical negligence litigation, generally the defendant will file an acknowledge-   **15.26**
ment of service and will be entitled to 28 days after service of the particulars of claim for filing the defence. CPR 15.5(1) provides that the defendant and the claimant may agree that the period for filing the defence will be extended by up to 28 days. If the claimant does not agree or if the defendant requires more time, the defendant must apply to the Court for a permissive order.

In considering whether or not to consent to an application for an extension of   **15.27**
time, regard must be had for the reasons given. If, for whatever reason, the claimant's own conduct has led to proceedings being served before the defendant had the three months allowed under the protocol to respond to the allegations, it would be reasonable to agree an extension that would restore the defendant to the position they would have been in had the protocol been complied with.

If the defendant has had proper notice of the claim, it is reasonable to object to a   **15.28**
request for more time to file a defence. The wider consideration is that it is in the

claimant's interest to progress the case as expeditiously as possible. Sooner or later, each side is likely to encounter some unavoidable delay; it is very desirable that avoidable delay does not add to the timescale. Any request for extra time should be considered critically—if the claimant believes the difficulty is no more than an inconvenience to the defendant, the application should be opposed.

15.29 The defence must comply with CPR 16.5 and CPR PD 16. The defence should be reviewed by the claimant, to establish whether it narrows any of the issues in the case or provides new information that was not given in the defendant's response to the letter of claim.

15.30 The claimant should consider whether or not the defendant has addressed all of the allegations made in the claimant's statement of case. If not, the defendant should be asked to confirm that the allegation is admitted.

15.31 The defence may put forward a new hypothesis as to the medical facts. For example, the claimant's case may rest on an allegation that the injury resulted from a thermal burn in theatre, whereas the defendant may in their defence contend that the lesion was the result of an infection. In this situation the claimant's experts must be asked to comment.

15.32 The defence may contain an account of the facts that differs from the claimant's and it will be necessary to address this by amending or supplementing the claimant's witness evidence, particularly if the defendant supports its case with reference to the medical records or other documents. In the interests of transparency, the amended statement should refer to the defence as the occasion for the amendment. As always, when amending witness statements, the earlier signed versions should be kept on the file.

D. Admissions

Pre-action Admissions

15.33 It is important to establish whether the defence reflects any pre-action admissions. If the admission was made up to 6 April 2007, the defendant may withdraw a pre-action admission. CPR 14.1A provides that after that date, the claimant is entitled to apply for judgment to be entered on the admission; the defendant may only withdraw a pre-action admission with the court's permission.

Full Admission

15.34 Where the defence contains an open admission of breach of duty and some, if not all, causation the claimant should prepare a Consent Order for judgment to be entered for the claimant, with provision in the order for the steps required in order that the court may assess damages. The quantum investigations may be brought forward and, depending on how complex they are and how lengthy, the claimant may want to consider whether an adjournment should be requested at allocation stage or whether the matter should proceed to a case management conference (CMC) with directions for quantification of the case.

Partial Admissions

The practitioner should analyse the defence and consider how far, if at all, the **15.35** admissions made improve the claimant's case. The question is whether any issues have been fully disposed of—for example, whether breach of duty has been conceded, in full or in part. If the claimant's position has been strengthened by virtue of any admission, the claimant's litigation risk should be reassessed and the improved position should be conveyed to the funding body and to the after-the-event insurer in the next report.

A view must be taken on whether the admissions made affect the line-up of **15.36** experts required for the later stages of the litigation. In the example given, it might be possible to stand down the expert who advised on breach of duty, but naturally this should not be done if that expert has any role in the causation argument, or in the assessment of the claimant's current condition and prognosis. In a higher value or complex matter, all experts should be kept on board for the duration of the proceedings, until counsel advises otherwise, in case other issues emerge on which the expert's view is required. No expense will be incurred in simply asking an expert to keep the file open and to remain committed to the case and it is better to keep the panel intact if there is any doubt at all that they may be required.

The experts will need to comment on the defence but if the defendant intends to **15.37** serve witness evidence from clinical staff, it is sensible for the defendants to be asked to consider those statements together with the defence rather than comment piecemeal. Until the allocation questionnaire is filed, it will not be clear whether the defendant is to call any factual witnesses but there is no reason why the claimant's solicitor should not enquire. This may seem a minor point, but it assists with case planning as, if the defendant is not serving any witness evidence, the experts can be asked to consider the defence immediately rather than in six weeks' time after the allocation questionnaire has been served.

E. Judgment in Default

CPR 15.3 provides that if a defendant fails to file a defence, the claimant **15.38** may obtain default judgment if CPR 12 allows it. The relevant considerations, under CPR 12.3 are that the time for service of the defence has passed and the defendant has not made an application to strike out the claimant's case, or for summary judgment, that has not yet been disposed of.

15.39 It is unusual for a defendant to fail to file a defence in clinical negligence litigation; it is more likely to occur in claims against defendants in the private sector who may be indemnified by less experienced insurers.

15.40 If this situation does occur, the claimant should not hesitate to file an application to enter judgment for an amount to be decided by the court on Practice Form N227. Although in many circumstances it will be almost inevitable that judgment will be set aside on the defendant's application, the claimant's advantage should not be thrown away; at best, the defendant will settle. At a minimum, the defence is likely to be run more efficiently for the rest of the case.

F. Following Judgment

15.41 Once judgment has been entered or there has been an admission which includes an element of causation of injury, if the claimant so wishes, negotiations should be opened with the defendant for a voluntary interim payment and treatment that may assist the claimant.

Medical Treatment and Rehabilitation

15.42 Although the Rehabilitation Code is annexed to the protocol governing personal injury claims and not to the clinical negligence pre-action protocol, it is possible to evoke the spirit of the Code in certain cases. Understandably, the NHS is in a difficult position if asked to expedite treatment for a particular class of patient. Nevertheless, on an economic basis, if a claimant needs treatment and is on an NHS waiting list, the defendant may sometimes take a proactive approach to this or may respond positively to a request that private treatment or expedited NHS treatment is undertaken and funded by the defendant. The advantage of treatment over interim payment is that there can be no dispute at a later date about the reasonableness of private treatment, and no discount on the sums involved for litigation risk, as might be the case if an interim payment were used for the purpose.

Psychiatric Treatment and Counselling

15.43 Where psychological difficulties persist and the claimant is awaiting treatment, or claiming future treatment costs, the defendant will often offer to fund that treatment immediately. The defendant may regard this as a test of the credibility of the claimant's claim in this respect. However, the claimant must be advised that any records made during the course of the treatment will be disclosable to the defendant. This fact is hardly conducive to the therapeutic aims of psychiatric treatment and is in fact a deterrent to seeking treatment before the claim is resolved. A solution is to secure the defendant's undertaking that treatment can proceed on the basis that disclosure of the records will not be sought.

Interim Payments

If the claimant has pressing needs, an interim payment should be obtained; **15.44** an application should be made if a voluntary payment is not forthcoming. Not all claimants want interim payments. The practitioner must advise the claimant on the effect that an interim payment may have on eligibility for means tested benefit, and the need to create a Personal Injury Trust. Receipt of an interim payment should be reported to the Legal Services Commission as a change in financial circumstances and may affect their assessment of the claimant's financial eligibility.

16

ALLOCATION AND DIRECTIONS

CPR 26 governs the preliminary stage of the court's case management function. **16.01** The key matters to be decided are what lay and expert witnesses should be called, what steps need to be provided for, and the timescale within which each step should be taken. These provide the overall framework for the presentation of each party's case. If case planning has been detailed enough, and updated regularly, the claimant's strategy should be decided and the steps required to take the case forward should be set down in the plan. However, these proposed steps should now be reviewed in the light of the defendant's intentions with respect to witnesses and experts.

When the defence has been filed, the Court will serve notice of the date of the first **16.02** case management conference (CMC), with an allocation questionnaire annexed.

A. Allocation

Allocation questionnaires are often sent out with short deadlines for return. **16.03** Under CPR 25.5.5, if a party fails to file an allocation questionnaire, the Court may give any direction it considers appropriate. It is helpful if the parties discuss the various issues arising from the questionnaire on an informal basis before each makes a final decision on the experts and witnesses required. Completed questionnaires should be served on the other party when they are filed at Court.

193

Track

16.04 Clinical negligence claims will almost invariably meet the criteria for allocation to the multi-track set out in CPR 26.3.

Stay

16.05 The parties should consider whether they wish to take advantage of the provision of CPR 26.4.1 that a written request may be made for proceedings to be stayed while the parties try to settle the case by alternative dispute resolution or other means. A stay will be for one month, or such other period as the court considers appropriate. The stay may be extended and the simplest way to deal with this is for the parties to write to the court and jointly request an extension of the stay.

Cost Estimate

16.06 The parties are required to state their costs to date and to estimate their costs to the conclusion of the matter. It is important to provide a realistic estimate of the costs on the assumption that the case will go to trial. It is essential not to underestimate costs; the estimates given at this stage are taken into account when costs are assessed at the conclusion of the case and the claimant may be in difficulties in recovering all costs incurred if the defendant was not on notice of the extent of the risk, see *Leigh v Michelin Tyres plc* [2003] EWCA Civ 1766.

Witnesses of Fact

16.07 The parties must provide a list of the witnesses of fact whom they intend to call. The claimant's witnesses will include the claimant or litigation friend, together with any other lay witnesses whose evidence the claimant will need to rely on to support their case. Although quantification may not have been undertaken in detail at this stage, the list of witnesses should include likely factual witnesses on quantum issues. The court is unlikely to look kindly on a long list of witnesses; every effort should be made to obtain any documentary evidence that would enable less important witnesses to be dispensed with.

16.08 The defendant's list of witnesses is of particular interest to the claimant. The case plan should show what witness evidence the claimant feels should be available as to the treatment which gave rise to the claim. If not in the plan, this should be checked against the conference note and any subsequent advice from counsel. If the defendant has omitted any witness the claimant wants, the defendant should be asked to call them, as they are in a better position to locate the witness and obtain a statement. If the defendant will not agree, the claimant should do so and the witness should be added to the claimant's list.

Expert Evidence

The claimant's list of experts may change in the light of the discussion between **16.09** the parties. Although the claimant will have expended considerable thought and planning on the expert panel, from time to time the defendant's list will include an expert from a different specialty from any that the claimant had intended to call. If the claimant is confident that the existing panel is able to deal with all the issues on at least an equal footing as the opponent's experts, no changes need be made, but first the reasons for the defendant's proposals need to be explored.

It should be borne in mind that the defendant's representative will have had very **16.10** much less time to investigate the claim; it may be that the choice of experts reveals a misunderstanding or mistake about the issues in the case. In this situation, it is best to discuss the experts required with the defendant's representative, in order to elucidate what has occasioned this difference of approach.

The defendant may be using an expert in a different specialty whose expertise **16.11** overlaps with one of with the claimant's experts. For example, a neurosurgeon and an orthopaedic surgeon might equally well be able to comment on causation or prognosis in respect of an injury or surgery to the neck. If the claimant is confident this is the case, no change to the claimant's expert panel is required. On the other hand, the defendant may be using an expert who will be able to give a more specialist opinion. In the example given, if the case concerned injury to the spinal cord during back surgery by an orthopaedic surgeon, one would expect that a neurosurgeon would be able to provide the more specialist opinion on both causation and prognosis. If the claimant does not convince the defendant that both parties should rely on orthopaedic opinion, a neurosurgeon should be provided for on the claimant's list. A final decision as to who should be instructed may be taken in due course.

The defendant may be instructing an expert to comment on an aspect of the **16.12** case that to date the claimant's team has not considered to be an issue. For example, where the claimant in the previous example suffers from diabetes, the defendant may intend to instruct a physician to advise on life expectancy. If the claimant does not consider this is a significant issue requiring a specialist medical opinion, the point should either be argued at the CMC (if there are other matters that require a hearing) or, again, the additional expert should be added to the claimant's list, but the point should be taken up again with the defendant afterwards.

Single Joint Experts

There is very limited scope for the single joint expert in clinical negligence **16.13** litigation. Their use is sometimes promoted in cases in which liability has been conceded and the case is to proceed to an assessment of damages; this may have a superficial attractiveness, particularly for the paying party. Whether or not this approach will be appropriate should be considered on a case-by-case basis.

16.14   Care needs often result in claims for significant amounts. There are many subjective and speculative aspects to a care assessment and it is to be expected that the parties will place different interpretations on the claimant's care needs. If the care claim is substantial enough to justify an expert report, it will be a contentious head of claim and each party should be entitled to call its own care expert.

16.15   Equipment needs form another important and expensive aspect of many claims. The means to obtain the best available equipment and to replace it at reasonable intervals are very important to the future well-being of the claimant and substantially increase the sums payable by the defendant. Where this is the case, a single joint expert is not appropriate. As many care experts are also qualified to report on equipment and simple adaptations, a separate occupational therapy report may not be required. Where there is to be a care report, the instruction of a combined care and occupational therapy expert may be helpful in resisting an order for a single joint expert occupational therapist.

16.16   Other quantum experts might include an educational psychologist, speech therapist, physiotherapist, IT expert, accommodation expert. The suitability for instruction of any of these as single joint experts will depend partly on the nature of the case and the likely contentiousness of that aspect of the claim, but also on the experts themselves. One would be entirely confident that certain experts would provide a report that was fair to the claimant and which would be the same report whether they were instructed by the defendant or the claimant. Other experts are perceived to be more defendant- or claimant-minded. Knowledge of experts can only be built up through experience and, if the question is likely to arise, it is helpful to discuss with counsel which if any specialties they feel could in principle be addressed by a single joint expert and which particular experts they consider would be acceptable in that role.

B. Directions

16.17   The costs associated with attendance at the first case management conference can be avoided if the parties can agree on proposed directions to put to the master or district judge. It is generally a relatively straightforward matter to agree proposed directions but there are some contentious issues that may arise. Master Onley and Master Yoxsall's suggested model directions can be found at <http://www.hmcourts-service.gov.uk> (accessed 2 April 2007). These are authoritative guidance although they are not intended to be prescriptive.

The timetable that is set down in the first directions order is the one against which **16.18** the progress of the case will be viewed by all concerned, not least the claimant. It is an unfortunate fact that many unexpected factors may arise during the course of the litigation; the tendency of clinical negligence claims is to become prolonged well beyond the length of time that it seems reasonable to predict when looking at the matter at the outset. Preventing or at least reducing those delays is one of the most important tasks of the claimant and the court's case management.

The overall timescale in the proposed directions should be realistic and should **16.19** allow time for work to be accomplished as the case progresses. The claimant should be aiming to pursue the case proactively but the claimant who cannot comply with the directions timetable will be on the back foot and unable to keep the case moving forward; the initiative will pass to the opponent. Nevertheless, delay should not be factored in as a general contingency measure, as this would have an adverse effect on the claimant and on the overall management of the case.

17

DISCLOSURE AND EXCHANGE OF WITNESS STATEMENTS

A. Disclosure

17.01 The claimant must be advised of their duty of disclosure under CPR 31 and should be reminded at appropriate stages that this is an ongoing duty.

17.02 The directions order will normally provide for standard disclosure as defined at CPR 31.6, that is, documents on which the party relies together with documents which adversely affect either party's case or support another party's case, and any other documents which must be disclosed in compliance with a practice direction. The list should be served using Practice Form N265.

17.03 The importance of pre-action disclosure in clinical negligence cases may result in the formal disclosure stage being dealt with as a simple routine. However, the claimant's position needs to be carefully considered in order to ensure compliance with the rules. The defendant's list may contain documents of which the claimant was unaware or may omit relevant documents which are thought to exist.

Claimant Disclosure

17.04   The claimant's representative will already be in possession of documents on which the claimant intends to rely, including those relating to the claimant's losses and expenses; these should be brought up to date if necessary. The client should also be asked to consider whether there are further documents which support or adversely affect the claim, for example diaries, personal journals, photographs, or notes of medical consultations. Under CPR 31.4 a document is defined as 'anything in which information of any description is recorded' and therefore recordings in any medium are potentially disclosable—for example, a voice recording of a meeting or consultation.

Defendant Disclosure

17.05   The defendant's list is generally almost bare. Usually, pre-action disclosure will have produced all the necessary medical records and the position with regard to any missing records will have been resolved. However, if there has been any disagreement about whether particular documents should be disclosed, or if any unfulfilled request for disclosure has been lost sight of, the disclosure stage provides the opportunity formally to request the documents and take appropriate steps if they are not forthcoming. The claimant should expect to see such internal documents which come with the scope of CPR 31.6 such as surgeon's logbooks, staff training programmes, minutes of clinical governance meetings. If these are likely to exist, have not been disclosed, and are likely to either support the claimant's case or adversely affect the defendant's case, they should be requested at this point.

B. Witness Evidence

The Claimant's Witness Statements

17.06   The rules governing the format and content of witness statements are set down in CPR 32. The claimant's factual evidence will consist of their own statement and the statement of any other witnesses as to the fact that the claimant intends to call to give evidence. The statements served may be the same statements that were sent to the experts and referred to in their reports. Alternatively, it may be appropriate to serve updated statements. General considerations that apply to the drafting and amending of witness statements are discussed elsewhere in this work.

17.07   An updated statement may be helpful if the claimant's medical condition has changed significantly, if their domestic or employment circumstances are substantially different or if there is any inaccuracy in any previous statement to be corrected. There may be factual assertions in the defence that the claimant can usefully comment upon.

Where there is a substantial claim for future loss that is yet to be fully quantified, **17.08** the statement served at this stage of the proceedings should refer to those future losses in general terms, identifying the heads of loss and briefly putting them in context. As discussed in Chapter 18, a separate quantum statement will be served with the updated Schedule of Loss.

Practice Direction 3.18.1 provides that the statement should be, as far as possible, **17.09** in the witness's own words. Matters to be covered in the claimant's statement will include:

- occupation and, if this has changed since the injury, previous occupation;
- brief description of marital and family circumstances, including dates of birth of any children;
- the claimant's account of the sequence of events relating to the treatment in question. Care should be taken to avoid importing text and phraseology from medical records or reports that the claimant would not use in the normal course of discussing the case;
- if the claimant's factual recollection of events differs in any important respect from the medical records, or from the version of facts set out in the defence, the statement should acknowledge this and comment upon those differences;
- the claimant should describe the effects of the injury; this will include the effects on his or her physical condition, emotional condition, the practicalities of every-day life, the claimant's financial affairs, family life, and future plans and projects.

Additional witnesses should state their relationship to the claimant. If a family **17.10** member is providing a statement which is corroborative of the claimant's account of events the witness should confirm that he or she has read the claimant's statement and state that he or she agrees with its contents, insofar as those are within his or her own knowledge. The statement should then deal with the issues of which the witness can give primary evidence.

While it is unavoidable that all the witness statements will need to be drafted and **17.11** tidied up, particular efforts should be made to keep the additional witness statements as far as possible in the own words of the witness; this will reduce the risk of a witness signing a statement without reading or understanding it, or without taking the trouble to ask for it to be amended.

The witness should be given an opportunity to correct any inconsistencies in **17.12** their statement before they are served. Even relatively trivial flaws of this kind may open up the possibility that the claimant's recollection is poor.

Mutual Exchange

17.13 The order for mutual exchange should be observed, as otherwise the opponent will have the advantage of prior knowledge of the factual evidence. A defendant may indeed have genuine difficulties in obtaining a signed statement from a doctor, who may have moved abroad, or may be working in another area, and whose motivation to assist is not high. Nevertheless, generally the claimant should not accept phased service of the defendant's factual witness evidence. A reasonable compromise is to accept service of a statement that is unsigned but has been approved, to be followed by a signed statement as soon as possible thereafter. In that event, the signed statement must be checked against the earlier version. If it differs in any material respect, service of the statement should not be accepted.

Defendant Witness Statements

17.14 If the defendant has failed to serve statements from the witnesses listed in the allocation questionnaire, consideration must be given to whether the omission is germane to the claimant's case. If so, the defendant should be asked to say why they have not served a statement and, if the reason does not preclude this, should be requested to do so, or to provide contact details to enable the claimant to proof the witness. Sometimes the defendant will say that they have not been able to find a particular witness. This may be the case, but it is impossible to know what steps have been taken to locate the person in question. In practice, an online search of the relevant professional register will establish whether the witness is in practice, a simple check in the Medical Directory may locate them, or it may be necessary to find them through the services of an enquiry agent.

17.15 The defendant's witness statements will provide a considerable amount of information about the defence. The doctor or health care professional's judgment and standing are on the line and the court will carefully consider their evidence on the facts. The statement should contain information about the witness's CV, qualifications, and current professional status. The witness should then say whether the statement is based on the witness's personal recollection of the events that gave rise to the claim, or whether it is based on the medical records and the witness's normal professional practice. The treating professionals will give their account of events and provide their justification for the acts or omissions that the claimant alleges were negligent. The doctor criticised and colleagues who give evidence will also describe the general circumstances surrounding the incident or treatment plan, including whether it was a particularly busy time for the doctor, team, ward, or department. The statement may also give the witnesses impressions of the claimant at the time in question, in particular their impressions of the claimant's wishes and understanding of the procedures and choices.

Omissions from the statement are almost equally interesting. Where issues raised **17.16** in the particulars of claim about the treatment are omitted from the defendant's witness statement, this is likely to indicate an area where a truthful answer would be disadvantageous to the defence.

The defendant's witness statements may contain explanations of events which **17.17** have not been fully set out in the defence. This and other matters in the statement need to be commented upon by the claimant's expert.

Expert Comment

A copy of the defence and the defendant's witness statements should be sent to **17.18** each of the experts for comment. The expert should be asked to say:

- whether any part of the defence is, in the expert's opinion, plausible or implausible, or alternatively opens new areas for investigation;
- whether each of the witness statements is, or is not, consistent and credible, and whether any statements disclose a reasonable justification for the treatment criticised;
- whether anything they have read in the defence or in the witness statement causes them to change their opinion.

The expert's comments and their reports should be sent to counsel with instruc- **17.19** tions to advise on whether the expert should be asked to amend their report. Counsel will also have regard to whether the merits of the case have been affected for better or worse in the light of the defence, the witness evidence, and the expert's further comments.

C. Exchange of Expert Evidence

Preparation for Disclosure

CPR 35 governs the form and content of the expert report. The provisions in **17.20** CPR PD 35 are detailed and highly relevant to the content of the expert's report in clinical negligence litigation. The expert reports will have been available for some time by this stage of proceedings but consideration must be given as to whether the expert reports are fully ready for disclosure. The experts will have had the benefit of conference with counsel before the issue of proceedings will have seen and approved the particulars of claim and subsequently seen and commented upon the defence and defendant's own witness evidence. During the course of these steps, their opinion will have been confirmed, expanded, or modified. It may be helpful for the expert to comment in his report on the defence. It may also be helpful for the expert to comment on the statements of the treating doctors. All these factors may lead to a need to revise the expert's report prior to disclosure.

17.21 Before it is ready for disclosure, the expert will need to provide a list of references to be annexed to the report and copies of those references which the expert has relied upon should also be annexed.

17.22 This is a good opportunity to ensure the expert has supplied a copy of a full and up-to-date CV. The expert's full CV should be appended to their report. Although a summary CV is acceptable for the purpose, a full CV will be required for the expert meeting and for the trial bundle and may therefore be served with the report if available. A report is ready for service when it has been verified by statement of truth, is signed and dated by the expert, approved by counsel, and authorised for disclosure by the client.

Mutual Exchange

17.23 As the purpose of mutual exchange is to ensure that neither party has the advantage of reviewing their own evidence in the light of knowledge of what their opponent's experts are to say, it follows that the reports should not simply be sent out on the due date.

17.24 The defence and the defendant's witness statements will have given a good indication of the nature of the arguments to be set against the claimant's case but it is only on disclosure of the expert evidence that the parties reach an understanding of the strengths and weaknesses of their respective positions. Time devoted to careful analysis of the disclosed reports will be well spent if it results in a thorough grasp of the arguments on each side of the case, as, from this point on, the main focus of the case will be on the details of expert evidence.

17.25 Under CPR 35.6 written questions may be put to an expert within 28 days of service of the report, for the purposes of clarification of the report. A copy of the questions must be sent to the other parties.

17.26 An expert's omission to deal with a significant aspect of the case is likely to be indicative of a weakness in the instructing party's case. Such an omission should be followed by a request to the expert for clarification.

17.27 A note should be made as to whether the experts have reviewed the same reference material. Where this is not the case, the experts should be asked to review the further material before the expert's meeting.

17.28 Where the experts have preferred different versions of textbooks, the justification for that preference should form part of the agenda for discussion.

Settlement negotiations often follow exchange of expert evidence. The defendant **17.29** may have delayed making an offer on a meritorious case until the claimant's evidence (or resolve) had been tested. Alternatively, the defendant may consider there is an increased litigation risk, and prefer to settle now and avoid the costs of the expert's meetings. Equally, the claimant should consider whether an offer should be made if the case is substantially strengthened or weakened at this stage.

Expert Discussions

The expert discussions may prove to be the turning point of a case. If one **17.30** party's expert accepts the other expert's arguments and so changes their own opinion on an important point, this will clearly have a major impact on one or more aspects of their instructing party's case. Even smaller shifts of opinion may have an impact, sometimes more psychological than real. If both experts maintain their previous positions, there is a real prospect the case will proceed to trial.

Drafting the Agenda

Generally, it is for the claimant's solicitor to draft a proposed agenda, although **17.31** this is not a hard and fast rule. Occasionally defendants do produce draft agendas and sometimes where there are many sets of experts to meet in a short period of time in a complex case, it is agreed that the work should be shared between the parties. It is sensible for the less experienced practitioner to instruct counsel to approve a draft or indeed to settle the agenda.

The Model Directions suggest that agenda questions should be framed wherever **17.32** possible to allow for yes or no answers. Unfortunately, this is a rule that cannot help but be honoured more in the breach than in the observance. Nevertheless, it is an excellent starting point; of the questions that must be put, the experts should not be asked questions that require essay answers, or invite regurgitation of large paragraphs from their reports. Questions should tend towards crystallising the differences where they exist and establishing points of agreement where possible.

Where there are significant factual matters at issue between the parties, it is **17.33** important to draft the agenda in a way that provides for the experts to answer the questions on the basis of each different factual scenario. The experts should be specifically reminded in the body of the agenda that factual issues are to be decided by the court. The sample agenda at the end of this work contains suitable wording for this situation.

17.34 If the current condition and prognosis evidence is essentially the same for each party, there may be no need for those experts to have a discussion at all and it should be possible for the current condition and prognosis evidence to be agreed in due course.

17.35 The claimant's draft agenda should be sent to the claimant's expert for comment before being agreed with the defendant, if time allows. Any comments received should be considered critically before being included and reworded if necessary. Experts frequently seek unwittingly to move the discussion on to more comfortable ground, especially tending to replace the legal test of probability to the more familiar concept of scientific certainty.

Agreeing the Agenda

17.36 As it is not a straightforward matter to draft an agenda, in any but the most straightforward cases, the defendants are likely to put forward further questions of their own (in fact, these are often the same questions in a different style), or to propose an alternative agenda altogether containing some but not all of the points the claimant wishes the experts to discuss. Defendants tend to favour agenda questions that require discursive answers. In this situation, little is gained by argument; the practical way forward is to append the defendant's agenda or additional questions to the claimants, numbering all the questions sequentially. The experts should be instructed to consider both sets of questions.

17.37 If the claimant's agenda refers to pagination in the medical records, unless the parties are working from the same paginated bundle, the defendant's expert will be at a disadvantage. The solution may be to provide the defendant with a copy of the claimant's bundle and the relevant records to append to the agenda, or to liaise with the defendant's solicitor who may wish to insert their own pagination into the agenda in addition. This problem can be avoided if the Masters' Model Direction on medical records is observed, as all reports will refer to the claimant's pagination.

Format of Expert Meetings

17.38 The Model Directions envisage that solicitors will not attend the expert meetings except by agreement or by order of the court.

17.39 In an ideal world, all meetings would take place face to face in a neutral venue. A formal arrangement invests the meeting with its proper significance and reduces the client's anxiety about a real or perceived 'easy compromise' being reached. However, such an arrangement is not always proportionate to the issues to be discussed and in any event may not be practically achievable.

In deciding the format, the matters to consider include: **17.40**

- the length of the agenda: a very short agenda may be more reasonably disposed of in a telephone call than a lengthy one;

- costs of the experts' travel and attendance: if this factor has been taken into account when it was decided to instruct the expert, distance should not be an obstacle in itself, unless the only outstanding issues to be discussed are minor or relatively straightforward;

- the expert's own preference for a face to face meeting;

- the need for a joint and simultaneous consideration of materials, such as scans or pathology specimens;

- whether more than two experts are involved in one discussion. If so, a conference call is no substitute for a meeting;

- the robustness of the expert and the strength of commitment to their role as expert. A telephone discussion may be perceived as a less weighty occasion than a meeting.

Venue

Although neutral territory is perhaps ideal, the offices of either party's solicitors   **17.41**
are perfectly suitable if geographically convenient and if the services required are available. This is a very cost effective option. The Royal Colleges, the Royal Society of Medicine, and the Law Society all have facilities for meetings. Other commercial suites and services exist in different cities and the experts may have their own suggestions.

Support

It is usually most practical to ask the experts themselves to agree a date for the   **17.42**
meeting, but otherwise the claimant should make the arrangements.

If there is to be a meeting between more than two experts, the discussion is bound   **17.43**
to take off in various directions rather than staying strictly with the agenda questions; it will be much more difficult to record the experts' answers. A meeting of several experts is likely to occur only on the large or more complex cases and in those circumstances a stenographer should be hired to be present at the meeting. This will enable the discussion to be reproduced in written form while the meeting is in progress. The cost is trivial compared with the time saved in the expert meeting. Unless agreed otherwise, it should be made clear to the experts when making these arrangements that the stenographer is a service for the experts and not the solicitors who will not see the verbatim record. The claimant should nominate one of the experts to take charge of circulating the draft joint statement

to the other experts and collecting and destroying any printout or disc produced by the stenographer once the experts have signed off the agenda.

17.44 The timing of the meeting needs thought, although the options will be constrained by expert availability and convenience. It is not sensible to arrange for a long meeting to start late on a Friday afternoon, as one of the participants is bound to need to leave early. A long agenda with four experts should not start later than 5 o'clock on a Monday to Thursday for the same reason.

17.45 If the experts are likely to be engaged for more than an hour or so, it is important to think of the comfort and convenience of the participants. A room with reasonable facilities and the provision of water, hot drinks, sandwiches, and fruit is essential. The room should be booked for long enough to enable a discussion to proceed without concerns about needing to vacate it. Lack of attention to any of these details can lead to a hasty meeting as opposed to a fully concentrated discussion.

17.46 Arrangements should be made to ensure the necessary documents and equipment are available at the venue. For example, does the radiology need to be available and is there an X-ray viewer at the venue? Is any other equipment needed, such as a microscope? The experts can probably arrange this themselves but this should not be assumed, they should be asked if they are able and willing to do so. If the experts are likely to produce the agenda or notes on a laptop, is a printer available? It may not be possible to provide everything that is required but if there are any facilities lacking, this should be explained to the experts and the defendant before the meeting.

17.47 These arrangements are not just a matter of courtesy, although that is an important consideration. In the absence of solicitor, client, and counsel, the experts need to motivate themselves to work through the frequently obvious, annoying, and scientifically unanswerable questions that the lawyers have put to them. The more reasonably comfortable and convenient the arrangements, the more likely it is that the experts will be able to give all necessary time and attention to the matter in hand.

Joint Statement

17.48 The experts should be encouraged to print off and sign the joint statement at the end of the meeting if possible, but generally more time is required. The claimant's nominated expert may need to be kept to the task of chasing it up.

17.49 The expert's meeting is effectively in session until the statement is signed off. That makes it a delicate matter to have a discussion with the expert after the meeting but before the joint statement is finalised. A full note should be kept of any conversation.

If the joint statement indicates that the claimant's expert has significantly changed **17.50**
his or her opinion, it is reasonable to ask for an explanation. If it emerges that the
expert did not expect the joint statement to carry the meaning that appears, or is
for some other reason unhappy with the statement, it is open to the expert to produce a corrected statement. If an expert wishes to amend a joint statement at a
later stage, perhaps after further evidence comes to light, it is open to the expert
to say they wish to amend the joint statement. The concern is that in this situation the expert will create an impression of weakness, whether real or imaginary.
This will be a factor to consider when re-assessing the claimant's litigation risk.

Under CPR 35.12(4) and (5) respectively, the contents of the discussion will only **17.51**
be admissible at trial by agreement of the parties and any agreement reached in
the discussion is not binding on the parties unless the parties expressly agree to be
bound. There is no requirement to file the joint statement at court.

18

THE PROCESS OF QUANTIFICATION

General Considerations

The valuation of claims for injuries sustained as a result of clinical negligence is no different in principle from that which is undertaken in personal injury practice. However, there are some distinguishing factors that need to be borne in mind when quantifying these claims. **18.01**

As the pre-existing condition and the precise nature of the injury are likely to be different in each case, it is often difficult to find quantum reports where the facts of the case are sufficiently similar to create a reliable precedent. The small number of mid-to-lower value cases going to trial means that judicial awards in these cases are relatively rare and more reliance must be placed on reported settlements, where the factors influencing the settlement figure may be unclear, particularly with respect to the extent of causation and damages for pain, suffering, and loss of amenity. **18.02**

Both parties have to work within these constraints and will be obliged to arrive at a valuation by identifying the most analogous cases in the usual sources and developing an instinct for the right figure through experience. **18.03**

The client is entitled to know the likely value of their claim and indeed must know this in order to take an informed decision on the risks and benefits of litigation, and to give informed instructions on offers. This means that it is necessary **18.04** to explain to the client the factors that will influence that valuation as the claim progresses and that in any event there is a broad range within which an award might be made by a trial judge. Sensitivity and tact are required to convey these unpalatable facts.

18.05 Medico-legal discussions on quantum not infrequently relate to reduced life expectancy and the prospects of full recovery. It is difficult for the client to hear such discussions, whether these relate to themselves or a member of their family, but most will approach this with fortitude if they have been forewarned and the potentially distressing nature of the discussion is acknowledged.

Difficulties in Quantification

18.06 The causation arguments in a case will determine how quantification is approached. As will be apparent from the discussion of the law of causation in Chapter 2, the quantification of a clinical negligence claim must be based on the difference between the likely course of events had the claimant received treatment of a reasonable standard and the actual course of events that ensued after the allegedly negligent treatment. As the causation issues are developed and then resolved, the overall value of the case should be kept under review.

18.07 It may be alleged that the claimant was in good health before the injury and that they would have continued in unimpaired health but for the negligence—for example, in a birth injury case where a healthy foetus was injured during delivery, or where the mother sustained a bladder injury due to urinary retention. Here the causation arguments are unlikely to affect the value of the claim.

18.08 Commonly, quantification is complicated by expert advice that on the balance of probabilities the claimant would not have made a full recovery, even with competent treatment. The experts' advice is needed to describe the difference between the actual and hypothetical scenarios. Valuation of the claim will be based on the pain, suffering, loss of amenity, and consequential losses attributable to that difference.

18.09 There may be more than one stage during treatment at which the claimant alleges a breach of duty occurred; until liability is determined, the extent of the injury and the valuation of the claim needs to be calculated, in the light of each separate breach, at least in broad terms.

18.10 Any of these situations may be further complicated by a pre-existing condition, if the claimant is suffering from impaired health unrelated to the medical problem that gave rise to the claim. This may not be a known factor at the outset of the case. For example, a claimant with a claim relating to management of a knee injury may be shown to have pre-existing arthritic changes, raising the possibility that the claimant's future mobility would have been impaired irrespective of the negligence. The expert evidence on the likely future impact of the arthritis will need to be considered. The valuation of damages for pain and suffering may need to be reviewed and the calculation of loss will be based on the costs attributable to the knee problem alone.

A. Damages for Pain, Suffering, and Loss of Amenity

The initial valuation of pain, suffering, and loss of amenity needs to be recon- **18.11** sidered as the case develops. Pre-existing, concurrent, or subsequent illness may affect the amount of damage that can be attributed to the negligence. Once liability reports have been obtained, a careful analysis of the causation evidence must be carried out to consider the expert's advice on the extent to which the claimant has been adversely affected by the alleged negligence. Active consideration needs to be given as to how far the evidence on this point impacts upon the initial valuation of damages likely to be awarded for pain, suffering, and loss of amenity.

In lower value claims, where financial losses are relatively small, the causation **18.12** evidence may support the case in attributing some injury to the alleged breach of duty, but only to a limited extent, with the effect that the value of the claim is so reduced that problems of proportionality, risks, and benefits have to be considered. Early settlement may be the only alternative to discontinuing the claim.

B. Financial Losses and Expenses

It is a good practice to assemble evidence of past losses and make some enquiry **18.13** into the extent of future loss and expense during the investigative stage. It is easy to overlook this while the liability evidence is being developed. There are many cases in which it will not be possible to quantify the case in any detail at this point, perhaps because of funding constraints, because the outcome of the claimant's condition remains uncertain, or because it is intended to proceed to a split trial. Nevertheless, making some progress in assembling the documentary evidence will assist in preserving the evidence that will be needed at a later stage, and will provide an indication of the strengths and weaknesses of the case for the losses claimed and put the claimant in a somewhat better position to consider early offers.

Discounted Settlements and Awards

If a claimant is to receive less than 100 per cent of their damages as a result of a **18.14** compromise on liability, the claim should be quantified in full and the quantum experts should be instructed to ignore any such factor when making their recommendations. The reduction is applied only after the final award is made or the full value settlement figure agreed. It follows that it is not easily open to the defendant to demand proof that certain services or items claimed are being purchased, as the claimant will be acting in accordance with the prospect of reduced damages, and how their life is adjusted to this reality is a matter for them alone.

Reviewing Quantum—Timing

18.15 In summary, quantum should be reconsidered at the following stages:

- on receipt of the claimant's experts' reports;
- on receipt of the experts' comments on the defence and witness statements, if there is a change in an expert's view on the timing of breach of duty or the extent of causation;
- following joint meetings of liability experts, if the claimant's experts change their views on timing of breach of duty, or the extent of causation, or the prognosis;
- after meetings of quantum experts, if the claimant's experts have modified their recommendations;
- after service of the defendant's schedule, when the defendant's arguments can be evaluated;
- when an offer is made or in contemplation, in the light of the limitation risk at that point.

Practical Issues in Quantification

18.16 Where quantum experts are to be instructed, arrangements should be made for a quantum conference with counsel, in good time before the date for service of the claimant's schedule of loss. Ideally this should be as soon as possible after the liability experts have produced their joint assessment. Counsel is likely to assume that the claimant intends the case to be put forward on the basis of the draft schedule unless the instructions say otherwise. Counsel should explicitly be instructed to advise on the claimant's draft schedule and to deal specifically with the format, the methodology, and the merits of the individual heads of claim; the specific recommendations should be explored with the relevant quantum expert. counsel should advise on any amendments to the schedule, on the overall settlement value, and on possible offers. This should avoid a situation where a substantial claim is put forward, only for counsel to advise when negotiations commence that the schedule was always unrealistic and must be slashed to achieve settlement.

19

ALTERNATIVE DISPUTE RESOLUTION

A. Introduction

Going to trial should always be seen as a last resort. A detailed risk assessment by **19.01** both parties should ultimately, in all but exceptional cases, allow a settlement to be reached. A number of factors need to be considered in approaching such a risk assessment.

In particular: **19.02**

  (i) the scope of settlement negotiations;
 (ii) the timing of settlement negotiations;
(iii) the mechanism of settlement negotiations.

B. The Scope of Settlement Negotiations

The main issue in respect of the scope of settlement negotiations will be whether **19.03** liability and quantum should be considered together or separately. This involves consideration of a number of factors.

As a general proposition, settlement of the entire litigation rather than liabil- **19.04** ity alone has an immediate attraction for both parties. It provides finality

215

to both parties, earlier compensation to the claimant, and saves costs for both sides.

19.05 If a split trial has been ordered by the Court the parties may not have expert evidence on the quantum issues. This will provide additional risks to both parties in settling quantum as well as liability. An order for a split trial, however, will not always be a total bar to achieving a settlement of the whole litigation.

19.06 In relatively low value cases or cases where the biggest head of loss is general damages both sides may be able to calculate damages without expert evidence. The parties will always have the medical records and if proceedings have been issued will have a report on condition and prognosis that has been served with the particulars of claim. This should allow an assessment of general damages to be made. Past losses will be provided by the claimant's records and receipts except in respect of past care costs where expert evidence will usually be obtained. However, if the claimant can provide an estimate of the number of additional hours of care, the local rates for care can be applied to calculate the overall value of past care. If the future need for care is modest it too can be approximately calculated by reference to local rates. Loss of earnings will usually not require expert evidence and will be calculated from documents the claimant has. This information should be capable of allowing a reasonable calculation of quantum to be made if necessary for negotiation purposes.

19.07 The advantage for the claimant of negotiating a percentage settlement on liability only is that there is then still scope for maximising the quantum of the claim without the anxiety that ultimately the claimant may lose altogether. The advantage in negotiating liability and quantum together is that the claimant may be in a better position to assess quantum earlier than the defendant. Further, the flexibility of running together quantum and liability issues may result in a better overall settlement.

19.08 For the defendant the advantage of negotiating quantum and liability together at an early stage is the very significant cost saving if neither party needs to incur the costs of a full quantum investigation. Further, in some cases, the defendant may consider the claimant's claim is only likely to increase with further investigation.

19.09 Decisions will always need to be made on a case-by-case basis as to whether the parties are prepared to negotiate quantum and liability together or only prepared to negotiate liability as a separate step. What is important is that each side is prepared to consider and discuss each possibility rather than approaching negotiations with rigid preconceptions.

C. The Timing of Settlement Negotiations

Each party has to consider what is the best point in the litigation to make the **19.10** assessment of risks. A balance has to be struck between the parties having enough information to make a responsible assessment of risks and the saving of costs by early settlement. In principle, the longer the litigation progresses the more information each side has, but the higher the costs.

Possible points at which the parties may find it particularly appropriate to **19.11** consider negotiations are discussed below. However, in practice the parties may consider negotiations at any time.

D. After Exchange of Letter of Claim and Response and Before Issue of Proceedings

This obviously allows the maximum saving of costs and in a relatively low value **19.12** case may be the only point at which settlement is likely. As costs overtake the quantum of the claim, settlement becomes more and more difficult.

For settlement to be achieved at this stage either the parties will need to be pre- **19.13** pared to exchange evidence ahead of the court timetable or the claimant will need to be prepared to provide supportive evidence ahead of exchange. If an early settlement is a priority for the claimant this may be justified in a particular case but the position will need to be carefully explained to the claimant.

If the claimant is a child or a patient proceedings will need to be issued in any **19.14** event so that the court, and, if the claimant is a patient, the Master of the Court of Protection, can be asked to approve the settlement. The procedure in CPR Part 8 can be used as described in CPR 8 Part PD 1.4.

E. After Exchange of Expert Evidence

If the parties have complied properly with the pre-action protocol the service of **19.15** particulars of claim and the defence will not add a great deal to the issues. The statements of case should, at least in theory, reflect the issues raised in the pre-action procedure. The exchange of witness statements will be particularly important for the claimant who will learn what the treating doctors, nurses, and midwives say about the events. However, usually in clinical negligence cases it is the opinion expressed in the expert reports that is likely to demonstrate the strengths of each side's case. Exchange of expert evidence is therefore often a good time for negotiations.

19.16 After exchange of expert reports costs begin to escalate as the next stage will involve:

(i)   the drafting of agendas for expert meetings;

(ii) conferences with the experts to discuss the opposing expert's report and to discuss the agendas;

(iii) the experts' meetings.

19.17 These steps all involve solicitor, expert, and counsel's costs and can increase the overall costs enormously. If liability and quantum are to be tried together the cumulative cost of this stage in the process can be very high. The balance of risk can change significantly for either side after the experts have met, and the outcome of the experts' meetings may be unpredictable for both sides. It is also possible that in some cases the experts' meeting may not take the case much further if both side's experts stand by their opinions. In such cases postponing negotiations until after the experts' meetings may have been a costly exercise which does not narrow the issues.

19.18 Negotiations after exchange of expert evidence may therefore strike a good balance. At this stage each party has a good basis for assessing the other side's case, but there are still very considerable costs to be saved by settling the litigation without expert meetings.

F. After Expert Meetings

19.19 This is the last sensible opportunity for negotiations before trial and should be possible in time to save the costs of preparation for trial as well as the trial itself. Provided the expert meetings have not been delayed, they should have occurred sufficiently early before trial so that bundles have not been prepared and brief fees not incurred. At this stage both sides should be in a strong position to assess the risks of going to trial and to take a realistic view of the prospects of success on liability and quantum issues.

19.20 Thereafter the door should not be closed on negotiations at any point but the costs savings become more and more marginal and the purpose of negotiations becomes to avoid the unpredictability of the trial judge's decision rather than the saving of costs.

G. The Mechanism of Settlement Negotiations

19.21 Negotiations can take place in a wide variety of ways, the following being the most common:

(i)   in correspondence between solicitors;

(ii) on the telephone between solicitors and confirmed in writing;

(iii) by written formal CPR Part 36 offers;

(iv) in round table meetings, with or without counsel;

(v) in formal mediation, with or without counsel.

In small value cases it is usually most cost effective to conduct negotiations in **19.22** correspondence or between solicitors on the telephone. Most small value claims will be settled in this way. The exception is a case where there are very strong feelings on either side or issues other than damages to be resolved. One example is a client to whom an apology or undertaking is very important. Another example is where indemnities in respect of public provision of services is necessary. In these cases a round table meeting or mediation may be appropriate.

CPR Part 36 sets out a comprehensive formal basis for claimants and defendants **19.23** to make offers and to provide some costs protection. In practice the position is much more flexible than that provided by the rules. The Court will take into account the parties' attitude to negotiations and attempts made by either party to settle. Formal Part 36 offers by either side are to be encouraged but they are only one of a number of ways of negotiating.

In any reasonably high value case (over £50,000) where settlement has not been **19.24** achieved in correspondence or by telephone a round table meeting should be attempted. The claimant, or litigation friend, should always be invited to attend if they wish to and to be present during negotiations if they wish to. A claimant who wished to attend a round table negotiation but was advised not to is unlikely to be happy with a settlement negotiated at such a meeting. Advice may need to be given in certain cases as to the advantages and disadvantages of the claimant being in the room throughout the negotiations. This is always a matter of client care and sensitive handling by solicitor and counsel.

A round table meeting is a good opportunity for each party to set out the strengths **19.25** of their case and to understand the strengths of the opposing case. Meetings usually work best where initially each party sets out their case and where there are no restrictions on the issues that can be discussed.

Where quantum is being discussed a schedule with each side's figures from the **19.26** schedule and counter-schedule and several columns for suggested compromise is necessary. Each side should be prepared to discuss a conventional lump sum or periodical payments unless there has been a previous agreement or order that one or other means of compensation is not appropriate to the particular case.

The claimant should consider whether they are able to provide the defendant with **19.27** a detailed breakdown of costs prior to a round table meeting and whether there is a possibility of settling the costs issues as well as the damages issues. Doing so will provide additional advantages to both sides in terms of finality and certainty.

19.28 Before a round table meeting it is important for the claimant to check that the defendant team will include somebody with authority to agree a settlement figure up to the maximum of the claim. The defendant should check that if the claimant or litigation friend is not attending the meeting there will be access to the claimant to agree any settlement figure that is proposed. If either side does not have a practical means to take instructions the round table meeting will be significantly hampered and far less likely to resolve the claim.

19.29 If both parties are represented by solicitors and counsel it is comparatively rare that a mediator is required at a settlement meeting. The circumstances where a mediator may be considered are:

(i) where a round table meeting without a mediator has failed;

(ii) where there are issues other than the quantum of the claim to resolve;

(iii) where both sides have particular confidence in a mediator.

20

TRIAL

A. The Barrister's Perspective

Bundles

The Court will usually have ordered that bundles should be lodged at court at **20.01** least seven days before trial. In any multi-track case with trial estimate of three days or more the preparation of bundles is likely to be a huge task. It is not simply a matter of including everything and getting the pagination chronological. The convenience and logic of the bundles can make a significant impact on the trial judge. Badly prepared bundles are an irritation to the judge and are unacceptable, they cause embarrassment to everybody on the claimant team.

Typical examples of aggravation and embarrassment are: **20.02**

- illegible page numbers;

- cut off page numbers;

- missing pages;

- duplicate pages;
- upside down pages;
- pages with the edge cut off;
- pages with the hole punch through the vital entry;
- pages copied with the corner turned over;
- pages that have inappropriate messages on them;
- pages copied with comments written on;
- double-sided documents not copied on the reverse;
- A3 pages copied in pieces.

20.03 It seems to be surprisingly difficult to avoid all of these problems but careful checking should minimise the problem, otherwise the chances are that the first page counsel takes the Judge to will have one of these problems.

20.04 Many firms have a house style for preparation of bundles which is tried and tested, if that is the case the following suggestions may be adapted to the house style or may be unnecessary.

20.05 Numbering bundles by beginning the first volume at 1000, the second volume at 2000 and the third volume at 3000, has the advantage that the page number will tell the judge the volume number as well as the page reference. References in the skeleton argument and chronology need only give one number to indicate both volume and number, eg [3046] will tell the judge the reference can be found at Volume 3 page 46. The most aggravating arrangement of bundles is one where each bundle is divided into sections and the numbering begins again in each section, for example it is necessary to give a reference: [Volume 3 tab 1 page 46] where Volume 3 also has a page 46 at tab 2 and tab 3. Using the same colour file for each Volume 1 and a different colour for each Volume 2 and Volume 3 has the advantage that counsel can refer to the bundles by colour and everybody in court can take the red bundle or the blue bundle and find the reference.

20.06 During the course of the trial inevitably further documents will surface that one or other party asks to add to the bundles. These may be added as 'a' numbers in the original bundles or a new bundle may need to be started. In either event a careful note needs to be kept of the further documents that have been added and where they are to be found.

20.07 The following is a suggestion for the content of bundles.

Volume 1: Pleadings and Orders

20.08 This bundle should only include those documents that are relevant and necessary. It does not need to be a copy of the solicitor's complete pleadings bundle and/or court file including the receipt for the issue fee. Where pleadings have been amended it is usually only necessary to include the amended versions. The final version as served with the date included should be in the bundle. If there have been requests for further information, the pleaded reply should include the questions and the request need not be included in the bundle. Only court orders that either party wants the Judge to look at should be included, not every case management decision. Care should be taken to exclude any order that mentions a payment into court or payment of an interim payment.

Volume 2: Witness Statements

All witness statements will need to be included. The claimant statements will **20.09** usually come first and then the defendant statements. Where there is an exhibit to a witness statement this must also be included, for example a defendant witness may have copied a page of medical notes or attached a CV, if this is not attached and requires reference to another bundle it is aggravating for everybody. Signed and dated copies of the witness statements must always be used.

Volume 3: Expert Reports and Points of Agreement and Disagreement

Final versions of expert reports with the date attached must always be used. Any **20.10** supplementary reports or separate letters should be included with the expert's original report including the answers to questions put to the expert. It is convenient to have the claimant and defendant reports in the same specialism following each other. Where the expert has referred to literature this will probably best be filed separately in a literature bundle. If it is included in the expert report bundle it will make the expert report bundle difficult to follow. Any diagrams, CVs, or other exhibits to the expert report should however be included with the report. The claimant's solicitor should ensure that each claimant expert has provided an up-to-date CV and that this is included in the bundle of expert reports. The points of agreement and disagreement resulting from expert meetings should be included in this bundle. The agendas for the meetings will only need to be included if the experts have not typed the questions in the final response. Where they have not, the agenda for the meeting should be included.

Volume 4: Medical Literature

Where there is a significant amount of literature this should be in a separate **20.11** volume and the index should indicate which expert refers to the literature. It may be that more than one expert has referred to the same literature and this is an added reason for not attaching the literature to each expert report but instead providing a separate bundle. It is important to check that each piece of literature is copied completely and that extracts from books have the front piece of the book with the date of publication and edition shown. It is vital that the Judge can identify the date of publication of each piece of literature included.

Volume 5: Protocols and Guidance

20.12   A separate bundle may be required for hospital protocols and Royal College of Obstetricians and Gynaecologists (RCOG) or other college guidelines on a particular topic.

Volume 6: Medical Records Core Bundle

20.13   Where there are several volumes of medical records a core bundle is essential. This should retain the original pagination from the main bundles of medical records in the bottom right hand corner but have new chronological pagination, 6001, 6002, etc, in a different place, for example in the top right hand corner. Where a manuscript note is important and not easily legible a typed copy should be included in the bundle with the note. The content should be agreed with the defendant in advance. In an obstetric case the CTG trace will need to be included in the core bundle of medical records. This will however need to be copied continuously and is usually most conveniently provided in a plastic wallet inside the bundle.

Volume 7,8,9, etc: Complete Medical Records Including General Practitioner records

20.14   A complete copy of the medical records will need to be available as well as the core bundle. This should retain its original pagination so that references in the expert reports and particulars of claim can be easily identified. The simplest way of correlating the pagination may be to add 7000, 8000, etc to the numbering. That is, if the first volume of medical records ran from pages 1 to 253 this will become pages 7000 to 7253.

X-rays, MRI scans

20.15   Arrangements will need to be made for the scans and X-rays to be in Court and a light box available for the Judge to view them. If any expert needs to use charts, models, or either party wishes the Judge to watch a video, arrangements need to be made in advance for how this is to be achieved.

Skeleton Argument

20.16   Counsel's skeleton argument will usually need to be lodged at court at least three days before trial and sometimes seven days before trial. Counsel should be asked to draft the skeleton in time for the solicitor, client, and if appropriate the experts, to approve the content. This means counsel will need the trial bundles at least two weeks before trial. Without the trial bundles being available there is a huge duplication of time by counsel in drafting the skeleton in a form that it can be lodged at court.

It is preferable to arrange the pre-trial conference at a date when counsel has **20.17** completed the first draft of the skeleton argument so that the content can be discussed with the client/litigation friend and experts at the conference. The skeleton can then be amended to reflect the views of the client and experts before being lodged at court.

In almost every case a detailed chronology will be needed as well as a skeleton **20.18** argument and possibly other schedules and summaries. Examples of a chronology and a schedule of labour are included in the Appendices.

Pre-trial Conference

This should take place at least seven days before trial so that the skeleton argu- **20.19** ment can be discussed and any necessary corrections made to the trial bundles before they are lodged at court. The client and each expert who is to give evidence must attend. If there are experts who are not required to give evidence consideration should be given as to whether they should nevertheless attend the pre-trial conference. For example, the evidence of neuro-radiologists may be agreed but in certain cases it may be helpful for the neuro-radiologist to attend the conference. That is, careful thought should be given as to who should attend, it should not be assumed that because an expert need not attend the trial he will not be needed at the conference.

The pre-trial conference is an opportunity to make a final attempt to explore **20.20** settlement proposals. There is likely to have already been a round table meeting that has failed to resolve the issues. However, it will always be worth considering whether any further proposals can be put to the defendant whether to resolve the whole case or individual issues.

Witness Order at Trial

The Judge and the defendant will anticipate in a case where the claimant does not **20.21** have a litigation friend that the claimant will be the first witness. Logically the claimant will usually be called first. However, it should not be assumed by the claimant team that this is the best course. The Judge's impression of the claimant will be a vital factor in his assessment of the case. There are cases where the claimant's personality has been affected by the injury in a subtle way that will not easily be understood by the Judge. Some claimants may come across as far less seriously injured than they are, others will come across aggressively because of the nature of the injury. In some cases it is tactically better to call the condition and prognosis expert to explain the claimant's condition before the claimant gives evidence.

20.22   In most clinical negligence cases it is sensible to agree with the defendant that witnesses of fact including treating doctors will all be called before the experts. This allows the claimant and defendant experts an opportunity to comment on the treating doctors'/nurses'/midwives' actions and explanations. Clearly the liability experts will need to be in court to hear this evidence in order to comment meaningfully on the evidence.

20.23   It is usually convenient for claimant and defendant experts in the same specialism to be called back to back so that the Judge can fully appreciate the arguments on each issue. Agreement for this course needs to be reached with the defendant well ahead of trial to enable both party to timetable expert witnesses economically.

B. Solicitor's Comments

Trial Listing

20.24   The directions order will have provided a due date for the parties to file at court details of the witnesses' and experts' availability for trial within a trial window. By this stage the solicitor should have a fairly clear idea of who is to be called. It is best to compile a table of *unavailable* dates and this is a secretarial task. The experts (and indeed witnesses) must understand that their role in the case implies a commitment to appear in the background of the hearing; the court accordingly expects to be given reasons for their unavailability on particular dates. Where the expert is unavailable because they are committed to another trial, they should be asked to state where that trial is taking place. If it is in the same Trial Centre, it should be possible for that expert to double up and give evidence in both matters. Experts who have indicated that they have immutable clinical commitments on given days in the week should be reassured—it is almost always possible to accommodate this by arranging the order of witnesses accordingly.

20.25   The claimant and their lay witnesses should be reminded that they must be present at the hearing, the claimant probably for each day. If the listing period includes any dates which would cause great difficulty, this must be included in the representations to the listing officer. If any lay witness is likely to encounter difficulties in obtaining leave of absence from work, they should be served with a witness summons. The same applies if the witness's attendance cannot be relied upon with complete confidence and this is probably true of any witness outside the immediate family of the claimant. Pre-booked holidays tend to be the most common difficulty; a witness summons should enable the witness to claim for compensation for cancellation or curtailment under their travel insurance.

20.26   The claimant will be relieved to have a date fixed for the trial, believing this will bring the case to a conclusion. It is important to warn the claimant at this point—and to remind them again in due course—that there is every likelihood judgment will be reserved and that they will not know the outcome of the case immediately, possibly not for some months after the hearing.

For cases to be heard at the Royal Courts of Justice, a listing appointment will **20.27** be given which would normally be attended by the clerk to each party's counsel, armed with details of expert availability and in this way counsel's availability will be accommodated. If the trial is fixed on a day that is in fact unsuitable, or that becomes unsuitable, an application must be made for the trial period to be vacated and a further listing appointment be arranged for the trial to be relisted.

In other Trial Centres, there is no listing appointment. The dates to avoid for **20.28** experts, witnesses, and counsel should be filed in accordance with the Directions Order. It is sensible to mention in the covering letter that as this is a clinical negligence matter it is important that the same counsel who has been involved throughout should be able to appear. It is more likely that counsel can be accommodated if the request is made before the listing. In due course, the Court will send out a Notice of Trial. If the date fixed is problematic for reasons known and disclosed when filing details of availability, the listing office of the court should be contacted immediately—a telephone discussion followed by a letter by fax is the best approach. This will usually result in a relisting. Delay in contacting the court makes this less likely.

Witness Summonses

Each expert and lay witnesses should be served with witness summonses as **20.29** soon as the trial is listed. The sooner the expert is served, the less the chance there is of the practitioner being pre-empted by experts receiving a summons for the same period on another case. Most experts are used to this procedure but occasionally an expert will be offended, assuming that their integrity is in doubt. The best course of action is for the practitioner to elect to serve the summonses rather than opt for court service and to explain the reasons for serving a summons in a standard letter to each witness.

Lay witnesses are likely to be alarmed on being served with a summons. It should **20.30** be explained in the covering letter that this is standard procedure and that the summons will assist them if they experience difficulty in attending, for example in taking time away from work.

Trial Costs

As always, the practitioner will have to work within the limits of the funding **20.31** body's financial authority at the trial stage. Unfortunately, however carefully a case is prepared, trials do develop unpredictably. Counsel will be focusing on what is required to present the case and it is the solicitor's responsibility to support counsel, the claimant, and lay and expert witnesses by making arrangements for attendance, producing additional documents and, in short, dealing with all contingencies, while keeping control of the costs.

20.32 The expenses of a trial can increase dramatically in the heat of the moment. It only requires an expert to attend for an additional day and one unplanned evening conference for costs to increase by several thousand pounds. In cases that are publicly funded, the costs limit for the trial has to be regarded as final; only in exceptional circumstances is there any real possibility that that authority would be extended at this stage. In cases that are funded by insurance, every effort must be made to secure a last minute authority from the funding body for the additional expenses. These additional costs, if reasonably incurred, will be recoverable if the case is won. If the case is lost and the expenditure has not been authorised the shortfall will be top-sliced from the practitioner's profit costs.

20.33 This possibility cannot be eliminated altogether but as always, careful case planning can reduce the exposure to risk. The practitioner should include a section in the trial brief dealing with the costs limits, setting out the experts' hourly and daily rates. Counsel should be invited to advise whether more expert time is likely to be required. This will enable the solicitor to make representations to the funding body in advance. The constraints imposed by the financial limits and how these should be dealt with can be discussed at the pre-trial conference.

The Trial

20.34 The trial is a time of high tension for all involved. Meticulous organisation and preparation will assist the team effort and reduce the amount of additional tension generated by problems with documents or misunderstandings about arrangements. Practitioners will have their own systems but the suggestions below may be useful. None of them is revolutionary but each is capable of helping to contribute to an atmosphere of calm efficiency in the background to the hearing:

- Ensure every expert has provided an up-to-date full CV for the trial bundle.
- Additional references to the medical literature are often produced during the course of the trial. Ensure that all textbook reference material includes the title page of the volume and all journal reference material carries the full reference details.
- Check in advance if the court can cater for any audio-visual requirements that have been agreed at the pre-trial conference, ie video evidence, computer link, computer graphics.
- If any models/diagrams are to be used, ensure that the courtroom will have or will accommodate the means to display them.

- Identify each volume with a different coloured file and each complete trial bundle with a different coloured strip—blue for the Court bundle, green for claimant's counsel for example—so that if the bundles are collected in for additional material to be added during the trial, the bundles can be easily returned to whom they came from.

- One spare trial bundle should be left in court and one in chambers. These must be amended in the same way as the bundles in use.

- A selection of different coloured Post-it notes should be available in court. Each expert should be allocated a different colour for their notes to counsel—this saves the intercepting solicitor having to check who sent a note and scribbling the expert's name on the note before passing it to counsel, by which time the moment for the contribution may have passed.

- If possible, a trainee or member of the solicitor's support staff should be in court on each day, to help to keep track of the documentation and bundles while the solicitor looks after the claimant and witnesses. They can also be sent on errands or make telephone calls as required. It may turn out that the full cost of their time cannot be recovered but the assistance will be invaluable to the legal team and the experience invaluable to them.

21

COSTS AND CASH FLOW

A. Cash Flow

It takes significantly longer to bring in costs in clinical negligence cases than in **21.01** most other types of work and this can create a real difficulty for the business. This is in addition to the fact that the cases themselves take long periods of time to conclude and are more difficult to risk assess and case manage than most personal injury claims. The process of cost recovery in clinical negligence is complex for a number of reasons, including the requirement to comply with Legal Services Commission procedures, and arguments about proportionality with the defendants (or more commonly their costs draftsman).

21.02 The cumulative effect of these difficulties is to make it very hard to project accurate cost targets for any given year. Most financial years reach a nail-biting finish. In the circumstances, it is hardly surprising that most clinical negligence practitioners will say that 'costs' cause more stress than any other aspect of their work.

21.03 Intrinsic difficulties of clinical negligence claims cannot be removed but if the process of billing and cost recovery is understood and a methodical approach is instituted to managing that aspect of the case, this can help to relieve the pressure.

21.04 Effective cost management starts at the beginning of the case, with a correctly drafted client care letter as the basis of a retainer, and then continues with regular application for interim payment of costs whenever that is allowed, and concludes with prompt billing, effective negotiation, and the confidence to go to detailed assessment if necessary.

The Private Paying Client

21.05 The costs agreement with a private client must be set out in detail in the client care letter and the standard terms of business. That agreement should include an explanation of how much the client must pay at the outset, whether that is on account of costs or costs and disbursements, and when the balance of costs will be payable. A reasonable arrangement for a £4,000 fixed costs agreement would be:

- £1,000 on account of costs at the outset;
- disbursements to be paid in advance as and when they arrive;
- quarterly interim bill for the balance of costs up to the agreed ceiling;
- new costs agreement to be entered into once the initial work is concluded.

21.06 Some arrangement for interim billing is advisable. It is also essential to ensure that the client is billed for any outstanding balance as soon as the agreed work has been completed. Although there may be reason to make some exceptions, as a general principle, agreeing to defer the cost of the investigation is a bad idea. Interim billing ensures that the client is fully aware of how costs are accruing and enables them to manage their financial commitment to the litigation. The interim costs received will make a modest contribution to the fee earner's or team's cash flow. Most importantly, interim billing reduces the occasion for disputes at the conclusion of the investigation. However regrettable, it is understandable that a client who has reached the conclusion of a negative investigation will react badly when presented with a bill for many hundreds or thousands of pounds. This is especially true if the bill arrives weeks or even months after they have been told their case cannot proceed. Inevitably, some clients will look for a reason not to pay and this could lead to a dispute over costs. The time taken up by resolving this upsetting situation will be considerable and will detract from work on other cases.

Different considerations apply once investigations have been found to support a claim. There is frequently further work to be done before a Conditional Fee Agreement can be agreed and after-the-event insurance obtained. In these circumstances, any flexibility that can be offered to bridge the gap can be justified as enabling the claim to go ahead. Just as with the initial arrangement for costs, your cost agreement must be in writing, must not breach the indemnity principle, and must comply with Law Society Rules. **21.07**

The Publicly Funded Client

A franchised firm will have systems in place that ensure experts and other suppliers are paid promptly. For each certificate that is granted, normally £250 net will be paid on account of costs. Recovery of costs on successful and unsuccessful cases is governed by Legal Services Commision (LSC) regulations and this section is concerned with working within those regulations so as to recover costs due as effectively and expeditiously as regulations allow. **21.08**

Disbursements can be claimed from the LSC using a CLSCLAIM4 up to three months in advance but it is probably more efficient to apply for the exact amount once the fee note is to hand. It is courteous to inform the supplier that funds have been applied for and that a cheque will be sent in four weeks or so. Most suppliers, including experts, provide that interest is payable on their fees if payment is delayed beyond a certain period. In publicly funded cases, the supplier's letter of instruction should include a paragraph on the following lines: **21.09**

> Mr Smith has the benefit of a certificate of public funding. Your fee will be claimed from the Legal Services Commission within 7 days of receipt at this office. We will forward to you a cheque to pay your fees within 14 days of receiving funds from the Legal Services Commission. You are advised that interest will not be payable on your fee unless we fail to comply with these terms.

Interim payments of profit costs are available on all certificates, except where the certificate was issued before the firm was awarded a clinical negligence franchise. The payment of interim payments is discretionary, but to date, there has been no indication that discretion would not be exercised. Some practitioners prefer not to make applications for interim payments, possibly because of the additional work involved or because when the payments are recouped, the effect is to reduce the final profit cost total received at that time. Both of these are understandable concerns but in business terms, interim payments improve profitability. **21.10**

21.11 Interim payments of profit costs should be applied for on a six-monthly basis during the lifetime of a case. This process can be built into the system for sending six-monthly cost letters to clients. There is a two-month window on either side of the half yearly date when applications are allowed. The payment made on a case will be 75 per cent of profit costs to date, at standard rates and up to the limit of the financial authority. This also includes cases which are under a high cost case contract.

21.12 Before submitting a CLSCLAIM4, it is important to ensure that the current level of costs is well within the limitation of the certificate and takes into account any disbursements that are likely to be incurred—for example, if an expert report has been commissioned but the invoice has not been received for the work completed. Otherwise it is all too easy to be paid costs on account, only to find money is owed to the LSC at the end of a case because it has been over claimed in error.

LSC Individual High Cost Case Contracts—End-of-Stage Payment

21.13 Where a case has been run under a high cost case contract with the LSC, costs to date may be claimed as soon as the contract is entered into. A CLSCLAIM1 for assessment of costs should be completed. Enhanced rates should be applied to reflect the complexity of clinical negligence litigation. Unfortunately this is usually not much more than a gesture of principle. The fact is that an enhancement may only be claimed for specific items of work. It may not be paid across the board on all the hours claimed; enhanced rates may only be paid up to the limit of the overall financial authority. The effect of this is almost to obliterate the supposed concession, given that the financial limits of publicly funded investigations are very low.

21.14 The high cost case contract also allows for 100 per cent of costs to be claimed at the completion of each stage of the case plan (clause 11). Costs are limited to the work in the case plan as agreed with the LSC. While costs and disbursements excluding VAT are below £25,000 (Very High Cost Civil Cases—Solicitors Information Pack and Guidance), costs are paid at the standard rate and an enhancement can be claimed. Once costs and disbursements exceed £25,000, the rate payable is reduced to £70 an hour. This is known as the 'risk' rate. Similarly reduced rates apply to counsel from this point.

21.15 The payment for each stage of the plan is in full and final settlement of costs at that stage. The indemnity principle is of course not applied if costs fall to be paid by the defendant, but if the claim is discontinued or fails, no retrospective increases will be paid by the LSC. The high cost case plan must be drawn up with great care but, even with the most expert planning, it is unlikely that every possible development can be anticipated, nor would the LSC be likely to agree to a contract that included all possible contingencies. When an unplanned development arises, requests must be made to the LSC for additional funding, before the cost limit for this stage is reached and before the extra work is carried out. Additional funding will only be given where the LSC specifies that the additional work was not reasonably foreseeable when the case plan was originally submitted (clause 8).

Before-the-Event Insurance—Interim Payments

Those firms that are on insurers' panels will have their own arrangements for payment. This section is concerned with individual cases funded by before-the-event insurance. It is important not to be limited to the insurer's hourly rate when a claim for costs is made at the successful conclusion of a case. The insurer's concerns will be to keep the exposure limited to an hourly rate that is unlikely to be close to the solicitor's standard hourly rate, or indeed the Court rate. Most insurers will also insist that the client should not be liable for the difference, ie for any shortfall at the conclusion of the case. It is possible to reach an effective agreement that allows recovery of an acceptable rate from the defendant but also achieves the insurer's objectives. The agreement should say that the insurer agrees with the solicitor's usual hourly rate but if the claim does not succeed, the insurer will limit payment to whatever is their proposed rate. If the client care letter is correctively drafted the result will be that the case is run at a risk rate probably higher than on a publicly funded case. **21.16**

Like the LSC, insurers expect a solicitor to work to agreed financial limits and within the authorised steps. The extent of control varies widely between insurers but none will be easy to persuade to meet additional costs retrospectively. Not all insurers even agree to pay interim profit costs but where they will do so, applications should be made at every opportunity, under the same financial principles that apply to publicly funded cases. **21.17**

B. Billing and Negotiating

All comments made in the previous parts of this book about the need for systems, meticulous case management, and maintaining momentum apply with, if anything, additional force to the billing stage. **21.18**

Billing on Unsuccessful Claims

If a claim is unsuccessful, it is important to get paid and close the file as soon as possible. **21.19**

21.20 If the case is being funded by the LSC and has concluded before the issue of proceedings, a CLSCLAIM1 form should be completed. The LSC will then assess costs claimed and pay monies due, less any funds paid on account of profit costs and disbursements. If the claim is publicly funded but not subject to a high cost case contract and it has been necessary to discontinue an issued claim, then the costs should be claimed on the CLSCLAIM1 form provided that the total amount requested is less than £2,500. However, in the vast majority of issued cases, this limit will have been exceeded and it is therefore necessary to apply to the court for assessment and a full bill should be prepared. Once the court has assessed the bill and provided a sealed assessment certificate, a CLSCLAIM1 should be sent to the LSC so that payment can be authorised.

21.21 In contracted high cost cases, a CLSCLAIM1 should be submitted to the LSC regardless of whether the claim was issued.

21.22 Where a claimant has had the benefit of legal expenses insurance, the insurer should be contacted to obtain details of their billing requirements. More often than not, a short form bill specifying the amount of profit costs and disbursements is sufficient.

Billing in Successful Cases

Claims Settled Before Proceedings

21.23 In these cases, just as with more substantial cases, it is important to remember to time-record the work involved in settling the costs and to make it clear that settlement includes payment of 'additional costs'—ie the time involved in arriving at agreement on costs. When a claim settles without the need to issue proceedings, in theory, it should be relatively straightforward to settle the costs. This may well be so if the defendant's claim handler or their solicitor deals with the costs. Unfortunately, this is not usually the case as defendants, ever more frequently, employ costs draftsmen. It must be presumed that they can tell a reasonable bill from one open to challenge, but costs draftsmen seem automatically to dispute virtually every aspect of every bill. This may or may not be related to the draftsman's costs agreement with the defendant's solicitors.

21.24 Additional costs should not be confused with 'additional liabilities' in a conditional fee agreement case. These are discussed below. Additional costs would include reviewing the points of dispute and considering proposals for settlement.

21.25 When a substantive claim settles, the defendant is likely to ask for a schedule of costs and indeed may urge against preparation of a formal bill. Except in the smallest of cases, this only tends to delay ultimate resolution of the costs. As indicated above, costs are rarely settled easily and a schedule does not provide sufficient detail for arguing the matter out. A detailed bill is almost inevitably required and six weeks or more can be saved if the bill is drawn up as soon as the claim is settled.

A detailed bill should be served on the defendant with all supporting documents, **21.26** including disbursement vouchers and information on additional liabilities, as soon as it has been prepared. As assessment proceedings have not been commenced, the defendant cannot be compelled to serve points of dispute but should be invited to do so, in order to assist in resolving any arguments on the costs.

As the claim was settled before proceedings have been issued, there is no authority **21.27** for the claimant's costs to be assessed. If settlement cannot be achieved, cost proceedings should be commenced as provided for under CPR Part 8 (CPR 44.12A and CPD17*).

Form N208, the claim form for Part 8 proceedings must: **21.28**

(i) identify the claim or dispute to which the agreement to pay costs relates;
(ii) state the date and terms of the agreement on which the claimant relies;
(iii) set out or have attached to it a draft of the order which the claimant seeks;
(iv) state the amount of the costs claimed; and
(v) state whether the costs are claimed on a standard or indemnity basis.

Once the claim form has been issued and served, the defendant should file an **21.29** acknowledgement of service disputing the amount of costs to be paid. In practice, the court will then make an order without a hearing, to the effect that the amount of costs to be paid by the defendant is to be decided at a detailed assessment hearing. The court will also give directions for lodging of the bill and service of points of dispute in accordance with the procedure referred to below.

Claims that Settle After Issue of Proceedings

This section does not deal with summary assessment of costs as most clinical **21.30** negligence claims will be subject to detailed assessment.

A flow chart showing the different steps of the detailed assessment procedure is at **21.31** the end of this section.

Preparation and Service of the Bill

It is possible to serve a 'without prejudice' schedule of costs on the defendant in **21.32** an attempt to settle the costs without the need to prepare a full bill. However, this is often counter-productive and results in increasing costs. The defendant is under no obligation to serve points of dispute and there is no Court timetable to keep things moving. If the schedule is to be of any use, it needs to be reasonably detailed and it is therefore time-consuming to prepare. Inevitably, the defendant will ask for clarification of certain aspects of the schedule, particularly if they have not been provided with sufficient information on other work completed. If an offer is forthcoming on the basis of the schedule, it is usually a very low one, because the defendant is not able accurately to evaluate the reasonableness of the costs claimed. In these circumstances, negotiations break down very quickly and a full bill then needs to be prepared.

CPR 47.7, CPR 47.8(2) and (3), CPR 47.6(2)

21.33 In any event, if settlement of costs has not been reached, notice of commencement must be served on the defendant within three months of judgment or acceptance of an offer. If costs proceedings are not commenced within three months, the defendant can ask the Court to apply sanctions, for example, reducing the amount of costs or interest to be paid. The notice of commencement must also be served on all 'relevant persons'. The claimant should, of course, be sent a copy of the bill because they have ultimate responsibility for payment of their costs and the publicly funded client may have to meet the statutory charge.

21.34 The costs draftsman or the in-house costs clerk should be instructed to prepare a detailed bill as soon as the claim settles. In discussion with the draftsman, a view should be arrived at as to the realistic figure that will probably be achieved if the claim went to detailed assessment. It is a convention to allow 12 per cent to represent the risk of reductions on detailed assessment. However, if time recording is accurate and the claim has been well conducted, a figure in excess of 90 per cent should be aimed for in negotiation. The figure to be achieved should be clearly recorded on the file—this will avoid the necessity of recalculating every time the file is picked up. The costs draftsman should also be alerted to the fact that clinical negligence claims inevitably require a greater amount of time spent on planning and on client care than a personal injury claim. It is also worthwhile drawing this to the defendant's attention, particularly if arguments on proportionality are anticipated.

21.35 The bill should be served on the defendant with the notice of commencement. Nothing is gained by serving the bill and holding back the notice of commencement. Serving the notice does not prevent cost issues being resolved through negotiation, and prompt commencement of the assessment process is conducive to prompt settlement.

CPR 47.6 and CPD 32.3, 32.5, and 32.7

21.36 In a case that has been conducted under a conditional fee agreement (CFA), at the time the bill is served, the defendant should be provided with details of additional liabilities claimed. This should include a copy of the certificate of insurance and details of the CFA, including the percentage of the success fee claimed and the reasons for the percentage increase.

Offers to Settle Costs

CPR 47.19

The defendant should be invited to put forward proposals for settlement at **21.37** the time the bill is served. If the initial offer from the defendant is too low, which is overwhelmingly likely, the choice is between entering into verbal negotiations or making formal counter offers. From this point onwards, the steps taken to progress the settlement depend upon individual style. The discussion below covers some general points.

The formal counter offer should be reasonably close to the figure that would be **21.38** considered acceptable. Each settled case contributes to the reputation of the fee earner's approach to costs. While it is important to make every effort to settle costs without the necessity of a court hearing, if a practitioner is confident of their initial offer, they should be confident to stand their ground. If the defendant is aware the practitioner is prepared to go to detailed assessment if the offer is not accepted, they are much more likely to take the first offer seriously. This can be much more effective than making a series of offers reducing each by a small amount—the latter approach gives the defendant the impression that the practitioner is not confident in their bill and will keep going lower.

It is reasonable to expect counsel to accept a like-for-like reduction in their fees **21.39** as contemplated for profit costs, but this must be discussed with counsel's clerk in advance. This is a matter of courtesy and counsel of course is entitled to the full amount unless there is prior agreement. The same principle applies to the after-the-event insurer. Where the claim is being conducted under a CFA and the claimant has a deferred insurance premium, the insurer must agree to any proposed reduction in the premium and confirm they will not claim the shortfall from the client.

Where the client may have to pay for the shortfall in relation to any profit costs **21.40** and/or disbursements, their authority has to be obtained before an offer is made or accepted.

Interest

CPR 40.8(1) and Section 17 of the Judgments Act 1838

Interest should be added to any offer made. The claimant is entitled to interest on **21.41** costs at 8 per cent per annum from the date of judgment or the consent order confirming terms of settlement.

Additional Costs

21.42 The claimant is also entitled to reasonable costs associated with the detailed assessment procedure.

21.43 As interest and additional costs can mount up rapidly, the defendant should be served with an up-to-date 'without prejudice' schedule of additional costs, and a calculation of interest to date, with every letter written during negotiations. Every offer made should be made or considered 'plus interest and additional costs' until a final acceptable global offer is proposed.

21.44 An offer under CPR 47.19 does not carry the same consequences where the claimant has the benefit of public funding, unless the court rules otherwise (CPD 46.4). However, in practice, the parties are still encouraged to attempt settlement of the inter partes element.

Points of Dispute

CPR 47.9(1), CPR 47.11

21.45 The defendant must serve the points of dispute within 21 days of service of the notice of commencement. If the points of dispute are not received within the time limit, the claimant can apply for a default costs certificate requiring the defendant to pay the sums claimed, together with an amount relating to the cost of commencing the detailed assessment procedure. Once the points of dispute have been received, they must be served on counsel within three days if counsel has been instructed under a CFA and the defendant is seeking a reduction in their success fee. A copy of the points of dispute should be sent to the claimant with an indication of which costs may not be recovered from the defendant and whether they may be deducted from the damages.

Replies

CPR 47.13

21.46 Replies to the defendant's points of dispute should be drafted in all but the most straightforward cases. They should be served within 21 days of receipt of the points of dispute. Once served, they often prompt the defendant to reconsider their position in relation to settlement.

Requesting a Detailed Assessment Hearing

CPR 47.14 (CPD 40)

21.47 A request for a detailed assessment hearing must be made within three months of expiry of the period for commencing detailed assessment proceedings. The request should be made on Form N258. The form specifies which documents should be filed. Technically, a hearing could be requested as soon as the points of dispute have been served, although it would be unwise to do so without having first served the replies, as the defendant could argue they were not given sufficient opportunity to attempt settlement before Court fees were incurred; this is something the Court can take into account when deciding what costs order to make.

When requesting a hearing, it is wise to consult the costs draftsman on the time **21.48** estimate to be included on the N258. The time estimate needs to take into account the Judge's reading time and it is better to err on the side of caution, rather than risk the case being part heard. The court will fix a date for the hearing and papers must be lodged within 7 to 14 days of the detailed assessment.

It is usually sensible for the costs draftsman that prepares the bill to represent the **21.49** practitioner's firm at the detailed assessment hearing. Where there is a significant proportion of the bill in dispute then it is worthwhile attending court to sit behind the costs draftsman to answer any questions that arise about the conduct of the file and to justify the time that has been spent dealing with the claim.

CPR CPD 42

After the hearing the bill must be amended to take into account items that have **21.50** been disallowed or reduced at the assessment. The amended bill must be lodged within 14 days of the hearing so that the final costs certificate can be issued.

Tips for Maximising Cost Recovery

The appropriate time for considering how to maximise costs recovery is not at the **21.51** billing stage but instead at the outset of the claim. It is no use trying to justify to a costs judge at the detailed assessment hearing why a certain party's investigation was so time-consuming when there is no attendance note on the file and the work was undertaken several years ago.

File management is crucial to obtaining good costs recovery. All time spent on the **21.52** file should be accurately recorded with detailed attendance notes. While it may be time-consuming preparing a full note for each item of work done, rather than just recording the time spent on a computer system with a line or two in the file, the costs judge is much more likely to allow recovery where the work has been clearly identified and where it is shown in the attendance note how the work claimed progressed the case.

For any item of work that has required a significant amount of time, the attend- **21.53** ance note should explain exactly what was done and why it took so long. For example, preparing an agenda for a meeting of experts can be extremely time-consuming. The attendance note should explain that all the medical evidence had to be read, the medical records and witness statements had to be reviewed, then the questions for the agenda were formulated. The more detail that is included in the note, the easier it is to justify why the time spent was necessary.

21.54   If time has been accurately recorded and attendance notes have been prepared in support of the time claimed, there should be no reason why a very high percentage of the costs should not be recovered from the defendant. This should also give the practitioner confidence in going to detailed assessment rather than accepting an offer from the defendant in order to avoid having a costs judge scrutinise their file.

Interim Payment of Costs

21.55   Costs issues can take several months to resolve and obtaining an interim payment from the defendant is a good way to improve cash flow while waiting for final payment of costs. Quite often the defendant will be prepared to make a payment on account of costs, once the substantive claim has been concluded, because this will reduce the interest that they have to pay on the total costs assessed or agreed. It can be more difficult to obtain a substantial interim payment if there are likely to be arguments about the level of success fee for a CFA case or the amount of an insurance premium. However, as a matter of course, the defendant should be asked for an interim payment as soon as the claim is successfully concluded. This will help the firm's cash flow—if an interim payment is not obtained, it could be up to six months before cost issues are finalised and payment is made for work. In publicly funded cases, it is important to keep up to date with claims for payments on account of costs to keep the money coming in. Unfortunately interim payments on account of costs are not helpful in such cases as accounts procedures make it impossible to apply the costs and they have to sit in client's account until the whole cost process has been concluded.

CPR 44.3(8)

21.56   After trial, or settlement approval hearing, in addition to the costs order against the losing party, it is possible to obtain an order for an interim payment to be made on account of costs. It is entirely at the Judge's discretion as to whether an order for an interim payment is made and if so, how much should be paid. A request to the trial Judge to make an order for a payment on account is much more likely to be successful than an application at a later date. This is because the trial Judge will already be aware of the particular complexities of the case and should have an idea as to the appropriate level of the claimant's costs. In considering whether or not to exercise discretion and make an order for an interim payment the Judge will consider all of the circumstances of the case including the financial position of each party. For further guidance, see the cases of *Rambus Inc v (1) Hynix Semiconductor UK Ltd (previously known as Hyundai*

Electronics UK Ltd) (2) Micron Europe Ltd [2004] EWHC 2313, *Dyson Appliances v Hoover Ltd* [2003] EWHC 624 (CH), and *Mars UK Ltd v Teknowledge Ltd (No.2)* [1999].

For cases that settle before trial but post-issue, it is often possible to obtain a **21.57** voluntary interim payment from the defendant and a request should be made in correspondence before the court application is made, once the bill is served. This is usually sufficient to obtain payment, because the defendant will be aware that if they refuse, they are unlikely to be successful in defending the court application, as the claimant is entitled to payment of their costs. A refusal and an unsuccessful defence of an application would result in the defendant having to pay the claimant's costs associated with the application.

If the defendant is initially unwilling to make a voluntary interim payment, the **21.58** best time to repeat the request is once the bill has been served and the defendant has responded with their points of dispute. The defendant has no grounds to resist making an interim payment for the amount allowed in their points of dispute.

Statutory Charge

The statutory charge may apply to all cases where the claimant has the benefit **21.59** of legal aid. The client will have been informed of the general risk of the statutory charge applying at the outset of the claim and will have been reminded at regular intervals such as in the six-monthly cost letter and before settlement of the claim. Nevertheless, the claimant is unlikely to have a full grasp of the meaning of this, and it is very important to be in regular communication, preferably verbal as well as written, so that the claimant understands how and why there may be something to pay from their damages and how the figure is arrived at. A proportion of their damages will have been retained in the client account to provide for any liability under the statutory charge. The amount of the statutory charge then has to be sent to the LSC before payment from damages will be authorised.

Where the case is not subject to a high cost case contract, the bill will be drawn **21.60** up with inter partes costs on one side and LSC costs on the other. The client should be sent a copy of the bill and it should be explained to them that they are responsible for the costs on the LSC side and that the precise amount they will have to pay will be determined after assessment by the LSC or the court.

In most cases, inter partes costs will be agreed with the defendant without a **21.61** detailed assessment hearing. In that event:

• complete form CLSCLAIM2 requesting LSC approval to retain the agreed inter partes costs and assessment of costs due under the statutory charge, if those costs are less than £2,500;

- advise the client of the maximum figure payable under the statutory charge and of their right to make representations regarding level of that figure;

- the LSC will send notice of their decision and will recoup profit costs and disbursements paid during the course of the claim. This completes the costs recovery process. The accounts department can finalise matters and the client can be sent the balance of their damages with a sum of money in lieu of interest.

21.62 If the LSC costs are more than £2,500 these costs must be assessed by the court:

- submit Form N258A to request the assessment;

- advise the client that they have the right to have a detailed assessment of costs;

- the court will provisionally assess the bill. It will then be necessary to:

- consider whether provisional assessment of the bill is acceptable;

- if counsel's fees have been reduced, send the bill to counsel for confirmation that they agree to the provisional assessment or that they wish to request detailed assessment;

- if provisional assessment is acceptable, Form EX80A should be completed and returned to the court for sealing, with the original bill and fee. The original bill needs to be recalculated and the summary page completed to reflect what items have been reduced on assessment;

- then send sealed assessment certificate EX80A to the LSC with a completed CLSCLAIM2 for authority to retain both inter partes costs and costs under statutory charge.

Cases Under LSC Contracts and the Statutory Charge

21.63 For cases where a high cost case contract has been entered into with the LSC, whether or not money can be recovered from the client under the statutory charge is governed by the terms of the contract.

21.64 Under a high cost case contract, if a claim is successfully concluded, a choice can be made between claiming costs from the defendant or claiming payment from the LSC. Subject to clauses 16 and 17 of the contract, which are explained below, this means that in practice, if a claim is made for costs from the defendant in order to recover inter partes rates, the statutory charge cannot be enforced against the client. This is an important difference from non-contracted cases.

21.65 Clause 16 does enable certain costs to be claimed from the LSC that have not been recovered from the defendant. The contract specifies that a claim can be made for costs where 'one or more of the issues that [the practitioner] reasonably pursued was not, at trial, covered by an order for costs, or was unlikely, at trial, to be covered by an order for costs'. This could include costs associated with, for example, amendment of the particulars of claim.

Clause 17 specifies that all claims for payment under clause 17 must be assessed **21.66** by the LSC and not by the Court. A CLSCLAIM1 should be submitted.

Retrospective Risk Review

It is good practice to review every case in the light of the original risk assessment, **21.67** any interim risk assessment, the outcome for the client, and the costs recovered at the conclusion of the case. If profitability data is available, this should be included in the review. If a case is successfully conducted under a CFA, it is worthwhile reviewing the level of the success fee that was recovered from the defendant. This can provide useful guidance as to the amount that may be recoverable from the defendant in a similar claim.

Costs Assessment Flow Chart

As soon as the claim is successfully concluded instruct costs **21.68** draftsman to prepare bill.
⇓
Within three months of judgment or settlement of claim serve the bill on the defendant with notice of commencement. Serve copy of bill.
⇓
Defendant must serve points of dispute within 21 days of service of the notice of commencement.
⇓
If no points of dispute are received from the defendant the claimant may file a request for a default costs certificate.
⇓
Upon receipt of the points of dispute the claimant may serve replies within 21 days.
⇓
As soon as the points of dispute are received a request can be made to the Court for a detailed assessment hearing on Form N258. However, if the request is made before replies are served this can be taken into account by the court.
⇓
Lodge papers for the detailed assessment between 7 and 14 days before the hearing.
⇓
After the hearing the bill must be amended to take into account items that have been disallowed or reduced at the assessment. The amended bill must be lodged within 14 days of the hearing so that the final costs certificate can be issued.

22

FATAL CASES

A. Introduction

The general principles applicable to claims arising out of deaths in hospital **22.01**
or elsewhere as a result of clinical negligence are the same as the principles applying to other fatal claims. Consideration always needs to be given to a claim on
behalf of the estate of the deceased pursuant to the Law Reform (Miscellaneous
Provisions) Act 1934 and on behalf of the dependants of the deceased pursuant
to the Fatal Accidents Act 1976. Particulars of claim in a claim on behalf of the
dependants of a mother who died in childbirth are attached at Appendix 1.

B. Secondary Victims

In addition to a claim under the Law Reform (Miscellaneous Provisions) Act 1934 **22.02**
and/or a claim under the Fatal Accidents Act 1976 in some cases there may be
a claim by a relative who is a secondary victim. That is, a relative who witnessed
the death or was closely involved in the aftermath may have suffered psychiatric
damage as a result of witnessing the events surrounding the death.

22.03 The specific criteria by which a secondary victim may bring a claim has been examined a number of times by the House of Lords in the last 25 years. The following cases provide the guidelines:

  (i) *McLoughlin v O'Brien* [1983] 1 AC 410;

 (ii) *Alcock v Chief Constable of South Yorkshire Police* [1992] 1 AC 310;

(iii) *Page v Smith* [1996] AC 155;

 (iv) *Frost v Chief Constable of South Yorkshire Police* [1999] 2 AC 455;

  (v) *W v Essex County Council* [2000] 2 WLR 201.

22.04 In the *Alcock* case, Lord Ackner set out the three criteria which need to be satisfied in cases of nervous shock:

  (i) the claimant needs to have a close personal relationship with the physically injured victim;

 (ii) the claimant needs to have seen or heard or come upon the immediate aftermath of the accident;

(iii) the 'nervous shock' needs to be suffered by means of seeing or hearing of the event or its immediate aftermath.

22.05 Lord Oliver explored in the *Alcock* case the difficulties in classifying psychiatric damage claims as 'liability for nervous shock' claims. At page 407C–408G he pointed out that:

> This may be convenient but in fact the label is misleading if and to the extent it is assumed to lead to a conclusion that they have more in common than the factual similarity of the medium through which the injury is sustained—that of an assault upon the nervous system of the plaintiff through witnessing or taking part in an event—and that they will on account of this factor, provide a single common test for the circumstances which give rise to a duty of care. Broadly they divide into two categories, that is to say, those cases in which the injured plaintiff was involved, mediately or immediately, as a participant, and those in which the plaintiff was no more than a passive and unwilling witness of injury caused to others.

22.06 None of the House of Lords cases were clinical negligence cases. However, a number of clinical negligence cases at first instance or in the Court of Appeal have looked at the criteria which govern whether a relative is a secondary victim and whether there is a claim for damages. These cases include:

  (i) *Sion v Hampstead Health Authority* [1994] 5 Med LR 170;

 (ii) *Tredget & Tredget v Bexley Health Authority* [1994] 5 Med LR 178;

(iii) *North Glamorgan NHS Trust v Ceri Ann Walters* [2003] Lloyd's Rep Med 49;

 (iv) *Julia Ward v Leeds Teaching Hospitals NHS Trust* [2004] Lloyd's Rep Med 530.

In the case of *Walters* Lord Justice Ward described how:

22.07

> The issue is whether a mother can recover damages for the pathological grief reaction which it is agreed by the psychiatrists she suffered after waking at her young baby's bedside in hospital at 3am when the child was having a fit and then, some 36 hours later, having the child die in her arms after life-support treatment was withdrawn. The hospital admitted that the child died as a result of its negligent treatment.

Ward LJ described how the Judge had addressed the issue as follows:

22.08

> The essence of what the claimant must show is that the psychiatric illness was brought about through the sudden appreciation by sight or sound of a horrifying event that affected her mind. Although the psychiatrists are agreed that she suffered 'shock' and I am satisfied that her mind was violently agitated, the question is whether what happened was a sudden appreciation by sight or sound of a horrifying event rather than an accumulation over a period of time of more gradual assaults on the nervous system and that it was that sudden appreciation that caused the pathological grief reaction.

The correct approach was set out by Ward LJ as follows:

22.09

> It is a matter of judgment from case to case depending on the facts and circumstance of each case. In my judgment on the facts of this case there was an inexorable progression from the moment when the fit occurred as a result of the failure of the hospital properly to diagnose and then to treat the baby, the fit causing the brain damage which shortly thereafter made termination of this child's life inevitable and the dreadful climax when the child died in her arms. It is a seamless tale with an obvious beginning and an equally obvious end. It was played out over a period of 36 hours, which for her both at the time and as subsequently recollected was undoubtedly one drawn-out experience.

And Lord Justice Clarke concluded:

22.10

> In my opinion the very close relationship between the claimant and her son Elliot, the sudden and unexpected shock or series of shocks over a short period and the presence of the claimant leading to the death of Elliot in her arms, which together had the devastating effect on her described by Ward LJ, lead to the conclusion that the judge was right to hold that she is entitled to recover damages for the pathological grief reaction which she suffered as a result of the appellant's negligence.

In cases of sudden death through the negligence of the defendant health authority or doctor it will be necessary to ascertain whether any qualifying relative was present at the death or during the immediate aftermath. It is then necessary to ascertain whether any such relative suffered recognised psychiatric damage as a result of witnessing the death or aftermath. In order to bring a claim the relative will need the report of a psychiatrist supporting the allegation that a psychiatric injury was sustained as a result of witnessing the events or being involved in the immediate aftermath.

22.11

C. The Inquest

The Need for an Inquest in the Context of Clinical Cases

22.12   By section 8(1) of the Coroners Act 1988 an inquest must be held where there is reasonable cause to suspect that a deceased person:

- has died a violent or unnatural death;
- has died a sudden death of which the cause is unknown;
- has died in prison or such other place or in such circumstances to require an inquest under any other Act.

22.13   By section 8(3) the coroner is required to summons a jury where:

- the death occurred in prison or in such a place or in such circumstances as to require an inquest under any other Act;
- the death occurred while the deceased was in police custody, or resulted from an injury caused by a police officer in the purported execution of his duty;
- the death was caused by an accident, poisoning, or disease notice of which is required to be given under any Act to a government department, to any inspector or other officer of a government department, or to an inspector appointed under section 19 of the Health and Safety at Work etc Act 1974; or
- the death occurred in circumstances the continuance or possible recurrence of which is prejudicial to the health or safety of the public or any section of the public.

22.14   In clinical negligence cases the most likely inquests to require a jury are:

- those occurring in prison where a prison doctor is alleged to have failed to provide proper care;
- those occurring in hospital where it is alleged that there has been a systems failure and there is a risk of recurrence.

22.15   In *R v Her Majesty's Coroner at Hammersmith ex p Peach* [1980] QB Lord Denning said at page 226 that a jury must be summoned: 'When the circumstances are such that similar fatalities may possibly recur in the future, and it is reasonable to expect that some action should be taken to prevent their recurrence.' And Bridge LJ said at page 227: 'The key to the nature of that limitation is to be found, I think, in the paragraph's concern with the continuance or possible recurrence of the circumstances in question.'

22.16   The jurisdiction of the coroner depends not on the fact of the death having occurred but on the coroner being informed of the fact that there is a dead body within his area. As the certification and coronial processes are separate from each other, the coroner has no information on or responsibility for deaths not reported to him. Thus, as was found in *Shipman*, there is little to stop an unscrupulous doctor from 'certifying his way out of trouble'.

The Coroners Act 1988 does not deal with the obligation to report such deaths. **22.17** The reporting process derives from registration legislation and under current legislation, the Registrar of Deaths is the only person subject to a statutory duty to report a death to the coroner. There is no statutory duty upon a doctor to report deaths to the coroner, but there is a common law duty to report a death to the coroner in circumstances where an inquest might be required. It applies to everyone. Furthermore, there is a specific duty in the case of a deceased person who has been 'attended during his last illness' by a registered medical practitioner to sign a certificate in the prescribed form stating to the best of his or her knowledge and belief the cause of death and to deliver it to the Registrar of Deaths. The Registrar of Deaths is then required to report deaths which appear to have occurred during an operation before full recovery from the effect of an anaesthetic *and* deaths which the Registrar has reason to believe to have been unnatural or to have been caused by violence or neglect.

The Need for the Inquest to Comply With Article 2 Requirements

For deaths after the implementation of the Human Rights Act 1998, that is for **22.18** deaths after October 2000, it is also necessary to consider Article 2 of the European Convention. In *In Re McKerr* [2004] UKHL 12, [2004] 1 WLR 807, the House of Lords confirmed that the provisions of the Convention did not apply to deaths before October 2000. Although the Court of Appeal had earlier held in *R (Khan) v Secretary of State for Health* [2004] 1 WLR 971 and subsequently has held in *Commissioner of Police v Hirst* [2005] EWCA Civ 890 that some of the requirements of Article 2 apply even to deaths before October 2000.

Article 2 provides that: 'Everyone's right to life shall be protected by law. No-one **22.19** shall be deprived of his life intentionally save in the exercise of a sentence of a court following his conviction of a crime for which this penalty is provided by law.'

The European Court of Human Rights in the case of *McCann v UK* [1995] 21 **22.20** EHRR 97 confirmed that the Article 2 right extends not only to the preservation of life but to the investigation of how a death came about. The Court stated:

> The court finds that the obligation imposed on the state that everyone's right to
> life shall be 'protected by law' may include a procedural aspect. This includes the
> minimum requirement of a mechanism whereby the circumstances of a deprivation
> of life by the organs of the state may receive public and independent scrutiny.

22.21   The House of Lords has confirmed in the case of *R (Amin) v Home Secretary* [2004] 1 AC 653 that the requirement of independent scrutiny for deaths which are the responsibility of the state includes a requirement for:

- an investigation into the circumstances of the death;
- an effective investigation;
- an independent investigation;
- a prompt investigation;
- public scrutiny in the investigation;
- involvement of the relatives in the investigation.

22.22   The House of Lords considered three other cases in 2004:

- *R (Middleton) v Her Majesty's Coroner for the Western District of Somerset* [2004] UKHL 10, [2004] 2 All ER 465;
- *R (Sacker) v Her Majesty's Coroner for the County of West Yorkshire* [2004] UKHL 11;
- *In Re McKerr* [2004] UKHL 12, [2004] 1 WLR 807.

22.23   In these three cases the House of Lords examined the interplay between coroners' inquests, the right to life, the right to a proper inquiry into a death, and the implementation of the Human Rights Act 1998. These decisions analyse the domestic and European law in respect of the obligations to carry out a proper inquiry into deaths. The House of Lords has found that to comply with the European Convention the verdict of a coroner should give a wide interpretation to the question 'how, when, and where the deceased came by his death' so as to include an explanation of the circumstances in which the death occurred, although it should not go as far as to provide a specific finding of criminal or civil liability. The finding must however be wide enough to prompt a reconsideration of a decision not to prosecute where that is appropriate. Effectively it should give a pointer to further investigation.

D. The *Middleton* Case

22.24   In the *Middleton* case the House of Lords set out the three central issues in that appeal as follows:

- What, if anything, does the Convention require (by way of verdict, judgment, findings, or recommendations) of a properly conducted official investigation into a death involving, or possibly involving, a violation of Article 2?

- Does the regime for holding inquests established by the Coroners Act 1988 and the Coroners Rules 1984 (SI 1984/552), as hitherto understood and followed in England and Wales, meet those requirements of the Convention?

- If not, can the current regime governing the conduct of inquests in England and Wales be revised so as to do so, and if so how?

Having posed these questions the House of Lords emphasised: **22.25**

> It should be observed that they are very important questions. Compliance with the substantive obligations referred to above must rank among the highest priorities of a modern democratic state governed by the rule of law. Any violation or potential violation must be treated with great seriousness. In the context of this appeal the questions have a particular importance also. For, as the facts summarised in paragraphs 39–43 below make clear, the appeal concerns an inquest into the suicide, in prison, of a serving prisoner.

The House of Lords examined the case law in respect of the requirements of an **22.26** inquest both in Strasbourg and in the English Courts. Against that background the government argued that:

> What is required, where the obligation arises, is a full, thorough, independent and public investigation of the facts surrounding and leading to the death but not necessarily culminating in any decision on whether the state or any individual is responsible. The duty is to investigate, no more. If the investigation yields evidence of delinquency on the part of the state or its agents, then the victim must have a remedy. But that is a requirement of article 13, not of the procedural obligation under article 2.

On behalf of the family of Mrs Middleton the argument was that: **22.27**

> If an investigation is to ensure the accountability of state agents or bodies for deaths occurring under their responsibility (Jordan, paragraph 105) and be capable of leading to a determination of whether the force used had been justified (Jordan, paragraph 107) and to establish the cause of death or the person or persons responsible (Jordan, paragraph 107), then it must culminate in a finding which, while it need not convict any person of crime nor constitute an enforceable civil judgment against any party, must express the fact-finding body's judgment on the cardinal issues concerning the death.

The House of Lords concluded that an inquest is of no value unless it allows a jury **22.28** to comment specifically on their findings of the circumstances in which a death occurred:

> It seems safe to infer that the state's procedural obligation to investigate is unlikely to be met if it is plausibly alleged that agents of the state have used lethal force without justification, if an effectively unchallengeable decision has been taken not to prosecute and if the fact-finding body cannot express its conclusion on whether unjustifiable force has been used or not, so as to prompt reconsideration of the decision not to prosecute. Where, in such a case, an inquest is the instrument by which the state

seeks to discharge its investigative obligation, it seems that an explicit statement, however brief, of the jury's conclusion on the central issue is required a verdict of an inquest jury (other than an open verdict, sometimes unavoidable) which does not express the jury's conclusion on a major issue canvassed in the evidence at the inquest cannot satisfy or meet the expectations of the deceased's family or next-of-kin. Yet they, like the deceased, may be victims. They have been held to have legitimate interests in the conduct of the investigation (Jordan, paragraph 109), which is why they must be accorded an appropriate level of participation (see also *R (Amin) v Secretary of State for the Home Department*, supra). An uninformative jury verdict will be unlikely to meet what the House in *Amin*, paragraph 31, held to be one of the purposes of an article 2 investigation: '… that those who have lost their relative may at least have the satisfaction of knowing that lessons learned from his death may save the lives of others'.

19. The second consideration is that while the use of lethal force by agents of the state must always be a matter of the greatest seriousness, a systemic failure to protect human life may call for an investigation which may be no less important and perhaps even more complex: see *Amin*, paragraphs 21, 41, 50 and 62. It would not promote the objects of the Convention if domestic law were to distinguish between cases where an agent of the state may have used lethal force without justification and cases in which a defective system operated by the state may have failed to afford adequate protection to human life.

20. The European Court has repeatedly recognized that there are many different ways in which a state may discharge its procedural obligation to investigate under article 2. In England and Wales an inquest is the means by which the state ordinarily discharges that obligation, save where a criminal prosecution intervenes or a public enquiry is ordered into a major accident, usually involving multiple fatalities. To meet the procedural requirement of article 2 an inquest ought ordinarily to culminate in an expression, however brief, of the jury's conclusion on the disputed factual issues at the heart of the case.

22.29 The House of Lords specifically considered whether the procedure under the Coroners Act 1988 and the Coroners Rules 1984 met the requirements of the European Convention. The House concluded: 'The conclusion is inescapable that there are some cases in which the current regime for conducting inquests in England and Wales, as hitherto understood and followed, does not meet the requirements of the Convention.'

22.30 The House of Lords went on to suggest that the defect in the present system should be met by the interpretation of 'how' the deceased met his death so as to include not only 'by what means' but also 'in what circumstances'. On the facts in the *Middleton* case, the House of Lords found that a verdict that the deceased had taken his own life in prison was not sufficient as there was no dispute in that regard, the issue was the circumstances in which he had done so. The House of Lords set out their conclusion as follows:

> There was no dispute at this inquest whether the deceased had taken his own life. He had left a suicide note, and it was plain that he had. The crux of the argument was

whether he should have been recognized as a suicide risk and whether appropriate precautions should have been taken to prevent him taking his own life. The jury's verdict, although strictly in accordance with the guidance in *Ex p Jamieson*, did not express the jury's conclusion on these crucial facts. This might have been done by a short and simple verdict (eg 'The deceased took his own life, in part because the risk of his doing so was not recognized and appropriate precautions were not taken to prevent him doing so'). Or it could have been done by a narrative verdict or a verdict given in answer to the coroner's questions. By one means or another the jury should, to meet the procedural obligation in article 2, have been permitted to express their conclusion on the central facts explored before them.

The conclusion in respect of the *Middleton* case is that this decision may be seen **22.31** as something of a compromise and each party succeeded on the appeal to some extent so that the House of Lords made no order for costs. However, it is an important decision in recognising that there is an obligation under the European Convention to investigate the circumstances of death so as to identify circumstances which could give rise to a reconsideration of criminal investigation or a civil claim. However, the role of the inquest remains inquisitorial and should still not seek to attribute criminal or civil responsibility. The fact that it should not do so provides safeguards for both individuals and the state. It would clearly be unsatisfactory if the opportunity to attribute blame was concentrated more on the inquest. The fact that the House of Lords has emphasised that the jury should make its findings clear enough to prompt further investigation can at least be seen as some help for the families of the deceased in seeking to understand the circumstances and cause of the death of a relative in an NHS Hospital or whilst undergoing medical treatment.

E. The *Sacker* Case

The facts in this case were that the deceased was a 22-year-old woman who was **22.32** held on remand in prison and was recognised as a suicide risk. She had been sent to the health care centre but a locum doctor referred her back to the residential wing of the prison where she had hanged herself. The House of Lords applied the reasoning in the *Middleton* case and found that the coroner should have been able to interpret 'how' the deceased came by her death as wide enough to include 'by what means and in what circumstances'.

The House of Lords described the circumstances of this death as follows: **22.33**

It is plain that Ms Creamer, like so many other women in prisons, fell within the profile of those who most commonly die while they are in custody. She was a young woman, she was unconvicted and she was withdrawing from drugs. It is plain too that she was placed on her own in a cell without a television set where material was available for her to hang herself. The tragedy which occurred in her case is that these factors came together to create the dark, desperate sense of isolation and hopelessness that drives a person to contemplate, and then to commit, suicide. There are signs in the report commissioned by Mr Clifford that this tragedy might have been prevented if there had been better communication between members of staff with each other and between staff and prisoners. It may be too that it was a mistake to rely on the routine system of half-hourly inspections in her case as this left ample time for prisoners, aware of the system, to take measures while they were unobserved that could lead to self-harm and ultimately to suicide.

22.34 The Conclusion reached reflected the decision in the *Middleton* case and the need to give a broader interpretation to the Coroner's Act 1988 than had previously been allowed. The House of Lords concluded:

> As Lord Bingham of Cornhill, giving the opinion of the Appellate Committee, has explained in *R v H M Coroner for the Western District of Somerset, ex p Middleton* [2004] UKHL 10, paras 34–35, the scheme for the conduct of inquests which has been enacted by and under the authority of Parliament must be respected, save to the extent that a change of interpretation is required to honour the international obligations of the United Kingdom under the Convention. The word 'how' in section 11(5)(b)(ii) of the 1988 Act and rule 36(1)(b) of the 1984 Rules is open to the interpretation that it means not simply 'by what means' but rather 'by what means and in what circumstances'. The provisions of section three of the Human Rights Act 1998 indicate that it should now be given the broader meaning, with the result that a coroner will be able to exercise his discretion in the way Lord Bingham has indicated in paras 36 and 37 of the opinion in that case.
>
> 28. The coroner in this case did not have an opportunity of inviting the jury to consider the issues in the way which Lord Bingham has now identified. This deprived the inquest of its ability, when subjecting the events surrounding Ms Creamer's death to public scrutiny, to address the positive obligation that article 2 of the Convention places on the State to take effective operational measures to safeguard life: *Osman v United Kingdom* (1998) 29 EHRR 245, paras 115–116. The inquest was not able to identify the cause or causes of Ms Creamer's suicide, the steps (if any) that could have been taken and were not taken to prevent it and the precautions (if any) that ought to be taken to avoid or reduce the risk to other prisoners. The most convenient and appropriate way to make good this deficiency is, as the Court of Appeal did, to order a new inquest.

22.35 This case gives a second further example of the wider interpretation that must now be given to the Coroner's Act 1988. It implements a wider jurisdiction for coroners and juries to specify the circumstances in which a death occurred so as to point to any further investigation of fault that might thereafter be required.

F. The *McKerr* Case

22.36 In the *Middleton* case and the *Sacker* case no issue arose as to the retrospective application of the Human Rights Act and the European Convention (although such points might have been taken). The Human Rights Act 1998 was assumed to be applicable. However, in the *McKerr* case the issue was whether the Human Rights Act 1998 provisions should be applied retrospectively to ensure a proper investigation into the circumstances of an unnatural death. The conclusion was that the Act did not apply retrospectively.

The position is summarised in the speech of Lord Steyn: **22.37**

> The retrospectivity issue now arises. Mr McKerr's case is founded on section 6 of the 1998 Act. Leaving aside proceedings taken at the instigation of a public authority, which are not under consideration, it is now settled law that section 6 is not retrospective: section 22(4) of the 1998 Act; *R v Lambert* [2002] 2 AC 545; *R v Kansal (No. 2)* [2002] 2 AC 69; *Wilson v First County Trust Ltd (No. 2)* [2003] 3 WLR 568 (HL). Mr McKerr's father was killed in 1982. The 1998 Act came into force on 2 October 2000. The Court of Appeal held that there is a continuing breach of Article 2 which requires to be addressed by the Government: para 13. In my view the Attorney-General has demonstrated that this reasoning cannot be sustained. The Government may have been in breach of its obligations under international law before 2 October 2000 to set up a prompt and effective investigation. But those treaty obligations created no rights under domestic law, not even after the right to petition to Strasbourg was created by the United Kingdom Government in 1966. The very purpose of the 1998 Act was 'to bring home rights' which were previously justiciable only in Strasbourg: The Government White Paper, October 1997 (Cm 3782).

The House of Lords therefore ruled that there was no right to investigation of **22.38** deaths occurring before 2 October 2000 and no continuing right to investigation as found in the cases of *R (Wright) v Secretary of State for the Home Department* and *R (Khan) v Secretary of State for Health*. The House of Lords found whatever the position in Strasbourg would be the rights in the UK to rely on Convention Rights could only apply after the implementation of the Human Rights Act 1998 and the right to investigate could only apply to deaths after 2 October 2000.

G. The *Hurst* Case

In the case of *R (on the application of Christine Hurst) v Commissioner of Police* **22.39** *for the Metropolis* [2007] UKHL 13, the Court of Appeal held that section 3 of the Human Rights Act 1998 required that sections 16 and 11 of the Coroners Act 1988 should be interpreted so as to require an inquest complying with the UK's international obligations under Article 2 of the European Convention on Human Rights no matter when the death occurred. The House of Lords reversed the Court of Appeal decision and held that the Convention rights applied domestically only to deaths occurring after the coming into force of the Human Rights Act 1998. Further, the right to proper investigation was an ancillary aspect of the right to life and only arose in respect of deaths occurring after 2 October 2000.

22.40   These four cases decide important points of principle in respect of the application of the Human Rights Act 1998 to the pre-existing domestic law. The Act should not be interpreted so as to have retrospective effect and, in the context of inquests, should only be applied to deaths occurring after 2 October 2000. In respect of inquests into deaths occurring after that date in order to render the Coroners Act 1988 compatible with the Human Rights Act 1998 it is necessary to give a broad interpretation to the concept of 'how' the deceased came by his death so as to allow findings of the circumstances in which unnatural death occurred. Whilst this should not extend to a finding of criminal or civil responsibility it should give considerable pointers as to whether on further investigation by civil or criminal proceedings such findings can be expected to be made.

22.41   A death in a hospital run by a public authority has the potential to be a death that is the responsibility of the state as was found in three Strasbourg cases:

  (i)   *Powell v UK* (App no 45305/99) ECHR 4 May 2000;
  (ii) *Sieminska v Poland* (App no 37602/97) ECHR 29 March 2001;
  (iii) *Calvelli v Italy* (App no 32967/96) ECHR 17 June 2002.

22.42   However, not every death in hospital will involve a breach of Article 2. The severity of the allegations of negligence (gross negligence as opposed to simple negligence) has to be assessed before it can be established that the Article 2 criteria apply. The position in respect of hospital deaths after the implementation of the Human Rights Act 1998 has been analysed in the cases of:

  (i)   *R (Goodson) v HM Coroner for Bedfordshire and Luton and Dunstable Hospital NHS Trust* [2005] 2 All ER 791;
  (ii) *R (Takoushis) v Her Majesty's Coroner for Inner North London* [2005] EWCA Civ 1440.

22.43   Further, the position when a severely disabled child died after delay in obtaining medical treatment was also found by the Court of Appeal not to engage Article 2 for the purposes of requiring an inquest: *R (Canning) v HM Coroner for Northamptonshire* [2005].

22.44   The Court of Appeal summarised the existing principles in the *Takoushis* case by reference to the findings of Richards J in the *Goodson* case as follows:

  • Simple negligence in the care and treatment of a patient in hospital, resulting in the patient's death, is not sufficient in itself to amount to a breach of the state's positive obligations under Article 2 to protect life. This is stated clearly in the *Powell* case. The position is or may be different in a case in which gross negligence or manslaughter is alleged: see eg *R (Khan) v Secretary of State for Health*.

  • Nevertheless, where agents of the state potentially bear responsibility for the loss of life, the events should be subject to an effective investigation. The reference to potential responsibility for loss of life must include a potential liability in negligence. Thus the need for an effective investigation is not limited to those cases where there is a potential breach of the positive obligations to protect life under Article 2.

• The requirement of an effective investigation is linked with the positive obligation to establish a framework of legal protection, including an effective judicial system for determining the cause of death and any liability on the part of the medical professionals. In order to comply with Article 2, the state must set up a system which involves a practical and effective investigation of the facts. The mere fact that the state has made it possible in law for the family to begin a civil action against those said to be responsible is not by itself a sufficient discharge of the state's obligation in every case. For example, it may not be practicable for the family to procure an effective investigation of the facts by the simple expedient of civil proceedings. Their claim may be for a comparatively small sum, as for example where the only claim is that of the estate of the deceased, such that it would not make practical or economic sense for civil proceedings to be begun, especially for a family who is not able to obtain legal aid. The facts may be such that liability has been admitted, with the result that there will be no trial and thus no independent investigation of the facts as part of the civil process.

• Although certain minimum criteria are laid down, the actual nature of an investigation required under Article 2 varies according to context; and the Strasbourg cases on deaths resulting from alleged medical negligence show that, if the procedural obligation does apply, the range of remedies available under the judicial system (criminal, civil, and possibly disciplinary) can be sufficient to discharge it. There is no separate procedural obligation to investigate under Article 2 where a death in hospital raises no more than a potential liability in negligence. In such a situation an inquest does play a part, though only a part, in the discharge of the state's positive obligation under Article 2 to set up an effective judicial system for determining the cause of death and questions of liability. But it does not need to perform the function of discharging a separate investigative obligation on the state under Article 2. It will only be in exceptional cases, where the circumstances give rise to the possibility of a breach of the state's positive obligations to protect life under Article 2, that the separate procedural obligation to investigate will arise and an inquest may have to perform the function of discharging that obligation.

The totality of available procedures, including most obviously the possibility of **22.45** a civil claim in negligence, must be looked at in order to determine whether the state has complied with the positive obligation to set up an effective judicial system pursuant to Article 2. In order to establish there should not only be an inquest but that the procedure must comply with Article 2 it is necessary to consider the alternative methods by which a full investigation might be achieved on the particular facts of the case.

H. Practical Considerations in Respect of the Inquest

22.46 The Coroners Rules provide for only a limited class of family to participate in an inquest, they include: parent, child, spouse, or personal representative; this raises issues under Article 8 and Article 6.

22.47 In order to represent a family properly at an inquest into the death of a relative it will be necessary to obtain:

- statements from the family members as to the circumstances of the deceased's death and the deceased's condition in the months or weeks preceding his or her death if the death results from an admission to hospital because of an illness.

- medical records relating to the deceased which should include:

    (i) the deceased's full GP records and in particular any records relating to a GP on call who attended the deceased including the log of emergency calls if relevant;

    (ii) the deceased's hospital records, from the hospital where the deceased died if he or she died in hospital, but also from any other hospital at which he or she was treated or any prison hospital records if he was in prison;

    (iii) any ambulance records including the ambulance log of calls to the service if relevant;

    (iv) any police reports or police medical records if the police became involved;

    (v) an expert's report in relation to the cause of her death and the responsibility and liability for it.

22.48 Without statements and medical records it will be impossible to:

- identify which witnesses the coroner should be invited to call at the inquest. It is not unknown for coroners to adduce evidence solely from the consultant in charge of the relevant unit without calling those who treated the deceased. Without the records it is impossible to assess which of the staff in the hospital, the GP, or the ambulance crew would be likely to assist in establishing how the deceased died;

- cross-examine properly the witnesses which are called.

22.49 There is no provision for any form of disclosure from the coroner of documentation—documentary evidence or statements—prior to the inquest.

The only exception relates to the post-mortem report which in principle (although there is still some debate in relation to this) and almost always in practice is released after a request is made pursuant to rule 57 of the Coroners Rules 1984.

There is provision for disclosure of the deceased's medical records pursuant to   **22.50**
the provisions of the Access to Health Records Act 1990 or the Data Protection Act 1998. The deceased's records will not contain other documents which are likely to have been created and which are likely to be highly relevant to the cause of death. For example, it is likely that the NHS Hospital or NHS Trust will have carried out an investigation for audit (as opposed to litigation) purposes into the circumstances surrounding the death. Disclosure of documents of this nature will only occur if an application for pre-proceedings disclosure is made pursuant to CPR Part 31.16.

The necessity of pre-proceedings disclosure in the context of the investigation of   **22.51**
the circumstances surrounding a patient's death and an inquest into that death was dealt with over a decade ago in *Stobart v Nottingham Health Authority and related cases* [1992] 3 Med LR 284 (QBD). Rougier J in giving judgment that disclosure should be made to the claimants commented that:

> Now, the following principles should, I think, be stated. First, the purpose of pre-action discovery is very different from that of what I might call ordinary discovery. Ordinary discovery takes place when by and large the plaintiffs have decided that their chances warrant the institution and the prosecution of proceedings and that discovery is ordered so that they may be in possession of appropriate discoverable material as indeed almost a weapon or at any rate one of the shots in their armoury in the forthcoming litigation. Pre-action discovery is primarily designed to allow the plaintiff's advisers to assess the possibilities of success at an early stage so that in many cases proceedings will not even be started and thereby a great deal of costs are saved.

> Secondly, it is a principle of both types of discovery that it can only be used in relation to the proper conduct of the action in which it is made and not for any ulterior or collateral purpose. For the present purposes it seems to me the question boils down to this. Within the remit of a coroner's inquest, are there any legitimate purposes for which disclosure of the documents are reasonably necessary for the plaintiffs to undergo the proper conduct of the action? I consider that part of the proper conduct of an action is all appropriate inquiries into the salient facts upon which the action will be based. I cannot accept the proposition that proper conduct of an action was not involved in investigation at an early stage.

> On behalf of the plaintiffs, one purpose alone is advanced. Because it must be borne in mind that a coroner's remit, as is shown by the Coroners Act 1887 and the rules made thereunder, is a narrow one and for present purposes is limited to ascertain the cause of death. The argument is that anybody who is advising a potential plaintiff in a fatal accident action, especially where the cause of action is likely to be what is sometimes called 'medical negligence', although the phrase is not a very happy one, will be concerned to know the cause of death. From there, it is argued that since the

coroner is also concerned to discover the cause of death, it is a legitimate purpose for the plaintiffs to have the relevant documents in attending the inquest, so that they, armed with appropriate expert advice, may take part in the inquisitorial proceedings and play their part in helping the coroner and themselves to establish what was the cause of death. That, it is claimed, is not an ulterior or collateral purpose. It is what I might call a direct purpose. (col1, 285).

22.52 Apart from ensuring that full and proper instructions are received from the family and that statements are taken from relevant family members, and that full documentary disclosure is obtained, it is essential that expert opinion is obtained as to the cause of death.

22.53 Rougier J stated that he considered that:

> It is a legitimate purpose for the plaintiffs to have the relevant documents in attending the inquest, so that they, armed with appropriate expert advice, may take part in the inquisitorial proceedings and play their part in helping the coroner and themselves to establish what was the cause of death.

22.54 It is not only legitimate but also a necessity that expert opinion is obtained (and even perhaps called at inquest) if the family are to be placed in a position to respond to the expert opinions of the treating doctors who are likely to be called by the coroner. Further, it may be that a verdict of death arising from natural causes contributed to by lack of care will need be considered: see *R v HM Coroner for Inner London North ex p Touche* [2001] EWCA Civ 383 (CA Civil Division). It would be clearly unfair for the family not to have the benefit of their own expert evidence in these circumstances. In the *Touche* case the Court of Appeal confirmed that a coroner should hold an inquest if the death was '(a) at least contributed to by neglect and thus (b) unnatural' (Lord Justice Simon Brown at paragraph 32 and 46). Lord Justice Simon Brown described a further category of case where an inquest was necessary and stated:

> Undoubtedly there will be cases which fall outside the category of 'neglect' and yet appear to call for an inquest on the basis already indicated, namely cases involving a wholly unexpected death from natural causes which would not have occurred but for a culpable human failure ... It is the combination of their unexpectedness and the culpable human failing that allowed them to happen which to my mind makes such deaths unnatural. Deaths by natural causes though undoubtedly they are, they should plainly never have happened and in that sense are unnatural.

22.55 The Court of Appeal in the *Touche* case expressed concern at the test used in *R (Thomas) v Poplar Coroner* [1993] QB 610b in which the test was whether the death was natural in the sense of whether what caused the death was illness that was not itself caused by the doctors. Lord Justice Robert Walker (as he then was) stated at paragraph 61:

> The expression 'unnatural death' in S.8(1)(a) of the Coroners Act 1988 does not have a single clearly defined meaning. ('As Lord Sumner said in a different context in

Weld-Blundell v Stephens [1920] AC 956 "everything that happens, happens in the order of nature and is therefore 'natural' ") Often unnatural means little more than abnormal and unexpected, and that rather muted shade of meaning would appear to be consistent with the legislative purpose of the Coroners Act 1988. In particular I doubt whether the naturalness or unnaturalness of a death should be determined exclusively in terms of causation, especially if that is seen as requiring a search for a 'single dominant cause of death'... the better way forward is to look for a combination of circumstances rather than a single dominant cause.

These passages from the Court of Appeal judgment are of direct relevance in seeking to identify the cases where a family is anxious that an inquest should be held after a death in hospital and the coroner may be reluctant to hold an inquest. The approach is also of wider interest in the context of causation in personal injury claims and mirrors developments in that area towards a less rigid approach to identifying a single cause of injury. **22.56**

I. Funding an Inquest

Obtaining public funding to attend an inquest can be extremely difficult. Perversely when public funding has been requested for a clinical negligence case the certificate may be refused pending the outcome of the inquest. However, when a further application is made pointing out that attending the inquest may be a vital step in establishing the clinical negligence claim this is frequently again refused. Sometimes the only step that can then be taken is to apply for public funding for an application for Judicial Review of the public funding decision. From such an application instead of a certificate for the Judicial Review application a certificate may ultimately be obtained for the clinical negligence claim. It is unattractive, to say the least, that one public authority should be refusing to grant the deceased's family sufficient funds to ensure that all aspects surrounding the death of the deceased are investigated properly before a hearing into the cause of his or her death at which another public authority, whose actions arguably contributed to the death, will be represented fully and will have had an opportunity to investigate matters fully before the hearing. **22.57**

In the case of *R (Khan) v Secretary of State for Health* [2004] 1 WLR 971, the applicant was the father of a three-year-old child who had died of a cardiac arrest whilst undergoing dialysis in an NHS Hospital. He was refused public funding for representation at the inquest on the basis he did not come within the eligibility criteria in the Community Legal Service (Financial) Regulations 2000. In Judicial Review proceedings the Court of Appeal found that a public investigation of the death of the child was required and the Court adjourned the case for the Secretary of State to provide either a public inquiry or an inquest in which the claimant could be legally represented. **22.58**

22.59 During the period of adjournment the Secretary of State introduced the Community Legal Services (Financial) (Amendment No 2) Regulations 2003 which introduced into the Community Legal Services (Financial) Regulations 2000 the following provisions:

  (i) This regulation applies to an application for the funding of legal representation to provide advocacy at an inquest into the death of a member of the immediate family of the client;

  (ii) Where this regulation applies, the Commission may, if it considers it equitable to do so, request the Secretary of State to disapply the eligibility limits in regulations 5(6) and 5A;

  (iii) In considering whether to make such a request, the Commission shall have regard in particular to any applicable Convention rights under Article 2 of Schedule 1 of the Human Rights Act 1998;

  (iv) On receipt of a request under paragraph (2) the Secretary of State may, if he thinks fit, disapply the eligibility limit.

22.60 These provisions are however in practice likely to be of limited application and reserved for exceptional cases where the family cannot realistically take part in the inquest without legal representation and where the facts are unusually complex or there are allegations of a 'cover-up'.

22.61 In the subsequent case of *R (Challender) v Legal Services Commission* [2004] EWHC 925, a challenge to the Legal Services Commission's failure to make a request to the Secretary of State to disapply the regulations was unsuccessful. Mr Justice Richards distinguished the *Khan* case and refused the judicial review application.

22.62 It is illogical for the merits of the deceased's family's claim to be reviewed, for public funding purposes, after the inquest given that the outcome of the inquest upon which it is proposed that the merits will be assessed will be affected by their being inadequately represented. Proper investigation of the cause of the deceased's death and proper representation at the inquest may well avoid or at least shorten any civil proceedings which may arise after the inquest, thereby saving costs. Often if the family are represented at the inquest and the strength of the case against a hospital or health authority is apparent at that hearing there will be an early admission of liability saving much unnecessary anxiety and further upset to the family.

22.63 In practice, representation at the inquest may either have to be provided on a pro bono basis or paid for on a private basis. In the event that there is subsequently a successful clinical negligence claim the costs of the inquest may be recovered as either special damages or costs in the civil proceedings. In two cases a costs Master has allowed the costs of legal representation at an inquest as part of the bill of costs in the civil proceedings, applying the principles set out by Mr Justice Clarke in

The Bowbelle [1997] 2 Lloyd's Rep 196: see *Stewart v the Medway NHS Trust* (LTL 20 September 2004) and *King v Milton Keynes General NHS Trust* (LTL 4 June 2004). However, the expenditure which was allowed was only the cost of legal representation, but not the cost of instructing an expert.

J. Damages

Stillborn Babies

Leading cases which illustrate the appropriate heads of damage are as follows: **22.64**

(i) *Bagley v North Hertfordshire Health Authority* [1986] New LJ 1014.
     £18,200 total award—stillborn baby after ten-hour labour, mother could not face having a further child and suffered psychiatric damage;
(ii) *Grieve v Salford Health Authority* [1991] 2 Med LR 295.
     £13,865 total award—stillborn baby after prolonged labour, aborted forceps delivery and Caesarean section to an unmarried mother with a vulnerable personality.

Further examples set out in the *AVMA Journal* and *Clinical Risk* include: **22.65**

(i)   *Re MH* [1991] *AVMA Journal*, July 1991, at p 7.
      £8,000 settlement—stillborn baby after Caesarean section, disputed abnormal grief reaction;
(ii) *Winter v Tower Hamlets Health Authority* [1991] *AVMA Journal*, July 1991, at p 6.
      £11,000 settlement—stillbirth of second twin, psychiatric damage to mother but she would have been likely to develop a puerperal illness in any event, although of less seriousness;
(iii) *Picken v Salford Health Authority* [1991] *AVMA Journal*, October 1991, p 7.
      £10,000 settlement—stillborn baby after nine-hour labour, psychiatric damage, following pregnancy mother underwent an abortion but thereafter had a healthy child;
(iv) *Parnell v North Warwickshire Health Authority* [1992] *AVMA Journal*, April 1992, p 12.
      £20,000 settlement—intra-uterine foetal death, stillborn baby induced, mother claimed loss of earnings during further pregnancy (award reflected £10,000 general damages, no psychiatric damage mentioned);
(v)   *Best v Waltham Forest Health Authority* [1992] *AVMA Journal*, July 1992, p 16.
      £17,500 settlement—stillborn baby delivered by Caesarean section, mother suffered clinical depression;

(vi) *Wheeler v Southampton and South East Hampshire Health Authority* [1995] *Clinical Risk and AVMA Medical and Legal Journal* vol 1 no 1.
£18,000 settlement—stillbirth to mother with vulnerable personality;

(vii) *Robson v Sunderland Health Authority* [1995] *Clinical Risk and AVMA Medical and Legal Journal* September 1995 vol 1 no 5.
£12,500 settlement—post-mortem described baby as stillborn but there was a dispute whether it had lived at all, psychiatric damage, Caesarean section;

(viii) *Hill v Dudley Health Authority* [1996] *Clinical Risk and AVMA Medical and Legal Journal* January 1996 vol 2 no 1.
£23,000 settlement—stillborn baby, ruptured uterus, mother sterilised to avoid risk of pregnancy and further rupture of the uterus, mother suffered post-traumatic stress disorder and depression;

(ix) *Griffiths v South Manchester Health Authority* [1998] *Clinical Risk and AVMA Medical and Legal Journal* July 1998 vol 4 no 4.
£18,500 settlement—claimant reported her waters had broken but was sent home from hospital for four days until admitted when there was no foetal heart rate and was delivered stillborn baby. The claimant suffered a pathological grief reaction. Liability was denied and the case settled very shortly before trial;

(x) *Joyce and Joyce v Sandwell Healthcare NHS Trust* [1998] *Clinical Risk and AVMA Medical and Legal Journal* vol 4 p 57.
£29,000 settlement on behalf of both parents: £23,000 for mother and £6,000 for father, both claims included general damages for psychiatric damage, counselling costs, loss of earnings. The parents' first child was stillborn or died very shortly after birth (the claim for bereavement was not pursued and the notes described the birth as a 'stillbirth'). The mother suffered moderately severe depression, she quickly became pregnant again but in view of the experience of the first birth underwent an elective Caesarean section for the second birth, involving additional pain and injury;

(xi) *Wilson v Rochdale Health Care Trust* [1999] *Clinical Risk and AVMA Medical and Legal Journal* vol 5 p 69.
£18,000 settlement—stillbirth after five hours of failure to progress and delivery by ventouse of stillborn baby. Mother suffered grief reaction and post-traumatic stress disorder, three years after the birth the prognosis was her symptoms would settle in a further 12–18 months. Mother also claimed loss of earnings for the period of a further pregnancy;

(xii) *Baylis v Worcester Royal Infirmary* [1999] *Clinical Risk and AVMA Medical and Legal Journal* vol 5 p 218.
£10,000 settlement—stillbirth of mother's fourth child after the hospital had failed to interpret blood tests and diagnose cholestasis. The hospital admitted liability and negotiated the settlement direct without intervention of solicitors;

(xiii) *G v A Hospital Trust* [2000] *Clinical Risk and AVMA Medical and Legal Journal* vol 6 p 163.

£23,000 settlement—stillbirth following foetal distress on the CTG which the midwife ignored. Both parents suffered distress but wished to claim swiftly and without claiming for future loss of earnings due to psychiatric damage or for the rigours of a further pregnancy;

(xiv) *F v Kingston Hospital NHS Trust* [2000] *Clinical Risk and AVMA Medical and Legal Journal* vol 6 p 210.

£40,000 settlement—stillbirth after induction at 39 weeks following failure to recognise intra-uterine growth retardation. This was the mother's first pregnancy achieved after three cycles of IVF. The mother suffered a serious ongoing depressive illness;

(xv) *M v Guy's and St Thomas' Hospital NHS Trust* [2000] *Clinical Risk and AVMA Medical and Legal Journal* vol 7 p 73.

£15,000 settlement—general damages following a stillbirth, mother suffered depressive episodes for the following year until she gave birth to a healthy baby;

(xvi) *Bacon v Nottingham Health Authority* [2000] *Clinical Risk and AVMA Medical and Legal Journal* vol 7 p 114.

£20,000 settlement on quantum following contested trial on liability, death of baby shortly before birth from a true knot in the cord, the baby should have been delivered prior to this by Caesarean section;

(xvii) *Begum v Luton and Dunstable NHS Trust* [2004] *Clinical Risk and AVMA Medical and Legal Journal* vol 10 p 242.

£76,000 settlement—stillborn baby after claimant's first pregnancy when the registrar misinterpreted CTG traces as normal on several occasions. An Ombudsman's report criticised the midwives for failing to challenge the Registrar's interpretation of the CTG trace. The Registrar was described as having 'very little insight' into what he had done wrong and the Ombudsman recommended an audit of the interpretation of CTGs in that hospital. A psychiatric report described the claimant as suffering from moderate to severe pathological grief reaction, she was unable to work but it was predicted with treatment she should be able to work after a further year.

Damages were assessed as follows:

General damages	£22,000
Special damages	£54,000
Including:	
Past and future loss of earnings	
Past and future care costs	
Past and future treatment costs	
Travel expenses	
Funeral costs	

22.66 Claims relating to stillborn babies are outside the Fatal Accidents Act 1976 and there is therefore no claim for bereavement. The cases reflect that a sum at least equivalent to the statutory bereavement sum will usually be awarded by some other means. In *Bagley v North Herts Health Authority* [1986] NLJ 1014 Simon Brown J awarded damages as follows:

(i) loss of the satisfaction and joy of a successfully concluded pregnancy and the arrival of a healthy planned baby;

(ii) loss of the prospect of adding a further child to her family;

(iii) damages for the physical suffering and depressive illness resulting from her loss which had already lasted four years at the date of trial.

22.67 In *Kerby v Redbridge Health Authority* [1993] PIQR Q1, Ognall J refused to order damages on the basis of (i) above as he found that would constitute double recovery for bereavement. Ognall J also doubted whether damages could properly be recovered on the basis of (ii) above but did not need to decide that point on the facts of the *Kerby* case. However *Kerby* was a case where the baby had lived and bereavement damages were recoverable, damages under (i) were awarded by Simon Brown J in circumstances where no bereavement damages were recoverable, so double recovery was not a risk. The doubt cast on both (i) and (ii) in the *Kerby* case was therefore obiter. Both Ognall J and Simon Brown J relied on *McLoughlin v O'Brian* [1983] 1 AC 410 in support of their viewpoint. *Alcock v Chief Constable of South Yorkshire* [1992] 1 AC was not referred to by Ognall J although decided three months before. Both are decisions at first instance.

22.68 Other heads that may be claimed by a mother where a baby dies shortly before birth are as follows:

(i) Psychiatric damages can include various elements, eg:
  - shock and distress in discovering her baby was dead and still inside her or shock and distress of discovering the baby is dead when it arrives;
  - pain, suffering, and distress during the period after the death of the baby and before it was stillborn, in cases where it is already dead and needs to be induced;
  - residual pain, suffering, and distress resulting in psychological disturbance and clinical depression after she returned home without her baby (which may be increased by the reaction of other children and the husband's reaction).

(ii) Physical pain and discomfort, eg:
  - milk continuing to fill the breasts;
  - womb not contracting back after the stillbirth;
  - infection;
  - an unnecessary Caesarean scar.

(iii) The cost, inconvenience, and risks of a further pregnancy which would be a reasonable course to take on her part to compensate her in some way for the loss of the baby (this may include loss of earnings in a further pregnancy).

(iv) Special damages:
  • cost of layette;
  • funeral expenses.

Both the father and mother may recover as secondary victims (see (xiii) above) if **22.69** they suffer recognised psychiatric symptoms for which damages will be recoverable if medical evidence is available in support.

Claims in Respect of Babies who Die soon after Birth

Leading cases which illustrate the appropriate heads of damage are: **22.70**

  (i) *Kralj v McGrath* [1986] 1 All ER 54;
  (ii) *Kerby v Redbridge Health Authority* [1994] PIQR Q1.

Further cases reported in the *AVMA Journal* and *Clinical Risk and AVMA Medical* **22.71** *and Legal Journal* are as follows:

  (i) *Phillips v Salford Health Authority* [1991] *AVMA Journal* April, p 14.
      £19,784 settlement—baby damaged at birth died after nine months, damages for psychiatric damage to mother, pain and suffering of further pregnancy, bereavement, funeral expenses, additional cost of care of a damaged child, layette;
  (ii) *Re N Ridley (dec'd)* [1992] *AVMA Journal*, January, p 15.
      £11,500 settlement—death after three hours of baby delivered by elective Caesarean, abnormal grief reaction, damages for bereavement under Fatal Accidents Act, funeral expenses, graveyard visits, loss of earnings, general damages £6,000;
  (iii) *Mrs M v Darlington Health Authority* [1992] *AVMA Journal*, April.
      £17,500 settlement—death after two hours after forceps delivery in which double fold of dura mater was torn, mother had pre-disposition to psychological damage;
  (iv) *Baker v Dartford and Gravesend Health Authority* [1992] *AVMA Journal*, April, p 14.
      £16,000 settlement—death after seven months of second twin who suffered severe asphyxia at birth, mother suffered cervical tears and very heavy bleeding, damages for bereavement, pain and suffering of child, cost of care for brief periods at home, travelling expenses, psychiatric damage;

(v) *Re Mrs M* (Scottish case) [1992] *AVMA Journal* October, p 13.

£45,500 settlement for mother and father—death after five days after failed forceps delivery and Caesarean section, psychiatric damage, mother could not have further children;

(vi) *Armitage v North Tees Health Authority* [1993] *AVMA Journal*, January, p 17.

£22,000 settlement for mother and father—death after ten days after forceps delivery, damages for bereavement, psychiatric damage to both parents, £500 pain suffering loss of amenity for the child, nursing care, funeral expenses;

(vii) *Re W* [1993] *AVMA Journal*, summer, p 9.

£40,000 settlement for mother and father—death after four months, bereavement damages, psychiatric damage both parents, cost of care;

(viii) *Re Lorna Charlesworth* [1994] *AVMA Journal*, winter, p 11, spring, p 11.

£22,500 settlement—death after nine weeks of second twin, coroner's verdict of misadventure exacerbated by lack of care;

(ix) *Re Griffiths (dec'd)* [1996] *Clinical Risk and AVMA Medical and Legal Journal*, January, vol 2 no 1.

£11,000 settlement—death after one hour after Caesarean section, damages for bereavement, loss of earnings, funeral expenses;

(x) *Nakakande v North Middlesex NHS Trust* [1995] *Clinical Risk and AVMA Medical and Legal Journal* vol 1 no 4, p 151.

£20,000 settlement—death after eight months, baby born after long and difficult labour, damages for pain and suffering of child £4,000, funeral expenses £4,000, visits to hospital meals and loss of earnings £4,500, bereavement £7,500, no claim for psychiatric damage;

(xi) *Re S* [1996] *Clinical Risk and AVMA Medical and Legal Journal*, March vol 2 no 2.

£15,000—settlement in respect of a baby who died on the day it was born, £7,5000 bereavement, together with damages for the rigours of a further pregnancy, and an abnormal grief reaction;

(xii) *T v Huddersfield NHS Trust* [1998] *Clinical Risk and AVMA Medical and Legal Journal*, January vol 4 p 29. Second twin died shortly after birth when there had been a delay in delivery, the hospital claimed that this was partly due to the lack of availability of an obstetric theatre. The case settled before the issue of proceedings.

£27,500 settlement to include bereavement damages, some loss of earnings for each parent immediately after the death, general damages including psychological damage for the mother and the need for another pregnancy and Caesarean delivery to complete her family;

(xiii) *B v Forest Healthcare NHS Trust* [1998] *Clinical Risk and AVMA Medical and Legal Journal*, March.

£25,000 settlement—claim arising out of the death of a baby after 35 days when there had been delay in delivery despite a bradycardic trace.

The claim was as follows:

General damages:

Pain and suffering for 35 days for the baby	£2,000
Post-traumatic stress disorder of mother	£14,000
Special damages	
Bereavement	£7,500
Burial costs and flowers	£50
Baby equipment	£200
Past travel to hospital and cemetery	£230
Future travel to cemetery	£500
Interest on past losses	£550

(xiv) *M v Ealing Hospital NHS Trust* [2000] *Clinical Risk and AVMA Medical and Legal Journal*, vol 6 p 36.

£30,000 settlement—baby died a few hours after birth from damage to the cranial vault and a haemorrhage caused by a combination of inept attempts at ventouse and forceps delivery. The mother suffered post-traumatic stress disorder;

(xv) *M v City Sunderland Hospitals NHS Trust* [2000] *Clinical Risk and AVMA Medical and Legal Journal*, vol 7 p 199.

£245,000 settlement—the claimant was a nurse whose first baby died a few hours after birth, she suffered profound and chronic psychiatric reaction diagnosed as post-traumatic stress disorder, she underwent counselling including residential counselling and drug therapy but this was all unsuccessful. The claimant went on to have two further children but this aggravated her psychiatric condition and she was unable to return to work again and needed care. The schedule of loss came to £500,000, general damages were assessed at £40,000–£50,000;

(xvi) *Okpara v Central Sheffield University Hospitals NHS Trust* [2000] *Clinical Risk and AVMA Medical and Legal Journal*, vol 7 p 118.

£20,000 settlement—death of baby three days after birth. The mother suffered a reactive depression for ten months following the death and for a few months during a subsequent pregnancy.

Damages were assessed as follows:

General damages for the mother	£6,100
General damages for the baby for three days	£600
Bereavement	£7,500
Special damages	£2,500
a. Interest	£3,300

(xvii) *K v Guy's and St Thomas' NHS Trust* [2002] *Clinical Risk and AVMA Medical and Legal Journal*, vol 8 p 40.

£94,000 settlement—death of a baby days after birth after administration of increasing amounts of Syntocinon with an abnormal CTG trace and foetal heart rate baseline at 110. The claimant suffered a ruptured uterus and required a hysterectomy thereafter and psychiatric damage;

(xviii) *HC v Scarborough & North East Yorkshire Healthcare NHS Trust* [2003] *Clinical Risk and AVMA Medical and Legal Journal*, vol 9 p 246.

£42,500 settlement—death of baby seven months after birth and rupture of the mother's uterus when a trial of scar labour was mismanaged and a request for a Caesarean section refused.

Damages assessed as follows:

General damages mother	£13,000
General damages baby	£10,000
Bereavement	£7,500
Special damages	£12,000

22.72 If the baby is born alive a claim is brought on behalf of the estate of the deceased baby to include a claim under the Law Reform (Miscellaneous Provisions) Act 1934 as well as a Fatal Accidents Act 1976 claim letter of administration are required. The claim for bereavement can be made by either the mother or father or shared between them but is only payable once.

22.73 In addition the mother may have her own claim for pain and suffering and financial loss and the father may have a claim for psychiatric damage.

22.74 In *Kralj v McGrath* [1986] 1 All ER 55, the claimant was 35 years of age and admitted to a private hospital for the birth of twins. The first twin was born perfectly satisfactorily and survived to be a healthy child. The second twin presented considerable difficulty as it was lying in a transverse position. The Consultant defendant placed his arm inside the plaintiff and attempted manually to turn the baby for a period of 40 minutes during which the plaintiff suffered excruciating pain and she had to be held down by other nursing staff. The baby still did not arrive and a Caesarean section was then performed. The baby that was born by the Caesarean section was very severely injured and only lived for eight weeks in an incubator and then died from the brain damage he suffered during the negligent delivery. The Consultant was found to be negligent in a number of respects. First, in trying to prematurely accelerate labour with a drip (which was thought to have been because he had other commitments the following day). Secondly, he was negligent in the painful manner he unsuccessfully tried to turn the twin. Thirdly, he was negligent in failing to turn the twin and needing to perform a Caesarean section which should not have been required.

The claimant in the *Kralj* case recovered damages under the following heads: **22.75**

• pain and suffering during labour;

• pain and suffering for the residual physical complaints after the delivery;

• nervous shock as a result of being told what had happened to her baby and seeing him in the deformed state that he was;

• inconvenience and distress in travelling to and from hospital to see her baby for the eight weeks it survived;

• grief as a result of the subsequent death of the baby;

• anticipated pain and suffering in respect of a future pregnancy if it were achieved;

• financial loss in respect of a further pregnancy, including loss of earnings and private hospital treatment.

Woolf J (as he then was) considered the possibility of included aggravated   **22.76** damages because of the very severe physical suffering the plaintiff had undergone but concluded that aggravated damages were not appropriate in claims for negligence and that damages were appropriate only as compensation.

In respect of damages for grief Woolf J explains the position as follows: **22.77**

> First of all there can be no doubt that the plaintiff is entitled to be compensated for the shock she undoubtedly suffered as a result of being told what happened to Daniel and of seeing him during her visits. Secondly while damages for grief are not payable in the same way as I indicated when dealing with aggravated damages in the situation where the plaintiff's injuries have on her a more drastic effect than they would otherwise because of the grief which she is sustaining ... that is something the Court can take into account.

As far as the loss claimed for a future pregnancy is concerned Woolf J found that   **22.78** this loss was not too remote and that the hospital could reasonably have foreseen that the plaintiff would want further children. As the plaintiff in that would have completed her ideal family of three had she had twins and been able to go back to work the Judge found she would need to extend this period by a further later pregnancy and consequently suffer loss of earnings. Woolf J awarded the sum of £18,000 in respect of the financial loss incurred by a further pregnancy. The plaintiff also recovered a sum for the time her husband took off work in order to look after her, she also received assistance from her mother and her sister. The Judge awarded £600 for the time taken off work by her husband and £180 for the assistance rendered by her mother and sister.

22.79 In the *Krajl* case the general damages awarded for pain and suffering and loss of amenity of the mother were £10,500. A sum of £2,500 was also awarded to the estate of the dead baby for the pain and suffering of the baby in the eight weeks he survived as a grossly disabled baby. In *Kerby v Redbridge Health Authority* a sum of £750 was awarded for pain, suffering, and loss of amenity to a baby who survived three days and was described by the Judge as having no insight into his condition. In *Nakakande v North Middlesex NHS Trust* [1995] (*Clinical Risk and AVMA Medical and Legal Journal*) a sum of £4,000 in damages was agreed as damages for pain, suffering, and loss of amenity for a baby who lived for about seven months. A brain damaged adult who survived for three months and never fully regained consciousness recovered £9,000 in the case of *Cooke v Prushki* (1992) *Kemp and Kemp* A2-011.

23

SEXUAL ASSAULTS

A. Recognition of the Problem

A sexual assault of a patient by a health care professional will always be a criminal **23.01** offence. Legislation now deals separately with assaults by those in positions of trust. The Sexual Offences (Amendment) Act 2000 creates a specific and new offence of sexual activity by a person in a position of trust. This legislation is a further step in the growing recognition of the problems arising from sexual abuse. The potential for abuse of both adults and children placed in a vulnerable position with respect to abusers had not previously been sufficiently appreciated. The damage such abuse may cause has now been better acknowledged and understood. The increased public awareness of the problem has led to developments in the criminal law as well as public inquiries and widespread civil litigation arising from sexual abuse.

23.02 The issues that arise in respect of sexual abuse are complex. The points that have been clearly recognised include the following:

- where one person is in a position of power or trust over a more vulnerable person the opportunity for sexual abuse may arise;

- the position of power or control that an abuser has over their victim may prevent the more vulnerable person being able to report the abuse for many years or at all;

- the fact that the opportunity for abuse arises also gives rise to the opportunity for false allegations to be made.

23.03 The task of investigation of sexual abuse is a particularly difficult one. The abuse typically takes place in private and the investigation often requires a judgment to be made between the account of the alleged victim and the account of the alleged abuser. It is obvious that a potentially vulnerable victim needs to be protected. Allegations of abuse, which may be painful and difficult for the victim to make, need always to be taken seriously. On the other hand, because of the opportunity for false allegations, the alleged abuser may also need protection. False allegations can have a devastating impact on the professional career of the alleged abuser as well as his/her personal reputation and family life. A very careful balance needs to be struck between the interests of the parties concerned.

23.04 Investigation of abuse has frequently included allegations of abuse against:

- teachers;
- care workers;
- social workers;
- prison officers;
- priests;
- doctors;
- dentists;
- nurses.

23.05 All of these professionals are placed in positions of trust over potentially vulnerable people and particularly children.

23.06 The Sexual Offences (Amendment) Act 2000 provides that an offence will be committed where a person over the age of 18 engages in sexual activity with a person under that age, if the older person is in a position of trust in relation to the younger person.

A position of trust arises where a person under 18 is looked after in a number of **23.07** different circumstances including:

- detention in an institution by virtue of a court order;
- placement in a home or accommodation under the Children Act 1989;
- placement in accommodation provided by a voluntary organisation;
- care in hospital;
- care in a residential care home, nursing home, mental nursing home, or private hospital;
- care in a community home, voluntary home, children's home, or residential establishment;
- receipt of full-time education in an educational institution.

A person over 18 is described as looking after a person under 18 for the purposes **23.08** of this offence if 'he is regularly involved in caring for, training, supervising or being in sole charge of such persons'.

A hospital is described as having the meaning given by section 128(1) of the **23.09** National Health Service Act 1977 and a nursing home and mental nursing home have the meanings given by sections 21(1) and 22(1) respectively of the Registered Homes Act 1984.

The ingredients of this new offence are described below. It is clearly intended **23.10** specifically to address, amongst other problems, the potential abuse of patients under 18 years of age by doctors and nurses. Prior to this offence prosecution of doctors or nurses occurred under the other general provisions discussed below. This new offence may now be used to cover any sexual activities between a doctor or nurse and his/her patients under 18 years.

B. Statutory Provisions in Respect of Criminal Offences of Indecent Assault and Indecency with Children

The Sexual Offences Act 1956 contains two separate offences of indecent assault: **23.11**

- section 14: Indecent assault on a woman;
- section 15: Indecent assault on a man.

The Indecency with Children Act 1960 as amended by section 39 of the Criminal **23.12** Justice and Court Services Act 2000 contains a separate offence of:

- Gross indecency with or towards a child under the age of 16.

23.13 The Sexual Offences (Amendment) Act 2000 creates the new offence involving sexual activity by a person over the age of 18 with a person under that age where the older person is in a position of trust in relation to the younger person. These provisions came into force on 8 January 2001 pursuant to the provisions of the Sexual Offences (Amendment) Act 2000 (Commencement No 1) Order 2000.

23.14 Following the Crime (Sentences) Act 1997 the maximum sentence for the offences of indecent assault on a man or a woman and indecency with children is ten years' imprisonment. For the new offence of sexual activity when in a position of trust towards a person under 18 the maximum sentence is five years.

C. The Offence of Indecent Assault on a Woman

23.15 Section 14 of the Sexual Offences Act 1956 (SOA 1956) provides that it is an offence for a person to make an indecent assault on a woman.

23.16 Section 14(2) of SOA 1956 specifically provides that a girl under the age of 16 cannot in law give any consent which would prevent an act being an assault.

23.17 A reasonable belief that the victim was 16 years of age will not constitute a defence to this offence.

23.18 Section 14(4) of the SOA 1956 specifically provides that a woman who is a 'defective' cannot give consent so as to prevent an act being an assault.

23.19 Defective is defined in section 45 of SOA 1956 as 'a person suffering from a state of arrested or incomplete development of mind which includes severe impairment of intelligence and social functioning'.

23.20 Whether a victim comes within this definition will be a matter of fact to be decided by a jury rather than a matter of technical expert opinion. Severe impairment is to be measured against the standards of normal persons.

23.21 It will be a defence for a defendant to show that he did not know that the victim was a defective and that he believed the victim was consenting to the act complained of. In the case of a woman over 16 years of age consent may be a defence. It will be sufficient in the case of a woman over 16 for the defendant to show the accused believed the woman was consenting to his conduct whether his belief is based on reasonable grounds or not unless:

- consent was procured by fraud as to the nature or quality of the act; or
- the indecent act to which consent was given consists of blows intended or likely to cause bodily harm.

To prove the offence of indecent assault on a female the prosecution must **23.22**
prove:

- that the accused intentionally assaulted the victim;
- that the assault in the circumstances in which it was committed is capable by right-minded persons as being considered indecent;
- the assault was indecent in itself or the accused intended to commit an assault that would be considered by right-minded persons as indecent.

An assault (or battery) is an act by which a person intentionally or recklessly **23.23**
causes another to apprehend (or sustain) immediate unlawful violence. It must
therefore be the defendant who touches or threatens to touch the victim. In the
case of *Fairclough v Whipp* 35 Cr App R 138 DC, [1951] 2 All ER 834, the
defendant exposed his penis to a girl of nine and asked her to touch it, which she
did. It was held that an invitation by the defendant to touch him could not
amount to an assault. This behaviour would now constitute an offence under
section 1 of the Indecency with Children Act 1960.

D. The Offence of Indecent Assault on a Man

This offence is contained in section 15 of the SOA 1956 and is in similar terms **23.24**
to the offence of indecent assault on a woman. Either a man or a woman may be
guilty of indecent assault on both a woman and a man: see *R v Hare* [1934] 1 KB
354, 24 Cr App R 108 CCA.

Neither a boy under 16 nor a defective can give consent to an indecent assault. **23.25**
In respect of a defective it is a defence that the defendant did not know the victim was a defective and believed the victim was consenting. Similarly to the
offence against a girl, it is no defence that the defendant believed the man was
over 16 years of age.

E. The Offence of Indecency with Children under the Age of 16

Section 1(1) of the Indecency with Children Act 1960 (as amended) provides: **23.26**

> Any person who commits an act of gross indecency with or towards a child under the
> age of [16], or who incites a child under that age to such an act with him or another,
> shall be liable on conviction on indictment to imprisonment for a term not exceed-
> ing 10 years.

This offence as distinct from an offence of indecent assault can be committed **23.27**
where the adult defendant invites or encourages a child to touch the defendant or

to participate in the adult's sexual activities. Examples of behaviour which would constitute this offence are:

- an adult who invites a child to touch his penis;

- an adult who allows a child who has voluntarily placed his hand on the defendant's penis to leave it there for period of time. In *R v Speck*, 65 Cr App R 161, CA, an adult allowed a child to continue to place her hand on his penis for a period of five minutes, the Court of Appeal held the jury should have been directed that the defendant's conduct might constitute an offence under this section if it amounted to an invitation to the child to continue this activity and if it amounted to an act of gross indecency;

- an adult who masturbates in front of a child and thereby obtains satisfaction from knowing the child was watching. See *R v Francis* 88 Cr App R 127;

- an adult who photographs children partially clothed and unclothed for the purposes of selling photographs to magazines. In *R v Sutton* 66 Cr App R 21, CA, the Court of Appeal found such action would not constitute an indecent assault on a man even if the boys were touched in order to place them in suitable poses if the touching was not threatening or hostile;

- any sexual activity between a person over 16 years and a person under 16, whether or not the person under 16 years is consenting.

23.28 The history of this offence and the ingredients were considered by the House of Lords in the case of *B (a minor) v DPP* [2000] 2 WLR 452, HL. In that case Lord Nicholls described how:

> An indecent assault on a woman is a criminal offence. So is an indecent assault on a man. Neither a boy nor a girl under the age of 16 can, in law, give any consent which would prevent an act being an assault. These offences have existed for many years. Currently they are to be found in sections 14 and 15 of the Sexual Offences Act 1956. They have their origins in sections 52 and 62 of the Offences against the Person Act 1861.
>
> In the early 1950s a lacuna in this legislation became apparent. A man was charged with indecent assault on a girl aged 9. At the man's invitation the girl had committed an indecent act on the man. The Court of Criminal Appeal held that an invitation to another person to touch the inviter could not amount to an assault on the invitee. As the man had done nothing to the girl which, if done against her will, would have amounted to an assault on her, the man's conduct did not constitute an indecent assault on the girl. That was the case of *Fairclough v Whipp* [1951] 2 AER 834. Two years later the same point arose and was similarly decided regarding a girl aged 11: see *Director of Public Prosecutions v Rogers* [1953] 1 WLR 1017. Following a report of the Criminal Law Revision Committee in August 1959 (First Report: Indecency with Children (Cmnd 835)), Parliament enacted the Indecency with Children Act 1960. Section 1(1) of this Act makes it a criminal offence to commit an act of gross indecency with or towards a child under the age of 14 [now 16], or to incite a child

under that age to such an act. The question raised by the appeal concerns the mental element in this offence so far as the age ingredient is concerned.

Lord Nicholls points out that the section says nothing about what shall be the **23.29** position if the person who commits or incites the act of gross indecency honestly but mistakenly believed that the child was over the requisite age (now 16) and goes on to point out that:

> In principle, an age-related ingredient of a statutory offence stands on no different footing from any other ingredient. If a man genuinely believes that the girl with whom he is committing a grossly indecent act is over 14, he is not intending to commit such an act with a girl under 14. Whether such an intention is an essential ingredient of the offence depends upon a proper construction of section 1 of the 1960 Act ... I cannot find, either in the statutory context or otherwise, any indication of sufficient cogency to displace the application of the common law presumption. In my view the necessary mental element regarding the age ingredient in section 1 of the Act of 1960 is the absence of a genuine belief by the accused that the victim was 14 years of age or above. The burden of proof of this rests upon the prosecution in the usual way. If Parliament considers that the position should be otherwise regarding this serious social problem, Parliament must itself confront the difficulties and express its will in clear terms.

A reasonable belief that the victim was 16 years of age will therefore constitute a **23.30** defence to an offence of indecency with children under 16. In the House of Lords Lord Nicholls also expressed some doubt as to the correctness of the decisions in *R v Maughan* 24 Cr App R 130, CCA. Other members of the House of Lords stressed the distinctions between sections 14 and 15 of SOA 1956 and section 1 of the Indecency with Children Act 1960. It was pointed out that the later Act has much wider implications in that it does not require a sexual assault to actually take place.

This distinction was subsequently adopted by the Court of Appeal in *R v K* The **23.31** Times, 7 November 2000, who held that the prosecution was not required to prove absence of the defendant's genuine belief as to the girl's age. The House of Lords however allowed the defendant's appeal and found that there was an overriding presumption of statutory interpretation that mens rea was an essential ingredient of every statutory offence, unless Parliament had indicated by express words or by necessary implication that it should be excluded; that no express words were contained in either section 14 or elsewhere in the 1956 Act which would exclude the need for the prosecution to prove absence of genuine belief by a defendant as to the age of an underage complainant: *R v K* [2001] UKHL 41, [2001] 3 WLR 471 (HL). The Court of Appeal had found that the position was that it was a defence to an offence of indecency with a child under the Indecency with Children Act 1960 for the defendant to show he did not believe the victim was under 16 years of age. But that it was not a defence under sections 14 and 15 of SOA 1956 for the defendant to prove he did not believe the victim was under 16 years of age.

23.32 The House of Lords found this position to be anomalous and found that in both cases the prosecution was required to prove absence of genuine belief on the part of the defendant that the girl was 16. The House of Lords gave an affirmative answer to the question:

> Is a defendant entitled to be acquitted of the offence of indecent assault on a complainant under the age of 16 years, contrary to section 14(1) of the Sexual Offences Act 1956, if he may hold an honest belief that the complainant in question was aged 16 years or over?

23.33 Lord Bingham summarised the position as follows:

> Nothing in this opinion has any bearing on a case in which the victim does not in fact consent. While section 14(2) provides that a girl under the age of 16 cannot in law give any consent which would prevent an act being an assault, she may in fact (although not in law) consent. If it is shown that she did not consent, and the defendant did not genuinely believe that she consented, any belief by the defendant concerning her age is irrelevant, since her age is relevant only to her capacity to consent.

23.34 Lord Bingham concluded that:

> Nothing in this opinion should be taken to minimize the potential seriousness of the offence of indecent assault. Whilst some instances of the offence may be relatively minor, others may be scarcely less serious than rape itself. This is reflected in the maximum penalty, now increased to 10 years and the mandatory requirement that those convicted be subjected to the notification requirements of the Sex Offenders Act 1997. See *R v K* [2001] 3 WLR 471 at 481F–482F.

F. The Ingredients of the Offence of Abuse of Position of Trust

23.35 Section 3 of the Sexual Offences (Amendment) Act 2000 provides that:

> It shall be an offence for a person aged 18 or over:
> (i) to have sexual intercourse (whether vaginal or anal) with a person under that age; or
> (ii) to engage in any other sexual activity with or directed towards such a person if (in either case) he is in a position of trust in relation to that person.

23.36 Position of trust is given an extensive definition in terms of the institutions that the person under 18 may be detained in or placed in as described above. The person in a position of trust is the person over 18 years who looks after the person under 18 in any of these institutions or places including schools, NHS Hospitals, private hospitals, care homes, mental nursing homes, other nursing homes, detention centres, community homes.

Sexual activity is defined in section 1(5) so that it: **23.37**

   (i) does not include any activity which a reasonable person would regard as sexual only with knowledge of the intentions, motives or feelings of the parties; but

  (ii) subject to that, means any activity which such a person would regard as sexual in all the circumstances.

Specific defences are provided in the legislation in an attempt to avoid some of **23.38** the difficulties in interpretation discussed above. It is a defence for the adult in a position of trust to prove:

   (i) he did not know and could not reasonably have been expected to know that [the other person] was under 18;

  (ii) he did not know and could not reasonably have been expected to know that [the other person] was a person in relation to when he was in a position of trust; or

 (iii) he was lawfully married to [the other person].

It is unlikely that a doctor or nurse would be able to show that he/she did not **23.39** know or could not reasonably have been expected to know the age of the patient or that he/she did not know or could not have been expected to know that he/she was in a position of trust in respect of the patient.

G. The Current Position

Increased awareness of the potential for sexual abuse of vulnerable people, in par- **23.40** ticular those assumed to be unable to consent to sexual activity, has led to further legislation in the area of criminal law. The age when sexual activity with a child is assumed to be unlawful has been raised to 16 and a new offence has been introduced covering sexual activity with persons under 18 years when the person over 18 years is in a position of trust towards the younger person.

The difficulties for professionals accused of such abuse remain stark and sus- **23.41** pension from employment frequently follows accusations. There is an obvious need for clear protocols to avoid doctors and nurses being placed in a position where such abuse could occur and such accusations could be made. However, the prospect of no professional ever being alone with a patient is both an unrealistic and unhelpful one. The need to maintain the balance between a relationship of trust between patient and doctor and a position where the patient is safe from abuse and the doctor safe from false accusations will always present a challenge.

H. Features of Civil Claims for Assault or Abuse

23.42 Claims arising out of sexual assaults differ from clinical negligence claims in a number of important respects:

- the medical records are unlikely to record the event, the evidence will depend entirely on the client's account;

- expert evidence will not be required to prove liability, the *Bolam* test does not apply;

- clients often are unable to report sexual assaults until many years after the event, as part of the damage caused by the assault is the inability to talk about it;

- the limitation period for a claim in assault against the doctor or other health care professional will have a six-year non-extendable limitation period;

- the limitation period for a claim based on vicarious liability for the health care professional by the employer will also have a six-year non-extendable limitation period;

- the health care professional's insurer may decline cover for a claim brought for deliberate sexual assault.

23.43 It will be necessary to investigate whether the claim can be brought in negligence against the employer (the NHS Trust or Health Authority or other) for failing to supervise or failing to investigate complaints about the health care professional. A claim in negligence will have a three-year limitation period extendable pursuant to sections 11 and 14 of the Limitation Act 1980.

23.44 It may also be necessary to consider whether the health care professional was negligent in failing to report their own abuse or failing to treat the patient for the psychiatric damage the professional has caused by the abuse.

I. Causes of Action against a Doctor who has Assaulted a Patient

23.45 A doctor (or other health care professional) will personally be liable in damages for any assaults deliberately carried out by him. In *Stubbings v Webb* [1993] AC 498, the House of Lords held that a claim for deliberate assault has a six-year non-extendable time limit, as discussed below under limitation. Under the existing state of the law a claim against an individual for assault can only be brought:

- within six years of the assault;
- within six years of the claimant attaining 18 years;

- if the claimant was a patient within CPR 21.1 and the Mental Health Act 1983 when the assault occurred and has remained a patient.

An individual cannot be found negligent in respect of actions that constitute **23.46** assaults. This was confirmed in the House of Lords in the cases of *Stubbings v Webb* and in *L and ors v Hesley Hall Ltd* [2001] 2 WLR 1311, HL. The position was further considered and affirmed in the Court of Appeal in the case of *KR and ors v Bryn Alyn Community (Holdings) Ltd and Royal and Sun Alliance plc* [2003] EWCA Civ 85.

In some cases it might however be argued that a doctor or other health care pro- **23.47** fessional who has sexually assaulted a patient was also negligent. For example, he may have been negligent in not having a chaperone when seeing female patients and thereby giving himself the opportunity to assault patients. It also might be argued that a doctor was negligent in not reporting his own abuse or in failing to refer a patient he had abused for counselling and psychiatric treatment after the abuse had occurred.

The argument in respect of an abuser not reporting his own abuse was raised in **23.48** the case of *L v Hesley Hall Ltd*. This was a point on which the claimants in the *L v Hesley Hall* case succeeded before the trial Judge. The Court of Appeal reversed the lower court and the House of Lords found it unnecessary to decide the point as they allowed the appeal on the basis that the defendant was vicariously liable for the abuser's deliberate acts without being addressed on the limitation problem raised by *Stubbings v Webb*. Lord Steyn at paragraph 29 of the judgment in the *L v Hesley Hall* case made clear that he considered that the failure to report argu- ment might require further consideration. Lord Hutton specifically agreed with the speech of Lord Steyn. Lord Hobhouse in paragraph 62 specifically stated that in his opinion 'the Court of Appeal were mistaken in not attaching more validity to this way of putting the plaintiff's case'.

Lord Millett was the only member of the House of Lords committee in the **23.49** *L v Hesley Hall* case who clearly found the failure to report argument artificial.

Faced with the argument that only one member of the House of Lords ruled out **23.50** the failure to report argument, there would be a reasonable basis for arguing in a suitable case that the failure to report was a significant breach of duty for which a doctor is responsible or any defendant who employed him is vicariously liable. Allegations of negligence would be subject to sections 11, 14, and 33 of the Limitation Act 1980. In circumstances where a claimant was unable to discuss the abuse for many years and was later required to give evidence in criminal pro- ceedings, there are, as discussed below, very strong arguments for an extension of the limitation period pursuant to sections 11, 14, and 33 of the Limitation Act 1980.

23.51 There are a number of circumstances where a claim might reasonably be brought against a doctor or health care professional personally rather than the Health Authority or NHS Trust that employs him:

- if the doctor is identified as having financial assets to meet a claim;

- the doctor has been convicted of the assault or the case against him is admitted; and

- the claimant was abused less than six years before the claim is brought, or became 18 years of age less than six years before the claim is brought or is a patient for the purposes of the Mental Health Act 1983;

- if there is a reasonable argument that the doctor was negligent or in breach of duty in:
    (i) not having a chaperone for female patients who legitimately required physical examinations; and/or
    (ii) not reporting his own abuse; and/or
    (iii) not referring patients he had injured for counselling and psychiatric treatment. These claims will be subject to sections 11,14, and 33 of the Limitation Act 1980;

- if a claim against the doctor's employer in negligence is not clear-cut as there is no evidence of any earlier suspicion of the doctor or previous complaints;

- if the doctor is self-employed.

23.52 When there are potential difficulties in establishing liability against the NHS body responsible for monitoring a doctor or other health care professional, it will be prudent to issue proceedings against the individual personally. In as far as such claims arise out of deliberate assaults carried out less than six years before issue of the claim the usefulness of doing so will of course depend on whether any assets can be identified.

23.53 In as far as the claims arise out of allegations of breach of duty or negligence are concerned it is possible that such claims will be met by the doctor's MDU or MPS insurance and this will also need to be investigated in individual cases.

J. Causes of Action against an NHS Body for Abuse by an Employee

23.54 The liability of an employer for sexual abuse perpetrated by an employee was established in the decision in *L and Ors v Hesley Hall Ltd* [2001] 2 WLR 1311, HL. In this case the House of Lords held that an employer will be vicariously liable for the acts of an employee who abuses children whilst in the course of purporting to carry out child care duties if the acts are carried out in the course of employment or are closely connected to it. Although this claim was not against an NHS body or a public authority the principles apply to claims against an NHS body in respect of health care employees who abuse patients in the course of their employment or in situations closely connected to their employment.

In the case of *L v Hesley Hall Ltd* the claimants were pupils at a privately owned **23.55** residential school and alleged they were subjected to sexual abuse by a warden at the school. The warden was convicted of sexual abuse and sentenced to seven years' imprisonment. In a claim against the school for damages HH Judge Walker held the school could not be vicariously liable for the sexual abuse of an employee but could be liable for the employee's failure to report the abuse. The Court of Appeal allowed the defendant's appeal and held that the failure to report was so closely connected to the sexual abuse itself that it was outside the course of the employee's employment and the defendant could not be vicariously liable. The House of Lords reversed the decision of the Court of Appeal, overruled the case of *T v North Yorkshire County Council* [1999] IRLR 98, and found that the defendant was vicariously liable for the warden's acts of abuse.

The House of Lords found that the warden of the school had such close contact **23.56** with pupils at the school that there was sufficient connection between the work he was employed to do and the acts of abuse he had committed for those acts to be committed within the scope of his employment. The defendant could therefore be vicariously liable for those acts.

Lord Hobhouse described the position as follows (at paragraph 54 of the **23.57** judgment):

> What these cases and *Trotman's* case in truth illustrate is a situation where the employer has assumed a relationship to the plaintiff which imposes specific duties in tort upon the employer and the role of the employee (or servant) is that he is the person to whom the employer has entrusted the performance of these duties. These cases are examples of that class where the employer, by reason of assuming a relationship to the plaintiff, owes to the plaintiff duties which are more extensive than those owed by the public at large and, accordingly, are to be contrasted with the situation where a defendant is simply in proximity to the plaintiff so that it is foreseeable that his acts may injure the plaintiff or his property and a reasonable person would have taken care to avoid causing such injury ...

> The fact that sexual abuse was involved does not distinguish this case from any other involving the care of the young and vulnerable and the duty to protect them from the risk of harm.

This claim against the owners and managers of a private school had failed in neg- **23.58** ligence as the Judge found it could not be shown that the defendants had been negligent in their care selection and control of the warden. The claim succeeded on the basis that the defendant was held vicariously liable for the abuse perpetrated by the warden. The speeches of Lord Steyn (with whom Lord Hutton agreed) Lord Clyde, and Lord Hobhouse describe the vicarious liability of the defendant in terms of breach of duty. Lord Clyde describes how:

> It appears that the [defendant] gave the warden a quite general authority in the supervision and running of the house as well as some particular responsibilities. His general duty was to look after and to care for, among others, the [claimants]. That function was one which the [defendants] had delegated to him. That he performed that function in a way that was an abuse of his position and an abnegation of his duty does not sever the connection with his employment. The particular acts that he carried out upon the boys have to be viewed not in isolation but in the context and the circumstances in which they occurred. Given that he had a general management of the house and in the care and supervision of the boys in it, the employers should be liable for the way in which he behaved towards them in his capacity as warden of the house. The [defendants] should then be vicariously liable to the [claimants] for the injury that they suffered at the hands of the warden.

23.59 Lord Millett however described the liability of the defendants as vicarious liability 'for the warden's intentional assaults, not (as was suggested in argument) for his failure to perform his duty to take care of the boys'. This left open the important issue as to whether the vicarious liability of the defendants in *L v Hesley Hall Ltd* gives rise to a cause of action for breach of duty with a three-year limitation period (and the extension provisions of sections 11, 14, and 33 of the Limitation Act 1980) or whether it gives rise to a cause of action in trespass with a non-extendable six-year limitation period. In the case of *KR and ors v Bryn Alyn Community (Holdings) Ltd and Royal and Sun Alliance plc* [2003] EWCA Civ 85, the Court of Appeal confirmed that the proper analysis was that the employer was vicariously liable for the criminal acts of the employee so as to involve the same unextendable six-year limitation period.

23.60 Provided a claim can be brought against the NHS body within six years of the assault occurring the claimant need only establish:

- that the assault occurred. If there has been a criminal conviction of the abuser the claimant can rely on section 11 of the Civil Evidence Act 1968 to prove the assault;

- that the abuser was employed by the NHS body at the time of the assault;

- that the assault occurred in the course of the abuser's employment or was closely connected to it. If the assault occurred in the course of treatment or on the hospital premises this is likely to be established.

23.61 However, if the claim is not brought within six years and the claimant needs to rely on allegations of negligence and sections 11, 14, and 33 of the Limitation

Act 1980, then evidence of negligence will be required. This will mean that the claimant will need to establish that the NHS body:

- with reasonable enquiry ought to have ascertained that the abuser was not a suitable employee and should not have employed the abuser at all;

- failed to supervise the abuser and ascertain or prevent the abuse;

- failed to investigate complaints about the abuser made before the claimant was abused and then to prevent the abuser continuing to work.

K. Causes of Action for Abuse by a General Practitioner

Section 29 of the National Health Service Act 1977 provides that: **23.62**

> It is the duty of every Family Practitioner Committee in accordance with regulations, to arrange as respects their locality with medical practitioners to provide personal medical services for all persons in the locality who wish to take advantage of the arrangements. Detailed provisions for the arrangements that should be made follow. These provisions are set out in full and analysed in the case of *Godden v Kent & Medway Strategic Health Authority* [2004] EWHC 1629.

The Judge in the *Godden* case, which arose out of the sexual abuse perpetrated   **23.63**
by Dr Clifford Ayling, analysed the statutory provisions and the authorities relating to provision of services by public authorities including *X v Bedfordshire CC* [1995] 2 AC 633, *Barrett v Enfield LBC* [2001] 2 AC 550, *Gorringe v Calderdale Metropolitan Borough Council* [2004] 2 All ER 326, and *Stovin v Norfolk County Council* [1996] AC 923. He then asked the question:

> Is it arguable that section 29 of the 1977 Act gives rise to a common law duty of care, that is a duty which would not exist but for statute? I put the question in that way because it appears to me that it is only from section 29 that it can be said that any such duty arises. There is no other source for the duty in the 1977 Act.

In respect of the provisions in section 29 the Judge found that no common   **23.64**
law duty of care arises because the provisions of the 1977 Act are concerned with the structure and administration of the National Health Service, and ensuring its comprehensiveness rather than with the provision of particular medical services.

The basis on which the Judge allowed the claim in the case of the *Godden* case to   **23.65**
proceed was that there was a free-standing common law duty of care on the part of the defendant based on vicarious liability for breaches on behalf of employees of the relevant Family Practitioner Committee. The Judge pointed out that 'the peg for the existence of the duty is the receipt of information about Dr Ayling and his activities' and pointed out that the particulars of claim alleged that 'by 1993

there existed a wealth of information, known to some at least of the health care workers employed by the first defendant, about the kind of threat which Dr Ayling posed for women under his treatment'.

23.66 Claims in respect of abuse by a general practitioner may therefore be difficult to establish. It will be necessary to investigate:

- a claim against the abuser himself for assault or negligence;
- whether there are partners who will be responsible for his actions or failing to supervise him;
- whether he was employed by an NHS body for any of his medical treatment;
- whether complaints were made to the Family Practitioner Committee.

L. Limitation

23.67 Following *Stubbings v Webb* and *L v Hesley Hall Ltd* there are particular limitation problems in abuse cases. In the case of *Various Claimants v Bryn Alyn Community Homes Ltd and Anor* (Connell J, 26 June 2001), Connell J found that the claim for deliberate acts of abuse for which the defendant was vicariously liable was subject to a non-extendable six-year limitation period. The Court of Appeal confirmed this position in a decision given on 12 February 2003 in *KR and ors v Bryn Alyn Community (Holdings) Ltd and Royal and Sun Alliance plc* and stated:

> In our view the correct approach is as Lord Millett has expressed it. Whether or not section 11 is in play, it is to identify the wrongful act, deliberate or otherwise, in respect of which vicarious responsibility is claimed and to assess the closeness of its connection to the employment in question. If the act is sufficiently closely connected with the employment, there is vicarious responsibility. In such circumstances and bearing in mind Lord Griffiths reasoning in *Stubbings v Webb* (para 99 above) there is no justification or need, for the purpose of establishing vicarious responsibility, to elide the duty in respect of which the employee's deliberate act is a breach of duty of care delegated or 'entrusted' to him by the employer. The 2 are quite distinct. Where section 11 is under consideration, it follows that claims for personal injury in respect of deliberate conduct, whether considered in the context of vicarious responsibility or not, are not caught by its provisions. Accordingly, in absence of some provable allegation of systemic negligence of the first defendant, we are of the view that its employee's deliberate abuse does not fall within section 11 and is, therefore, governed by a non-extendable 6 year period of limitation rather than an extendable 3 year period.

23.68 Permission to appeal this decision was refused by the House of Lords. The decision was followed by the Court of Appeal in the case of *C v Middlesborough Council* [2004] EWCA Civ 1746. The House of Lords has now granted the claimant permission to appeal in the case of *C v Middlesborough Council*.

In three other cases: **23.69**

   (i) *A v Iorworth Hoare* [2006] EWCA Civ 395;
  (ii) *H v Suffolk County Council and Secretary of State for Constitutional Affairs* [2006] EWCA Civ 395; and
 (iii) *X & Y v London Borough of Wandsworth* [2006] EWCA Civ 395,

the Court of Appeal has granted permission to petition the House of Lords. In each of these cases the claimants suffered psychiatric damage from sexual abuse that was proved or not in dispute. However, in all cases the claims were found to be limitation barred because of the decision in *Stubbings v Webb* [1993] AC 498.

The Master of the Rolls delivered the judgment of the Court (the other members   **23.70**
being Lord Justice Brooke and Lady Justice Arden).

In the judgment the Court stated: **23.71**

> The Court expressed itself willing to grant all the claimants permission to appeal to the House of Lords, so that the House of Lords, which would not be constrained by binding case law, could consider how the issues raised by these appeals could be addressed without the intervention of Parliament.

The Court explained that they hoped: 'The House of Lords itself may be able to   **23.72**
remedy some of the very serious deficiencies and incoherencies in the law as it stands today in a way that we cannot.'

The judgment reviews the history of the cases before and after *Stubbings v Webb*   **23.73**
and the Law Commission recommendations. It pointed out that the Law Commission report was published in 2001 but Parliament has done nothing for five years. In considering the effect of *Stubbings v Webb* the Court pointed to the case of *S v W* and commented:

> It might be thought that in any rational legal system the 3 year extendable limitation period should apply to the claim against the abusing father as well as to the claim against the negligent mother, and that a claimant who does not possess the relevant knowledge before the expiry of the primary limitation period should be permitted in an appropriate case to advance a claim against both such parents and not merely against the less guilty one.

The Court considered the arguments that a teacher could be in breach of duty as   **23.74**
well as committing trespass to the person in some circumstances. In particular when, in his capacity as teacher, he groomed a boy for abuse and did not report his abuse. In respect of these arguments the Court stated:

> On the face of it principle and justice seem to require that when a teacher, in flagrant breach of the duty he owes a pupil in his charge, grooms him and encourages him to perform indecent acts in front of him or watch pornographic videos with him and

performs indecent assaults on him and follows a prolonged policy of favouring him and protecting him from justified complaints by other teachers, so that the child truants in the short term and suffers serious psychiatric harm in the long term, in addition to losing the normal benefit of education, the law should not provide a more relaxed limitation regime for the less serious breaches of duty and a more stringent regime for the more serious breaches.

Unrestrained by authority we would be inclined to follow what appears to be the approach of the majority in *Lister v Hesley Hall* and hold that such a claimant should recover damages for breach of duty in respect of the cumulative effect of all these activities, so that recovery is not confined to those improper activities that do not constitute intentional assaults.

23.75   Further, the Court considered whether it could get round the difficulty, however it concluded:

> In our judgment we are not free to take this course. In *KR v Bryn Alyn* this court expressly preferred the approach of Lord Millett in the *Lister* case as to the non-viability of an alternative claim based on breach of duty ... We considered whether we were able to depart from that part of the judgment in *Bryn Alyn*, but even if we were free to do so we think it would be very much better to leave it to the House of Lords to consider this area of the law as a whole, rather than for different divisions of the Court of Appeal to provide different answers in relation to what is, after all, only one part of a larger scene.

23.76   The limitation position in sexual abuse claims brought in negligence is also governed by the decision of the Court of Appeal in *Bryn Alyn*. The decision of the Court of Appeal in *Bryn Alyn* reviewed and revised the decision of Mr Justice Connell in respect of the application of sections 11, 14, and 33 of the Limitation Act 1980. The position now is that in the area of sexual abuse it is necessary to examine the date on which the claimant was first able to appreciate the significance of what had happened to him; that is when he appreciated the extent of the psychiatric damage that could be attributed to the events. The following passages from the judgment of the Court of Appeal illustrate this point:

> 42. Application of the section 14(2) meaning of 'significance' to child victims of abuse is often the more difficult because many of them, as in the case of these claimants, come to it already damaged and vulnerable because of similar ill-treatment in other settings. For some such behaviour is unpleasant, but familiar. As Mr Owen put it in his supplemental submissions, such misconduct was for many of these claimants 'the norm'; it was committed by persons in authority; and they, the claimants, were powerless to do anything about it. Some victims of physical abuse may have believed that, to some extent, they deserved it. And, in cases of serious sexual abuse unaccompanied by serious physical injury of any permanent or disabling kind, it is not surprising, submitted Mr Owen that they did not see the significance of the conduct in section 14(2) terms, and simply tried to make the best of things.
>
> 43. However artificial it may seem to pose the question in this context, section 14 requires the court, on a case by case basis, to ask whether such an already damaged

child would reasonably turn his mind to litigation as a solution to his problems? The same applies to those, as in the case of many of these claimants who, subsequent to the abuse, progress into adulthood and a twilight world of drugs, further abuse and violence and, in some cases, crime. Some would put the abuse to the back of their minds; some might, as a result or a symptom of an as yet undiagnosed development of psychiatric illness, block or suppress it. Whether such a reaction is deliberate or unconscious, whether or not it is a result of some mental impairment, the question remains whether and when such a person would have reasonably seen the significance of his injury so as turn his mind to litigation in the sense required by section 14(1)(a) and (2) to start the period of limitation running. At this stage the section 14(1)(b) issue of actual or constructive knowledge of attributability becomes more of a live issue than it would have been at or shortly after the abuse, because in some cases it might only be after the intervention of a psychiatrist that a claimant realises that there could have been a causal link between the childhood abuse and the psychiatric problems suffered as an adult, an argument accepted by the Court of Appeal, but which Lord Griffiths found difficult to accept, in *Stubbings v Webb*.

The Court of Appeal, therefore, accepted the argument that had been rejected by **23.77** Mr Justice Connell that victims of abuse often do not have the requisite knowledge to start the limitation period running against them until they can begin to talk about the abuse, and can take medical and legal advice. There is no reason why this should be confined to child victims. Much of what is stated in the passage quoted above would also apply to adult victims of abuse by health care professionals.

The Court of Appeal in *Bryn Alyn* went on to analyse the position in the 14 indi- **23.78** vidual cases. The following is a typical example of this analysis:

> As to limitation, the claimant issued proceedings in January 1998, that is 18 months earlier than most of the other claimants. The last of the abuse in respect of which he claimed was in 1981 some 17 years before. The Judge held that he had the requisite knowledge under section 14 before he left *Bryn Alyn* in early 1981, which, if correct, put his claim nearly 12 years after the expiry of the limitation period. The Judge said, at paragraph 95 of his judgment:
>
>> I accept ... that the claimant must have known in respect of the sexual abuse that what was done to him was wrong and that he had suffered significant injury. He must have known this before he left *Bryn Alyn*. Equally he knew that the injury suffered was at least in part attributable to the failure of the staff to protect him. That said, what he did not realise until he saw his solicitors and the doctors thereafter instructed was the extent of the damage that this wrongful abuse had caused him. In February 1997 the claimant saw a psychiatrist at his own request whilst in prison. This was shortly after he had made his statement to the Waterhouse Inquiry on 31st January 1997.

Further the Court of Appeal stated: **23.79**

> For the reasons we have given earlier in this judgment and on the available evidence in this claim, we are of the view that the Judge wrongly concluded that DJ had

knowledge of significant injury for the purpose of section 14 by the end of the abuse in 1981 or within 3 years after his majority, by 1986, so as to prevent him from relying on that provision. More accurately, in our view, on the evidence before the Judge as to the nature and circumstances of the claimant, the manner of the abuse and the time at which it occurred, he would not have reasonably considered that the abuse, despite its seriousness, would justify the institution of proceedings. The Judge's distinction in saying that he did not know 'the extent of the damage' until much later does not engage the meaning in section 14(1)(a) and (2) of the 'significance' of the injury, as explained by Bingham LJ, as he then was, in *Stubbings v Webb*, in the passage that we have set out in paragraph 36 above. Even allowing for the seriousness of the abuse alleged, the Judge's approach also overlooks the fact that such test has to be applied to conduct taking place in a wholly different climate of public opinion and attitudes over twenty years ago. And it is plain from the Judge's remarks and assessment of damages further on his judgment, at paragraph 97, that the only 'extent' of damage which he had in mind was lately developed post traumatic stress disorder: In my view this claimant has suffered significant distress since early 1997, which distress is likely to recur, albeit on a diminishing scale, for the indefinite future. The doctors agree that his tendency to lose control when in temper has been precipitated by his experiences of racial abuse as a child and his experiences of sexual and physical abuse at *Bryn Alyn*. Having seen the claimant in the witness box over half a day, I conclude that he is likely to mature further and to overcome his difficulties as time proceeds, getting on with his life in a more constructive way than hitherto. I take the view that he had in essence blocked out his memories of abuse between 1981 when he left *Bryn Alyn* and 1996/7 when he learned of the Waterhouse Inquiry. His suffering as a result of the *Bryn Alyn* experiences in that period of time was not such in my view as to merit compensation. He has however suffered significantly over 4½ years now and he will suffer on a reducing scale as time goes on. Given the length of time over which these problems have persisted, and bearing in mind the length of time over which the abuse described took place I conclude that the claimant's symptoms do justify the description of a post traumatic stress disorder which cannot be described as severe in the light of the claimant's constructive manner and positive outlook for the future.

In our view, the abuse suffered by DJ at *Bryn Alyn*, though serious and prolonged, and painful and harrowing, was not of significance to him within the meaning of that word in section 14(2). What became of significance to him much later, in about 1996 and within 3 years of his commencement of proceedings in January 1998, was his delayed post-traumatic stress disorder, prompting him then to frame a claim for damages for it.

23.80   The Court of Appeal specifically considered a number of actions by various claimants which did not indicate a date of knowledge sufficient to precipitate statutory awareness under sections 11 and 14 of the Limitation Act 1980. These included:

- the fact that a claimant sought his social services files from a potential defendant authority (paragraph 145 of the judgment);

- the fact that a claimant has made a statement to the police about the abuse he has suffered (paragraphs 169, 231, 301 of the judgment);

- the fact that the claimant had made a claim to the Criminal Injuries Compensation Board (paragraphs 169, 231 of the judgment);
- the fact that a claimant had made a complaint at the time of the abuse to a social worker and to the police (paragraph 181 of the judgment).

In the *Bryn Alyn* cases where the date of knowledge was relatively recent, but more than three years before the issue of proceedings, then the Court of Appeal considered that the period of limitation may be extended by a further period pursuant to section 33 of the Limitation Act 1980. See paragraph 233 of the judgment. **23.81**

Further, in a case where the total time since the abuse was nine or ten years, and the claim brought five years outside the primary limitation period, the Court of Appeal would have allowed the claim to proceed, pursuant to section 33 of the Limitation Act 1980, even if they had not found a later date of knowledge. See paragraphs 183, 192, 311, 322 of the judgment. **23.82**

Two further recent decisions of the Court of Appeal have reviewed the decision in *Bryn Alyn* following the decision of the House of Lords in *Adams v Bracknell Forest Borough Council* [2005] 1 AC 76. Some doubts have now been expressed about the correctness of the decision of the Court of Appeal in *Bryn Alyn* but it has not been overruled. **23.83**

In the case of *Catholic Care and the Home Office v Kevin Raymond Young* [2006] EWCA Civ 1534 and in the case of *Jason McCoubrey v Ministry of Defence* [2007] EWCA Civ 17 the point from *Bryn Alyn* that was reviewed by the Court of Appeal was the extent to which the test under section 14(2) of the Limitation Act 1980 is an objective test. It was decided by the Court of Appeal in the *Catholic Care and the Home Office* case that following the findings of the House of Lords in the *Adams* case that as the test under section 14(3) of the Limitation Act 1980 is a largely objective test, the test under section 14(2) must also be a largely objective test. The House of Lords in the case of *Adams* referred in passing to the *Bryn Alyn* case without expressing any doubts as to its correctness. This was recognised by the Court of Appeal. However, the Court of Appeal in the *Catholic Care and the Home Office* case found that the reasoning in *Adams* affected the correctness of the reasoning of the Court of Appeal in *Bryn Alyn* as to whether the section 14(2) test was largely subjective or largely objective. It could be argued that the decision in *Catholic Care and the Home Office* cannot overrule the decision in *Bryn Alyn* in any respect. However, the Court of Appeal have now twice stated that the law has been modified so that an objective test is the correct approach. **23.84**

In other respects the decision in *Bryn Alyn* remains the benchmark for assessing the limitation position in child abuse cases under sections 11 and 14 of the Limitation Act 1980. Although Lord Justice Buxton in the Court of Appeal in the *Catholic* **23.85**

Care and the Home Office case expressed some doubts about the decision he accepted that it was binding. He stated:

> We are bound, as the Judge was bound, to apply the *Bryn Alyn* test as amended by implication by the House in Adams: that is, when a reasonable man in the circumstances of the claimant would reasonably turn his mind to litigation; and
>
> third because the House was not directly concerned with section 14(2) it did not address the analysis of section 14(2) that is to be found in *Bryn Alyn* and in particular did not pass on what has been identified as 'the *Bryn Alyn* test' that is, when such an already damaged child would reasonably turn his mind to litigation as a solution to his problems; see para 50 above. The only amendment to that formula that follows from Adams is to express it in terms of the reaction in respect of litigation of a hypothetical reasonable child in the position of the claimant.

23.86 A point given considerable emphasis in the *Catholic Care and the Home Office* case was that applying an objective test to the date of knowledge of a claimant who suffered sexual abuse as a child requires the Court to take into account the effect that the type of injury inflicted by the defendant would have on a claimant. For example, Lord Justice Dyson stated:

> On the other hand if the injury affects the claimant's ability to acquire knowledge or to seek expert advice, these are matters that can be taken into account; and
>
> The Adams approach to reasonableness indicates that if a person who has suffered a particular type of injury would reasonably be inhibited by the injury itself from instituting proceedings, then that is a factor that should be taken into account in deciding whether he or she would reasonably have considered it sufficiently serious to justify proceedings. The standard that has to be applied is that of the reasonable behaviour of a victim of child abuse who has suffered the degree of injury suffered by the claimant in question and of which he has knowledge.

23.87 This point was also subsequently emphasised by Mr Justice Holland in the case of *AB and ors v the Nugent Care Society (formerly Catholic Social Services Liverpool)* [2006] EWHC 2986 in which he said at paragraph 9:

> An important gloss on the terms of the statute was adumbrated by Lord Hoffmann in Adams and adopted in Young by Dyson LJ at paragraph 34. The practical effect can be expressed: 'In deciding whether it was reasonable for the claimant to seek such medical or other appropriate expert advice, if the injury itself would reasonably inhibit him from seeking advice then that is a factor which must be taken into account'.

23.88 In the case of *McCoubrey v Ministry of Defence,* the Court of Appeal were not dealing specifically with child abuse. However, the judgment of Lord Justice Neuberger in that case (with which the other Judges, Lord Justice Ward and Lord Justice Tugendhat, agreed) again cast doubt on the *Bryn Alyn* decision. Mr Justice Neuberger stated:

> First as appears to be agreed between the parties (plainly rightly in my opinion), the decisions in the *Adams* and *Young* cases mean that the law as it had been previously

understood and applied, at least in the *Bryn Alyn* case, purportedly following in particular the *McCafferty* case, has changed. The test under section 14(2) is substantially objective and is not the mixture of subjective and objective in the way in which the analysis of Geoffrey Lane LJ in the *McCafferty* case was interpreted as indicating in a number of cases culminating with the *Bryn Alyn* case.

Therefore the decision in *Bryn Alyn* must now be applied subject to the comments of the Court of Appeal in the *Young* and *McCafferty* cases so that a more objective test is applied to the reasons why the claimant has not been able to commence proceedings before.   **23.89**

In the decision of the Court of Appeal in *T v Girls and Boys Welfare Society* [2004] EWCA 1747, it was pointed out that when considering an extension of time under section 33 the Court will take into account the entire period of delay even if the period since the claimant acquired the relevant knowledge is relatively short. By way of example, if the claimant could show knowledge dated from when he first reported the abuse to a psychiatrist and understood the significance of it in 1993, then he would have had three years from then to bring a claim, ie 1996. The Court, in exercising its discretion under section 33, would not just take into account any delay since 1996 they would take into account the delay since 1992 when the claimant was aged 21, it would then consider whether this period was too long.   **23.90**

In the *T v Girls and Boys Welfare Society* case the Court of Appeal found as follows: **23.91**

> By the time the claim was brought, 28 years had passed since the events that gave rise to the claim, and the service of the claim was the first notice that *B* had of those allegations. It was no answer to say that the prejudice had only been marginally increased by the fact that the claim was made 2 years after the limitation period had expired. Parliament had determined in s.11 and s.14 of the Act where the balance of prejudice should normally be struck. It followed that s.33 was only available in special cases and it was for the claimant in any particular case to establish that his claim was one of those special cases. The mere fact of being asked to deal with a stale claim was itself prejudice, and the staler the claim the greater the prejudice. The policy of the law was to permit people and organizations to arrange their affairs on the basis that there came a time when they should not be asked to meet such claims. The judge was fully entitled to conclude that the instant case did not come within the category of those where an exception could be made under s.33.

Therefore unless a claimant can show her date of knowledge was less than three years before the date of issue of proceedings, when the events took place over 20 years ago, it is likely to be difficult to persuade a court to exercise its discretion to allow the claim to proceed. Once a claimant is outside the three-year period from his date of knowledge (actual or constructive) the court will look at the whole period of delay since the primary period of limitation expired.   **23.92**

The issue of whether limitation should be tried as a preliminary issue provides a particular problem in cases involving sexual assaults. To hear the limitation   **23.93** issues will almost inevitably involve hearing evidence from the claimant and the requirement for the claimant to give evidence twice in respect of the details of sexual abuse can be oppressive in cases where this causes great distress.

23.94 In the cases of *Ablett and ors v Devon County Council* (21 September 2000), Mr Justice Toulson considered an application by the defendant for the trial of limitation as a preliminary issue. These cases involved child abuse in an approved school between 1957 and 1985. Mr Justice Toulson refused the application and pointed out that in order for the Court to exercise its discretion it would need a profound understanding of what happened at the time and the consequences for the claimant. To carry out this exercise requires a detailed trial on liability and without such a trial and an assessment of the strength of the case on liability it is not fair to either party to decide on the exercise of discretion in respect of limitation.

23.95 In the *Ablett* case the defendant applied to the Court of Appeal for permission to appeal. Lord Justice Latham refused permission on paper and Lord Justice Sedley refused permission at an oral hearing.

23.96 At the oral hearing Lord Justice Sedley stated that:

> In my judgment Toulson J was not only entitled to reach this conclusion, which is enough for present purposes; if I had to consider the question I would say that he reached an undoubtedly correct conclusion. Latham LJ considering these applications on paper, took the same view.

23.97 Further, in examining the question of limitation in respect of the defendant's application for permission to appeal, Lord Justice Sedley made the following comments:

> Inevitably there is a problem of limitation in these proceedings. I say 'inevitably' because it is in the nature of abuse of children by adults that it creates shame, fear and confusion, and these in turn produce silence. Silence is known to be one of the pernicious fruits of abuse. It means that allegations commonly surface, if they do, only many years after the abuse has ceased ...
>
> What is not inevitable is that a defendant especially when that defendant is a public authority, will plead limitation rather than accept responsibility for as much or as little as can be reliably established at such a distance of time.

23.98 In the *Bryn Alyn* case the Court of Appeal allowed all the claims to proceed (except one where there was only an allegation of vicarious liability). The Court was not deciding whether limitation should be decided as a preliminary issue but did comment obiter on the fact that there may be circumstances where limitation can be considered as a preliminary issue at paragraph 74. The Court acknowledged: 'It may not always be feasible or produce savings in time and cost for the parties to deal with the matter by way of preliminary hearing, but a judge should strain to do so whenever possible.'

However, the Court of Appeal contemplated that such a preliminary hearing **23.99** should be by reference to the pleadings and written witness statements and importantly the extent and content of discovery.

In many cases to ascertain whether the claim is limitation barred will require **23.100** evidence from most of the same witnesses who will be required to give evidence at trial. If after determination of the issue of limitation the claim is found not to be limitation barred there will be very considerable overlap in a second trial to determine the issues of liability and quantum. Cost far from being saved will be significantly increased. Further, the distress to the claimant in being required to give evidence will be very significant in many cases. Careful consideration therefore needs to be given to the issue as to whether limitation should be heard as a preliminary issue.

M. Anonymity

Section 1 of the Sexual Offences (Amendment) Act 1992 as amended provides **23.101** that:

> Where an allegation has been made that an offence to which this Act applies has been committed against a person, neither the name nor the address, and no still or moving picture, of that person shall during that person's lifetime:
>
> (i) be published in England and Wales in a written publication available to the public; or
> (ii) be included in a relevant programme for reception in England and Wales.
>
> If it is likely to lead members of the public to identify that person as the person against whom the offence is alleged to have been committed.

Section 6 of the Act defines a written publication as follows: 'written publication **23.102** includes a film, a sound track and any other record in permanent form but does not include an indictment or other document prepared for use in particular legal proceedings.'

In the North Wales inquiry into abuse of children in North Wales, *Lost in Care,* **23.103** published in February 2000, the issue of anonymity was raised. At paragraph 1.08 the report records that the tribunal specifically indicated at the start of the proceedings that it would be contempt of court to publish any material which would enable any living person to be identified as a person who had made an allegation of sexual abuse.

23.104   In these proceedings concerning sexual abuse, a claimant should be protected by section 1 of the Sexual Offences (Amendment) Act 1992 from being named in the media. However, if any claimant is particularly anxious about their name appearing on the claim form it is possible to apply to the Court for an order that the claimant be referred to only by an initial. Such an application would need to be made when proceedings are issued.

23.105   In the case of *HM Attorney-General v British Broadcasting Corp and anor* (December 2001 DC), the Court imposed a fine of £25,000 on the BBC and £500 on an individual journalist for disclosing the name of a complainant in a sexual abuse trial. The defendant was being tried at the Crown Court on charges of indecent assault and buggery of children. Witnesses, including T, were concerned about the publication of their names and had been told that they would benefit from anonymity for life under section 1 of the Sexual Offences (Amendment) Act 1992 ('the 1992 Act'). There were reporting restrictions in place under section 4 of the Contempt of Court Act 1981 ('the 1981 Act') that applied to references to earlier trials. Section 2 of the 1992 Act provided that strict liability applied to a publication which created a substantial risk that the course of justice in the proceedings in question would be seriously impeded or prejudiced. Contrary to section 2 the second respondent, M, reported details of the names of T and his age during two broadcasts on the evening of the first day of the trial. The judge noted the 'catastrophic error' which had 'caused untold damage to the witness' and directed the matter to be referred to the Attorney-General, the applicant. The Attorney-General contended that the identification of T in the two programmes amounted to contempt of court under the strict liability rule in that it had created a substantial risk that T would be unwilling to return to court to complete his evidence, he would be unable to do himself justice in the giving of his evidence, and that one or more of the other complainants would be unwilling to give evidence. The respondents admitted liability and the Divisional Court was required only to determine the appropriate penalty.

24

COST OF UPBRINGING CASES

A. Introduction

Cost of upbringing claims are claims arising out of negligent medical treatment **24.01** which has resulted in the birth of a child who with competent care would not have been born. The claimant is the parent of the child. The loss claimed is the expense of bringing up a child that the claimant would not have had to care for in the absence of negligent treatment. Whether a parent should be entitled to recover for the cost of the upbringing of a child has always been a controversial issue. The law in this area has radically developed and changed over the last 25 years since the Court of Appeal decision in *Emeh v Kensington & Chelsea & Westminster Area Health Authority* [1985] 2 WLR 233 confirmed that there was no public policy reason why the parent could not recover. The most recent House of Lords decision in *Rees v Darlington Memorial Hospital NHS Trust* [2004] 1 AC 309 has confirmed the restriction on cost of upbringing claims introduced by *McFarlane v Tayside Health Board* [2000] 2 AC 59 but has still left the position somewhat uncertain. Any client with a cost of upbringing claim needs to be warned that the law in this area may change further and that it is possible that in the future the cost of upbringing may cease to be recoverable in any circumstances.

In order to appreciate and understand the changes it is necessary to examine the House of Lords cases of *McFarlane* and *Rees* in some detail and to consider how first instance judges and the Court of Appeal have tried to apply these authorities.

24.02   The present position is that a doctor or other health care professional owes a duty of care to a patient not to cause personal injury. Causing a woman to become pregnant or continue a pregnancy and undergo labour when she would not otherwise have done so, constitutes a personal injury. The level of damages for such an injury will be relatively modest. The extent to which the duty of care extends to saving the woman (and her partner) from the financial consequences of bringing up an additional child is now severely restricted. Only where the child has disabilities and additional costs because of the disabilities will there be a possible cost of upbringing claim.

24.03   It has been well established since the Court of Appeal decision in the case of *McKay v Essex Area Health Authority* [1982] 2 WLR 890 that no duty of care is owed to a child to prevent it being born. A child, even if he has severe disabilities, cannot claim damages for having been born when with competent care the foetus would have been terminated. In the *McKay* case the Court of Appeal held that section 4(5) of the Congenital Disabilities (Civil Liability) Act 1976 deprived a child of such cause of action and the sanctity of life of a viable foetus was preserved by section 5(1) of the Abortion Act 1967 notwithstanding recognition by the Act that it would be better for a child with such deformities not to be born at all. A defendant health authority was not under a duty to the child to give an opportunity to the mother to terminate the birth.

24.04   There is potentially a personal injury claim for a mother and a cost of upbringing claim for the parents if the child is born disabled in the following circumstances:

- a woman seeks to avoid pregnancy but is given negligent advice in respect of contraception leading to conception, pregnancy, and the birth of a child;
- a woman seeks to avoid pregnancy by undergoing a sterilisation procedure and the procedure is negligently performed so as to result in conception, pregnancy, and the birth of a child: see *Rees v Darlington Memorial Hospital NHS Trust* [2003] UKHL 52;
- a man undergoes a vasectomy procedure which is negligently performed or in which he is not given adequate advice about the risks of failure and this results in his partner conceiving, undergoing a pregnancy, and the birth of a child: see *Thake v Maurice* [1986] 2 WLR 337, *Newell and Newell v Goldenberg* [1995] 6 Med LR 371, and *McFarlane v Tayside Health Board* [2000] 2 AC 59;
- a woman who is already pregnant undergoes investigation for foetal abnormalities and the investigation is negligently performed so as not to identify

abnormalities which would have led to the woman choosing to undergo a termination. This results in the birth of a child who would have been aborted: see *Rand v East Dorset Health Authority* [2000] Lloyd's Law Rep Med 181;

- a woman who is already pregnant requests investigation for foetal abnormalities but is offered an inadequate test to identify abnormalities which would have led to the woman choosing to undergo a termination. This results in the birth of a child who would have been aborted: see *Carver v Hammersmith & Queen Charlotte's Special Health Authority* (Nelson J, 10 April 2000);
- a woman who has a risk of giving birth to a child with foetal abnormalities is not given adequate advice about the risks and conceives, goes through a pregnancy, and gives birth to a child with congenital abnormalities: see *Nunnerly v Warrington Health Authority* [2000] Lloyd's Law Rep Med 170;
- a doctor fails to identify a woman is pregnant and to give advice about termination at an early stage so that the woman continues with the pregnancy and birth: see *Greenfield v Flather and ors* [2001] 1 WLR 1279; *Groom v Selby* [2002] Lloyd's Rep Med 1, *Saxby v Morgan* [1997] 8 Med LR 293;
- a doctor refuses to offer an abortion to a woman who wishes to terminate a pregnancy: see *Barr v Dr Matthews* [2000] 52 BMLR 217.

B. Limitation

A cost of upbringing claim is always a claim by a parent or parents. It is possible **24.05** the claimant mother is still a child or is an adult patient, however, usually the claimant will be an adult with capacity. The three-year limitation period for a personal injury claim pursuant to sections 11 and 14 of the Limitation Act 1980 will apply to the claim. Although the cost of upbringing part of the claim is an economic loss claim the courts have held both before and after the *McFarlane* case that the claim for economic loss cannot be separated so as to allow a six-year limitation period pursuant to section 2 of the Limitation Act 1980.

In *Walkin v South Manchester Health Authority* [1995] 1 WLR 1543, the Court **24.06** of Appeal refused to allow a claimant to abandon the personal injury claim and only claim for economic loss. In *Godfrey v Gloucestershire Royal Infirmary NHS Trust* [2003] EWHC 549, Mr Justice Leveson confirmed that the decision in the *Walkin* case was not altered by the *McFarlane* case.

The limitation period will usually run from the date of birth of the child. In most **24.07** circumstances that will be the relevant date of knowledge that the claimant has suffered personal injury and economic loss consequent on the birth of a severely disabled child.

24.08 The possibility of a claim for the cost of upbringing of a severely disabled child may first be considered by a parent during the investigation of a claim for birth injury to the child. The sequence of events may be as follows:

- A client with a severely disabled child consults you with a view to investigating a claim for birth injury.
- The expert paediatric evidence shows that the child's disabilities were not the result of events during labour or delivery.
- The expert paediatric neurologist advises the MRI scans show a serious congenital disability which should have been apparent on ante-natal ultrasound.
- The expert obstetric evidence confirms there has been no negligence in the conduct of the birth and delivery.
- The obstetrician confirms that the child's disability should have been diagnosed ante-natally and the mother given advice on termination.
- The claim for the child therefore cannot be pursued but there may be a claim by the parents for negligence in the ante-care in failing to diagnose abnormalities and give advice on termination.

24.09 As the original investigation will not have had any limitation constraints it is very important to consider the possible alternative claim for cost of upbringing at the outset to preserve the limitation position. If the child is close to three years when the client first instructs you, the possibility of an alternative cost of upbringing case will need to be investigated urgently.

24.10 If the child is already more than three years of age careful consideration will need to be given to ascertaining the date of knowledge pursuant to sections 11 and 14 of the Limitation Act 1980. Proceedings may need to be issued to protect that date or agreement reached with the defendant for limitation to operate from a particular date.

24.11 Some initial questioning may rule out a cost of upbringing claim, for example if the mother would not in any event have undergone a termination. However, in most cases, the possibility that a disability was not caused at birth but could have been diagnosed ante-natally will require an MRI scan or some expert investigation on causation.

24.12 A further difficulty is that a cost of upbringing claim will not be able to investigated under a public funding certificate for a child. If there needs to be an alternative investigation of a cost of upbringing claim a separate public funding certificate for the parent will be required. If the parent is not eligible for public funding another means of funding the investigation will need to be found, for example, either private funding, legal expenses insurance, or a conditional fee agreement.

C. The House of Lords Decision in *McFarlane*

The first decision of the House of Lords on the right to recover damages after **24.13** failed sterilisation or vasectomy was delivered on 25 November 1999. The decision relates to a case from Scotland (hence the use of the terms delict, pursuer, and solatium) but Lord Slynn pointed out that:

> Although the judgments refer to the law of Scotland (which obviously was the applicable law) it is as I understand it accepted that the law of England and that of Scotland should be the same in respect of the matters which arise on this appeal. It would be strange even absurd if they were not.

The speeches in the *McFarlane* case provide an extensive review of the cases **24.14** relating to failed sterilisations and failed vasectomies in England, Scotland, the USA, the Commonwealth, and Europe. They do not however touch on any human rights issues either with direct reference to the European Convention or prospectively under the Human Rights Act 1998. Earlier the same year in the case of *Barrett v London Borough of Enfield* [1999] 3 WLR 79, Lord Browne Wilkinson made clear that the impact of the Convention was a significant factor in the House of Lords determination of areas of public authority liability. It is perhaps surprising that no reference is made to the possible implications in this respect.

The House of Lords analysed the claim for damages resulting from the birth of a **24.15** child following a failed vasectomy as comprising effectively two separate claims. The claim for the mother's pain, suffering, loss of amenity, and special damages during pregnancy and birth (which was said to be valued at £10,000) and the claim for cost of upbringing of the unplanned child (which was said to be valued at £100,000). Effectively the House of Lords found (by a majority of 4 to 1) the former was a personal injury claim and gave rise to a sustainable claim on conventional principles. The latter was categorised as a claim for economic loss and unanimously the House of Lords held this claim was not sustainable.

The analysis of claims following unplanned births as comprising two separate **24.16** claims, one for personal injury and one for economic loss was not a novel one. In *Allen v Bloomsbury Health Authority* [1993] 1 All ER 651, Brooke J (as he then was) described the claim in this way. He pointed out that his analysis would lead to there being two separate limitation periods for the two different claims (three years for the personal injury claim and six years for the economic loss claim). This led to the argument in the case of *Walkin v South Manchester Health Authority* [1995] 1 WLR 1543 that a claimant could pursue the economic loss claim only and rely on a six-year limitation period. The Court of Appeal did not believe this was the position when considering the limitation point alone. Lord Justice Auld stated:

> In my view Brooke J's suggestion in this obiter passage that an unwanted pregnancy creates 2 different causes of action according to the nature of the damages claimed is not supported by the authorities nor by his own analysis of them. Postnatal economic loss may be un-associated with 'physical injury' in the sense that it stems from the cost of rearing a child rather than any disability in pregnancy or birth but it is not un-associated with the cause of both, namely pregnancy giving rise to the birth of a child.

24.17   Lord Justice Roch expressed some disquiet with the position in stating:

> I have some difficulty in perceiving a normal conception, pregnancy and the birth of a healthy child as any disease or any impairment of a person's physical or mental condition in cases where the only reasons for the pregnancy and subsequent birth being unwanted are financial.

24.18   Further anxiety about claims for costs of upbringing had been expressed by the Court of Appeal in the case of *R v Croydon Health Authority* [1998] Lloyd's Rep Med 44. In that case the claimant became pregnant when she was suffering from negligently undiagnosed primary pulmonary hypertension. Had she been advised of this condition which gave her a very substantially reduced life expectation and gave rise to high risks of death in pregnancy, she would have sought to avoid pregnancy and aborted any unexpected pregnancy. She recovered for the pain, suffering, and complications of pregnancy but not for the resultant cost of upbringing. The reasoning in that case was that the negligent radiologist who missed the obvious symptoms on a chest X-ray did not owe a duty of care which extended as far as the claimant's personal life.

24.19   Lord Slynn in the *McFarlane* case in analysing the position as two separate claims stated:

> I do not find a real difficulty in deciding the claim for damages in respect of the pregnancy and birth itself. The parents did not want another child for justifiable economic and family reasons; they already had four children. They were entitled lawfully to take steps to ensure that did not happen, one possible such step being a vasectomy of the husband. It was plainly foreseeable that if the operation did not succeed ... the wife might become pregnant ... The object of the vasectomy was to prevent [this] happening. It seems to me that in consequence the wife, if there was negligence, is entitled by way of general damages to be compensated for the pain and discomfort and inconvenience of the unwanted pregnancy and birth and she is also entitled to special damages associated with both—extra medical expenses, clothes for herself and equipment on the birth of the baby. She is also entitled to compensation for loss of earnings due to the pregnancy and birth.

24.20   In passing Lord Slynn endorsed the approach of Slade LJ in *Emeh v Kensington and Chelsea Hospital Management Committee* [1985] 1 QB 1012 that the chain of causation was not broken by the wife's failure to have an abortion.

In considering the second claim, that is the economic loss claim, Lord Slynn stated: **24.21**

> Whether the parents should be entitled as a matter of principle to recover for the costs of maintaining the child is a much more difficult question. Logically the position may seem to be the same. If she had not conceived because of the board's negligence there would not have been a baby and then a child and then a young person to house to feed and to educate.

Again Lord Slynn rejected the idea that the chain of causation might be broken   **24.22** by the failure to place the child for adoption. He also rejected the argument that damages should not be awarded in case the child later learnt that their birth was unwanted. The resolution of this difficult issue came for Lord Slynn, as it did for the Court of Appeal in *R v Croydon Health Authority*, from a restriction of the ambit of the duty of care and an examination of the principles in *Caparo Industries v Dickman* [1990] 2 AC 728. Lord Slynn stated:

> It is remembered on this part of the claim your Lordships are concerned only with liability for economic loss. It is not enough to say the loss is foreseeable as I have accepted it is foreseeable … in respect of economic loss in order to create liability there may have to be a closer link between the act and the damage than foreseeabil-ity … there should be a relationship of proximity … the relationship depends on whether it is fair just and reasonable to impose the duty … the doctor undertakes a duty of care in regard to prevention of pregnancy: it does not follow that the duty includes also avoiding the costs of rearing the child if born and accepted into the family … I consider that it is not fair just or reasonable to impose on the doctor or his employer liability for the consequential responsibilities, imposed on or accepted by the parents to bring up a child. The doctor does not assume responsibility for those economic losses. If a client wants to be able to recover such costs he or she must do so by an appropriate contract.

Lord Steyn came to the same conclusion by a rather different analysis. He consid-   **24.23** ered the case against the background of the duty of care cases and pointed out that the *Emeh* case pre-dated the retreat from *Anns v Merton London Borough Council* [1978] AC 728 in *Murphy v Brentwood District Council* [1991] 1 AC 398 and he pointed out that the cost of upbringing claim was an economic loss claim. He then stated that:

> It is possible to view the case simply from the perspective of corrective justice. It requires someone who has harmed another without justification to indemnify the other. On this approach the parents' claim for the cost of upbringing must succeed. But one may also approach the case from the vantage point of distributive justice. It requires a focus on the just distribution of burdens and losses among members of a society.

Lord Steyn considered the attitude of the commuter on the Underground   **24.24** (the end of millennium replacement for the man on the Clapham Omnibus) and surmised that the 'traveller on the Underground would consider the law of tort has no business to provide legal remedies consequent upon the birth of a healthy child, which all of us regard as a valuable and a good thing'. Lord Steyn states:

> Judges ought to strive to give the real reasons for their decision. It is my firm conviction that where courts of law have denied a remedy for the cost of upbringing of an unwanted child the real reasons have been grounds of distributive justice ... In my view it is legitimate in the present case to take into account considerations of distributive justice. That does not mean I would decide the case on grounds of public policy. On the contrary I would avoid those quick sands. Relying on principles of distributive justice I am persuaded that our tort law does not permit parents of a healthy unwanted child to claim the costs of bringing up the child from a health authority or a doctor. If it were necessary to do so I would say that the claim does not satisfy the requirement of being fair just and reasonable.

24.25 Lord Steyn therefore reached the position of saying effectively that this was an action based on the *Anns* case principles which was no longer good law after the *Murphy* case. Examination in the light of the modern test of duty of care from *Caparo* or *Hedley Byrne* left the parents without a cause of action in tort.

24.26 Lord Steyn did however point out that it was conceded by the Health Authority that the position might be different if the child was born disabled and stated there might be force in that concession but it did not arise in this appeal and should await determination in a suitable case. In distributive justice terms the result might be different (and the Underground traveller have a different response) in terms of strict legal logic it might be difficult to formulate the reasons why the result should be different in terms of duty of care.

24.27 Lord Hope also analysed the principles in terms of the *Caparo* test and found it would not be fair, just, and reasonable to impose liability for cost of upbringing. He concluded that his reasoning was similar to that of Lord Steyn.

24.28 Lord Millett did not consider that importance should be attached to the issue whether the economic loss was categorised as pure or consequential. He described that distinction as 'technical and artificial if not actually suspect. In the circumstances'. Whilst not referring to distributive justice or the traveller on the Underground Lord Millett applied a similar reasoning to Lord Steyn when he stated: 'I suspect that most people would regard it as reasonable for a surgeon who performed a sterilization to attempt to exclude liability for the costs of upbringing of a child whose birth he negligently failed to prevent.'

24.29 On the other hand, Lord Millett suggested it would be unacceptable for a surgeon to seek to limit by contract the damages for which he might be liable for professional negligence. Lord Millett concluded that the law must take the birth of a normal healthy baby to be a blessing not a detriment and that it is morally offensive to regard a normal healthy baby as more trouble than it is worth. Lord Millett did not agree that there was a separate claim for pain and suffering during pregnancy that gave rise to a recognised personal injury claim. However, he found that there was a small claim for the loss of freedom to limit the family for which the claimant would be entitled to the sum of £5,000. Further, Lord Millett found there was a claim for special damages for the cost of buying baby equipment that the parents had disposed of after completing their family.

Lord Clyde and Lord Hope on the other hand in agreement with Lord Steyn **24.30** and Lord Slynn categorised the mother's claim for pain and suffering in pregnancy and childbirth as a recognisable personal injury claim and allowed those items to be recovered in a conventional way. They too dismissed the claim for cost of upbringing.

Lord Clyde accepted there was a claim for pain and suffering of the mother. He **24.31** stated however 'the claim for financial loss seems more difficult'. He found such recovery went beyond 'what would constitute a reasonable restitution for the wrong and that the expense of child rearing would be wholly disproportionate to the doctor's culpability' so that limited damages were the solution. This was an approach rejected in terms by Lord Millett who pointed out that 'the harm caused by a botched operation may be out of all proportion to the seriousness of the operation', clearly a minor operation going wrong can have devastating consequences, it also does not require any particular additional culpability, and shades of culpability are generally avoided by the courts.

The speeches in this case highlight the very significant practical difficulties that **24.32** arise in the application of the simple principles set out in *Livingstone v Rawyards* [1880] 5 App Cases 25 that:

> Where any injury is to be compensated by damages, in setting the sum of money to be given for reparation of damages you should as nearly as possible get at that sum of money which will put the party that has been injured, or who has suffered, in the same position as he would have been if he had not sustained the wrong for which he is now getting his compensation.

The uneasiness expressed by judges examining cost of upbringing claims for a **24.33** healthy child since the decision in the *Emeh* case (which itself involved a disabled child), were finally resolved in favour of a compromise position. However, the difficulty that the House of Lords had in discerning the principles and the variation in approach did little to assist practitioners in deciding which arguments could still be run in this difficult area. The difficulties are demonstrated by the subsequent cases and the need for the House of Lords to examine the issue again four years later in the case of *Rees v Darlington Memorial Hospital NHS Trust* [2004] 1 AC 309 (see below).

24.34   Following the *McFarlane* case the principles established were:

- a claimant mother who can show breach of duty in the performance of a sterilisation procedure, where a pregnancy and birth follows, has a personal injury claim for pain, suffering, and loss of amenity during pregnancy and birth;
- a claimant mother may also claim as part of her personal injury claim loss of earnings and consequential damages during the period of pregnancy and recuperation from childbirth;
- a claimant mother who suffers serious complications in pregnancy or psychiatric repercussions can recover for these and logically if she dies in pregnancy or childbirth her estate may recover;
- if the child is healthy, further damages are limited to the costs of equipping the nursery and a sum for losing the right to restrict the size of the family. The damage suggested under this head of loss was the sum of £5,000. Thereafter the child is integrated into the family and the daily costs of upbringing are not recoverable;
- the position where the child is unpredictably born disabled, or where disabilities are negligently missed on foetal scanning was simply not determined by the decision in the *McFarlane* case and was expressly reserved by Lord Steyn.

D. The Cases Following *McFarlane*

24.35   The first three cases in which the costs of upbringing for a disabled child born as a result of the defendant's negligence were considered in the High Court after the *McFarlane* case were:

- *Rand v East Dorset Health Authority* [2000] Lloyd's Rep Med 181;
- *Carver v Hammersmith & Queen Charlotte's SHA* (25 February 2000);
- *Hardman v Amin* [2001] 59 BMLR 58.

24.36   The Court of Appeal then considered the position in:

- *Parkinson v St James & Seacroft University Hospital NHS Trust* [2002] QB 266;
- *Groom v Selby* [2002] Lloyd's Rep Med 1;
- *Greenfield v Flather* [2001] 1 All ER 159.

The *Rand* Case

24.37   The facts in the *Rand* case were that a claim was brought by the parents of a child born with Down's syndrome against the hospital authority responsible for the mother's ante-natal care. In January 1988 doctors wrongfully omitted to inform the claimants of the results of a scan carried out in the course of the routine provision of medical care and management of Mrs Rand's pregnancy. The scan disclosed the likelihood that she would give birth to a Down's syndrome baby. It was accepted by the defendant health authority that the negligent omission deprived the claimants of the opportunity to terminate the pregnancy. Further, it was accepted by the defendant that had they been told of the likelihood that Mrs Rand would give birth to a Down's syndrome baby, she would have had an abortion.

The argument advanced by the claimant's counsel after the decision in the **24.38** *McFarlane* case was that there was no reason why all the claims for the cost of upbringing of the child should not succeed. It was submitted that the reasoning in the *McFarlane* case had no application where the child born as a result of a wrongful birth was born seriously disabled. The claimant relied upon seven cases, each concerning the birth of a disabled child:

(i) *Salih v Enfield Health Authority* [1991] 3 All ER 400, CA;

(ii) *Fish v Wilcox* (Swinton Thomas J, 9 April 1992);

(iii) *Emeh v Kensington and Chelsea and Westminster Area Health Authority* [1985] 1 QB 1012;

(iv) *Anderson v Forth Valley Health Board* [1998] SLT 580;

(v) *McClelland v Greater Glasgow Health Board* (Lord Macfadyen, 24 September 1998);

(vi) *Nunnerly v Warrington Health Authority* [2000] Lloyd's Rep Med 170;

(vii) *Taylor v Shropshire Health Authority* [1999] Lloyd's Rep Med 96.

The claimant in the *Rand* case submitted that in each of these cases the ordinary **24.39** principles of damages had been applied so as to allow claims in the same legal category as the claims in the *Rand* case. In each case the court had allowed the total cost of upbringing and other losses to the parents. In the *Rand* case, the schedule amounted to £800,000, Mr Justice Newman considered each of the cases referred to above in detail and then reached the following distinction as to the position in the *Rand* case and the *McFarlane* case:

> I have concluded that there is a difference between the choice available to parents to limit their family on the grounds of size alone, and the choice available by virtue of the Abortion Act 1967 to terminate a pregnancy on medical grounds. The exist-ence of the Act is sufficient to introduce into the relationship between the health authority responsible for a pregnancy and the parents, a duty to take reasonable steps to ensure the parents can exercise their choice under the Act. The lawful and proper operation of the Abortion Act anticipates and requires the opinions of medical experts to be available and is firmly placed in the area of medical expertise. Although the scan of Mrs Rand was not deliberately carried out to detect whether she was carrying a disabled foetus, in my judgment, the existence of the Abortion Act, and the potentiality for it serving a purpose relevant to Mr and Mrs Rand's rights under the Act, are sufficient to liability for financial consequences flowing

from the failure to draw the relevant risk of disability to their attention. For these reasons I reject the argument that there was an insufficient relationship of proximity between the negligence and the loss complained of. The defendant was under a duty of care to save the claimants from the consequences of the birth of a disabled child. The quantification of any damage must be carried out in accordance with established principles. I do not accept, as [the defendant] submitted, that there is an inconsistency in allowing recovery for the parents (subject to the proper limits to which the parents' action must be limited) where there is no recovery for the child. The claim has to be treated for all purposes as the parents' claim. I shall have to revert to this when dealing with quantum. I reject the suggested undesirable consequence that a child might perceive a recovery in damages as being based on a contention that he or she should have been aborted. When old enough to do so he or she will recognize that what was lost by its parents was an opportunity which Parliament had decided should be available to them. The express purpose of the statute can hardly be regarded as an offensive legal basis for compensation.

24.40   Mr Justice Newman then summarised his conclusions as follows:

(i)   The claim for the full cost of the maintenance and upkeep of Katy is not maintainable in law;

(ii)   Mrs Rand has a legally maintainable claim for general damages for pain and suffering;

(iii)   The claimants have a legally maintainable claim based upon the extended principle of *Hedley Byrne & Heller* for financial consequences flowing from the admitted negligence of the defendant, limited to the consequences flowing from Katy's disability;

(iv)   The claim advanced for the cost of maintenance and the cost of care for Katy is a claim for pure economic loss, as is the claim advanced for loss of profits.

24.41   The Judge awarded the total sum of £118,000: £50,000 of this was for general damages and £50,000 concerned loss of profits in respect of a hotel run by the family. The remaining items covered physiotherapy, a computer, and holiday costs. Most of the costs of care for the child were not allowed on the basis that they did not arise from the child's disability but would also have arisen for a healthy child.

The *Hardman* Case

24.42   In the case of *Hardman v Amin* (2001) 59 BMLR 58, a decision of Mr Justice Henriques, different principles were applied. Mr Justice Henriques specifically departed from the reasoning of Mr Justice Newman and re-examined the principles in very considerable detail.

24.43   The facts in the *Hardman* case were that during the mother's pregnancy she had contacted a rubella infection. She called her general practitioner (the defendant) who failed to diagnose the infection. The defendant conceded negligence in failing to arrange serological tests. Further, it was conceded that if such tests had been arranged the rubella infection would have been diagnosed and the mother would have undergone a termination had she been advised of the severe effect the infection was likely to have on her baby. In the event no tests were carried out, the mother gave birth to a very seriously disabled baby who had no hearing, was partially sighted, and had severe cognitive and behavioural changes. The child was a particularly stressful child to care for and screamed most of the time including at night. This precluded the mother from being able to return to work when she would otherwise have wished to.

The only issue at the trial was the calculation of damages arising from the admit- **24.44** ted liability of the general practitioner. The court examined every aspect of the damages claimed and addressed the following questions:

(i) Can the claimant get damages for the suffering and inconvenience of pregnancy and childbirth?

(ii) Can the claimant get special damages for loss and expense (including loss of earnings) consequent on pregnancy and childbirth?

(iii) Can the claimant get damages for the past and future cost of providing for the child's special needs and care related to his disability?

(iv) Can the claimant get damages for the past and future cost of the child's basic maintenance?

(v) Is any award for cost of upbringing limited to the amount which the would be able to contribute to such costs in an absence of an award of damages to meet them?

(vi) Can the mother get damages for past and future care under *Housecroft v Burnett* principles or by way of damages for loss of amenity?

Mr Justice Henriques reviewed the cases examined by Mr Justice Newman in *Rand* **24.45** and reviewed the case of *Rand* itself. He came to the following conclusions:

The mother can recover general damages for the pain suffering and inconvenience of childbirth but on the facts of this case these should reflect that she would have required a termination if the defendant had not been negligent. Further she (unlike the failed sterilisation cases including *McFarlane v Tayside Health Board*) would have chosen to undergo a further pregnancy in the hope of later having a healthy child. She would however have avoided the shock of realising her child had been born seriously disabled.

• The mother had suffered a personal injury and could recover consequent loss and expense (including loss of earnings) resulting from the personal injury, that is from the pregnancy and childbirth itself. However, again in this case where the mother would have undergone a further pregnancy she must offset any loss and expense she would have incurred in that pregnancy. The Judge specifically indicated that this could (but not necessarily would) reduce the damages to nil.

• The Judge found that the mother could recover the past and future cost of providing for the child's special needs and care required to meet his disabilities.

The defendant argued that following *McFarlane v Tayside Health Board* the mother could recover nothing under this head. The Judge found that for a disabled child effectively the position was as it had been before *McFarlane v Tayside Health Board.* Like Mr Justice Newman he examined the cases of: *Emeh v Kensington and Chelsea and Westminster Health Authority, Taylor v Shropshire Health Authority, Salih v Enfield Health Authority, Fish v Wilcox,* and *Nunnerly v Warrington Health Authority.*

- The Judge specifically rejected the principle applied in *Rand* that the calculation of such costs should be capped by the family's means in the absence of damages. Mr Justice Henriques pointed out that in none of the pre-*McFarlane v Tayside Health Board* cases had such a principle been applied and there was no basis on which *McFarlane v Tayside Health Board* introduced such a principle. The effect of *McFarlane v Tayside Health Board* was to treat the cost of upbringing as a claim for economic loss. In such claims damages are assessed pursuant to the principles in *Hedley Byrne & Co v Heller and Partners* [1964] AC 464, *Henderson v Merrett Syndicates* [1995] 2 AC 181, *Williams v Natural Life Health Foods Ltd* [1998] 1 WLR 830. That is, should be assessed on the basis that responsibility has been assumed and reliance placed and damages should compensate for such economic loss as flows from the breach of duty. Mr Justice Henriques stressed that the fact that the child in the case of *Hardman* was born disabled while the child in the case of *McFarlane v Tayside Health Board* was born healthy leads to different considerations when the three-stage test in *Caparo Industries v Dickman* [1990] 2 AC 605 is applied. That is that it is fair, just, and reasonable to award damages to the mother of a disabled child even though considerations of distributive justice preclude such damages for a healthy child. The Judge therefore concluded that damages for the costs arising from the child's disability could be recovered.
- The costs of basic maintenance could not however be recovered for the reasons advanced in *Salih v Enfield Health Authority* [1991] 3 All ER 400. The loss amounts only to the additional costs resulting from the negligence, not to costs of upbringing which would in any event have been incurred for another child.
- There should be no cap on the amount recoverable by way of damages set by reference to the family's means. The Judge described the anomaly that would result from the defendant's argument by stating that the result would be that a family who managed to borrow money could recover more than a family who could not persuade their bank to lend as much. To limit the damages to what the family could afford is entirely contrary to the normal principles by which damages are awarded to meet the consequences of a tort and to place the claimant as nearly as possible in the position they would have been in but for the tort.

- The mother can recover damages for the gratuitous care she provides for the disabled child either (a) on the same principles as in personal injury cases calculated in accordance with *Housecroft v Burnett* or (b) by way of damages for loss of amenity consisting in the stress, anxiety, and disruption of her life resulting from the obligation to bring up a disabled child.

The Judge ended his judgment by stating that throughout his deliberations he **24.46** had had regard to Article 8 of the European Convention on Human Rights and that he considered he had by the common law reached a solution entirely compatible with Article 8. Had he not provided compensation to the Hardman family in the circumstances of this case there would have been a disruption to their family life and the family would 'have been deprived of its autonomy vesting all major decisions as to care in the state'.

The *Parkinson* Case

In the case of *Parkinson v St James & Seacroft University Hospital NHS Trust* **24.47** [2002] QB 266 the Court considered preliminary issues as to the costs of upbring- ing of a child born after a failed sterilisation who suffered from a heart murmur and behavioural problems.

The Court of Appeal addressed for the first time the interesting and important **24.48** post-*McFarlane* question of whether the costs of upbringing in respect of a dis- abled child could still be recovered and if so on what basis. This case set the parameters in respect of the principles to be applied to the cost of upbringing of a disabled child for the time being.

In the *Parkinson* case, the Court of Appeal accepted that the House of Lords in **24.49** *McFarlane* had not ruled out claims for the cost of upbringing of a disabled child born after a failure to diagnose the disabilities. Lord Justice Brooke described how:

> Like the judge, we have had the opportunity of considering the judgments of English judges in what are called 'wrongful birth' cases which were decided at first instance after the decision of the House of Lords in *McFarlane*. These cases are different from 'failed sterilisation' cases because the opportunity that is lost to the parents in 'wrong- ful birth' cases is the opportunity to terminate a pregnancy which they would have enjoyed if the impugned professional services had not been negligently performed. In *Rand v East Dorset Health Authority* [2000] Lloyd's Med Rep 181, Newman J was concerned with a Down's Syndrome child. In *Hardman v Amin* [2000] Lloyd's Med Rep 498, Henriques J was concerned with a child who was born very severely dis- abled after his mother contracted rubella during her pregnancy. In *Lee v Taunton and Somerset NHS Trust* (October 2000) Toulson J was concerned with a child born with a large spina bifida lesion and hydrocephalus. All three judges held that the decision in *McFarlane* did not preclude an award of compensation for child-rearing costs to these parents, although they differed when assessing the scale on which compensa- tion should be awarded.

24.50 Lord Justice Brooke then analysed what the Court of Appeal considered the correct basis for recovery in cases where a child is born suffering a severe disability. The test was said to apply both to failed sterilisations and failed diagnosis of foetal abnormality. Brooke LJ stated:

> I would apply the battery of tests which the House of Lords has taught us to use, and arrive at the same answer. My route would be as follows:
>
> (i) For the reasons given by Waller LJ in *Emeh*, the birth of a child with congenital abnormalities was a foreseeable consequence of the surgeon's careless failure to clip a Fallopian tube effectively;
>
> (ii) There was a very limited group of people who might be affected by this negligence: viz Mrs Parkinson and her husband (and, in theory, any other man with whom she had sexual intercourse before she realised that she had not been effectively sterilised);
>
> (iii) There is no difficulty in principle in accepting the proposition that the surgeon should be deemed to have assumed responsibility for the foreseeable and disastrous economic consequences of performing his services negligently;
>
> (iv) The purpose of the operation was to prevent Mrs Parkinson from conceiving any more children, including children with congenital abnormalities, and the surgeon's duty of care is strictly related to the proper fulfilment of that purpose;
>
> (v) Parents in Mrs Parkinson's position were entitled to recover damages in these circumstances for 15 years between the decisions in *Emeh* and *McFarlane*, so that this is not a radical step forward into the unknown;
>
> (vi) For the reasons set out in (i) and (ii) above, Lord Bridge's tests of foreseeability and proximity are satisfied, and for the reasons given by the Supreme Court of Florida in *Fassoulas*, an award of compensation which is limited to the special upbringing costs associated with rearing a child with a serious disability would be fair, just and reasonable.
>
> (vii) If principles of distributive justice are called in aid, I believe that ordinary people would consider that it would be fair for the law to make an award in such a case, provided that it is limited to the extra expenses associated with the child's disability.

24.51 Lord Justice Brooke, with whom the other members of the Court of Appeal agreed, concluded:

> I can see nothing in any majority reasoning in *McFarlane* to deflect this court adopting this course, which in my judgment both logic and justice demands. Although Mr Hone had a cross-appeal in which he sought full recovery for his client, and not the limited recovery ordered by the judge, he did not press his cross-appeal very vigorously, and in my judgment it would not be fair, just and reasonable to award compensation which went further than the extra expenses associated with bringing up a child with a significant disability.
>
> What constitutes a significant disability for this purpose will have to be decided by judges, if necessary, on a case by case basis. The expression would certainly stretch to include disabilities of the mind (including severe behavioural disabilities), as well as physical disabilities.

Lady Justice Hale (as she then was) also gave a detailed judgment in which she   **24.52**
described how the decision in *McFarlane* provided an exception to the normal
rules for recovery of damages:

> The true analysis is that this is a limitation on the damages which would otherwise
> be recoverable on normal principles. There is therefore no reason or need to take that
> limitation any further than it was taken in McFarlane. This caters for the ordinary
> costs of the ordinary child. A disabled child needs extra care and extra expenditure.
> He is deemed, on this analysis, to bring as much pleasure and as many advantages
> as does a normal healthy child. Frankly, in many cases, of which this may be one,
> this is much less likely. The additional stresses and strains can have seriously adverse
> effects upon the whole family, and not infrequently lead, as here, to the break up of
> the parents' relationship and detriment to the other children. But we all know
> of cases where the whole family has been enriched by the presence of a disabled
> member and would not have things any other way. This analysis treats a disabled
> child as having exactly the same worth as a non-disabled child. It affords him
> the same dignity and status. It simply acknowledges that he costs more.
>
> It also provides a solution to the problem of degree: how disabled does the child
> have to be for the parents to be able to make a claim? The answer is that the law
> has for some time distinguished between the ordinary needs of ordinary children
> and the special needs of a disabled child. Thus, for the purposes of the services to
> be provided under Part III of the Children Act 1989, a child is taken to be 'in need'
> if, among other things, 'he is disabled': see s 17(10)(c). For this purpose, 'a child is
> disabled if he is blind, deaf or dumb or suffers from mental disorder of any kind
> or is substantially and permanently handicapped by illness, injury or congenital
> deformity or such other disability as may be prescribed': see s 17(11). This or very
> similar definitions have been used since the legislation establishing the welfare
> state in the late 1940s to identify those whose special needs require special services.
> Local social services authorities are used to operating it, for example when maintain-
> ing the register of disabled children required by Sched 2, para 2 of the 1989 Act.
> I see no difficulty in using the same definition here.
>
> Another question is when the disability must arise. Mr Stuart Smith QC. argued
> that there was no rational cut-off point, as any manner of accidents and illnesses
> might foreseeably affect a child throughout his childhood. But that is part of the
> ordinary experience of childhood, in which such risks are always present, and the
> balance of advantage and disadvantage is deemed to be equal. The two serious con-
> tenders are conception and birth. The argument for conception is that this is when
> the major damage was caused, from which all else flows. This was what the defendant
> undertook to prevent. But there are at least two powerful arguments for birth. The
> first is that although conception is when the losses start, it is not when they end.
> The defendant also undertook to prevent pregnancy and childbirth. The normal
> principle is that all losses, past, present or future, foreseeably flowing from the tort,
> are recoverable. The second is that it is only when the child is born that the deemed
> benefits begin. And it is those deemed benefits which deny the claim in respect of
> the normal child. In practice, also, while it may be comparatively straightforward to
> distinguish between ante and post natal causes of disability, it will be harder to
> distinguish between ante and post conception causes. Further, the additional risks to

mother and child (for example because of the mother's age or number of previous pregnancies) may be among the reasons for the sterilisation. I conclude that any disability arising from genetic causes or foreseeable events during pregnancy (such as rubella, spina bifida, or oxygen deprivation during pregnancy or childbirth) up until the child is born alive, and which are not novus actus interveniens, will suffice to found a claim.

24.53   The principles that can be derived from the *Parkinson* case can therefore be summarised as follows:

(i)   The cost of upbringing of a disabled child raises different principles of distributive justice from the costs of upbringing of a healthy child. While distributive justice or questions of 'just fair and reasonableness' may preclude the costs of upbringing of a healthy child they do not preclude the cost of upbringing for a disabled child.

(ii)   The same principles apply whether a child is born disabled by reason of the failure to diagnose abnormalities by antenatal scanning or whether the child is born disabled after a failed sterilisation procedure.

(iii)   The point at which to determine whether the child is healthy or disabled is the point of birth not the point of conception.

(iv)   The recoverable costs are the additional costs occasioned by the disability of the child not the total costs of upbringing, in that way the disabled child is treated in the same way as the healthy child, the difference is the disabled child costs more.

24.54   A number of points however were not addressed in terms by the Court of Appeal:

(i)   *Should the costs of upbringing terminate when the child reaches 18?*
This point had been conceded by the defendant in *Parkinson* before Longmore J and followed the decision on this point by Morrison J in *Nunnerly v Warrington Health Authority* [2000] Lloyd's Law Rep Med 170.

(ii)   *Should a cap be applied to reflect the means of the family?*
This was a point applied in the case of *Rand* which had been highlighted by the parties for consideration in *Parkinson* but not decided by the Judge as he found it was not within the terms of the preliminary issue ordered to be determined. The reasoning of the Court of Appeal in *Parkinson* is however inconsistent with such a cap being imposed. Both Lord Justice Brooke and Lady Justice Hale in effect treated the restriction on costs of upbringing imposed by the House of Lords in *McFarlane* as an exception to the usual rules for recovery of damages. Lady Justice Hale stated in terms that 'there is no reason to take the limitation any further than it was taken in *McFarlane*'.

(iii) *Should the costs of upbringing be determined using a multiplier based on the life expectancy of the child or the mother?*

In the case of *Hardman*, Mr Justice Henriques considered that 'this should be placed in a position in which she can care for her disabled child's reasonable needs during the duration of their joint life span'. This would appear to indicate that Henriques J's view was that a claim for economic loss can only persist for the time when both mother and child are both still alive.

(iv) *How should the state benefits available to the mother and/or the child be taken into account in determining the economic loss to the mother?*

As the claim is an economic loss claim not a personal injury claim there is a good argument for making reductions for any economic benefit which reduces the financial consequences of the loss.

Groom v Selby

In *Groom v Selby* [2002] Lloyd's Rep Med 1, the Court of Appeal considered **24.55** questions of causation and in particular whether costs of upbringing were recoverable for a baby born apparently healthy who then developed an infection.

The claimant in this case underwent a sterilisation operation when she was already **24.56** pregnant and no test was carried out to ascertain the pre-existing pregnancy. Negligence in this respect was admitted.

The claimant's child was born on 26 May 1995 and appeared healthy. On 21 June **24.57** 1995 she became unwell and was admitted to hospital, where she was diagnosed as suffering salmonella meningitis complicated by bilateral frontal brain abscesses. The Judge found that the baby had been in contact with bacteria colonising in the mother's birth canal and perineal area and that the baby had contracted infection during birth when she was particularly susceptible to infection through her prematurity. The issues for the judge were:

(i) Is the mother entitled to damages for cost of upbringing?
(ii) Was the baby born with congenital abnormalities which increased her need for care?

The Court of Appeal confirmed that the Judge was correct to find that the baby's **24.58** meningitis was a natural though rare consequence of birth and that the chain of causation had not been broken between the negligent act and the resultant damage to the baby. Whilst it was right to categorise the claim as a claim for economic loss not personal injury this did not alter the principles applying to personal injury claims in respect of causation as set out in *Jolley v Sutton London Borough Council* [2000] 1 WLR 1082.

24.59   Lord Justice Brooke in the Court of Appeal applied the principles he had found in the *Parkinson* case and stated:

> (i) in the absence of evidence of any new intervening act, the birth of a premature child who suffered salmonella meningitis through exposure to a bacterium during the normal processes of birth was a foreseeable consequence of Dr Selby's failure to advise the claimant that although she had been sterilized she was in fact pregnant;
>
> (ii) there are no difficulties about proximity;
>
> (iii) there is, as in *Parkinson*, no difficulty in principle in accepting the proposition that Dr Selby should be deemed to have assumed responsibility for the foreseeable and disastrous consequences of performing her services negligently;
>
> (iv) Dr Selby knew that the claimant had been sterilized and wanted no more children (let alone children with serious handicaps) and Dr Selby's duty of care when advising on the symptoms of which the claimant made complaint must be deemed to include the purpose of ensuring that if the claimant was indeed pregnant again she should be informed of this fact, so as to enable her to take appropriate steps to prevent the birth of another child if she wished;
>
> (v) as in *Parkinson*, no radical step into the unknown is in question here;
>
> (vi) as in *Parkinson*, an award of compensation which is limited to the special upbringing associated with rearing a child with a serious disability would be fair, just and reasonable.

24.60   Lady Justice Hale confirmed the principles applicable were as follows:

> The principles applicable in wrongful birth cases cannot sensibly be distinguished from the principles applicable in wrongful conception cases. This court has already decided, in *Greenfield v Irwin (A Firm) and others* [2001] 1 FLR 899, that the principle in *McFarlane v Tayside Health Board* [2000] 2 AC 59 applies to the wrongful birth of a healthy child. The facts were similar to those of this case, in that there was a negligent failure to discover that the mother was pregnant before prescribing her a course of contraceptive injections. Her pregnancy was therefore not discovered until it was too late to terminate it. In such cases, unlike the usual run of wrongful birth cases, there is no direct connection between the negligence and the disability. In cases such as *Rand v East Dorset Health Authority* [2000] Lloyd's Rep Med 181, *Hardman v Amin* [2000] Lloyd's Rep Med 498, or *Lee v Taunton & Somerset NHS Trust* [2001] 1 FLR 419, there has been a negligent failure to diagnose the disorder which leads to, or to screen properly for, the disability in question. Here the negligence consists in allowing the pregnancy to continue when the claimant did not wish to be pregnant at all.
>
> Nevertheless, in *Parkinson v St James and Seacroft University Hospital NHS Trust* [2001] EWCA Civ 530, [2001] 3 WLR 376, this court took the view that the principle in *McFarlane* could properly be confined to the ordinary costs of bringing up a healthy child in a wrongful conception case. The extra costs of bringing up a disabled child could be claimed even though there was no direct link between the negligence and the disability.

Greenfield v Flather

24.61   In *Greenfield v Flather* [2001] 1 All ER 159, HH Judge Langham QC considered the position where a mother of an unplanned healthy child claimed loss of earnings.

In the *Greenfield* case it was argued that the loss of earnings of the mother whilst caring for her healthy but unplanned child were part of the mother's own loss. It was argued they were in a different category to the economic loss claim for cost of upbringing. The Court of Appeal dismissed this argument and applied the House of Lords decision in *McFarlane v Tayside Health Board* on a broader basis.

Lord Justice Buxton stated: **24.62**

> In my view it is overwhelmingly clear from *McFarlane* that the claim in that case was not dismissed on grounds that narrowly related to the economic nature of the claim, or narrowly related to the fact that the expenditure was not directly a loss suffered by the parent. The claim was rejected in *McFarlane* by the House of Lords on grounds of very broad principle, broad principle reaching certainly beyond, in my judgment, the particular circumstance of an unwanted pregnancy. But even within that particular circumstance it is really quite impossible to distinguish between our case and *McFarlane* in any terms that protect this case from the broad view of liability and the broad view of the nature of the application of the law of tort that was adopted by all of the judges, in one manner or another, in the *McFarlane* case. For that reason (which I think will not improve by being expanded on further) it is absolutely clear to me that this appeal must fail.
>
> There is another and different ground, it seems to me, why the appeal is also misconceived. Even on the basis that this is a claim for losses contingent upon physical injury, it seems to me simply not to be the case in any realistic terms that the cost of the existence of a child, whether it be costs of rearing or the contingent loss of the parent who has to give up a job to bring the child up, is in law caused by the pregnancy: which is the matter to which the complainant in this case complains. It is caused rather by the existence of the child, just as the family's expenditure on its other children is caused by their existence. That again is a short point, but it seems to me that it demonstrates again that this case cannot be solved in the plaintiff's favour by characterising it as a case of physical damage with contingent loss.

The Court of Appeal therefore confirmed that attempts to circumvent the **24.63** decision in *McFarlane v Tayside Health Board* by describing the consequences of the birth of an unplanned healthy child as something other than 'economic loss' or 'costs of upbringing' will be unlikely to place those losses in a distinguishable category.

E. The House of Lords Decision in *Rees*

On 16 October 2003 the House of Lords gave their decision in the case of *Rees v* **24.64** *Darlington Memorial Hospital NHS Trust* [2004] 1 AC 309. The case raises further difficulties and produces further uncertainties for cost of upbringing claims in clinical negligence. The case was considered by seven judges in the House of Lords: Lord Bingham, Lord Nicholls, Lord Steyn, Lord Hope, Lord Hutton, Lord Millett, and Lord Scott.

24.65 Whilst it might have been hoped that this decision would clarify the law in respect of cost of upbringing claims, it has in effect highlighted the difficulties in this area and the divergence of opinion amongst judges as to how to determine these issues. The case has emphasised the problems that arise when the courts depart from a strictly logical approach to the application of tort law and stray into areas of policy and morals.

24.66 In the *Rees* case a mother who was herself blind underwent a sterilisation to avoid becoming pregnant. The sterilisation was negligently performed and she became pregnant and gave birth to a healthy child. The issue was whether additional costs of upbringing occasioned by the mother's own blindness could be claimed where her child was a healthy child.

24.67 The House of Lords allowed the appeal by the NHS Trust and decided by 4:3 to overturn the Court of Appeal decision (which was a decision by a 2:1 majority). The House of Lords restored the decision of the Judge at first instance that the mother could not recover any additional costs of upbringing. Overall, six Judges ruled out the claim and five would have allowed it. However, the House of Lords acknowledged that a mother who has a child she would not have had in absence of clinical negligence has suffered a wrong for which there should be a remedy. The House of Lords therefore suggested by way of remedy a standard award of £15,000 analogous to the bereavement award of £10,000 and considerably higher than the award of £5,000 suggested by Lord Millett in the *McFarlane* case.

24.68 In the course of their opinions the House of Lords specifically considered three categories of case:

  (i) The case where a healthy child is born to healthy parents after the parents have sought to avoid further children after completing their family: *McFarlane v Tayside Heath Board*.
  (ii) The case where a healthy child is born to a mother with a severe disability where the mother has sought to avoid ever having a child because of her severe disability: *Rees v Darlington Memorial Hospital NHS Trust*.
  (iii) The case where a child with severe disabilities is born after a mother has sought to avoid having further children: *Parkinson v St James and Seacroft Hospital NHS Trust*.

24.69 In the *McFarlane* case the House of Lords decided that the cost of upbringing of a healthy child was not recoverable after a failed sterilisation, the position in respect of a disabled child was specifically reserved. The Court of Appeal in the *Parkinson* case had already distinguished the *McFarlane* case and found that if a child was born disabled after negligent advice or treatment then the additional costs of upbringing to cater for the disability were recoverable. In the *Rees* case the

Court of Appeal found by a majority that a disabled mother should be able to recover the additional costs of upbringing incurred through her disability. The House of Lords however held that the mother's disability does not distinguish her position from that in the *McFarlane* case. Unfortunately the House of Lords have left open the issue as to whether the *Parkinson* case was rightly decided and whether the additional costs of upbringing of a disabled child can be recovered. This is likely to continue to cause considerable difficulties in this area of litigation.

In the course of the seven Judges' opinions the following points were decided. **24.70**

Unanimously it was decided that the decision in the *McFarlane* case should not **24.71** be overturned. It was confirmed that the *McFarlane* case was rightly decided. Further, it was stated that it was too soon to reconsider the decision.

It was acknowledged that the decision represented a departure from the ordin- **24.72** ary law of tort. Lord Bingham stated: 'An orthodox application of familiar and conventional principles of the law of tort would, I think, have pointed towards the acceptance [that full damages against the tortfeasor for the cost of rearing the child may be allowed].'

By a majority of 4:3 it was found the appeal should be allowed, the disabled **24.73** mother should not recover the additional costs of upbringing of a healthy child. The basis of this decision was one of 'policy' although the Judges tried to ensure this was seen as 'legal policy' rather than 'public policy', the distinction is not easy to understand. It was said by Lord Bingham that:

> The policy decisions underpinning the judgments of the House [in *McFarlane*] were, as I read them, an unwillingness to regard a child (even if unwanted) as a financial liability and nothing else, a recognition that the rewards which parenthood (even if involuntary) may or may not bring cannot be quantified and a sense that to award potentially very large sums of damages to the parents of a normal and healthy child against a National Health Service always in need of funds to meet pressing demands would rightly offend the community's sense of how public resources should be allocated.

By a majority of 4:3 it was decided that a new 'conventional' award of £15,000 **24.74** should be introduced where a child was born as a result of clinical negligence. This will apply whether a mother is healthy or not and whether the child is a healthy or a disabled child. The proposed award was described by Lord Bingham as not being 'compensatory'. It was justified by Lord Scott on the grounds of human rights and he stated:

> I regard the proper outcome of all these cases is to award the parents a modest conventional sum by way of general damages, not for the birth of the child but for the denial of an important aspect of their personal autonomy, viz the right to limit the size of their family. This is an important aspect of human dignity, which is increasingly being regarded as an important human right that should be protected by law.

24.75 There was no agreement as to whether the Court of Appeal decision in *Parkinson* was correct and whether the cost of upbringing of a disabled child should now be recoverable or not.

24.76 The following different positions were adopted by the seven Judges. This leaves unresolved the issue as to whether the *Parkinson* case was correctly decided. However, as the House of Lords did not specifically overrule the *Parkinson* case the present position remains that the parents of a disabled child can recover the costs of upbringing.

24.77 Lord Bingham found it was anomalous that Mrs Parkinson should recover and there should be no differentiation for either the child or the parent who is disabled. He stated that in every case there should simply be an award of £15,000.

24.78 Lord Nicholls agreed with Lord Bingham but did not comment on the *Parkinson* case at all.

24.79 Lord Steyn specifically agreed with the decision of the Court of Appeal in the *Parkinson* case.

24.80 Lord Hope agreed with the decision in *Parkinson* and did not see any difficulty in awarding the additional costs of upbringing for a disabled child even if the costs of upbringing of a healthy child were not recoverable.

24.81 Lord Hutton specifically stated that he considered the decision in the *Parkinson* case was right.

24.82 Lord Millett stated:

> It is not necessary for the disposal of the present appeal to reach any conclusion whether *Parkinson* was rightly decided and I would wish to keep this point open.

24.83 Lord Scott stated that he did not consider that there was any sufficient basis on the facts of the *Parkinson* case to distinguish the case of *McFarlane* and he did not consider the costs of upbringing of a disabled child should be allowed if the negligence was the cause of the pregnancy but not of the disability itself. Lord Scott suggested however that the position might be different if: 'the avoidance of the birth of a child with a disability is the very reason why the parents sought the medical treatment or services to avoid conception.'

24.84 Unfortunately the unsatisfactory result of this case is therefore that in respect of the cost of upbringing of a disabled child three of the Judges thought the decision in *Parkinson* was correct, two of the Judges thought the decision was wrong, one of the Judges did not specifically comment but agreed with the Judges who thought it was wrong, and the seventh Judge specifically left the question open. As the *Parkinson* case was not specifically overruled it should at least be considered a binding authority of the Court of Appeal.

F. Summary of Issues in Cost of Upbringing Claims

Duration of the Period of Loss

The duration of the period of loss where a seriously disabled child is provided for **24.85** by his parents will depend on ascertaining both the life expectation of the child and that of the parents.

If the life expectation of the child is shorter than that of his parents then the maxi- **24.86** mum period for recovery of future losses will be the life of the child.

If the life expectation of the child is longer than that of the parents then the future **24.87** losses can only be recovered for the life of the parent. The claimant is not entitled to claim the cost of somebody else looking after the child after the parent dies.

In addition there are likely to be issues as to whether the parents will in fact care **24.88** for the disabled child once he reaches adulthood or whether he will then be cared for in a residential home at public expense.

The argument that there is no obligation for the parents to care for a child after **24.89** the age of 18 has been raised in two cases. In *Rand v East Dorset HA (No1)* [2000] LLR Med 377 and *(No 2)* [2000] LLR Med 181, Mr Justice Newman found, as a matter of law, losses were not restricted to the child's 18th birthday.

When hearing the permission to appeal application in *Gaynor v Warrington* **24.90** *Health Authority* [2003] LLR Med 365, Lord Justice Pill and Lady Justice Hale found it would be contrary to the general rules of the law of negligence and dam- ages to enforce a cut-off when the child reaches 18 years.

Hale LJ stated that: **24.91**

> I would add only that the argument that damages should be limited up to the age of 18 years was based on a very narrow view of what might or might not be the respon- sibilities of parents towards children, particularly those children who sadly suffer a disability. There is a great deal in family law to indicate that liabilities not only towards those children, but also the parent who is looking after those children (should there have been a marriage as there was in this case), may indeed endure long after the age of 18. But in any event I would have thought that there is no basis for departing from the normal principles of reasonable forseeability of the loss in question in this case.

State Provision of Benefits and Services

The state may provide services and/or benefits to a disabled child or his parents **24.92** in a variety of ways.

(i) in the form of welfare benefits to the child or the parents;

(ii) in the form of services provided to the child during childhood by:

- the relevant local authority:
  - pursuant to section 17 of the Children Act 1989; and/or
  - pursuant to the Education Act 1996; and/or
- the NHS;

(iii) in the form of services provided to the child after the age of 18 by:
- the relevant local authority pursuant to sections 29 of the National Assistance Act 1948 and section 2 of the Chronically Sick and Disabled Persons Act 1970; and/or
- the NHS.

24.93   In relation to the receipt of state welfare benefits, the child's position must be considered separately to the parents. There is no appellate decision in relation to the issues which arise in relation to the receipt of state welfare benefits; and there is limited assistance from first instance decisions. However, in respect of receipt of welfare benefits by the child in the *Rand* case, Newman J found that these were not to be deducted from the award given that no award had been made to the child. Whilst correct, this finding begs the question whether, if viewed from a different perspective, welfare benefits received by a child which are then expended on, for example, aids and equipment result in there being no loss to the parents. See, for instance, *Cunningham v Harrison* [1973] QB 942.

24.94   In respect of receipt of welfare benefits by the parents, Newman J found In *Rand (No 2)* that these were to be deducted from the award, on a 'like for like basis' but not otherwise, that is, in accordance with the decision of the House of Lords in *Hodgson v Trapp* [1989] AC 807. Therefore benefits received by the parents or likely to be received by them throughout the child's lifetime must be taken into account and deducted from the claim.

24.95   In respect of the receipt of state services during childhood the position is as follows. In relation to local authority provided non-education services:

(i) These may be provided to a child in need pursuant to section 17 of the Children Act 1989. A local authority is not, however, under a duty to do so: see the recent House of Lords decision in *Re A*.

(ii) The services which may be provided are wide-ranging. They may include care at home or respite care. Further, instead of providing services, a local authority may choose to make direct payments in lieu of the services: see section 17A of the 1989 Act.

(iii) If the local authority elects to provide services or make direct payments, it may levy a charge for them either on the parents before the child attains the age of 16, and thereafter to the age of 18 on the child only: sections 17A and 29 of the 1989 Act; and *Kidd v Plymouth Health Authority and Cornwall County Council* [2001] LLR Med 165 (QBD).

(iv) Therefore *if* a service is provided by the local authority to a child, it may choose to charge the parents, resulting, for the purposes of the proceedings, in a loss being incurred by the parents.

In relation to educational services, a local authority must provide these services **24.96** pursuant to the Education Act 1996. The provision may encompass a wide range of services, including transport to and from school; classroom assistance; aids and equipment; and therapies. See, for example, section 454 of the 1996 Act. No charge may be made for them (see section 451 of the 1996 Act). Therefore no loss will be incurred by the parents in relation to these services if provided.

In relation to NHS provided services to the child, if NHS paediatric treatment is **24.97** sufficient, a claim for private treatment will be difficult to sustain. Given that the claim is not for personal injuries, but is an economic loss claim, section 2(4) of the Law Reform (Personal Injuries) Act 1948 cannot be relied upon to permit a claim for private treatment expenses where there is equivalent NHS treatment available.

Further, in addition to the provision of treatment, it is possible that the defendant **24.98** will argue that, in the future, the child will require specialist nursing care which should be provided free: see *R v North and East Devon Health Authority, Ex parte Coughlan* [2001] QB 213 (CA).

In relation to the receipt of state services during the child's adulthood: **24.99**

(i) a local authority is obliged to carry out an assessment of a person who appears to be in need of care and attention pursuant to section 47 of the National Health Service and Community Care Act 1990. Provision of care and attention, includes the provision of accommodation and care connected to its provision;

(ii) if the assessment pursuant to of the National Health Service and Community Care Act 1990, established that the child was in need of accommodation the local authority *must*, unless accommodation is otherwise provided for, provide accommodation pursuant to section 21 of the National Assistance Act 1948; see: *Abdul Wahid v The Mayor and Burgesses of the London Borough of Tower Hamlets* [2002] EWCA Civ 287. However, if the child has been provided with accommodation in childhood as an adult he will only become in need of accommodation if the parents are no longer prepared to provide accommodation;

(iii) if the assessment carried out pursuant to section 47 of the National Health Service and Community Care Act 1990, established that the child was in need only of care and non-accommodation services:
  • these *may* be provided pursuant to section 29 of the National Assistance Act 1948 and section 2 of the Chronically Sick and Disabled

Persons Act 1970. There is, however, no statutory duty to provide the services: see *R v Gloucestershire County Council Ex parte Barry* [1997] AC 585 (HL);
- *if* the local authority exercised its discretion to provide care and non-accommodation services (and, of course, it would be entitled periodically to review this decision and, having regard to its resources, decide not to provide services), it would be entitled to charge the child, but not her parents, for them pursuant to section 17 of the Health and Social Services and Social Security Adjudications Act 1983;
- therefore, *if* care and other non-accommodation services are provided, there would be no loss to the parents in relation to any claim for equivalent care and non-accommodation services for the child;

(iv) in relation to *NHS* provided services: the NHS will provide treatment free of charge, however it may in some cases still be argued that the treatment likely to be provided by the NHS is not adequate to meet the level of provision the parent reasonably wishes to provide for the child.

Calculation of Care Costs

24.100 Before the decision of the House of Lords in *McFarlane v Tayside Health Board* [2000] 2 AC 59 the cost of care for a child born after a failure to sterilise was recoverable in full. That is, the parents were put in the position they would have been if the negligence had not occurred and they had saved all the costs of bringing up a child. However, in cases of failure to terminate a pregnancy where abnormalities were detected where the mother or parents would have gone on to have another child after the termination of a particular pregnancy for abnormalities only, the additional costs brought about by the disability were recoverable: see *Salih v Enfield Health Authority* [1991] 3 All ER 400.

24.101 The position after the *McFarlane* case was that the Court of Appeal in the case of *Parkinson v St James Hospital NHS Trust* stated that even where the parents would have avoided bringing up an additional child in the family only the costs occasioned by the child's disability could be claimed. Effectively it is postulated that the costs of bringing up a healthy child are offset by the benefits and rewards of doing so.

24.102 In most cases the additional costs of care occasioned by the disability which are recoverable will be calculated by a care expert. The calculation will be the same as the care costs for an injured child making a claim on its own behalf, for example a cerebral palsy birth claim. The costs increase as the child gets older as the amount of care the child would have required had the child been a hypothetical healthy child decreases.

In the cases since *McFarlane* the courts have discussed three ways of calculating   **24.103**
care in cost of upbringing claims:

> (i)   additional costs of care as calculated in birth injury cases and including
>   commercial and non-commercial care;
> (ii) parents' loss of earnings;
> (iii) a lump sum to compensate the parents for having to care for a disabled
>   child when they would have chosen to avoid doing so.

In the case of *Rand v East Dorset HA* [2000] Lloyd's Rep Med 181 Newman J   **24.104**
found that parents could not recover the gratuitous cost of care as it was not an
economic loss. Mr Justice Newman found that the parents could recover the loss
of profits in running their family business, as they had given up work to care for
their disabled child. In that case Newman J found they could not recover costs of
gratuitous care.

In *Hardman v Amin*, Henriques J took a different view and found costs of care   **24.105**
could be recovered on the same basis as where they are provided to disabled
children who themselves have a claim. The costs of care were assessed as being
such costs as would allow the claimant 'to be placed in a position in which she
can care for her disabled child's reasonable needs during the duration of their
joint life span'. Further Henriques J found that the mother could recover for the
non-commercial costs of care on the principles set out in *Housecroft v Burnett*.
Newman J had found that a parent could not recover costs of care they themselves
provided as it was not care the child could claim for. He argued that if the mother
could claim for commercial care then it must follow she could also claim for non-
commercial care she herself provides. Henriques J found that the basis of recovery
was similar to that in a personal injury claim and stated:

> In an ordinary claim where a child claimant is injured and a mother gives up work
> and looks after the child, the damages would be measured either by the amount
> of loss of earnings which she has lost, or if it not very much earnings and she has
> put in a lot of hours by the amount of care she has provided there is not an overlap
> (*Housecroft v Burnett*). It is said that these are simply two ways of quantifying the
> same head of damage.

Henriques J then considered a third way of quantifying the loss to the parents   **24.106**
brought about by bringing up a disabled child which was to quantify the loss by
means of a lump sum awarded for the 'stress anxiety and disruption to life resulting from the obligation to bring up a disabled child'. This was the approach that
Newman J had applied in *Rand* and had awarded £30,000 to the mother and
£5,000 to the father on this basis. Henriques J concluded that the mother could
get either the non-commercial care costs or the lump sum for the task of bringing
up a disabled child.

Eligibility for Periodical Payments

24.107   It is doubtful whether a cost of upbringing claim will qualify for a periodical payments order. Section 2(1) of the Damages Act 1996 provides: 'A court awarding damages in an action for personal injury may, with the consent of the parties, make an order under which the damages are wholly or partly to take the form of periodical payments.'

24.108   Section 100 of the Courts Act 2003 substitutes section 2(1) for the provision:

> A court awarding damages for future pecuniary loss in respect of personal injury:
>
> (i)   may order that the damages are wholly or partly to take the form of periodical payments, and
> (ii) shall consider whether to make that order.
> (iii) A court awarding other damages in respect of personal injury may, if the parties consent, order that the damages are wholly or partly to take the form of periodical payments.

24.109   The question that arises is whether damages for the cost of upbringing of a disabled child born as a result of the defendant's negligence can properly be described as 'future pecuniary loss in respect of personal injury'. It is curious that the wording in section 100 of the Courts Act 2003 specifically changes from the previous wording in the Damages Act 1996 which was 'future pecuniary loss in an action for personal injury'.

24.110   In the *McFarlane* case the House of Lords analysed the position as follows:

> (i)   Lord Slynn: '… your Lordships are concerned only with liability for economic loss'.
> (ii) Lord Steyn: 'Here the father's part of the claim for the cost of upbringing the unwanted child is undoubtedly a claim for pure economic loss. Realistically despite the pregnancy and childbirth, the mother's part of the claim is also for pure economic loss'.
> (iii) Lord Hope: 'The child rearing costs: This is a claim for economic loss. The first named pursuer does not claim that he suffered any physical or mental injury'.
> (iv) Lord Clyde: 'That leads immediately to the fifth consideration which relates to the nature of the two claims made in the present case. I have already noted one is a claim for solatium with a further element of financial loss, while the other, the joint claim is a claim purely for a financial loss. They both arise from an allegation of the making of a negligent statement'.
> (iv) Lord Millett: 'It is also true that the claim for the costs of upbringing of Catherine is a claim in respect of economic loss, and that claims in delict for pure economic loss are with good reason more tightly controlled than claims in respect of physical loss'.

24.111   In the *Parkinson* case Lord Justice Brooke in distinguishing the *McFarlane* case for the cost of upbringing claims where a child was born with serious disabilities stated: 'There is no difficulty in principle in accepting the proposition that the surgeon should be deemed to have assumed responsibility for the foreseeable and disastrous economic consequences of performing his services negligently.'

To categorise the costs of upbringing as 'future pecuniary loss in respect of per-   **24.112**
sonal injury' particularly if they relate to the father requires some considerable distortion of the language of section 100 of the Courts Act 2003.

In practice it would seem that the provisions for periodical payments could be   **24.113**
made to fit the criteria for costs of upbringing of a disabled child which are calculated much in the same way as where the claimant is the child himself/herself. That is, additional care costs could be awarded by way of periodical payments and constrained by the alternative time periods of the life of the child and the life of the parents. There would not appear to be any policy reasons why periodical payments should not apply to cost of upbringing claims and it might well be thought that the intention was to include such claims.

25

PUBLIC PROVISION

A. Introduction and Background

One of the major issues in the assessment of damages in cases of serious injury **25.01** is the extent to which specially adapted accommodation, care, and other services will be available through state services. There is then the issue as to whether the claimant is entitled to choose private provision rather than accept state provision and to force the defendant to pay the full cost of private provision. The difference between damages assessed on the basis that a claimant will remain in an NHS Hospital or local authority residential home for the rest of their lives and damages assessed on the basis that the claimant will live in their own home and be provided with privately funded 24-hour nursing care can be many millions of pounds.

In the combined appeals of *Sowden v Lodge* and *Crookdake v Drury* [2005] Lloyd's **25.02** Rep Med 86, the Court of Appeal spelt out that if the defendant seeks to argue that the claimant should be accommodated in local authority housing and utilise local authority care provision, then it is for the defendant to:

- raise the issue well in advance of trial;

- investigate the extent to which the relevant local authority can provide any suitable accommodation or care;

- investigate and cost the appropriate top-up care that might be provided and how it would work;

- plead the case for local authority accommodation and care and give the claimant the opportunity to respond to the case in detail.

25.03 The position was summarised by Lord Justice Pill as follows:

> While claimants and those advising them, must be expected to co-operate with local authorities discharging their statutory duties, they are entitled to claim in the action that to which they believe the claimant is entitled and there is no legal burden on them first to disprove that statutory provision will be adequate. It may of course be prudent to call evidence, as in any situation where a judgment upon the facts is to be made, as to why statutory provision is inadequate.

25.04 Although the Court of Appeal in the *Sowden* cases confirmed that the burden of proof was on a defendant to prove that the state would provide services which met, entirely or in part, a claimant's needs so as to fulfil the test in *Wells v Wells* [1999] AC 345, it is usually reasonable for a claimant to investigate what is available from a local authority in order to meet the defendant's case.

25.05 The defendant's argument in the *Sowden v Lodge* and *Crookdake v Drury* cases related to the provision of local authority accommodation and care pursuant to section 21 of the National Assistance Act 1948. The defendant relied on the first instance decisions in *Firth v Geo Ackroyd Junior Ltd* [2000] Lloyd's Law Rep Med 312, *Ryan v Liverpool Health Authority* [2002] Lloyd's Law Rep Med 23, *Bell v Todd* [2002] Lloyd's Law Rep Med 12, which confirmed that the local authority could not render any charge to the claimant for the provision of care and accommodation if the claimant's only assets were personal injury damages which were to be invested in and administered by the Court of Protection. In these circumstances the local authority was not entitled to take such damages into account when assessing the claimant's ability to make a contribution pursuant to section 22 of the National Assistance Act 1948 to the cost of such accommodation and care.

25.06 The issues in respect of public provision for disabled claimants are no longer confined to provision of accommodation and care pursuant to section 21 of the National Assistance Act 1948. The argument that the claimant should utilise public provision is now raised in respect of all types of local authority facilities, even when a charge can be rendered to a personal injury claimant with funds in the Court of Protection. Further, the argument is raised in respect of a range of NHS provision and in respect of provision under section 117 of the Mental Health Act 1983. Set out below are the different criteria that apply to these different public schemes.

B. National Health Service Provision

In respect of any National Health Service provision the starting point is section 2 **25.07** of the Law Reform (Personal Injuries) Act 1948. This provides that:

> In an action for damages for personal injuries … there shall be disregarded in deter-mining the reasonableness of any expenses, the possibility of avoiding those expenses or part of them by taking advantage of facilities available under the National Health Service Act 1977.

This provision which followed the recommendations of the Monckton **25.08** Committee, specifically allows a personal injury claimant to choose to ignore the availability of National Health Service provision. The rationale for this provision in 1948 was that it would be invidious to expect the Court to determine whether private health care provision was better quality and more beneficial to the claim-ant than the NHS provision before allowing the cost of private provision.

The section 2(4) provision was considered by the Court of Appeal in *Eagle v* **25.09** *Chambers* [2004] EWCA Civ 1033. The Court of Appeal pointed out that under this section the question is whether on the balance of probabilities the claimant will obtain the services from the NHS. The Court of Appeal pointed out that it cannot be enough for the defendants to say there is no evidence that the services will not be available from the NHS or social services.

Where a defendant argues that NHS provision is suitable for the claimant's needs **25.10** the defendant must establish that, even if put in funds to pay privately for the provision, the claimant would utilise NHS care. This issue is frequently raised in respect of surgery or medical treatment that a claimant will require in the future. If the claimant can show, if put in funds, he would use private medical treatment he is entitled to recover this cost from the defendant. The same argument applies in respect of long-term care in a hospital at the expense of the NHS. If the claim-ant can establish he would in fact move to a private home and employ private medical treatment, the claimant will be entitled to recover the cost of private care at home. Section 2(4) simply provides that the Court must 'disregard' that the cost might otherwise be met by the NHS.

Section 2(4) remains in force as far as NHS provision is concerned. It has survived **25.11** suggestions for its amendment or repeal in:

(i) the Pearson Committee Report, Cmnd 7054–1, paragraphs 340–342;

(ii) the House of Lords in *Lim Poh Choo v Camden Health Authority* [1980] AC 174; and

(iii) the Department of Health Consultation Paper: *Making Amends*, Report of the Chief Medical Officer, June 2003.

25.12 The Law Commission Report, *Damages for Personal Injury: Medical, Nursing and Other Expenses; Collateral Benefits* (Law Com No 262, 1999), concluded that, following *Woodrup v Nicol* [1993] PIQR 104, 'the scope of section 2(4) is therefore not in doubt and we maintain our view that the courts have adopted a clear, uniform and correct interpretation of section 2(4).'

C. Section 117 of the Mental Health Act 1983 Provision

25.13 In addition to the section 2(4) argument, in respect of section 117 of the Mental Health Act 1983, it is necessary to take into account that the obligations on a health authority to provide accommodation and care pursuant to section 117 of the Mental Health Act 1983 are less prescriptive than the obligations of a local authority under section 21 of the National Assistance Act 1948 and allow the health authority to take into account resources. The distinction between the two statutory provisions was considered by Mr Justice Leveson in the case of *Tinsley v Sarkar* [2005] EWHC 192 (QB).

25.14 In that case Mr Justice Leveson pointed out at paragraph 110 that:

> Furthermore the duty under section 117 is not open ended. When dealing with the level and nature of services to be provided under section 117, Lord Phillips MR, in *R v Camden and Islington Health authority ex parte K* [2001] EWCA Civ 240 (at paragraph 29):
>
> > In my judgment section 117 imposes on health authorities a duty to provide after-care facilities for the benefit of patients who are discharged from mental hospitals. The nature and extent of those facilities, must, to a degree, fall within the discretion of the health authority, which must have regard to other demands on its budget. In relation to the duty to satisfy conditions imposed by a tribunal, I would endorse the concession made by the respondent authority as to the extent of its duty. Thus resources are not irrelevant.

25.15 Mr Justice Leveson further pointed out in paragraph 111 that:

> The problem about resources was recently underlined by Scott Baker LJ in *W v Doncaster Metropolitan Borough Council* [2004] EWCA Civ 378, at paragraph 59, in these terms; unfortunately there is neither a bottomless pit of funds nor an adequate supply of suitable accommodation and support to deal with these difficult cases. Stretched local authorities and health care providers have to do as best they can with the facilities and resources that are available.

In the *Tinsley* case Mr Justice Leveson concluded that there was not an apt **25.16** analogy between section 117 of the Mental Health Act 1983 and section 21 of the National Assistance Act 1948. He further concluded it was not reasonable to expect Mr Tinsley to accept what the NHS trust proposed in terms of treatment. The Judge rejected the claimant's proposals for a regime with his own private accommodation and 24-hour support team. However, the Judge allowed the claim on the basis that the claimant should be able to pay for private residential care and his own nursing regime within a private care home. The Judge assessed that in addition to the charge made for the basic regime at a residential unit known as Redford Court the claimant should also recover the cost of additional care for seven hours during each day, three hours each evening, and a further flexible six hours a week. This top-up care would provide 2:1 support for many activities. The weekly care package the Judge allowed for was:

Basic line fee Redford Court	£1,275
Vocational activities	£50
Additional support 76 hrs p/w @ £11.50 per hour	£ 866
Administration fee (2.5%)	£ 55
Total weekly cost	£ 2,246

The defendant argued that no award should be made in respect of these costs as **25.17** the NHS would make adequate provision under section 117. The Judge rejected this argument after consideration of the provisions of section 117, the specific way that the Trust in Manchester operated these provisions he concluded:

> I simply do not know what the Trust will decide is an appropriate placement for Mr Tinsley or what it will be prepared to fund. In the light of the evidence to his reaction to the attempt to examine him, it is clear that he has not been interested (for whatever reason and perhaps not unconnected to the litigation) in pursuing a Trust option. Further it is beyond doubt that the financial position of the Trust is such that there is no question of it funding a regime which Mr Tinsley would be prepared to accept, or even the regime which I have found to be reasonable to meet his needs. Further absent statutory provision to allow money to be put in a different regime, I am not prepared to accept that it is reasonable to require Mr Tinsley to accept what the Trust proposes and assuming that he is not unreasonably failing to mitigate his loss by accepting alternative provision, there is no basis for deducting what might be the cost of what the Trust might offer.

Mr Justice Leveson added to this analysis of the position: **25.18**

> I leave this analysis with one further comment. Given the obligations of the Trust, the shortage of resources to meet all those obligations and the likelihood that the need will continue to rise without commensurate increase in resources, I am pre-pared to confess that, although I will dutifully apply my view of the law to the facts of any case (and I do not apologize for advancing the arguments in *Firth*) I am one of those judges to who Longmore LJ was referring in *Sowden v Lodge* at paragraph 92 when he said: 'Some judges also have an instinctive feeling that if no award for care

is made at all, on the basis that it will be provided free by local authorities, the defendant and his insurers will have received an undeserved windfall'.

D. Local Authority Provision

25.19 Whilst a distinction needs to be made between local authority provision under section 21 of the National Assistance Act 1948, which is provided to a patient of the Court of Protection with no assets other than personal injury damages, and other local authority provision, the distinction is not as clear-cut since the decision of the Court of Appeal in *Crofton v NHSLA* [2007] EWCA Civ 71. It is only section 21 of the National Assistance Act 1948 which was considered in the *Bell v Todd, Ryan v Liverpool,* and *Firth v Ackroyd* cases. Other provision may be resource sensitive or may be charged for. Some of the arguments in the *Tinsley* case may also apply to local authority provision other than that provided to a patient under section 21.

E. Capacity

25.20 The starting point must be whether the claimant has capacity pursuant to CPR Part 21 and the provisions of the Mental Health Act 1983. The test being as described in *Masterman-Lister v Brutton & Co* [2003] 1 WLR 1511.

25.21 If the claimant has capacity and wants to be housed in private accommodation then any submission by the defendant that he should reside in state funded accommodation and/or should be content with state funded care, will usually be difficult to sustain. A court is unlikely to wish to restrict the ability of a claimant, who has capacity, to choose where he lives and how he is cared for. It will usually be reasonable for a claimant to insist on private provision where the claimant has the capacity to make their own choice as to how their damages are spent.

25.22 However, there are two circumstances where the argument as to state funded care may still arise with a claimant with capacity and where it is necessary to investigate whether the claimant will in fact have to pay for the state provision once they receive an award of damages as they will not be protected by the ring-fencing provisions considered in the *Bell v Todd* line of cases.

25.23 First, it may be the case that the claimant wishes to remain in a state funded residential care facility and is happy with the provision of services there. If this is the claimant's position it will be necessary to give careful consideration as to the consequences for the future. If the provision later becomes unsatisfactory after the claim has been settled the claimant will no longer be able to look to the defendant for alternative provision.

Secondly, it may be that the claimant was accommodated in state funded accommodation prior to the injury. For example, the claimant may have had a previous injury or congenital disability that meant he was provided with state funded accommodation and care before sustaining the injury his claim relates to. In these circumstances it is necessary to consider whether his injuries are such as to justify a change in provision and an argument that state funded accommodation will no longer meet his needs. If it will not, it will still be necessary to consider whether once a damages award is received by the claimant he may need to pay for his state provision and he previously was provided with it free of charge because he had no funds. **25.24**

The following issues will need to be considered whether the claimant has capacity or not. **25.25**

F. The Claimant

It is necessary to consider: **25.26**

(i) the claimant's background, lifestyle, and aspirations prior to the injury; and
(ii) his status, capacity, needs, and wishes post-injury.

G. Pre-injury Considerations

The purpose of the award for accommodation and care is to meet the claimant's needs which arise as a result of the injury, and to restore the claimant, insofar as it is possible to do so, to the position he would have been in but for the injury as confirmed by the House of Lords in *Wells v Wells* [1999] AC 345. **25.27**

If the claimant is in state funded accommodation and/or in receipt of state funded care, or it is proposed by the defendant that the claimant should be so accommodated and/or cared for, the state funded accommodation and/or care must both meet the claimant's needs and restore him to the position he would have been in had he not been injured. **25.28**

In order to assess whether the existing or proposed state funded accommodation and/or care meets these objectives it is vital that comprehensive evidence is obtained as to the claimant's pre-injury situation, for example: **25.29**

(i) family situation before the injury in order to ascertain the future need to be able to live with/have access to partner/children/close friends in an environment that promotes, as far as possible, the family life/social life that existed before the injury;
(ii) educational background;

(iii) occupational background;

(iv) pre-injury accommodation and aspirations.

25.30   It will be against this backdrop that all other issues should be assessed.

H. Post-injury Position

25.31   The claimant's capacity or lack of it is the starting point. It is important to establish whether the claimant is a 'patient' for the reasons given above, and because there are important distinctions in the way in which patients and non-patients may be charged for any statutory services provided to them.

25.32   If the claimant is a patient it is essential to assess:

- his level of insight and understanding;

- his capabilities and, in particular, ability to make choices;

- his needs for support in a medical, care, and social context;

- the wishes of the immediate family in as far as it is reasonable and in the claimant's interests to take these into account.

25.33   The claimant's abilities may only be realised with the assistance of a care regime, aids and equipment, and assistive technology. Alternatively, medical treatment and/or psychological therapy may assist in maximising the claimant's ability. The early appointment of a case manager may help to assess the claimant's capabilities. Statements will need to be taken from family and friends who have regular contact with the claimant and from any nursing staff, physiotherapists, carers who are prepared to help in assessing the extent of the claimant's post-injury capabilities. If the family disagree with the expert's assessment of capability it may be helpful to arrange for the experts to see the claimant with the family and assess the level of communication achieved by the family.

25.34   Once the claimant's abilities have been assessed the extent to which the claimant will benefit from a privately funded accommodation and care regime should be apparent. If at all possible this should be supported by evidence of a trial period at home or a move to private accommodation with an interim payment if that can be achieved.

25.35   The extent to which the state funded accommodation and care regime meets the claimant's needs and caters for his or her abilities should also be apparent. Details of difficulties with the state funded regime may be gathered from the medical and care notes, family observations, the case manager if one has been appointed should be asked to document difficulties and provide a statement setting out the steps they have taken to try to resolve them.

The parties and the Court should then be in a position to determine how the **25.36** claimant should be compensated having regard to:

- the life and aspirations he would have had but for the injury;
- his or her post-injury level of understanding and ability;
- the adequacy of the state funded accommodation and care provision to meet the above considerations.

If the claimant is not a patient, it remains important to conduct a detailed factual **25.37** enquiry into the nature of her or his post-injury life so that it can be compared with the life he would have had but for the injury. For example, the paraplegic claimant with capacity may have lived in local authority housing prior to the injury which is not now suitable. It may be proposed that she or he does so again. The proposed accommodation may or may not, however, be suitable: there may be no access to his or her adapted vehicle, for example.

I. The Claimant's Family

It is necessary to consider: **25.38**

(i) the existence of family: does the claimant have a family; is there any possibility that she or he will do so in the future?
(ii) the involvement of the family: are they involved in the care of the claimant and/or will they become involved?

The existence of a committed family, who will assist in the recreation of the **25.39** 'but for' life and who will play a part in maintaining a stable private care regime, provides good evidence of the need for and benefits of a privately funded accommodation and care regime.

The family's wishes and the nature and extent of the family's involvement in **25.40** caring for the claimant and managing her or his affairs must be ascertained. What do they want? Have they been involved? If so, to what extent? If not, have they wanted to be involved but been hindered by something beyond their control? If so, what? For instance, it may be that the family have not been able to travel to the state funded rehabilitation unit that the claimant is currently accommodated in. Alternatively it may be that it has not been possible for the claimant to spend time with his or her children in the residential accommodation setting in which she or he is accommodated.

The extent to which the claimant's current family wish to be involved and will **25.41** be involved in the future must be assessed. The potential for the claimant, if she or he does not have a partner and/or children, to have a partner and children must be assessed. These matters have a direct bearing on the suitability of any proposed state funded accommodation and care regime.

25.42 In the case of *Freeman v Lockett* [2006] EWHC 102 (QB), Tomlinson J decided there should be no reduction in that claimant's damages to reflect the possibility of direct payments by the local authority by taking into account the specific wishes of the claimant. The Court of Appeal in *Crofton v NHSLA* [2007] EWCA Civ 71 considered the reasoning of Mr Justice Tomlinson in *Freeman v Lockett* and stated:

> In *Freeman v Lockett*, Tomlinson J decided there should be no reduction in the claimant's damages to reflect the possibility of direct payments by the local authority. A sufficient basis for his decision was his finding that, provided that no deduction on account of the possible receipt of state or local authority funding was made from her award of damages, the claimant would withdraw her application for funding; she wanted to rely exclusively on private funding for her care.

25.43 In the case of *Ahsan v University Hospitals Leicester NHS Trust* [2006] EWHC 2624, the Court accepted that the claimant who was in a permanent vegetative state should be cared for at home with a private care package. Her family who were devout Muslims wished to care for her in a way that was consistent with the claimant's beliefs and cultural background.

J. The Medical Evidence

25.44 The medical expert team will be involved in relation to:

- capacity;
- condition and prognosis, including life expectancy;
- provision for needs.

25.45 The defendant may contend that the claimant's medical needs or behaviour, now or in the future, are/is such that he or she can only be cared for in a residential setting.

25.46 It is necessary to ascertain:

(i) what the claimant's particular current medical needs are;

(ii) whether those needs render it necessary for the claimant to be cared for in a residential setting. Alternatively, why would accommodation in his/her own home not meet those needs?

(iii) if the claimant's current medical needs or behaviour are/is such that care in a residential setting is required, whether the claimant's condition and/ or behaviour will improve. What will the effect of rehabilitation and/or therapy be? Will a care regime established in the claimant's own home which has a nurse as a team leader meet any concerns about his or her medical needs?

(iv) if the claimant is currently able or, with rehabilitation, etc, will become able to be accommodated in his own home, whether there are any events which are likely to occur during his lifetime which may influence whether this will remain the case. For instance:
- is it likely that the condition will deteriorate so as to necessitate care in a residential setting in later life?
- is it likely, although this is not strictly a medical question, that family circumstances will change which would create a significant risk that the claimant will not be able to be cared for in his own home?

K. Accommodation and Care Needs

In respect of accommodation, it is necessary to assess the claimant's needs and requirements with reference to the following criteria: **25.47**

(i) In relation to his condition, these are likely to be:
- physical needs, for example single level accommodation;
- psychological needs including whether the claimant is suited to living in a residential setting with others who have learning disabilities, traumatically acquired brain injuries, or who are elderly.

(ii) In relation to the need to recreate the life of the claimant as it would have been if he was uninjured the issues are:
- Will accommodating him in a residential setting fulfil this objective?
- Will he have sufficient privacy, space, and facilities?

(iii) If the claimant requires care which can only be provided in a residential setting the issues are:
- What are the potential accommodation settings, eg is it proposed the claimant will be placed in a small unit with other people of his own age and gender or is a large mixed residential unit proposed?
- What does the accommodation proposed to be provided by the state comprise, eg will the claimant just have a bedroom or will he have his own bathroom and his own sitting room as well?
- Is the proposed accommodation within a reasonable distance of family and friends?
- Does the accommodation fulfil, insofar as it can, the needs of the claimant and recreate his or her former life, eg does he have a garden, access to shops, clubs or the type of facilities he would still be able to enjoy?
- Can the accommodation be made to fulfil the claimant's needs if the defendant provides top-up funds, eg to enable the claimant to purchase

a room with his own bathroom and with facilities for his own private carer?

(iv) Alternatively is there privately funded accommodation which more appropriately meets the claimant's needs and recreates his or her former life?

25.48 In respect of care, the issues that arise in respect of the claimant's needs and requirements are:

(i) In relation to his or her condition, whether a medically qualified carer or nurse team leader is required.

(ii) In relation to the care team, the level of qualifications and experience that will be necessary, the number of carers that will be required for transfers and other tasks, whether the claimant needs carers of a particular gender.

(iii) In relation to the need to recreate the life of the claimant if uninjured, the issue will be whether accommodating him in a residential setting will provide him with sufficient care, qualitatively and in terms of quantity, which will fulfil this objective.

25.49 A suitable expert will need to be instructed to determine the claimant's accommodation and care needs. A neuro-rehabilitation expert or paediatric neurologist will usually be required in a catastrophic injury case. Joint instruction should be avoided as it will be necessary for the medical expert to discuss the issues in conference with the care experts, educational psychologist, neuro-psychologist, and other experts instructed by the claimant.

25.50 The neuro-rehabilitation expert, in association with a neuro-psychologist or educational psychologist and care expert, is best qualified to consider the claimant's medical, care, and accommodation needs in a social and domestic context. The care expert must have experience in assessing and setting up home care packages and in comparing the home care package with the publicly provided facilities.

25.51 The experts should be provided with statements detailing the claimant's life as it would have been and life as it is; medical records; records of the residential institution in which the claimant is accommodated.

L. Accommodation

25.52 The first issue is to consider the claimant's current accommodation:

(i) If the claimant is already in state provided accommodation (excluding ordinary rental accommodation provided by the local authority under their Housing Act function), then will this be suitable on a long-term basis?

(ii) If the claimant is in private accommodation, is this suitable or not, having regard to his disability?

(iii) If the claimant's present accommodation is appropriate, as no alternative provision needs to be made, the duty to accommodate by statutory services will not apply so the issue needs no further investigation. A defendant may, of course, argue that statutory services should provide care in the claimant's own, private accommodation, but this provision is discretionary, raises issues as to how a statutory services/private care regime can co-exist, and raises further issues as to whether a charge may be made by statutory services for any care provided.

(iv) If the claimant's accommodation is not suitable, and further alternative accommodation needs to be arranged, then the issues arise as to the need for alternative suitable accommodation.

M. Child Claimant

The first issue which must be addressed is what are the current accommodation arrangements, and, if necessary, what are the potential future accommodation arrangements: **25.53**

(i) If the child is accommodated already in local authority accommodation, this will probably have been provided pursuant to section 17 of the Children Act 1989. The question here will be the extent to which this accommodation:
   • meets the child's needs arising from the injury; and
   • recreates the life that the child would have had if uninjured (see all sections above).

(ii) If the child is accommodated in private accommodation which is unsuitable and which cannot be adapted so as to render it suitable, it may be contended by the defendant that the state should accommodate the child pursuant to section 17 of the Children Act 1989. Two questions arise:
   • Will the accommodation, if adapted, meet the child's needs arising from the injury, and recreate the life that the child would have had if uninjured?
   • What are the implications of the defendant's contention that the state should accommodate the child?

(iii) If the child is accommodated in private accommodation which is unsuitable but which is capable of being rendered suitable, the defendant may contend that the local authority may exercise its jurisdiction under section 2 of the Chronically Sick and Disabled Persons Act 1970. Two questions arise:
   • Will the accommodation, if adapted, meet the child's needs arising from the injury, and recreate the life that the child would have had if uninjured?

345

- What are the implications of the defendant's contention that the state should accommodate the child?

25.54   In relation to the scenarios set out in (ii) and (iii) above:

(i) the local authority is not under a duty to provide for the claimant. Section 17 of the 1989 Act provides for a target duty owed to children generally, not a specific duty to an individual child. The local authority therefore has a discretion in relation to any child as to whether and, if so, how it might provide for that child;

(ii) this power may or may not be exercised in any given year depending on the local authority's resources;

(iii) if the power is exercised so as to provide some level of care to an applicant, the local authority is entitled to charge for the care pursuant to sections 17(5) and 29 of the Children Act 1989. The charge falls to be met by the parents of the child if under 16; and by the child if over 16. The local authority is entitled to charge whether the child is a patient or not.

25.55   The provisions whereby the local authority can charge for provision to children were considered by the Court of Appeal in the case of *R on the application of Spink (by his litigation friend Henrietta Spink) and anor v The London Borough of Wandsworth* [2005] EWCA Civ 302. In that case Mr and Mrs Spink had two severely disabled children aged 17 and 13 who were looked after by their parents at home. The home needed a range of adaptations in order to be suitable for the children's needs. The parents contended that the local authority was under a duty to carry out the adaptations. The local authority refused to do so without assessing the extent to which Mr and Mrs Spink could pay for the adaptations and without full details as to their means. The provisions relating to children were set out in detail in the judgment of the Court of Appeal and the Court held that:

> Where a local authority provides services in accordance with obligations imposed by section 2 of the Chronically Sick and Disabled Persons Act 1970 by exercising functions under section 17 of the Children Act the provision of those services is subject to such rights to charge as are conferred by section 29 of the Children Act.

25.56   In considering the charging provisions the Court of Appeal concluded:

> As a general proposition a local authority can reasonably expect that parents, who can afford the expense, will make any alterations to their home that are necessary for the care of their disabled children, if there is no alternative source of providing these ... we agree with Richards J that a local authority can, in circumstances such as those with which we are concerned, properly decline to be satisfied that it is necessary to provide services to meet the needs of disabled children until it has been demonstrated that, having regard to their means, it is not reasonable to expect their parents to provide these.

The position for children is therefore different from the position of adults com- **25.57**
ing within section 21 of the National Assistance Act 1948. Where the child has a
personal injury claim issues may arise as to the means of both the parents (through
payment of past care in the litigation) and the child through the litigation.

N. Adult Claimants with Capacity

In some cases the non-patient adult claimant may be in state accommodation. **25.58**
In most cases, a non-patient adult is unlikely to be in accommodation provided
by the state, other than that provided pursuant to the Housing Act, but may well
be in unsuitable private accommodation.

If the non-patient adult claimant is in state accommodation then: **25.59**

(i) it may be that the claimant is in temporary state accommodation, for instance
a rehabilitation unit. The question arises as to the claimant's permanent
accommodation needs once discharged from this hospital or unit:
   • if, on discharge, the claimant's home or other private accommodation will
be suitable, no further issue arises in relation to accommodation;
   • if, on discharge, the claimant's home or other private accommodation will
be unsuitable and cannot be adapted so as to render it suitable then the
issue arises as to how the claimant will be placed in suitable accommodation and whether that accommodation can be purchased by an interim
payment;
   • if, on discharge, the claimant's home or other private accommodation will
be unsuitable and can be adapted so as to render it suitable, then the issue
arises as to whether the cost of adaptations can be met by an interim
payment;
(ii) it may be that the claimant is in permanent state accommodation, that is
accommodation either provided or paid for by the state, and this is what the
claimant wants. Care will need to be taken to ensure that the claimant understands the implications of this decision. It will be necessary to consider
obtaining an indemnity from the defendant to cover any future change in
the claimant's accommodation;
(iii) alternatively, it may be that the claimant is in, what is alleged to be, permanent state accommodation, and does not wish to remain there. The following questions arise in respect of the accommodation:
   • Does it meet the claimant's needs arising from the injury? This will involve
an assessment of those needs and of the manner in which they are being
met by the state.
   • Does it recreate the life that the claimant would have had if uninjured?

- What are or may be the charging implications? Is the local authority charging the claimant? If not, is there any possibility that it will attempt to do so?

(iv) further, what is the intention of the current accommodation provider in relation to the claimant's accommodation? In essence, can it guarantee that the claimant will be accommodated in the present accommodation permanently?

25.60 If the claimant needs to be re-accommodated:

(i) the local authority must assess the need;

(ii) the local authority must, if it finds that there is a need for accommodation, that accommodation is not otherwise provided to the claimant, and that no other public body should meet this need, exercise its functions under section 21 of the National Assistance Act 1948;

(iii) under such statutory provision, the local authority has a duty to provide such accommodation and care as its assessment identifies as the claimant's needs;

(iv) a local authority may decide to discharge its duty by deciding to accommodate the claimant on a short-term basis, for example until an interim payment application has been heard or damages have been assessed;

(v) there is a discretion by the local authority as to how such services are provided in practice. It does not have to meet the *Wells v Wells* requirement that a claimant should be restored to the position in which he was and would have been in. Instead it only has to discharge the much lower standard of acting in a manner which is unreasonable, ie the *Wednesbury* test.

(vi) the provision of such services will be charged for by the local authority in accordance with:

- the legislation, both primary and subordinate, which governs the provision of the services;
- the guidance and/or directions which may have been issued by the relevant government department to local authorities. Note, such guidance is issued in respect of charging for the provision of services in residential accommodation and the provision of services in a person's own home;
- the local authority's own policy in relation to charging;

(vii) in respect of the treatment of a non-patient adult claimant's damages received for personal injury, these damages are subject to means testing by local authorities. The damages are not ring-fenced and protected unless:

- held in a special needs trust; or
- comprise periodical payments (but note that the lump sum element of any structured settlement is not excluded from means assessment);
- they fall within the guidance in *Fairer Charging Policies for Home Care and Other Non-Residential Social Services*.

In relation to the income and capital which the non-patient adult claimant **25.61** may receive the distinction between the section 21 and 29 provision is no longer clear-cut. The Court of Appeal in the *Crofton* case whilst recognising the difference in wording between sections 21 and 29 of the National Assistance Act 1948 found:

> We cannot accept that it is necessary to infer from the difference in legislative history that Parliament intended that an award of damages for personal injury should be disregarded at the threshold stage in relation to section 21 of NAA but taken into account in relation to section 29 of NAA and section 2 of CSDPA.

The Court of Appeal concluded on this point that the local authority is obliged **25.62** to disregard personal injury damages administered by the Court of Protection when deciding the threshold question. That is, in looking at the claimant's needs the award of damages is irrelevant. However, when it comes to the means testing stage the position is more complicated. The Court of Appeal simply found on the facts in *Crofton* the extent to which the personal injury award would be taken into account at the means testing stage by the local authority was unclear as there was insufficient evidence to decide the point.

The Court of Appeal concluded that: **25.63**

> The Judge was right to hold that the Council could and would make direct payments to meet the claimant's needs despite the award of damages and that these payments should be taken into account in the assessment of damages.

It is still the case that the local authority is entitled, in certain circumstances, and **25.64** may choose to test the means of a claimant's husband or wife.

In the vast majority of cases, any provision by the state will fall far short of **25.65** what the claimant can reasonably expect in order to recreate his or her uninjured life. Accommodation in a residential setting would usually be unacceptable. Accommodation in the community, if provided by the state, may be in poor quality housing and/or in an area in which the claimant would not have chosen to live in but for the injury. Further, although a defendant may suggest that it will top-up any state provision so as to ensure that better quality housing in the right locality is provided, the mechanics of this process are likely to prove difficult to put into place. For example, will the accommodation be rented, with the rent shared between the local authority and the defendant? If so, could the local authority, at some future date, choose to relocate the claimant to a different rental property; and, if so, with what effect on the shared rental arrangement? If it is proposed that the accommodation be purchased, will a local authority wish to commit significant capital in one budgetary year and, if so, how will the capital sum be calculated? Further, who will own the property? What would occur if the claimant wished to move? These, and other questions, are the questions which, should a defendant raise 'top-up' as the solution to the difficulty, will need to be answered by the relevant local authority in statement form.

25.66 If the claimant's accommodation can be rendered suitable by adaptations, and the defendant contends that the local authority should exercise its jurisdiction, under section 2 of the Chronically Sick and Disabled Persons Act 1970, to do so:

(i) provision of adaptations by a local authority pursuant to the 1970 Act is discretionary. There is a power, not a duty to carry out adaptations;

(ii) the local authority may charge for the adaptations.

O. Adult Patients Requiring Accommodation

25.67 If the adult patient claimant is in state accommodation:

(i) it may be that the claimant is in temporary state accommodation, for instance a rehabilitation unit. The question arises as to the claimant's permanent accommodation needs once discharged from this hospital or unit:

- if, on discharge, the claimant's home or other private will be unsuitable and cannot be adapted so as to render it suitable;

- if, on discharge, the claimant's home or other private accommodation will be suitable, no further issue arises in relation to accommodation;

- if, on discharge, the claimant's home or other private accommodation will be unsuitable and can be adapted so as to render it suitable;

(ii) it may be that the claimant is in permanent state accommodation, that is, accommodation either provided or paid for by the state, and this is what the litigation friend and claimant wants. Great care will need to be taken to ensure that the litigation friend understands the implications of this decision. An indemnity will need to be considered to cover any change in future provision and top-up provision will need to be considered. It is very unlikely there is no improvement that could properly be made, eg the provision of a case manager/additional care/private vehicle/extra physiotherapy;

(iii) alternatively it may be that the claimant is in, what is alleged to be, permanent state accommodation, and does not wish to remain there. The following questions arise:

- Does the accommodation:

(a) meet the claimant's needs arising from the injury? This will involve an assessment of those needs and of the manner in which they are being met by the state.

(b) recreate the life that the claimant would have had if uninjured?

- Further, what is the intention of the current accommodation provider in relation to the claimant's accommodation? In essence, can it guarantee that the claimant will be accommodated in the present accommodation permanently?

If the claimant is accommodated in private accommodation which is unsuitable **25.68** and which cannot be adapted so as to render it suitable, it may be contended by the defendant that the state should accommodate the adult pursuant to section 21 of the National Assistance Act 1948. Two questions arise:

(i) Will the accommodation, if adapted, meet the adult's needs arising from the injury, and recreate the life that the adult would have had if uninjured?

(ii) What are the implications of the defendant's contention that the state should accommodate the adult?

25.69

If the claimant needs to be re-accommodated:

(i) the local authority must assess the need;

(ii) the local authority must, if it finds that there is a need for accommodation, that accommodation is not otherwise provided to the claimant, and that no other public body should meet this need, exercise its functions under section 21 of the National Assistance Act 1948;

(iii) under such statutory provision, the local authority has a duty to provide such accommodation and care as its assessment identifies as the claimant's needs;

(iv) a local authority may decide to discharge its duty by deciding to accommodate the claimant on a short-term basis, for example until an interim payment application has been heard or damages have been assessed;

(v) there is a discretion by the local authority as to how such services are provided in practice. It does not have to meet the *Wells v Wells* requirement that a claimant should be restored to the position in which he was and would have been in. Instead it only has to discharge the much lower standard of acting in a manner which is unreasonable, ie the *Wednesbury* test;

(vi) the provision of such services will be charged for by the local authority in accordance with:
    - the legislation, both primary and subordinate, which governs the provision of the services;
    - the guidance and/or directions which may have been issued by the relevant government department to local authorities. Note, such guidance is issued in respect of charging for the provision of services in residential accommodation and the provision of services in a person's own home;
    - the local authority's own policy in relation to charging.

351

25.70 If the adult patient claimant's accommodation can be rendered suitable by adaptations, and the defendant contends that the local authority should exercise its jurisdiction, under section 2 of the Chronically Sick and Disabled Persons Act 1970, to do so:

    (i) provision of adaptations by a local authority pursuant to the 1970 Act is discretionary. There is a power, not a duty to carry out adaptations;

    (ii) the local authority may charge for the adaptations.

P. Care

25.71 Similar issues arise in relation to the provision of state care to a claimant.

25.72 If the claimant is a child, care will be provided pursuant to section 17 of the Children Act 1989. The same considerations apply as discussed in respect of accommodation.

25.73 If the claimant is an adult with capacity:

    (i) if, in the cases where the claimant is accommodated or will be accommodated in state accommodation pursuant to section 21 of the National Assistance Act 1948:

- the state is obliged to provide care which is ancillary to that accommodation;
- in practice this will mean that if a claimant is in a residential home they will have basic daily needs met by a team of carers employed in the home, ie they will be dressed, bathed, given medication, fed. Exactly what is provided and the expertise and turnover of carers needs to be investigated. If the claimant has a particular need for one-to-one care this will almost certainly not be provided, and the issue will arise as to whether it can be provided within the residential setting by top-up care. Some physiotherapy and speech therapy may be provided, but almost inevitably experts will recommend a higher level as reasonably necessary if it can be privately funded. If a vehicle can be bought for the claimant this will allow him/her to go out more often than the constraints of residential care allow. A privately paid case manager will usually be justified;
- whatever the precise nature of the local authority's obligation, the question of top-up will require investigation. In particular, the practical issues as to who controls a care team which comprises carers provided (or paid for) by a local authority and privately employed carers, how the care team will be managed, etc, will all require consideration by the care expert. The issue will arise as to whether the residential home will allow the claimant to have her own carers, does this interfere with the other

residents' arrangements and the ethos of the home? If the claimant has a private carer will the residential home expect to make use of that additional carer for other residents if it becomes necessary? Most residential homes will have no experience of top-up and whether and how it would work needs to be carefully investigated;

- further, the question of whether and, if so, how the claimant would be charged for the basic local authority provision and for any top-up provision will require consideration. There may be a considerable doubt as to whether the residential home will allow the claimant to employ his/her own carers direct. If they are employed by the local authority then local authority rates are sometimes as expensive, if not more so, than those quoted by a care expert for a privately employed regime;

(ii) if the claimant is accommodated in their own accommodation which is not provided by the state, the defendant may contend that the claimant should be content with care services provided by the local authority. Provision of these services is governed by section 29 of the National Assistance Act 1948:

- The local authority is not under a duty to provide for care for the claimant. It has a discretion as to whether and, if so, how it might provide for the claimant.

- This power may or may not be exercised in any given year depending on the local authority's resources.

- If the power is exercised so as to provide some level of care to a claimant, it must be assumed that the local authority is entitled to charge for the care. Again the charge may be at least as much as private provision but have the disadvantage that the claimant or his/her case manager has no choice about the carers and there may be different carers every day/week.

25.74 If the claimant is an adult without capacity, the same considerations apply as those discussed above with the exception that an adult claimant patient cannot be charged from his/her personal injury damages for the care provided pursuant to section 21 of the National Assistance Act 1948.

Q. The Cases Since *Sowden v Lodge*

25.75 In a number of decisions since *Sowden v Lodge*, High Court Judges have refused for a number of different reasons to reduce the costs of care by allowing the defendant to insist on the claimant utilising local authority provision.

25.76 In the case of *Freeman v Lockett*, Mr Justice Tomlinson reviewed the case of *Sowden v Lodge* and pointed out in paragraph 38 of his judgment that the decision of the Court of Appeal in that case was restricted to provision made to an adult under section 21 of the National Assistance Act 1948. The Judge further pointed out that in any case where it is reasonable for the claimant to be provided with care at home the provision of direct payments or other assistance from the local authority is subject both to discretion and to change in the future, it cannot provide a secure basis for a claimant's future needs.

25.77 At paragraph 40 of the judgment Mr Justice Tomlinson stated:

> In my judgment nothing said in *Sowden* was intended to be of guidance in a case such as the present ... The starting point in the present case is that it is reasonable for the claimant to be provided with care in her own home. Nothing said in *Sowden* gives the court any assistance as to how it should approach and evaluate the possible continued availability of direct financial assistance from the local authority towards the provision of care.

25.78 The Judge in the *Freeman* case drew the distinction between the section 21 provision for a cognitively impaired claimant who is a patient of the Court of Protection and the provision of care to a claimant with retained cognitive function. He stated in respect of a severely cognitively impaired claimant in residential accommodation the availability of continuing provision was secure. In the case of a claimant whose cognitive and intellectual powers have not been injured, 'it is axiomatic that she must be assisted in the attainment of so normal a family life in her own home as is reasonably possible'.

25.79 Whilst recognising there was a possibility of double recovery if the claimant continued to receive local authority direct payments the Judge commented that he would anticipate that the local authority would withdraw payments on receipt of a copy of the judgment. The Judge also pointed out that the defendant had refused to provide the claimant with an indemnity in the event that local authority payments should cease in the future. He commented: '[The defendant] wished in that regard to cast onto the claimant the entirety of the risk, whatever it may be. No principle of law either requires or encourages the Court to reach that result.'

25.80 In *Walton v Calderdale NHS Trust* [2005] EWHC 1053 and *Tinsley v Sarkar* [2005] EWHC 102, Mr Justice Silber and Mr Justice Leveson each held that local authority provision other than pursuant to section 21 of the National Assistance Act 1948 simply did not provide the necessary security for the future for injured claimants.

25.81 Mr Justice Tomlinson stated in the *Freeman* case:

> I would have expected that the purpose of an award of damages against a tortfeasor would in these circumstances be to relieve the victim of his negligence of the necessity to resort to state funding of his or her care, thereby incidentally relieving the state of the necessity to fund the care of that victim and ensuring that the state's limited and hard pressed resources are available to fund care in the case of those whose injury or affliction has not come about as a result of the actionable fault

of another who is by statute required to purchase insurance against the risk of his negligently injuring persons whilst engaging in the activity in question, here driving a motor vehicle on the public highway.

In respect of the argument that a claimant has a duty to mitigate her loss by utilising state benefits Mr Justice Tomlinson stated: **25.82**

> I recoil from the notion that a failure to avail oneself of a state benefit could in the circumstances be characterized as an unreasonable failure to mitigate loss. I should have thought that such conduct was praiseworthy and moreover calculated to contribute to the sense of wellbeing of the person concerned.

In the case of *A (by his litigation friend C) v B NHS Trust* (May 2006), Mr Justice Lloyd Jones assessed the costs of care for a cerebral palsy child. The Judge found that no deduction should be made for any possible care to be provided by the local authority. **25.83**

> The defendant has not produced evidence that care in future will be provided by the local authority. I find myself in the same position as Tomlinson J in *Freeman v Lockett* [2006] EWHC 102 in that there is no principled basis on which I am able to esti-mate what provision would be made by the local authority in the future. In any event, I consider that the local authority would be entitled to charge and would charge for any care made available following the award of damages. Accordingly, even if care were to be provided by the local authority, it could only have a bearing on the rate at which the defendant should reimburse the claimant. In these circum-stances, no adjustment is to be made to the calculation of the cost of care on the basis that care will be provided by the local authority.

The impact of the section 29 provision has therefore been considered by the courts in a number of cases since *Sowden v Lodge*. Judges have refused for a number of different reasons to reduce the costs of care by allowing the defendant to insist on the claimant utilising local authority provision. In the case of *Crofton v NHSLA*, HH Judge Reid QC reduced a claimant's care claim on the basis the claimant would continue to receive direct payments from the local authority. As discussed below, the Court of Appeal has allowed the appeal and remitted the case to the Judge for further evidence from the local authority and so that the local authority can be joined in the litigation. **25.84**

In the *Crofton* case, the Judge at first instance heard evidence from the local authority with reference to the issue of whether local authority residential care was suitable for the claimant. HH Judge Reid QC awarded the claimant a private care regime but made a reduction for direct payments. He relied on the fact that the local authority witness had indicated these would continue to be made pursuant to the guidance currently in force: *Fairer Charging Policies for Home Care and Other Non-Residential Social Services*. The Judge concluded that as the local authority employee had stated that the local authority would continue to have obligations to provide for the claimant's assessed needs he would continue to receive these. **25.85**

However, the Judge himself acknowledged that there could be future costs pressures on the local authority which would reduce such payments. The Court of Appeal have now pointed out that: 'It is by no means far-fetched to suggest that, at some time in the future, the ministerial policy of ring-fencing personal injury damages and/or the council's approach to the policy will change.'

25.86 The details of what the local authority will provide will need to be re-examined in the *Crofton* case now that the Court of Appeal have remitted it to the Judge for fuller investigation.

25.87 The reasoning of Mr Justice Tomlinson that the provision of future care by a local authority was too precarious for a personal injury claimant to rely on was applied in a number of other first instance decisions including by:

   (i) Mr Justice Silber in *Walton v Calderdale NHS Trust* [2005] EWHC 1053;

   (ii) Mr Justice Leveson in *Tinsley v Sarkar* [2005] EWHC 192 QB;

   (iii) Mr Justice Keith in *Martin Redhead (by his litigation friend Carole Redhead) v Alan Rawcliffe* [2006] EWHC 2695 QB;

   (iv) Mr Justice Lloyd Jones in *A (by his litigation friend C) v B NHS Trust* (2006) unreported.

25.88 Each of these Judges held that local authority provision other than pursuant to section 21 of National Assistance Act 1948 simply did not provide the necessary security for the future for injured claimants.

25.89 In the light of the Court of Appeal decision in *Crofton* the position will continue to need detailed investigation on a case-by-case basis. The issue in that case was whether the court should take into account direct payments for care made by a local authority to an injured claimant, who was living at home with a private care package. At first instance the Judge had reduced the award for care to take into account the availability of direct payments to the extent of making a reduction of £1,387,525. By contrast in the case of *Freeman v Lockett*, Tomlinson J decided there should be no reduction in that claimant's damages to reflect the possibility of direct payments by the local authority. The Court of Appeal did not disagree with the reasoning of Lord Justice Tomlinson in *Freeman v Lockett* but stated:

> In *Freeman v Lockett*, Tomlinson J decided there should be no reduction in the claimant's damages to reflect the possibility of direct payments by the local authority. A sufficient basis for his decision was his finding that, provided that no deduction on account of the possible receipt of state or local authority funding was made from her award of damages, the claimant would withdraw her application for funding; she wanted to rely exclusively on private funding for her care.

25.90 The decision reached by Tomlinson J was endorsed as a reasonable decision on the facts of that case. The Court of Appeal went on to explain that Tomlinson J was also influenced 'by the fragility of the policy from which the right to receive direct payments derived' in concluding it would not be reasonable to take them into account in assessing personal injury damages. In this respect the Court of Appeal commented:

> We would accept that there may be cases where the possibility of a claimant receiving direct payments is so uncertain they may be disregarded altogether in the assessment of damages. It will depend on the facts of the particular case. But if the court finds that a claimant will receive direct payments for at least a certain period of time and possibly much longer, it seems to us this finding must be taken into account in the assessment. In such a case, the correct way to reflect the uncertainties to which Tomlinson J referred is to discount the multiplier. We did not understand Mr Taylor to contend otherwise.

Effectively the Court went back to the principles in *Hodgson v Trapp* [1989] 1 AC **25.91**
807 and pointed out that:

> It is trite law that a claimant is entitled to recover the full extent of his loss. That involves asking what the claimant would have received but for the event which gave rise to the claim and which he can no longer get; and what he has received and will receive as a result of the event which he would not have received but for the event. The question then arises whether the latter sums must be deducted from the former when assessing damages. *Parry v Cleaver.* In *Hodgson v Trapp* Lord Bridge said that it was elementary that if in consequence of the injuries he has sustained a claimant enjoys receipts to which he would not otherwise have been entitled, then prima facie those receipts are to be set against the aggregate loss and expenses in arriving at the measure of damages. To this basic rule there are certain well established exceptions, none of which is of application in the present case.

The claimant in *Crofton* appealed against the Judge in making a deduction for **25.92**
direct payments which the Judge had calculated the claimant would receive in the future. The claimant won the appeal because the Judge had not had sufficient evidence to properly assess what the claimant would actually receive by way of direct payments. That is, he had had insufficient evidence as to how the payments would be affected by the claimant having a large award of damages. The case has been remitted to the Judge to carry out a detailed assessment in this respect on the facts of this case. The Court of Appeal pointed to the fact that the issue was raised by the defendant at the last minute in the course of trial and there should have been more detailed consideration of it. However, the Court accepted it was an issue that should be investigated. Further, the Court of Appeal accepted that the uncertainties as to the future of local authority provision would require the Judge to make 'a substantial discount' to the multiplier.

The Court of Appeal concluded on this point that the local authority is obliged **25.93**
to disregard personal injury damages administered by the Court of Protection when deciding the threshold question. That is, in looking at the claimant's needs the award of damages is irrelevant. However, when it comes to the means testing stage the position is more complicated. The Court of Appeal simply found on the

facts in *Crofton* the extent to which the personal injury award would be taken into account at the means testing stage by the local authority was unclear as there was insufficient evidence to decide the point.

25.94 Further the Court of Appeal concluded that:

> The Judge was right to hold that the Council could and would make direct payments to meet the claimant's needs despite the award of damages and that these payments should be taken into account in the assessment of damages.

25.95 In summary the position following the decision of the Court of Appeal in *Crofton v NHSLA* is that:

(i) each case will depend on its own facts;

(ii) it cannot be said with certainty that direct payments never need to be taken into account in assessing personal injury damages;

(iii) in some cases where the facts are similar to the *Freeman* case a claimant will be able to say that they do not want to utilise public funding; they can then withdraw any application for public funding and notify the local authority of the personal injury award; that is, the claimant may specifically argue he/she wants to rely exclusively on a private regime;

(iv) where direct payments have been made and will continue to be made by a local authority to a claimant they need to be taken into account in order to avoid double recovery thereby reducing the claimant's losses; it will be for the defendant to show what will be provided;

(v) the extent to which direct payments need to be taken into account requires detailed evidence as to how the local authority will carry out the means testing exercise after the claimant has received his/her award of damages; in order to ascertain this it may be necessary to join the local authority in the proceedings so that the judge can hear evidence as to what the local authority will provide and for what period of time;

(vi) there will always be uncertainty as to the future receipt of direct payments this will need to be reflected in a significant reduction in the multiplier.

25.96 The Court of Appeal judgment in *Crofton* ended with the following remarks:

> We cannot conclude this judgment without expressing our dismay at the complexity and labyrinthine nature of the relevant legislation and guidance as well as (in some respects) its obscurity. Social security law should be clear and accessible. The tortuous analysis in the earlier part of this judgment shows that it is neither.

25.97 The result would appear to be that the problem of grappling with this legislation will not go away and it will continue to be a feature of all high value personal injury and clinical negligence claims. Whilst the principle that the claimant should not recover the private costs of care from the tortfeasor and recover the same cost from the local authority is clearly right, the practical difficulties in ascertaining what the local authority will in fact pay and for how long are very considerable. The Court of Appeal suggested the local authority should be joined as a party to the proceedings in the *Crofton* case. The position will continue to be determined on a case-by-case basis but in the case of seriously injured claimants who wish to be cared for at home the authorities support the arguments that local authority provision does not have to be utilised in preference to a private regime by way of reduction of damages. If on the other hand the claimant will in fact utilise local authority provision then clearly damages have to be calculated on this basis.

26

OTHER AREAS OF MEDICAL LAW

This chapter touches briefly on three areas that fall outside of mainstream clinical **26.01** negligence practice: health and safety regulations, Human Rights Act applications, and judicial review. These aspects of medical law are less commonly encountered and beyond the scope of this work. What follows is not a guide to the legal processes involved, but is a brief commentary intended to alert the reader to these aspects of the law which may be relevant to a client's concerns. Health and safety legislation may provide a way forward in some hospital-based claims; the Human Rights Act elements may arise, although perhaps in fewer cases than may have been thought would be the case when the Act came into force. The need for Judicial Review may arise in connection with public funding or health care provision. For these reasons, the clinical negligence practitioner should have some awareness of these areas of law, in order that the client may be provided with timely advice, and referral if necessary.

A. Other Liabilities

Claims arising from trips, slips, food poisoning, injuries due to defective prod- **26.02** ucts, and other mishaps to patients and visitors (and staff) will follow the usual course of personal injury litigation. These will be managed on behalf of the Trust by the National Health Service Litigation Authority under the Liabilities to Third Parties Scheme (LTPS).

Health and Safety Regulations: MRSA Claims

26.03 Historically, it has been difficult to succeed in claims arising from infection with MRSA organisms contracted as a result of exposure in a health service setting. In essence, the difficulty is that the pathogen responsible for MRSA infection is present in many environments and frequently found on the skin of asymptomatic patients. Even where it is possible to demonstrate that the proposed claimant has been exposed as a result of breach of duty on the part of the Trust, it is extremely difficult to establish that but for that breach the patient would not have been infected. This is in contrast with some other infections, such as Legionnaire's disease, which may be traced to a probable source.

26.04 It is suggested that health and safety regulations may provide a more effective route to bring claims for damages for patients who have contracted the MRSA infection in hospital, as staphylococcus aureus (of which MRSA is a variant) has been included in the health and safety committee's list of dangerous pathogens which can cause human disease and may be a hazard to employees. This approach was discussed in Sapna Malik, 'MRSA Claims: An Alternative Approach', *Clinical Risk AVMA Medical and Legal Journal* 11(1) January 2005, 34–36.

26.05 'Nosocomial infection' is the generic term for an infection acquired in hospital, that is, an infection secondary to the patient's presenting condition that becomes symptomatic after 48 hours of hospitalisation. There are numerous organisms which may cause infection in the hospital patient; in addition to MRSA and Legionnaires disease; there is the increasingly prevalent clostridium difficile, staphylococcus aureus, candidiasis, influenza, pneumonia, and the common cold. The infective micro-organisms may be transmitted by several routes and many organisms are capable of being transmitted by more than one route, including person-to-person contact, contact with contaminated surfaces or equipment, in food and drink, or through the air in droplets or dust and from the patient's own skin surface.

26.06 Risk factors for an individual succumbing to infection include:

    (i)   pre-existing poor state of health;
    (ii) treatment which lowers immunity;
    (iii) invasive procedures which breach the body's natural defences;
    (iv) exposure to large numbers of sick people.

26.07 Avoidable environmental risk factors include:

    (i)   inadequate infection control procedures;
    (ii) human failure to correctly implement infection control measures;
    (iii) technical failure of infection control measures;

(iv) admission to a hospital or ward for elective surgery at the time of an outbreak of infection (two or more cases).

The starting point will be the identity of the infective organism and the routes by **26.08**
which it may be transmitted. It may be possible to advance a claim that, on the
balance of probabilities, an infection was acquired as a result of flawed procedures, if the claimant was infected by an organism with an identifiable mode of
transmission or one where colonisation should be preventable, such as clostridium difficile. The key to the investigation will be pre-action disclosure of the
documentation related to the control of infection and management of outbreaks,
in particular the protocols and guidelines in place at the relevant periods, and the
minutes of the hospital's Control of Infection Committee. Most of this information is either not patient-specific or may be anonymised; disclosure may be
requested under the Freedom of Information Act.

It may be helpful to instruct the consultant microbiologist expert early in the **26.09**
investigation, to advise on the completeness of disclosure and the merits of the
case in the light of the preliminary fact-finding.

Where there is no evidence of an avoidable exposure to infection, or of a poorly **26.10**
controlled outbreak, or of failure in infection control systems, it is unlikely a
claim would succeed, as it would be impossible to dispose of the non-negligent
explanations for the infection and thus it could not be said that 'but for' the
breach of duty the infection would have been avoided.

It is suggested that the exposure of patients to MRSA may in some circumstances **26.11**
amount to a breach of the Control of Substances Hazardous to Health (COSHH)
2002. If a patient has acquired an infection in circumstances where there has
been breach of COSHH regulations and the breach can be shown to have mat-
erially increased the risk of infection, a remedy may lie in damages without
the necessity to establish causation by disposing of the non-negligent routes of
transmission.

To the writer's knowledge this analysis has yet to be tested in the courts but may **26.12**
provide an alternative route to remedy where is there is at present little likelihood
of success. In principle, it may prove possible to extend this approach to other
claims that arise from a patient's exposure to hazardous situations or substances.

B. The Human Rights Act 1998

The Human Rights Act was expected to have a significant impact on the devel- **26.13**
opment of UK individual health care rights after it came into force in October
2000. In practice this has not proved to be the case, other than in connection with

the coronial inquest, as discussed in Chapter 22. Institutionally, however, the effect of the Act may be seen in the guidelines in force for decision making, for example, see Department of Health, *Human Rights in Health Care—a Framework for Local Action* (2007), which can be found on <http://www.doh.gov.uk> (accessed 2 April 2007). This describes the rights enshrined in the Act and how these apply to health services' policies and procedures at Trust level.

26.14 Detailed discussion of the application of this branch of public law to medical treatment is outside the scope of this work. The comments below are confined to a brief outline of the ways in which actions for breach of a Convention right under the Act may be relevant to the concerns of a client who consults a clinical negligence practitioner.

26.15 Under the Human Rights Act, section 6 (i) it is unlawful for a public authority to act in a way which is incompatible with a Convention right. By and large, cases that have been brought in relation to medical treatment concern access to health care or personal autonomy in health care decision making.

The Articles

26.16 The articles most likely to be engaged in a case relating to health care are:

  (i)   Article 2: Everyone's right to life shall be protected by law. No one shall be deprived of his life intentionally save in the execution of a sentence of a court following his conviction of a crime for which this penalty is prescribed by law;

  (ii) Article 3: No one shall be subjected to torture or to inhuman or degrading treatment or punishment;

  (iii) Article 8: Everyone has the right to respect for his private and family life, his home, and his correspondence;

26.17 A breach of a Convention right is actionable. The remedy ordered by the Court on a successful action will depend upon the facts of the case before the Court and will be aimed at achieving a balance between the rights of the individual and the public interest. The Court is charged with affording 'just satisfaction' to the injured party for violation of the Convention, if found. Pecuniary loss, non-pecuniary loss, costs and expenses may be awarded but just satisfaction may be achieved by the court finding a violation.

Standing

26.18 Under section 7(3) an application may be brought only where the applicant is, or would be, affected by the act or omission complained of.

Limitation

Under section 7(5) the limitation period for bringing an action is 12 months **26.19**
from the date on which the act complained of took place.

C. Judicial Review

Judicial review is a remedy of last resort against a public authority. All other rem- **26.20**
edies should have been considered and all genuine routes to remedy should have
been pursued before an application is made for a judicial review—one of the
factors to take into account is whether the client's needs are very urgent; in
which case a formal alternative remedy may not be a realistic option but alternative dispute resolution may be appropriate.

The procedural rules governing applications for judicial review can be found in **26.21**
CPR 54.

It should be borne in mind that judicial review is not a review of the merits of **26.22**
the decision complained of; it is a review of the process of decision making. The
Court will consider whether the decision-making process was based on illegality,
unfairness, or irrationality.

   (i)   An authority acts illegally if it exceeds the scope of its powers, misapplies the
         law, delegates a non-delegable function, or similar.
  (ii)   The question of unfairness of decision making is based on whether there was
         a procedural impropriety, a breach of natural justice, or an abuse of power.
 (iii)   The test of irrationality rests on the definition of unreasonableness in *Associated
         Provincial Picturehouses Ltd v Wednesbury Corporation* [1948] 1 KB 223.

In arriving at their decision on an application for judicial review the Court may **26.23**
have regard to the claimant's conduct, whether there is evidence the claimant has
suffered any substantial hardship, the requirements of good administration, and
the likelihood of a different decision resulting from proper process.

Standing

Under section 31(3) of the Supreme Court Act 1981 anyone with sufficient **26.24**
interest in the matter under review may bring judicial review proceedings. If the
judicial review includes Human Rights Act elements, the application may only
be made by a direct 'victim', under section 7(5) of the Act.

Limitation

Under CPR 54.5 an application for judicial review must be filed promptly and **26.25**
in any event not later than three months after the grounds to make the claim

first arose. CPR 54.7 provides that the claim form must be served within seven days of being issued.

26.26　The occasion to bring a judicial review will occur rarely in general clinical negligence practice but if it does arise, steps must be taken as a matter of urgency. If the claimant is not to be referred internally or externally to a public law specialist, advice may be obtained from the specialist support and advice line: public law specialist support is available to any firm or organisation that holds a general civil contract or general help with casework kite mark with the Legal Services Commission. Further information about the public law project and the advice available can be found at <http://www.publiclawproject.org.uk> (accessed 2 April 2007).

Appendices

APPENDIX 1

Particulars of Claim in a Claim where the Mother Died in Childbirth

IN THE HIGH COURT OF JUSTICE   Claim no
QUEEN'S BENCH DIVISION
B E T W E E N:

XY
(administrator of ZY deceased)

Claimant

- and -

J HOSPITALS NHS TRUST

Defendant

PARTICULARS OF CLAIM

1. The Defendant was at all relevant times responsible for the management control and administration of J Hospital, and was under a duty to provide medical, nursing, midwifery and other services at and for the purposes of the said hospital.
2. The Claimant is the administrator of ZY (referred to as "the Deceased") who died on 15 July 2003 in the circumstances set out below. Letters of Administration were granted to the Claimant on 1 November 2003 out of J District Registry.
3. The Claimant brings this claim on behalf of the estate of the Deceased pursuant to the Law Reform (Miscellaneous Provisions) Act 1934 and on behalf of the dependants of the Deceased pursuant to the Fatal Accidents Act 1976.
4. Each of the doctors midwives and nurses who was responsible for any part of the care of the Deceased in the circumstances set out below owed to the Deceased a duty of care and the Defendant is vicariously liable for any breach of such duty by their servants or agents.
5. The Deceased was born on 12 May 1978 and was married to the Claimant on 1 October 2002.
6. On 12 November 2002 the Deceased attended her general practitioner and reported her last menstrual period was 3 October 2002, she was diagnosed as 7 weeks pregnant and her estimated date of delivery was assessed as 10 July 2003. It was noted she should have a first trimester scan.
   [page 8]
7. The general practitioner referral letter dated 20 November 2003 and states that the Deceased was a 25 year old prima gravida who recently married and delighted to be pregnant. It gave a past medical history of a benign breast lump and colposcopy following an abnormal smear.
   [page 15]
8. On 28 November 2003 the Deceased attended her general practitioner and reported vaginal bleeding for 1 week, her general practitioner referred her for a viability scan.
   [page 8]

9. On 2 January 2003 the Deceased was seen at the booking clinic of J Hospital, it was noted she had a 5 year history of fibroids, bleeding in pregnancy, her estimated date of delivery and scan date were both 10 July 2003, she was 5' 2" tall and her weight was then 9 stone 8oz. [page 26]

10. Thereafter the Deceased did not suffer any complications in pregnancy other than a small quantity of glucose in urine on 2 April 2003 and peripheral oedema from 30 June 2003. [page 9, 27–28]

11. On 15 July 2003 the Deceased telephoned J Hospital at 0300 and reported she had had contractions since 0115, no spontaneous rupture of membranes [SROM] and no show, she agreed to stay at home and mobilise and telephone when she wanted to be admitted. [page 35]

12. At 0900 on 15 July 2003 the Deceased was admitted to J Hospital, the admission note records:
    "Admitted with contractions since 0120, now 1:5, no show no
    SROM, T36.5 P 97, BP 150/95
    fundus = term, long lie
    cephalic 3/5th ROL FHHR (fetal heart rate heard)
    CTG commenced".
    [page 38]

13. The CTG was discontinued at 0945 and at 1045 the note records:
    "VE [vaginal examination] to assess
    Cx [cervix] slightly posterior, effaced, 2–3 cms dilated, head –2,
    membranes intact, FHHR
    BP 150/100 P.I.H [pregnancy induced hypertension] bloods
    taken and sent".
    [page 38]

14. At 1145 on 15 July 2003 the note records:
    "BP 150/100 FH 126, feels nauseated, given bowl, may want
    epidural soon".
    [page 38]

15. At 1230 on 15 July 2003 the note records:
    "BP 150/95 FH 132
    would like an epidural
    Lab rung re FBC [full blood count]
    Hb [haemoglobin] 12.7;
    WC [white cell] 14.4;
    Plat [platelets] 153.
    Anaesthetist contacted, would like clotting result prior to epidural
    [the Deceased] informed.
    [page 38]

16. At 1300 the lab rang with the clotting result recorded as:
    "Prothrombin time   0.88
    APTT   0.91
    Fibrinogen   5.3"
    [page 39]

17. At 1410 on 15 July 2003 the epidural was sited, the Deceased's blood pressure was recorded as 160/105 and FH as 132.
    [page 39]

18. At 1440 on 15 July 2003 the note records:
    "VE to assess, cervix unchanged
    2–3 cms dilated. Head –2 ↑ [above] spines,
    ARM [artificial rupture of membranes] discussed and performed
    blood stained liquor draining
    CTG normal".
    [page 39]
19. At 1600 on 15 July 2003 the note records:
    "Top up. . . .Grade 1–11 meconium ++ on pad.."
    [page 39]
20. At 1650 on 15 July 2003 the Deceased was seen by Doctor X, registrar in obstetrics and gynaecology, the note records the third vaginal examination:
    "VE to assess, catheterised 400 mls urine, cervix unchanged
    head –2 ↑ I meconium +++
    to commence Syntocinon"
    [page 39]
21. At 1720 on 15 July 2003 Syntocinon was commenced at 10 units in a litre at 15mls per hour. The foetal heart was recorded at 150bpm.
    [page 40]
22. At 1735 on 15 July 2003 the note records the Deceased's blood pressure as 139/73 and pulse as 122.
    [page 40]
23. At 1750 on 15 July 2003 the note records:
    "Tachycardia (foetal) temp 37.5 BP 128/62
    ? late decelerations ? foetal activity ++
    conts [contractions] 4:10. Synto ↑ 30 mls/hr".
    [page 40]
    At the same time the CTG trace is annotated with:
    "Syntocinon 30 mls
    maternal pulse 127
    temp 37.5".
    The CTG records a foetal heart rate between 180 and 190 and late decelerations.
    [page 54]
24. At 1800 on 15 July 2003 the note records that Doctor X was informed of the CTG and at 1810 it is recorded:
    "seen by Doctor X. For reassessment if CTG continues".
    [page 40]
25. At 1820 on 15 July 2003 the notes record a fourth vaginal examination and the note reads
    "VE – in view of CTG and meconium grade 11 – no change".
    [page 40]
26. At 1830 on 15 July 2003 the note records:
    "Baseline 180 with late ↓ 140 but accs with contractions ^
    difficult to interpret.
    Conts. 4:10, Synto ↑ 45 mls/hour".
    [page 40]
    The CTG at 1820 does not show accelerations with contractions but shows consistent late decelerations, the baseline is 180–190.
    [page 53]

27. At 1845 on 15 July 2003 Doctor X was contacted but did not answer, the CTG was described as "still the same".
    [page 40]
28. At 1900 on 15 July 2003 the note records:
    "Requesting top up, grade 2 meconium now ++. Baseline 170
    settling – less ? late decelerations BP 133/78, P 120".
    [page 40]
    The CTG at 1900 shows the baseline continuing at around 180.
    [page 54]
29. At 1920 the note records:
    "BP 129/75 P 110 T 37.5 FH 177
    Syntocinon remains at 45 mls/hour
    Cont[ractions] 5:10
    one late dec[eleration] noted at 1932".
    [page 40]
    The CTG at 1934 shows a broad late deceleration.
    [page 56]
30. At 1945 on 15 July 2003 the note records:
    "[BP] 120/84 P 117 FH 160–180.
    Some coupling of contractions Synto ≠ 60 mls /hour. Dr X busy at present to do
    the next VE".
    [page 40]
31. At 1955 on 15 July 2003 the note records:
    "FH 160–170, reactive, [contractions] 4:10 Grade 11–111
    meconium now on pad +++. Bloodstained show.
    Dr X in with another delivery".
    [page 40–41]
32. At 2020 on 15 July 2003 the note of the fifth vaginal examination records in Doctor X's
    handwriting:
    "CTG – Tachycardic but reactive
    PA [per abdomen] – ceph 2/5th
    VE os – 3 cms
    Cx central 1 cm long
    station at the spine
    plan to be reviewed in one hour if no progress → LSCS [lower
    segment Caesarean section].
    [page 41]
33. At 2035 on 15 July 2003 the note records:
    "FH settled 149-156 reactive, no decelerations Conts 5:10
    grade 11–111 meconium persists
    maternal pulse 105 BP 130/68
    Ep top up".
    [page 41]
    At 2035 the CTG shows a baseline above 160, occasional late
    decelerations and occasional couplings of uterine contractions.
    [page 57]

34. An epidural top up was given at 2050 on 15 July 2003, at 2100 the Deceased's catheter was emptied and found to have an offensive smell.
    [page 41]

35. At 2125 on 15 July 2003 there was a change of midwife. Care was taken over by midwife K who noted the Deceased was shivering and there were late decelerations on the CTG, the Syntocinon (running at 60 mls/hr) was turned off and Doctor X asked to assess the Deceased.
    [page 41]

36. At 2128 on 15 July 2003 the midwife noted a further late deceleration in the foetal heart and a reduction in the foetal heart rate to 95 bpm, the Deceased was turned onto her left side and vomited ++. Doctor X arrived and noted:
    "CTG – prolonged bradycardia
    v/e no change os- 3 cm
    Plan emergency LSCS"
    [page 41]

37. Thereafter the anaesthetist was fast bleeped and the midwife was asked to inform the consultant Doctor L.
    [page 42]

38. At 2152 the Deceased's baby girl was delivered by Caesarean section under general anaesthetic. The baby had Apgar scores of 5 at 1 minute, 9 at 3 minutes, 9 at 5 minutes and 10 at 10 minutes, she was transferred to the special care baby unit.
    [page 42 and 46]

39. At 2201 on 15 July 2003 the note records:
    "placenta + membranes delivered, cord x 3 vessels –
    Query complete. In pieces, small amount of, obtain cord blood.
    EBL [estimated blood loss] 1000 mls
    closed in layers drain inserted"
    [page 42]
    The operation note records:
    "Cephalic 2/5th
    Grade 111 meconium
    baby girl → Paed. → cord Ph
    Multiple submucous fibroids
    Placenta – adherent – removed in pieces . . . .".
    And the total blood loss originally recorded as 1800 mls (or 800 mls) has been altered to 1000 mls.
    [page 61]

40. At 2245 on 15 July 2003 the note records:
    "Transferred back to room P 144, BP 114/49, saturation 91%
    oxygen 40% commenced
    urine output measurements commenced 120 mls drained".
    [page 42]

41. Thereafter the following was recorded in respect of the Deceased's post natal progress on 15 July 2003:
    "2247: BP 111/35, P144 maternal bloods taken
    22.55: BP 81/27, P 136
    2300: BP 88/48 – anaesthetist recalled to room

373

    2304:   BP 68/36, P125, Hemacell increased infusing stat.
                Turned onto left side end of bed elevated
    2305:   BP 81/48, P120 saturation 99%
    2307:   BP 82/26, P121 Espan stat. Commenced.
                Syntocinon infusing slowly
    2312:   Temp. 38.5° . . . C –tepi sponged saturation 91% BP
                84/40 P136 Fan commenced
                FBC results HB 101 WCC 5.1 Platelets 96
    2315:   Transferred to ICU [intensive care unit].
    [page 42]

42. The anaesthetic record states under post operative instructions:
    "* septic * unwell . . . .→ ICU".
    [page 64]

43. At 2330 on 15 July 2003 the ICU note records:
    "Admitted to ICU following
    an emergency LSCS under GA ? septic SV on 60% pyrexial
    (38.4) BP 80 systolic. HR 140 (ST) Saturations poor. Pain
    (abdo).
    +++. Drowsy and flushed 1x revac, minimal drainage. Urine
    output poor, catheterised, Haemacell x 4.0 given + 1.0 Hespan
    prior to ICU. Syntocinon in progress".
    [page 88]

44. At 0200 on 16 July 2003 the ICU note records:
    "HR ↑ to 190bpm suddenly BP ↓ to 70 systolic, rousable, Xe.
    ABG deteriorated (BE –13). Sodium bicarbonate given,
    Haemacell + N/saline BP became unrecordable – fast bleeped
    Dr Elkin. Intubated and ventilated on 100% 1 x DC shock for 190
    svt HR slowed to 60bpm Hb ↓ 2, 9 units of blood infused.
    Adreneline commenced to 40 mcg I min. Husband present".
    [page 89]

45. At 0215 on 16 July 2003 Doctor M recorded:
    "Fast bleeped – sudden deterioration d/w Doctor S ✓
    Doctor L informed ✓
    ≠ HR 170 ↓ ↓ BP unconscious Xe +++
    Art BP un-recordable
    → intubated & CPR commenced
    1 mg Adreneline given
    HR slowed to 60–70 BP 40/20 . . . . .".
    [page 90]

46. Thereafter the notes record the Deceased deteriorated rapidly and at 0445 on 16 July 2003 Doctor Z certified she had died.
    [page 90]

47. The cause of the Deceased's death was severe haemorrhage and the post-mortem report incorrectly found the cause of death to be amniotic fluid embolism, subsequent examination of the 184 slides taken for the post-mortem do not provide convincing evidence that the Deceased died from amniotic fluid embolism.

48. The death of the Deceased in the circumstances described above was caused by the negligence of the Defendant its servants or agents.

Particulars of Negligence

A. Prior to Delivery

(a) Failing to monitor the Deceased's progress in labour competently and to take into account that she was a high risk patient by reason of:
  (i) Her age – she was a primigravida of 25 years.
  (ii) Her small stature – she was 5' 2" tall (the pathology report is erroneous in stating she was 5' 4").
  (iii) She had uterine fibroids of significant size.
  (iv) She had had bleeding during the first trimester of pregnancy.
  (v) She was past her estimated date of delivery.
  (vi) She had pregnancy induced hypertension on admission.
(b) Failing to treat the progress of labour as suspicious and requiring particularly careful monitoring from 1600 on 15 July 2003 when there meconium ++ draining and no progress in labour since admission at 0910, the cervix remaining only 2–3 cm dilated.
(c) Increasing the Syntocinon infusion at 1748 when there were the following worrying factors:
  (i) a maternal pulse of 127.
  (ii) a maternal temperature of 37.5°.
  (iii) a foetal tachycardia of 180–190bpm.
  (iv) regular late decelerations.
  (v) a coupling of contractions which indicated hyperstimulation.
(d) Failing to arrange for review by an obstetrician at about 1830 (when Doctor X was not responding), review by an obstetrician should have led to arrangements for immediate delivery of the Deceased's baby soon after 1830 on 15 July 2003 when:
  (i) The Deceased's cervix had not dilated further since 0900.
  (ii) The Syntocinon infusion had been running in excess of 1 hour.
  (iii) There was persistent meconium staining grade 1–11.
  (iv) There was persistent foetal tachycardia of 180bpm.
  (v) There were repeated late decelerations.
  (vi) The foetal head remained high.
(e) The midwives again failed to arrange for the urgent attendance of an obstetrician at 1955 when Doctor X was with another patient and very urgent review was required. A consultant should have been contacted immediately if the registrar was unavailable. Review by an obstetrician should have led to arrangements for immediate delivery. Dr X failed to arrange for immediate delivery at 2020 when:
  (i) the cervix remained only 3cms dilated.
  (ii) the CTG showed prolonged tachycardia, repeated late decelerations, coupling of contractions.
  (iii) Syntocinon had been running for 3 hours since 1720.
  (iv) meconium grade 11–111 +++ was noted.
  (v) assessment per abdomen identified the baby's head as 2/5th Xpable (the position being confirmed and unchanged at Caesarean section at 2152) and the assessment of the "station at spine" was clearly incorrect as it was inconsistent with the assessment 2/5th per abdomen.

375

B. After Delivery

(f) Failed to assess properly the extent of the Deceased's blood loss and shock; the blood loss was recorded as 1000ml and then altered to 800 or 1800 (it is illegible), on any view the blood loss was excessive.

(g) Failed to administer a blood transfusion to the Deceased immediately after the delivery in circumstances where the placenta was removed piecemeal, the blood loss was excessive and the Deceased showed signs of shock. By 2245 the Deceased should have been receiving blood transfusion of at least 2 pints of blood as rapidly as possible with a further 4 units of blood being requested urgently and a clotting screen undertaken.

(h) Failed to appreciate the seriousness of the Deceased's condition after delivery and to treat it accordingly by immediate transfer to the intensive care unit. Between 2140 and 2315 the Deceased had developed the following symptoms:

    (i) abnormally high pulse rate.

    (ii) low blood pressure.

    (iii) metabolic acidosis.

    (iv) decrease in haemoglobin concentration from 12.7 to 10.1 g/dl.

    (v) rising temperature.

    (vi) decreasing platelet count from 153 to 96, ie to an abnormally low figure associated with poor blood clotting.

    (vii) requirement for additional oxygen.

    (viii) reduction in blood volume that was so severe that she was given colloid solution for blood expansion.

(i) Failed to arrange for the Deceased to be seen urgently by a consultant anaesthetist and a consultant obstetrician in the operating theatre in order to establish a proper diagnosis and treatment plan.

(j) Allowed the Deceased's blood pressure to fall dramatically before she was transferred to the Intensive Care Unit; the Deceased's blood pressure was recorded during a period of 30 minutes prior to transfer at 81/27; 88/48; 68/36; 81/48; 82/26; and 84/40.

(k) Failed to appreciate the seriousness of the Deceased's condition after transfer to the intensive care unit to treat it accordingly. In particular failed to arrange for the Deceased to be examined immediately by a Consultant Anaesthetist and/or Obstetrician.

Particulars of Causation

(a) If the Deceased's baby had been delivered by Caesarean section promptly (ie within 30–45 minutes) either after 1830 or 1955 or 2020 when the clinical signs required delivery at each of this examinations for the safety of the Deceased and her baby then the Deceased would not have suffered the life-threatening haemorrhage (or ambiotic embolism – if contrary to the Claimant's case that was the cause of death) and would not have died.

(b) Further whether or not delivery had occurred earlier as it ought to have done competent consultant care of the Deceased after delivery would and should have avoided the Deceased's death.

(c) If a Consultant Anaesthetist and Consultant Obstetrician had attended the Deceased whilst she was still in the operating theatre they should and would:

    (i) have arranged for her immediate resuscitation on the Intensive Care Unit with central line to monitor central venous and pulmonary pressure;

    (ii) have given a blood transfusion as soon as the blood was available (which should have been before 2300);

    (iii) performed a laparotomy between midnight and 0100 on 16 July 2003, followed by a hysterectomy which would have terminated the blood loss; had these steps been taken on the balance of probabilities the Deceased would not have died.

46. By reason of the negligence of the Defendant's servants or agents the Deceased suffered pain distress and injury between 1830 on 15 July 2003 when her baby ought to have been delivered safely and her death and the Claimant claims damages for this pain and suffering on behalf of the Deceased's estate pursuant to the Law Reform (Miscellaneous Provisions) Act 1934. Details of her pain and suffering appear from the Defendant's medical notes.

47. Further by reason of the negligence of the Defendant its servants or agents the Claimant, who was the husband of the Deceased has suffered bereavement and claims damages for bereavement pursuant to the Fatal Accidents Act 1976.

48. Further the Claimant and the Deceased's child C, born on 15 July 2003 in the circumstances set out above, and the Claimant were dependants of the Deceased and have suffered loss and damage by reason of her death.

Particulars Provided Pursuant to the Fatal Accidents Act 1976

    (a) The Deceased was born on 12 May 1978, the Claimant was born on 2 August 1972 and the Deceased's only child C was born on 15 July 2003.

    (b) The Deceased was 25 years of age at her death and had until her death been employed as a management consultant earning £30,000.00 net per annum. She would have returned to work within 3 months of C's birth and £30,000.00 per annum would have been available for the Claimant and C's care.

    (c) Further, the Deceased would until C reached 5 years of age have been responsible for her full time care and thereafter have been responsible for her care after school, the cost of providing this care is now £15,000.00 per annum.

    (d) Further, the Deceased would have provided mothering services to C and wifely services to the Claimant.

    (e) Further the funeral expenses were £3,000.00.

49. And the Claimant claims interest pursuant to Section 35A of the Supreme Court Act 1981 at such rate and on such sums for such period as the Court considers fit.

And the Claimant claims:

(1) Damages pursuant to the Law Reform (Miscellaneous Provisions) Act 1934.
(2) Damages pursuant to the Fatal Accidents Act 1976.
(3) Interest.

Served the   day of

Chronology

Date	Time	Entry	Ref.
15.12.64		Ms Z's date of birth. At the time of the events described below she was aged 22.	
02.02.87		Ms Z attended her general practitioner. The Lloyd George record notes inter alia "?preg".	[3/5]
05.02.87		Ms Z was referred to Mr R at the Negligent Hospital ("NH") by her general practitioner, Dr R. Her last menstrual period was 11.12.87. The estimated date of delivery was 16.09.87. Dr M was happy to share Ms Z's ante-natal care.	[1/2] [3/17]
11.03.87		Ms Z was booked at NH. The midwife who carried out the interview was Midwife C. Ms Z was booked under Mr R, Consultant Obstetrician. Her last menstrual period was 09.12.87. Her estimated date of delivery was 16.09.87. She was a primigravida. The Ante-natal record states: 13 weeks gestation; 62.7 kgs; no urine albumin or sugar; BP 95/65. The haematology report is at [1/59].	[1/5], [1/9], [1/10]
24.03.87		The Ante-natal record states: 15 weeks gestation; 64.8 kgs; no urine albumin or sugar; BP 110/70. The record maker's signature is illegible. The Ante-natal ultrasound scan report is at [1/49]. Scan = Dates.	[1/9], [1/10]
14.04.87		The Ante-natal record states only that there was a scan. The record maker's signature is illegible. The scan report is at [1/50]. A bacteriological report (reported 21.04.87) is at [1/71]: rubella antibody was detected.	[1/9]
26.04.87		The Ante-natal record states: 19+ weeks gestation; 67.6 kgs; no urine albumin or sugar; BP 110/50; 20 height fundus. The record maker's signature is illegible.	[1/9]
24.05.87		The Ante-natal record states: 23+ weeks gestation; 71.3 kgs; no urine albumin or sugar; BP 120/70; 23 height fundus. The record maker's signature is illegible.	[1/9]
30.06.87		The Ante-natal record states: 29 weeks gestation; 73.5 kgs; no urine albumin or sugar; BP 110/60; height fundus not recorded; presentation and position was cephalic; relation of presenting part to brim was free; FH was heard; and foetal movements were noted. The record maker's signature is illegible. The birth plan was given. The haematology report (sample received on 01.07.87; report dated 20.07.87) is at [1/60].	[1/5], [1/6], [1/9], [1/10]

Date	Time	Entry	Ref.
26.07.87		The Ante-natal record states: 33 weeks gestation; 76.2 kgs; no urine albumin or sugar; BP 120/75; height fundus was not recorded; presentation and position was cephalic; relation of presenting part to brim was noted as free; the foetal heart was heard. The record maker's signature is illegible.	[1/9]
09.08.87		The Ante-natal record states: 35 weeks gestation; 77.2 kgs; no urine albumin or sugar; BP 125/70; height fundus was 35; presentation and position was cephalic; relation of presenting part to brim was noted as free; the foetal heart was heard; oedema was noted L>R. The record maker's signature is illegible.	[1/9]
16.08.87		The Ante-natal record states: 36 weeks gestation; 78 kgs; no urine albumin or sugar; BP 130/70; height fundus was 36; presentation and position was cephalic; relation of presenting part to brim was 3/5; the foetal heart was heard; oedema was not recorded. The record maker's signature is illegible.	[1/9]
23.08.87		The Ante-natal record states: 37 weeks gestation; 78.5 kgs; no urine albumin or sugar; BP 125/85; height fundus was 37; presentation and position was cephalic; relation of presenting part to brim was 3/5; the foetal heart was heard; oedema is recorded illegibly. The record maker's signature is illegible.	[1/9]
25.08.87		The Ante-natal record states: 37 weeks gestation; 77.3 kgs; no urine albumin or sugar; BP 120/70; height fundus was not recorded; presentation and position was cephalic; relation of presenting part to brim was 3/5; the foetal heart was heard; oedema was noted to be +. The notes state "Well". The record maker's signature is illegible. The haematology report (sample received on 26.08.87; report dated 29.08.87) is at [1/61]. A second haematology report (sample received on 26.08.87; report dated 12.09.87) is at [1/62]. An immunological report (sample received 26.08.87; reported 01.09.87) reports a serum ferritin level of 5 ng/ml (female bracket being 14–150ng/ml).	[1/8], [1/9], [1/10]
26.08.87		The GP Lloyd George record notes "Itchy limbs–faint rash. [?] [?] BD 37/40" This entry is followed by a record which is illegible.	No ref.
28.08.87	Untimed	A record entitled Labour Record states: "Admitted from home with history of having a rash since Wednesday. On admission condition satisfactory. On inspection–has rash all over body. Patient says it's very itchy. Commenced CTG at 12.15 pm". The record maker's signature is illegible.	[1/12]

Date	Time	Entry	Ref.
	1300	A record entitled Labour Record states: "Seen by Dr Fleming may go home". The record maker's signature is illegible.	[1/12]
	1305	A record entitled Labour Record states: "CTG monitoring discontinued. FH baseline 140–150 bpm good reactivity. Awaiting an outside prescription and then going home". The record maker's signature is illegible.	[1/12]

	1305	A record entitled Case Admitted in Pregnancy or Emergency in Labour states:
		
		"Seen on labour ward
		
		C/o Gen rash.
		
		Rash started on Wednesday on bottom of legs. Now on armpits & groin & back. V. irritating. Otherwise well. Fm's ✓
		
		O/E Apyrexial
		   Abdo–uterus 38/40
		    Ceph long lie
		Rash. Maculopapular rash on legs, groin, armpits & back. Red. [no] Vesicles.
		Slight SOA.
		
		CTG–Reactive
		D/w Dr Hill.
		   No obvious cause for rash was allergic to iron in early pr.
		   Only on folic acid–stop this Rx–Ancoloxin 25mg
		T nocte → Home
		to come back if Rash gets much worse. "
		
		The maker's signature is illegible.
		CTG tracing taken on this day is at [1/79].
		A further trace (annotated with "seen by Dr Fleming 13-08") is at [1/80].
			[1/17]

30.08.87		The Ante-natal record states: 37+ weeks gestation; 79.4 kgs; positive urine albumin but not sugar; BP 140/90; height fundus was 38; presentation and position was cephalic; relation of presenting part to brim was 3/5; the foetal heart was heard; oedema was noted to be +. The record maker's signature is illegible.	[1/9]
31.08.87		The GP Lloyd George record notes ""Rash" on face and neck–vomiting + peticheal hages on [?]+?urtic rash on face BP 110/70– On Iron pills ?cause– Worried about German measles Observe See SOS ROM" This entry is followed by a record which is illegible.	No ref.

Date	Time	Entry	Ref.
06.09.87		The Ante-natal record states: 38+ weeks gestation; 79.4 kgs; no urine albumin or sugar; BP 125/90; height fundus was 39; presentation and position was cephalic; relation of presenting part to brim was 3/5; the foetal heart was heard; oedema was noted in the feet. The notes record "[?]++. [?] LA.". The record maker's signature is illegible.	[1/9]
13.09.87		The Ante-natal record states: 39+ weeks gestation; 79.4 kgs; urine albumin was noted as "Tv-"; no urine sugar; BP 130/90; height fundus was 39; presentation and position was cephalic; relation of presenting part to brim was 3/5; the foetal heart was heard; oedema was noted to be less. The record maker's signature is illegible.	[1/9]
15.09.87		The Ante-natal record states: 39+6 weeks gestation; 79 kgs; urine was noted to be "Prot+"; BP 50/90; height fundus was not recorded; presentation and position was cephalic; relation of presenting part to brim was 2/5 ≠; the foetal heart was heard; oedema was noted to be mild. The notes record "Long, closed Cx Knee jerk normal" and "Admit, observe. If BP stays ≠ PGE2 tomorrow". The record maker's signature is illegible.	[1/9], [1/10]
	1835	The Problem Evaluation/Progress Sheet records: "Admitted from clinic with a raised B/P swollen ankles and proteinurea. BP on admission 130/80 CTG recorded to be clerked by Dr Rudolphy 24 hr urine collection". The record maker's signature is illegible.	[1/11]
	1915	The Clinical Notes record: "Admitted from ANC ≠ BP proteinuria +1 well–[no] headache [no] flashing lights mild oedema. Good FMs No PV loss CVS Resp N [No] Drugs [?] Allergic, FE504 [?] O/E Well BP now 120/80 CVS LL [no] SOA 1+2LO Resp Trachea+ Exp/Perl R=L NAD BS–vesicular Abdo 40/60 uterus Head Eng. Imp ≠ BP only mild proteinuria No other symptoms or signs of pre-eclampsia	[1/18]

Date	Time	Entry	Ref.
		Observe overnight Bloods mane" The signature of the maker of this record is illegible.	
	2130	The Problem Evaluation/Progress Sheet records: "Observations satisfactory. FHH 140R". The record maker's signature is illegible. The Ante-natal Observation Chart for this day is at [25] It notes, inter alia, protein +; and that CTG recording was carried out. CTG tracing taken on this day approximately between (machine time) 1832–1900 is at [1/81].	[1/11]
16.09.87	0700	The Problem Evaluation/Progress Sheet records: "Slept for short periods only. BP settling 24 hr urine collection commenced at 0800. [?]+ [?].". The record maker's signature may be M. Bate.	[1/11]
	Untimed	The Clinical Notes state: "S/B Mr R BP 130/90 SOA++ proteinuria For FBC, plat - to stay in U&E - for induction if condition worsens Wate Creatinine C ✓ TP ✓"	[1/19]
	0915	The Problem Evaluation/Progress Sheet records: "Observations satisfactory B/P 120/90 CTG performed. S/B Mr R. Blood taken for Hb U+E & urates ✓ 24 hr urine collection in progress for VMA to be completed tomorrow mane. A further urine collection to be commenced on Sunday am, same completed sample should be sent to lab together with serum creatinine blood sample on Monday am. Prescribed for Fesulphate + Folic acid FH 158R BP 120/80". The record maker's signature is illegible.	[1/11]
	1900	The Problem Evaluation/Progress Sheet records: "BP 130/86. FHH Fe not given as Pt stated she's allergic to it to D/W Drs about it". The record maker's signature is illegible. The Ante-natal Observation Chart for this day is at [1/25] It notes, inter alia, that CTG recording was carried out; and that BP was 120/90. The chemistry report is at [1/52]. Adrenaline is low. The haematology report (sample received on 16.09.87; report dated 19.09.87) is at [1/64]. A second report (same dates) is at [1/65]. It notes: "FE deficiency picture persists" CTG tracing taken on this day approximately between (machine time) 0828 and 0900–0910 is at [1/82].	[1/11]

Date	Time	Entry	Ref.
17.09.87	0600	The Problem Evaluation/Progress Sheet records: "Temazepam given to settle. Slept for short periods only. FHH BP ↓". The record maker's signature is M Bate.	[1/11]
	0930	The Problem Evaluation/Progress Sheet records: "Blood taken for U 2 E". The record maker's signature may be O'Brien.	[1/11]
	0940	The Problem Evaluation/Progress Sheet records: "S/B Mr R–no new instructions". The record maker's signature may be O'Brien.	[1/11]
	1145	The Problem Evaluation/Progress Sheet records: "CTG recorded". There is no record maker's signature.	[1/11]
	1830	The Problem Evaluation/Progress Sheet records: "Bed rest maintained". The record maker's signature is illegible.	[1/11]
	2200	The Problem Evaluation/Progress Sheet records: "BP 130/80 FHH Regular". The record maker's signature may be A Sullivan.	[1/11]
		The Ante-natal Observation Chart for this day is at [1/25] It notes 2/5 engagement; trace protein; and BP 130/90.	
		A chemistry report is at [1/53]. A second chemistry report received on this day but reported on 19.09.87 is at [54]. Urate is high (0.52; the bracket is 0.15–0.40). Alkaline phosphatase is high (321; the bracket is 0–125).	
		CTG tracing taken on this day approximately between (machine time) 1112 and 1130/1140 is at [1/83].	
18.09.87		The Clinical Notes state: "SB Mr H Bp/80 & 85 [?] of problems [No] [?] [no] epigastric Well FMs–Await CTGs Continue with bed rest Review mane." The signature of the maker of this record is Dr G.	[1/19]
	0915	The Problem Evaluation/Progress Sheet records: "Seen by Dr H and Dr G. For review by Mr R Observations satisfactory. BP 120/80. + Protein in urine. Oedema in ankles. Baby active. For CTG. 24 hour urine in progress for Total Protein and Creatinine Clearance". The record maker's signature is illegible.	[1/11]
	PM	The Problem Evaluation/Progress Sheet records: "BP 120/85. FHH 120R". The record maker's signature is illegible.	[1/11]

Date	Time	Entry	Ref.
		The Ante-natal Observation Chart for this day is at [1/25] It notes 2–3/5 engagement; + protein; and BP 120/80.	
		The chemistry report is at [1/55].	
		CTG tracing taken on this day approximately between (machine time) 1020 and 1050/1100 is at [1/84].	
19.09.87		The Ante-natal record states "Admitted with BP ≠ + Protein". The record maker's signature is illegible.	[1/10]
	0720	The Problem Evaluation/Progress Sheet records: "Slept well–Temazepan given as prescribed BP 120/70". The record maker's signature may be White.	[1/11]
	Untimed	The Clinical Records state: "Protein neg today Traces nil BP [?] home see Thursday." The signature of the maker of this record is illegible.	[1/19]
	Untimed	The Problem Evaluation/Progress Sheet records: "S/B Mr R Home–ANC 3/7 CTG reactive BP 120/86". The record maker's signature is illegible.	[1/11]
		The Ante-natal Observation Chart for this day is at [1/25] It notes 2–3/5 engagement; CTG tracing carried out; and BP 120/80.	
		The chemistry report is at [56]. Urate is high (0.48; the bracket is 0.15–0.40). Calcium is low (2.08; the bracket is 2.20–2.60). Alkaline phosphatase is high (328; the bracket is 0–125).	
		CTG tracing taken on this day approximately between (machine time) 1112–1140/1150 is at [1/85].	
20.09.87		The Ante-natal record states: 40+4 weeks gestation; 79.8 kgs; urine albumin was noted to be "Tv-"; no urine sugar; BP 120/70; height fundus was 40; presentation and position was cephalic; relation of presenting part to brim was 2/5; the foetal heart was heard; oedema was noted to be slight. The notes record "Admit". The record maker's signature is illegible.	[1/9]
22.09.87		The Ante-natal record states: 40+6 weeks gestation; 77.8 kgs; no urine ulbumin or sugar; BP 125/90; height fundus was recorded as T; presentation and position was cephalic; relation of presenting part to brim was 1/5; the foetal heart was heard; oedema was noted as +. The notes state "Cx long londil post membranes intact for IOL Monday. HVS ✓" and "Active baby [?] 0.48 0.52 Creatine clearance 74 Cx 1cm membranes intact Long posterior	[1/9] [1/10]

Date	Time	Entry	Ref.
		HVB ✓ CTG ✓ Discussed [with] LDR For I.O.L on Monday " The record maker's signature is illegible. The CTG trace taken on this day at (machine time) 1633 to 1650/1700 is at [1/86].	
24.09.87	0220	A record entitled Labour Record states: "Readmitted from home with a history of no foetal movements since 2200 hrs and contractions. Since on admission T36.5 P100 BP 120 [?140]/80. Contracting 1–2 in 10 weak. H/O SROM, membranes are intact. Foetus long. Lie Cephalic presentation 3/5 Palpable. L.O.P F.H. 13[?] R". The record maker's signature is illegible.	[1/12]
	0220	The Problem Evaluation/Progress Sheet records: "Readmitted from home with a history of no foetal movements since 2200 hrs and contractions". The record maker's signature is T R.	[1/13]
	0230	A partogram record records: Foetal heart rate: 115 BP: 120/70 Maternal pulse: 90 Temperature: 37.4 Urine: -	[1/23]
	0233	A record entitled Labour Record states: "Attached to H/P 1768 Urine Prot++." The record maker's signature is illegible.	[1/12]
	0300	A partogram record records: Foetal heart rate: 120 BP: 120/80 Maternal pulse: 100 Temperature: - Urine: -	[1/23]
	0325	A record entitled Labour Record states: "+Vs Spec VE by Dr P–tightenings [?] Transferred to M4". The record maker's signature is illegible.	[1/12]
	0325	The Problem Evaluation/Progress Sheet records: "Spec HVS VE by Dr P Transferred to M4 [with] tightening only". The record maker's signature is illegible.	[1/13]

Date	Time	Entry	Ref.

	0330	The Clinical Record states:
		
		"Seen on L/W T+7
		- contns 2/10 weak for 6 hours
		- no FM for 4 hours
		- previous adm for proteinuria & ≠ BP
		- due for induction 3/7 time
		O/E BP 120/80 not distressed
		[diagram] Ceph long lie 2/5
		  CTG ✓
		  VE–Q high soft, long, closed
		    Mucous cervical discharge
		    o/liquor
		→ ward & observe."
		
		The signature of the maker of this record is illegible.
			[1/19]

	0330	A partogram record records: Foetal heart rate: 120 BP: 125/80 Maternal pulse: 100 Temperature: - Urine: -	[1/23]
	0400	A partogram record records: Foetal heart rate: 130 BP: 120/80 Maternal pulse: 100 Temperature: - Urine:-	[1/23]
	0430	A partogram record records: Foetal heart rate: 120 BP: 120/85 Maternal pulse: 100 Temperature: - Urine: -	[1/23]
	0500	A partogram record records: Foetal heart rate: 130 BP: - Maternal pulse: - Temperature: - Urine: -	[1/23]
	0530	A partogram record records: Foetal heart rate: 150 BP: 130/85 Maternal pulse: 100 Temperature:- Urine: -	[1/23]

Date	Time	Entry	Ref.
	0600	A partogram record records: Foetal heart rate: 145–150 BP: 130/80 Maternal pulse: 100 Temperature: 37.6 Urine: -	[1/23]
	0630	A partogram record records: Foetal heart rate: - BP: 130/80 Maternal pulse: 100 Temperature: - Urine: -	[1/23]
	0700	The Problem Evaluation/Progress Sheet records: "Unsettled night. Tightenings not so regular now. BP 110/70 P 84 T36.5 FHR 136. Membranes intact". The record maker's signature is S.	[1/13]
	0730	A partogram record records: Foetal heart rate: - BP: 130/80 Maternal pulse: - Temperature: - Urine: -	[1/23]
	0830	A partogram record records: Foetal heart rate: 140 BP: 110/80 Maternal pulse: - Temperature:- Urine: ++ Acetone	[1/23]
	0900	A partogram record records: Foetal heart rate: - BP: 110/70 Maternal pulse: - Temperature: - Urine: -	[1/23]
	0930	A partogram record records: Foetal heart rate: - BP: 130/80 Maternal pulse: 90 Temperature: - Urine: -	[1/23]
	0956	A CTG tracing was commenced, according to the machine, at about 0956 to about 1020/1030.	[1/87]
	1000	The Problem Evaluation/Progress Sheet records:	[1/13]

Date	Time	Entry	Ref.
		"BP 130/90 P87 T36.8 FHR122. No oedema. C/o tightenings + backache S/B Mr R, if not in labour by Monday, for IOL. S/B Dr M/DrP D/w Mr R Pt may be induced if L/W has bed available". The record maker's signature is illegible.	
	1510	The Problem Evaluation/Progress Sheet records: "Temp = 37.4[?] P=106 c\o feeling cold & shivery & weak FH–150. Feeling like this since 11am Dr Pipper informed". The record maker's signature may be O.	[1/13]
	1520	The Problem Evaluation/Progress Sheet records: "SROM Clear liquor seen on pad". The record maker's signature is illegible.	[1/13]
	1530	The Clinical Record states: "SROM 15.25 Not contracting Feels well No headache/flashing lights No epg pain FMF O/E well Temp 37.4°C Not distressed CVS/pulse 108/min Ry PP 120/85 Reflexes brisk No oedema Resp/chest clear Abdo [diagram] Ceph [?] Eng 2/4 palp. FHH Spec–liquor seen Clear - midwife agrees HVS taken Check urinalysis–protein + Observe temp Rpt CTG (satisfactory this am) To D/W Reg ?For IOL now." The signature of the SHO maker of this record is illegible.	[1/20]
	1555	The Problem Evaluation/Progress Sheet records: "S/B Dr P speculum clear liquor seen. Urinalysis Protein+ HVS ✓ reflexes brisk BP 120/85. CTG commenced. To discuss [with] Registrar Dr M ?To Labour Ward. Having irregular tightening". The record maker's signature is illegible.	[1/13]

Date	Time	Entry	Ref.
	1600	A CTG tracing was commenced, according to the machine, at about 1600 to about 1630/1640.	[1/87]
	Untimed	The Clinical Record states: "D/W Dr M–for transfer to LW for IOL temp now 38.4°C for IV antibiotics–Centuroxime 750m tds 　　　　　　　　　　–Metronidazole 500 mg tds HVS taken Send blood cultures 　FBC 　G+S 　U+E 　Clotting studies Results 　Na 134　Hb 9.8 　K+3.8　WCC 13.4 　U 3.2　Plts 237 　Glu 5.0　Pt 15 (15) 　Creat 83　PLCCT 39 (43) For epidural Syntocinon" The signature of the maker of this record is illegible.	[1/21]
	1730	The Problem Evaluation/Progress Sheet records: "L:.W. rang. [illegible but struck through] to go to Rm1 Temp = 37.6". The record maker's signature may be O.	[1/13]
	1745	The Labour Record records that: "Transferred from ward M4 for augmentation On admission <u>T38.4</u> P106 BP 120/90 Urinalysis + Protein slight oedema On palpation LOA 2/5 palpable FHHR Has thick '<u>Green discharge</u>' noted and draining liquor++ CTG commenced." The record maker's signature is illegible.	[1/14]
	1815	The Labour Record records that: "CTG reactive for EPV" The record maker's signature is illegible.	[1/14]
	1820	A record entitled Labour Record records that a vaginal examination took place: Dilatation: "1.5cm" Thickness of cervix: "1cm"	[1/12]

Date	Time	Entry	Ref.
		Height of presenting part: "-2cm" Position: "Not defined" Membrane intact or ruptured: "I" Remarks: "V. tight vagina [therefore] difficult [?]VE FHHR following procedure" The record maker's signature is illegible.	
	1845	The Labour Record records that: "Awaiting Syntocinon infusion meanwhile CTG discontinued temporarily. Analgesia discussed would like Epidural BP 120/60 [?80] FHH 143 bpm" The record maker's signature is illegible.	[1/14]
	2015	The Labour Record records that: "POSITIONED FOR EPIDURAL EPIDURAL SITED BY DR M" The record maker's signature is illegible. The epidural chart states that the indication was for increased blood pressure and MR [1/26]. The test dose and initial injection are timed at 2035 and 2042 [1/27].	[1/14]
	2019	The Labour Record records that: "TOP UP DOSE GIVEN WITHOUT EVENT" The record maker's signature is illegible. The epidural chart is at [1/26], [1/27].	[1/14]
	2115	The Labour Record records that: "Taken over care of patient T 37.4 P 100 BP 120/70 FHHR 120–130 bpm baseline." The record maker's signature is illegible.	[1/14]
	2135	The Labour Record records that: "Syntocinon infusion commenced. N/saline with 6 units Syntocinon at 0.5 ml Hr." The record maker's signature is illegible. The infusion therapy chart is at [1/40].	[1/14]
	2150	The Labour Record records that: "Contractions weak 2:10 Synt 1ml hr." The record maker's signature is illegible.	[1/14]
	2206	The Labour Record records that: "Syntocinon at 2ml/hr." The record maker's signature is illegible.	[1/14]
	2230	The Labour Record records that: "Syntocinon at 3ml/hr." The record maker's signature is illegible.	[1/14]

Date	Time	Entry	Ref.
	2238	The Labour Record records that a vaginal examination took place: Dilatation: "3cm" Thickness of cervix: "thick effaced" Height of presenting part: "-2" Position: "H/D" Membrane intact or ruptured: "R" Remarks: "B/s liqour" The record maker's signature is illegible.	[1/12]
	2238	The Labour Record records that: "VE Done. Findings on previous page. FSE applied working well FHHR 130/140 baseline" The record maker's signature is illegible.	[1/14]
	2245	The Labour Record records that: "Syntocinon at 4ml/hr Contractions weak." The record maker's signature is illegible.	[1/14]
	2300	The Labour Record records that: "Syntocinon at 5ml/hr." The record maker's signature is illegible.	[1/14]
	2345	The Labour Record records that: "Syntocinon at 8ml/hr. BP 120/80 Contractions painful would like top up." The record maker's signature is illegible.	[1/14]
	2350	The Labour Record records that: "1st Top up Marcain 0.5[?] 8 mls given. B/P later on 120/90 P120 150." The record maker's signature is illegible. The epidural chart at [1/27] shows that an 8ml top up was given at 2350. The chemistry report of a sample taken on this day and reported on 26.09.87 is at [1/57]. A second chemistry report of a sample taken on this day and reported on 26.09.87 is at [1/58]. Urate is high (0.50; the bracket is 0.15–0.40). Calcium is low (2.15; the bracket is 2.20–2.60). Alkaline phosphatase is high (357; the bracket is 0–125). The haematology report (sample received on 24.09.87; report dated 26.09.87) is at [1/66].	[1/14]

Date	Time	Entry	Ref.
25.09.87	0010	The Labour Record records that: "Turned to left side BP 130/85 P100 FH120 FH ↓ 100 picked up" The record maker's signature is illegible.	[1/14]
	0020	The Labour Record records that: "Syntocinon to 10mls/hr Temp 37.6 P102" The record maker's signature is illegible.	[1/14]
	0030	The Labour Record records that: "Seen Dr SHO M, Type 2 Dips *100[?]" The record maker's signature is illegible.	[1/14]
	0035	The Labour Record records that: "Seen by Sister turned to Rt side oxygen given via face mask [?] picked up baseline 120–130 bpm" The record maker's signature is illegible.	[1/14]
	0100	The Labour Record records that: "Syntocinon at 11 mls/psv hr" The record maker's signature is illegible.	[1/14]
	0115	The Labour Record records that: "Seen by Dr M would like Syntocinon to be increased by 2ml/hr" The record maker's signature is illegible.	[1/14]
	0015 (but presumably should be 0115)	The Labour Record records that: "Syntocinon at 13 ml/hr" The record maker's signature is illegible.	[1/15]

	0120	The Clinical Record states:
		
		"SRM at 1515 hrs yesterday
		  Augmentation 1745 for ≠ temp
		  See AN notes
		Slow progress. CTG OK now. Had
		a prolonged deceleration following epidural
		top up
		[?] up Syntocinon to effect good contractions please"
		
		The signature of the maker of this record is illegible.
			[1/22]

	0145	The Labour Record records that: "BP 130/100 P 100 Persistent Type I Dips" The record maker's signature is illegible.	[1/15]

Date	Time	Entry	Ref.
	0200	A record entitled Labour Record records that a vaginal examination took place: Dilatation: "8/9" Thickness of cervix: "thinning" Height of presenting part: "+2" Position: "Lot" Membrane intact or ruptured: "R" Remarks: "thick vaginal yellowish discharge clear liquor FSE applied" The record maker's signature is illegible.	[1/12]
	0200	The Labour Record records that: "3rd VE done findings on previous page. FSE reapplied oxygen given by face mask" The record maker's signature is illegible.	[1/15]
	0200	The Labour Record records that: "Syntocinon increased to 14 [?]" The record maker's signature is illegible.	[1/15]
	0205	The Labour Record records that: "Synt ↓ 13 [illegible but struck through] mls Hr" The record maker's signature is illegible.	[1/15]
	0208	The epidural chart shows that an 8ml Marcain top up was given at 0208. The foetal heart rate fell after this from 150 at 0213, to 140 at 0218 to 100 at 0225.	[1/27]
	0230	The Labour Record records that: "Persistent type Dips. Drs informed oxygen given" The record maker's signature is illegible.	[1/15]
	0250	The Labour Record records that: "Patient commenced pushing. Prepared for forceps delivery" The record maker's signature is illegible.	[1/15]
	0300	A record entitled Labour Record records that a vaginal examination took place: Dilatation: "9" Thickness of cervix: "ant lip" Height of presenting part: "+2" Position: "LOT" Membrane intact or ruptured: "R" Remarks: "Caput" The record maker's signature is illegible.	[1/12]

Date	Time	Entry	Ref.
	0300	The Clinical Record states: "Asked to reassess Late decelerations on CTG Baseline 160 VE–9 cm Ant lip – PP + 2 D/w Dr M–to review." The signature of the maker of this record is illegible.	[1/22]
	0330	The Labour Record records that: "FH ↓ 100–90 with slow recovery to 150–160 bpm O.S Fully dilated" The record maker's signature is illegible.	[1/15]
	0353	The Labour Record records that: "Ventouse extraction of an alive male infant aided by episiotomy by Dr M" The record maker's signature is illegible.	[1/15]
	0356	The Labour Record records that: "Placenta and membranes delivered by controlled cord traction placenta + membranes complete Blood loss 200mls Perineum sutured Post del obs T38.0C P100 B/P 140/85 Epidural catheter removed Checked complete IVI Hartmans cont'd to fet vein opened On W antibiotics Baby born floppy at birth. Attended by paed. Suction ++ Apgar 3/1m 6/5m 8/10ms [?] Konakion given 0400 BW 3.375 kg Transferred to SCBU." The record maker's signature is illegible and partly cut off due to poor copying.	[1/15]
		The delivery record which appears to have been completed by two doctors, one of whom was Dr M, anaesthetist. It records that the Claimant was born "floppy" with an Apgar of 3 at 1 minute (although the 3 has been altered), 6 at 5 minutes (the six has also been altered) and	[1/24]

Date	Time	Entry	Ref.
		8 at 10 minutes. It records "blue extremities"; "flaccid" tone; respiration established 0354 to 0357 with the comment "at birth not regular [with] recession"; the time and nature of cry was "weak cry".	
		Dr M comments that it was a ventouse delivery indicated by "Foetal tachycardia with loss of variability variable deceleration & meconium." The operation was described as follows:	
		"At 9 cms + 1stn LOL R mediol at episotomy Ventouse extraction of a boy covered with meconium. Complete delivery of secunduis. Layered repairs of the Episiotomy."	
		The midwives were identified as S/M A and sister W[?].	
		The summary of labour records that membranes ruptured at 1745; labour commenced at 2130 on 24.09.87; full dilatation occurred at 0330 on 25.09.87; the placenta was expelled at 0356. The first stage was timed at 6 hrs. The second stage was timed at 23 minutes. The third stage at 3 minutes.	
	Not timed	A paediatric record records Apgar scores of 3 at 1 minute, 6 at 5 minutes, 8 at 10 minutes and states:	[2/46]
		"Called to Ventouse delivery for foetal distress	
		Maternal pyrexia [no]PROM 05.53 delivery live male infant, pale floppy. HR >100 irreg resp effort meconium at end of delivery	
		Intubated–[?] meconium drained Liquor–v. little below cords.	
		Ventilated 3 mins. Then bagged [with] O2 Suction ++	
		IM Konakion given.	
		→ SCBU"	
	0400	The paediatric records note "Konakion 1mg Iv"	[2/46]
	0500	The paediatric records note:	[2/49]–[2/50]
		"Admitted to SCBU via labour ward	
		Mother 21 Primip VDRL –ve Rubella LMP 9/12/87 EDD 16/9/87	
		19/9/87 T+6 admitted [with] ≠ BP + protein in urine 29/9/87 → T+8 SROM 15.25 29/9/87 → IOL	

Date	Time	Entry	Ref.
		Before delivery Temp 38.4 HVS taken Rx Cefuroxime Metranidazole Ventouse extraction at 04.53 Poor condition at birth Pale floppy HR, 100 irreg resp effort Intubated–mec stained liquor–little below chords Ventilated 3 min Apgar 31 65 810 OA → SCBU → Seen at 35–40 min of age. OE Pale + grunting but pink Temp 37.2 BM 3.5 CVS pale–poor perfusion HS I + II + 0 HR 170 [?] [?] [?]✓✓ RS grunting++ [?] RR 70 AER[?]L [diagram of abdomen annotated with inter alia "?liver palpable"] CNS pale + floppy poor response to handling. Skull–moulding ++ post ventouse extraction [no] dysmorphic feats … Imp ?Severe Asphyxia ?Infection …"	
	0630	The clinical notes record that an X-ray and lumbar puncture had been carried out. Chest and abdominal X-rays are reported at [2/228]. A left pneumothorax and a large right lobe were detected.	[2/51]
	0715	The SCBU nursing notes commence. Severe head moulding noted.	[2/119]
	1000	A document entitled Post-natal Record states: "Day 1 Post Ventouse: Maternal Pyrexia foetal tachycardia + variable decelerations loss of variability + meconium = Temp 35.0C. No source of infection identified yet. BABY FITTING" This record is not signed. The entry in the clinical notes is at [2/52].	[1/16]
27.09.87		An ultrasound scan of the Claimant's kidneys was carried out and reported subsequently as being normal.	[2/226]
29.09.87		The clinical notes record that a cranial ultrasound scan was taken which showed "cerebral oedema only". The scan is reported at [227]: "… The ventricles were barely visible	[2/58]

Date	Time	Entry	Ref.
		consistent with cerebral oedema. No other abnormality seen. Cerebral echo pattern within normal limits."	
07.10.87		The Claimant was discharged from SHH.	[2/125]
		The Discharge Summary stated that the Claimant was born at 0353 on 25.09.87 having been delivered by vacuum extraction. The Apgar scores are recorded as 3, 6, 8. He weighed 3.375 kgs. The record notes "Baby admitted to SCBU with cerebral irritation and fitting. Going home on Phenobarbitone. Out Patients with Dr O in 4/52."	[1/1]
Not dated		On a date unknown Dr O, Consultant Paediatrician, wrote to the Claimant's GP, Dr G:	[2/3]

"(1) Severe birth asphyxia.
(2) Neonatal Seizures.
(3) Hypocalcaemia
(4) Hyponatraemia.

Mother:	22 years' old. Primigravida.
Pregnancy:	Uncomplicated until term.
	Raised blood pressure and proteinuria
Delivery:	Term plus 8 days. SROM. Ventouse extraction.
Baby:	Birth weight 3.57 kgs.
Problems:	(1) <u>Birth Asphyxia & Neonatal</u>
Seizures	Apgars–3 at 1, 6 at 5 and 8 at 10 minutes.

IPPV 3 Minutes. Post resuscitation– floppy, grunting poor response to handling. Arterial PH in first hour = 7.152–consistent severe asphyxia. Screened for infection at birth, cultures subsequently negative, antibiotics (Penicillin, Gentamicin and Cefuroxime) for a total of 8 days. Seizures and recurrent apnoeic attacks from 5 hours to 72 hours. Treated with Phenobarbitone and fluid retention. Cranial ultrasound showed cerebral oedema only but no bleed or ischaemic lesion.
(2) <u>Hypocalcaemia</u>
Lowest level (1.61 mmol/1) recorded at 24 hours.
Intravenous calcium supplements given and calcium subsequently normalised. Unfortunately developed a small calcium burn on the right ankle due to extravasation of calcium containing fluid. Subsequently healing satisfactorily.

Date	Time	Entry	Ref.
		(3) <u>Hyponatraemia</u> Sodium fell to extremely low levels (118 mmol/1) on day 4. Subsequently corrected with additional saline infusions. <u>Overall Progress</u>: Marked clinical improvement by day 9. Subsequently fed spontaneously and discharged from hospital on day 14. <u>Discharge</u> Phenobarbitone 10.5 mgs. b.d. <u>Recommendation:</u> <u>Follow-Up</u>: One month ..."	
13.10.98		An EEG report records: "... multifocal epileptiform phenomena. The left, seen over mid &* posterior temporal regions. The right, more centrally and extending to superior frontal regions. The presence of such changes does increase the risk of epilepsy but they may be of less standing as a consequence of events near birth."	[2/231]
15.01.99		The Claimant was admitted for an MRI scan. The scan was reported on 20.01.99: "MRI BRAIN: Axial proton density and T2W images were supplemented by coronal T2W images through the brain and a sagittal T1W localiser sequence. There was a significant amount of high signal within the right mastoid air cells and a small amount of high signal within the left mastoid air cells (images 4–6). Appearances consistent with mastoiditis. There are incidental polyps in the right maxillary antrum. No other sinus abnormality seen. In the brain high signal is seen in the white matter of the left occipital parietal region. (Axial images 14–18 and coronal images 15–19.) This is associated with mild dilatation of the posterior horn of the left lateral ventricle and widening of the overlying sulci. The appearances are consistent with infarction due to possible birth ischaemia. Less marked high signal is seen on the coronal images around the anterior horns (coronal images 9 and 10). Again, this is compatible with birth ischaemia. No other abnormality seen. CONCLUSION: High signal within the periventricular white matter particularly on the left consistent with infarction due to birth ischaemia. Has the patient had an EEG? If so, it would be interesting to know whether there were any epileptiform foci."	[2/92], [2/279]
08.06.00		Mr R's letter to the Trust: "... At around midnight there was a period of quite marked variability in the CTG and the SHO doctor, Dr M, was called and I suspect that the variability was related to the top up of the epidural at 2350.	

Date	Time	Entry	Ref.
		For a short period between 0134 and 0200 the CTG is within normal limits, however, from 0200 there are marked decelerations which were variable with some loss of baseline variability. She was examined at 0200 hours and was found to be 8–9cms with slightly bloodstained liquor. She thus made quite satisfactory progress. The Syntocinon was nevertheless increased to 14mls an hour but shortly afterwards reduced again because of the decelerations in the trace. The CTG is marked at 0249 as being seen by Dr Per. The patient was given oxygen and the SHO asked Dr M, I think the correct spelling of the Registrar on call, to see the patient who was 9 cms with an anterior lip and late decelerations on the CTG. I would agree with this assessment at this time and the patient was in fact starting to push. The trace thereafter runs for some 50–60 minutes and has very little variability, is tachycardic with late decelerations. According to the notes, at 0250 the patient commenced pushing and was prepared for a forceps delivery. However, it would seem that this Ventouse extraction was not accomplished until 0353 … For the majority of the labour the CTG was quite satisfactory until the last hour before delivery when the trace became abnormal …"	

APPENDIX 3

Summary of Labour

Page V.11 (i)	Date	Time	Bishop's score	Dilatation	Abd	Station	Presentation & Position	FH	Mecon	Observations	Syntocinon	Contractions
64	19.7.91	2130			2/5 palpable		cephalic ROL – A	FHH 140 CTG baseline FH 140 with good variability	draining mec grade 1	requesting a top-up	Syntocinon running at 20 dpm	palpated 4/5 in 10
64	19.7.91	2150								epidural top-up		
83	19.7.91	2200		5–6				144–142 bpm	mec gr 1		20 dpm mu/min	4:10
65	19.7.91	2215						144 bpm		appears quite exhausted, requesting rest, is in bed, pump alarming persistently not functioning	20 dpm	strong 1:2
65	19.7.91	2230		5–6		-2	Vertex	CTG reactive	mec gr 1	500 mls urine obtained		
65–66	19.7.91	2250						baby had a deceleration ↓ 95 follow up contraction lasted approx		encouraged to sit out in rocker, coping well	Syntocinon now recommence this new pump now working	

400

	Date	Time				FHH / bpm	mec	Notes	mu/min	Ratio
83	19.7.91	2300				138 bpm–150 bpm	mec 1	20 sec but recovered well	30 mu/min	5:10
66	19.7.91	2195						requesting epidural top up		
66	19.7.91	2330				145 bpm		patient resting comfortably		
66	19.7.91	2345				FHH Reg 140–150 although tracing appears fairly very variable		patient asleep		
83	19.7.91	2400		10		140–150 bpm	mec 1		32 mu/min	5:10
66	1.8.91	0030			Vertex			requesting epidural top up, assisted back into bed, top up given		
67	1.8.91	0045	-1	10	ROL	FHH reg	mec	seen by Dr to inform him re progress? narrow pubic, arch moulding observed, urine 150 mls ketones ++		
83	1.8.91	0100				138 bpm–150 bpm	mec 1–11		32 mu/min	5:10 shivering with contractions

Page V.11(i)	Date	Time	Bishop's score	Dilatation	Abd	Station	Presentation & Position	FH	Mecon	Observations	Syntocinon	Contractions
67	1.8.91	0115						FHH reg 138 bpm		reported feeling extreme pressure and pain at the back lower spine and symphysis pubis		encouraged to breathe with contractions
67	1.8.91	0130								epidural top up given, upright		
67	1.8.91	0140						FHH reg 136 bpm		still distress with pain in the suprapubic area		
67	1.8.91	0150						FH reg 140				difficult to remain comfortable with contractions
68/83	1.8.91	0200				Vx low advancing slowly with each push		160 bpm– 150 bpm FHH reg	mec	pushing commence	32 mu/min	5:10
68	1.8.91	0205				Vx at spines moulding present		FHH reg 130 variability		pushing well		

68	1.8.91	0215	no signs of obvious descent	FHH reg		continues to push well		
68	1.8.91	0220	no obvious descent	FHH reg 140 bpm		mother complaining of feeling exhausted		
68	1.8.91	0230	no progress observed, no descent	FHH reg 160 bpm		mother exhausted		
68	1.8.91	0240				pushing but not effectively, pt very exhausted and becoming distressed		
68	1.8.91	0245				pushing but not effectively. Drs informed of this, allowed to push for one hour		
68	1.8.91	0250				pushing continues but no progress, Dr has arrived		
68/83	1.8.91	0300			mec 11	epidural top up given delivery keillands forceps	32 mu/min	5:10

Page V.11(i)	Date	Time	Bishop's score	Dilatation	Abd	Station	Presentation & Position	FH	Mecon	Observations	Syntocinon	Contractions
69	1.8.91	0195				+2 moulding lamboidal sutures not sagittal	LOL	foetal heart rate decelerating ↓78	thick mec	procedure commenced for forceps delivery … difficult forceps application		
69	1.8.91	0325								transfer to theatre for emerg LSCS		
60	1.8.91	0342								emergency LSCS for failure to progress, failed forceps. Female infant with poor Apgars transfer to SCBU		

APPENDIX 4

Draft Particulars of Claim in a Case of Failure to Treat a DVT

IN THE HIGH COURT OF JUSTICE   CLAIM NO
QUEEN'S BENCH DIVISION

BETWEEN:

XYZ
(A Patient suing by her husband and litigation friend JJZ)   <u>Claimant</u>

AND

K GENERAL HOSPITALS NHS TRUST   <u>Defendant</u>

Draft/ PARTICULARS OF CLAIM

References in [   ] are to the two bundles of medical notes from K District Hospital. References in {   } are to other medical records. Medical abbreviations from the notes marked with * are defined in the glossary which is arranged alphabetically and attached to these particulars.

The Claimant

1. The Claimant was born on 17 May 1946. As a result of the events referred to in these particulars of claim the Claimant is now a patient within the meaning of the Mental Health Act 1983 and Civil Procedure Rules 21.1. The Claimant's husband XY acts as the Claimant's litigation friend in these proceedings.

The Defendant

2. The Defendant was at all relevant times responsible for the management, control, and administration of K General Hospital, and for the employment of doctors, nurses, and other medical specialists including surgeons at and for the purpose of the said hospital.

Duty of Care

3. Each of the doctors, nurses, midwives, and other staff employed at the Hospital who treated the Claimant at the Hospital owed the Claimant a duty of care. This duty included a duty in respect of:
   a. The advice given to the Claimant.
   b. The diagnosis made in respect of the condition of the Claimant.
   c. The treatment prescribed for the Claimant and advice as to the effects of the treatment.
   d. The monitoring of the Claimant whilst treatment was given to the Claimant.

4. The Defendant is vicariously liable for any such breach of duty on behalf of any of its employees.

The Sequence of Events

5. On 26 June 2001 the Claimant was admitted to K General Hospital Accident and Emergency Department. The admission note records the time of the Claimant's arrival as 0845 and she was seen by Doctor P at 0930. The note records:
   "Swollen painful left calf and thigh
   Suddenly developed over the past 24 hours.
   O/e* o* nv* deficit
   leg grossly swollen
   somewhat cyanosed
   DP* pulse palpable
   (n) sensation
   Imp*. ? Ileo femoral DVT*
   Plan: (1) Doppler US* scan
   *   (2) Refer RMO**
   ??? may need vascular opinion if limb is threatened
   wpc*: 11.8
   Hb*: 11.4
   Plt*. 332
   D-dimer 4.1"
   [page 2]

6. A further untimed note records the Claimant's medical history and makes a diagnosis of DVT* (extensive above knee), records an ECG*, chest X-ray, Doppler scan, and blood tests and the result of the ultrasound scan of the left leg is recorded as:
   "Extensive left ileo-femoral DVT
   (flow in the IVC*+)."
   [page 4]

7. At 1515 on 26 June 2001 there is a note of a surgical review with a consultant Mr Q. The observations recorded beside a diagram of a swollen left leg were:
   "Left leg swollen and tender from thigh to calf.
   Cooler than right leg.
   Pulses present
   Sensation intact.
   Motor function intact.
   IMP*: extensive ileo-femoral DVT*
   ? susceptible to thrombolise
   ? IVC* filter
   D/W* Mr Q
   To ask radiology to insert a catheter into clot for thrombolysis
   Admit to vascular team
   Anticoag with Clexane
   D/w Doctor Willard (Cons. Radiologist)
   can insert catheter and IVC* filter tomorrow".
   [page 5–6]

8. On 27 June 2001 an untimed note records:
   "leg swollen
   good dors pedis* +tib*

today thrombolysis".
This was followed by a note of a ward round with the direction;
"Surgeons will kindly continue care"
[page 6]

9. A further note on 27 June 2001 records;
   "(L) DVT* thrombolysis + IVC* filter placement
   5F sheath (L) popliteal vein. SF* lysis catheter advanced
   to pelvis.
   Cavagram left in common iliac vein for lysis.
   Cavagram shows clot in lower IVC* up to L ¾
   Catheter left in common iliac vein for lysis.
   As clot in IVC, filter placed from RIJV*
   5 mls 1% Lignocaine
   9F sheath [illegible] temporary filter at L2
   Difficult to find vein but eventually achieved.
   5mg rTPA* bolus given through lysis catheter ✓
   For infusion 8 mg rTPA in 40mls N saline at 5 mls/h
   =1mg/h
   Heparin 250u/h through side of arm popliteal sheaf
   I will check progress tonight
   signed Willard"
   [page 6–7]

10. A note at 2130 on 27 June 2001 records that thrombolysis procedure and states:
    "Good progress in clearing iliac vein but there is thrombus still in the IVC*
    Therefore catheter left in situ for now. Continue TPA*
    She is developing a haematoma around the neck puncture which will need to be
    watched carefully. If becomes a problem stop TPA* and watch"
    [page 7]

11. A further note on 27 June 2001 records:
    "Patient's haematoma has grown. No stridor but uncomfortable. Stop anti-coagulation to apply
    local pressure
    D/W Mr Q"
    [page 8]

12. A note on 28 June 2001 records:
    "Recheck bloods – Hb* + clotting
    No further progress in haematoma size – still some dysphagia.
    Dr L to see again"
    [page 8]

13. A later note on 28 June 2001 records:
    "Unfortunately all progress made yesterday has reversed
    therefore neckto [illegible]
    → 5 mg TPA bolus given
    to recommence [illegible]
    I will review 5pm"
    [page 8]

14. At 1305 on 28 June 2001 the notes record:
    "-tpa running
    -no further deterioration in neck haematoma
    → continue
    → needs thrombophilia screen"
    [page 8]

15. At 1620 on 28 June 2001 it was recorded that the Claimant's haemoglobin level was 8.1 and she needed 3 pints of blood transfused.
    [page 8]

16. At 1720 on 28 June 2001 the note records:
    "Good progress with lysis, now clear to below inguinal ligament but there is a tongue of throm-
    bus still in the lower inferior vena cava. Catheter pulled back; [illegible] will review tomor-
    row morning"
    [page 9]

17. A further untimed note on 28 June 2001 records:
    "- swelling in neck region has ? increased in size
    - the skin surrounding catheter entry has become tighter
    Px*not c/o* any pain/SOB*
    No stridor – oxygen sats normal
    Observations stable
    Px concerned Bloods –INR* 1.6 APTT* 32, ration 1.2
    Plan to discuss with senior, apply local pressure with cold pad and review"
    [page 9]

18. A further note at 1940 on 28 June 2001 records:
    "ATS on request of nursing staff
    Feeling very tight in her neck
    Some difficulty swallowing
    o/e* There is a definite enlargement of the neck haematoma extending into right
    posterior and mastoid area as well as the pre-tragial area. No stridor.
    Plan –As discussed with BRG(Mr Gwynn)
    - stop TPA and continue local Heparin. Target APTT* ratio about 3"
    [page 10]

19. At 7.30 on 29 June 2001 there is a note:
    "ARREST call 6.58
    - Respiratory arrest
    - v. oedematous neck
    2 ° to trauma from vena cava filter insertion
    initials → sinustrom
    - attempts made to establish airway – v. difficult"
    Adreneline was administered and the Claimant taken to the operating theatre for a tracheostomy.
    [page 11–12]

20. There is a note of a discussion with the Claimant's husband in which it was noted the Claimant was making a respiratory effort and:
    "that the outcome is difficult to judge at this stage, there is a possibility of damage to the brain"
    [page 12]

21. On 3 July 2001 there is a note described as a retrospective note pertaining to the arrest call on 28 June 2001. It states:
    "There appears to be no note from the on-call anaesthetist, the sequence of events is as follows.
    Arrest call approximately 7.0 am
    Arrived at ward 7
    Dr L in attendance
    O/E Airway obstruction 2 º external compression
    Heparin infusion stopped
    Difficulty maintaining airway due to obstruction and trimus
    Attempted maintenance with face mask and guedel airway
    LMA*requested by Dr M from theatres
    LMA arrived within approximately 2 minutes
    LMA inserted + able to maintain airway
    Reasonable air entry ausculated in apices
    ET* tubes (paediatric size) obtained
    LMA removed and intubation attempted
    Grade 4 laryngoscopy/
    LMA re inserted /c laryngoscopy. Airway again maintained
    Dr M contacted by Mr K
    Plan – Attempt to stabalise
    Transfer to theatre for emergency tracheostomy
    Doctor M will come in
    Transferred to theatre 5
    Scout monitoring for transfer –SaO2 (oxygen saturations)
    NIBP
    ECG
    Emergency tracheostomy performed under GA
    Spontaneous technique on LMA
    (R) radial arterial line inserted
    Transfer post op to ITU"
    [page 13]

22. On 3 July 2001 a report from Doctor G recorded:
    "Thank you for asking me to see this very sick lady who is currently on the Critical Care Unit. Although her seizure activity has resolved clinically she needs to maintain intravenous Phenytoin . . .
    I gather that she developed a left ileofemoral venous thrombosis on 26/02/2001. This was two days after she had returned from Spain by air. On 27/06/2001, she had thrombolysis. This had to be stopped and restarted on 28 June. She had developed a haematoma in her neck. Sadly the haematoma increased in size on 28/06/2001. At 7.30 on 29 June, she had a respiratory arrest. She required an emergency tracheostomy.
    On examination now, she had CPAP for ventilatory support. She had a bilateral lash reflex. She withdraws to pain in her arms. She had some rigidity in the lower limbs. Plantar responses are flexor.
    An EEG on 2/07/2001 was diffusely slow. She has intermittent spike charges."
    {page 51 general practitioner notes}

23. On 3 September 2001 the Claimant was transferred from K District Hospital to L Hospital for rehabilitation.
24. In January 2002 the Claimant returned home where she has remained severely disabled from the brain damage she sustained following the respiratory arrest in June 2001. The Claimant remains in a wheelchair and requires help with all daily tasks and requires full time nursing care.
{page 74 general practitioner notes}
25. A report from Doctor A dated 16 November 2001 concluded that the Claimant was suffering from a brain injury. He described how the CT scan on the 20th October showed evidence of bilateral fronto temporal atrophy with minor progress from previous scans and there were some cerebellar atrophic changes as well. Further he diagnosed the Claimant was suffering from psychotic depression.
{page 46–47 general practitioner notes}.
26. In a letter dated 2 July 2003 written on behalf of the Defendant it was admitted that the Defendant was in breach of duty in respect of the failure of the Defendant to prevent the Claimant suffering a respiratory arrest, followed by a cardiac arrest and ultimately brain damage.
27. The Claimant relies on the above admission of liability on behalf of the Claimant and the following matters in support of the claim that the Defendant's breach of duty was caused by the negligence of the Defendant, its servants or agents for whom the Defendant is vicariously liable:

Particulars of Negligence

a. The Defendant failed to administer the Claimant intravenous Heparin on her admission to hospital. With competent care the Defendant should and would have administered the Claimant intravenous Heparin from her admission to hospital on 26 June 2003. Had the Defendant done so her own fibrinolytic system would have allowed the clot to dissolve.
b. Having decided to use fibrinolytic treatment which carried established risks of bleeding the Defendant failed to monitor the Claimant adequately so that when the haematoma was first recognised in the Claimant's neck the fibrinolytic treatment should have been discontinued. Had the treatment been discontinued the Claimant would on the balance of probabilities have avoided the respiratory arrest.
c. When the haematoma in the Claimant's neck increased in size there were signs of tracheal compression and steps should have been taken to avoid the respiratory arrest suffered by the Claimant.

28. The Claimant has suffered severe injury loss and damage as a result of the negligence of the Defendant which is now admitted and the matters set out in particulars of negligence above. If the Claimant had been competently treated and monitored she would not have suffered a respiratory arrest or cardiac arrest and would have made a complete, or alternatively almost-complete recovery from her DVT.
29. As a result of the Defendant's negligence the Claimant has suffered injury, loss, and damage. Particulars of the Claimant's injury loss and damage are set out in the report of Professor A and the preliminary schedule attached. On the balance of probabilities if the Claimant had been competently treated by the Defendant she would have made a full recovery or would have suffered only minor injury in her legs.

30. Further and pursuant to Section 35A of the Supreme Court Act 1981 the Claimant claims interest on general damages at 2% from the date of service of these proceedings; and interest on special damages which have accrued on the date that they accrued at the full special account rate and on continuing losses at half the special account rate.

And the Claimant's claim

(a) **damages**

(b) **interest**

Dated this   day of   2006

The Claimant's litigation friend believes the matters set out in the particulars of claim are true

Signed

Glossary of medical abbreviations arranged alphabetically

o	No
APTT	Activated partial thromboplastin time
c/o	Complaining of
Dp	Dors. Pedis, Dorsalis pedis
DVT	Deep vein thrombosis
D/W	Discussed with
ECG	Electrocardiogram
ET	Endo-tracheal
Hb	Haemoglobin
IVC	Inferior vena cava
LMA	Laryngeal mask airway
Nv	Neurovascular
o/e	On examination
Plt	Platelets
Px	Patient
RIJV	Right internal jugular vein
RMO	Resident medical officer
RSO	Resident surgical officer
SOB	Shortness of breath
Tib	Tibial pulses
US	Ultrasound
Wbc	White blood cells

APPENDIX 5

Letters and Document Precedents

1. LETTER CONFIRMING APPOINTMENT

Dear Ms Client

Your Claim

I refer to our telephone conversation on 8 March 2007 and confirm your appointment to see me on 12 March 2007 at 11 am.

I enclose:

1. Our leaflet describing the Clinical Negligence Team;
2. A map showing the location of our office;
3. A Consumer Association leaflet "Medical Accidents".

I confirm that your initial appointment will be free of charge. During our meeting we will discuss the concerns you have about your treatment, the options you have as to what to do next, and the costs that would be involved if you were to proceed.

Please bring to the meeting any relevant documents or correspondence and your household, building and contents, and credit card insurance policies and schedules. I need to see those before I can advise about funding options.

I am Head of the Clinical Negligence Team and a member of the Law Society's Special Clinical Negligence Panel.

We aim to offer all clients a friendly and efficient service. If at any time you have any complaint about the services provided by the firm, please first raise the matter with me. If any problem remains please contact L . . . . . M . . . . . Complaints Partner.

If there is anything you wish to discuss before our meeting please do not hesitate to contact me.

Yours sincerely

2. CLIENT CARE LETTER

Dear Ms Client

Your Clinical Negligence Claim

Thank you very much for coming to see me last week. I am happy to act for you in your clinical negligence case against Pleasantown NHS Trust.

I enclose the following documents:

For you to keep:

- Information sheet about clinical negligence claims.
- Costs Information for claimants.

Please sign and return:

- Form of authority for release of medical records.
- Form of authority for release of your tax and business documents.
- Our Terms of Business in duplicate; one copy is for your records. You should read this carefully and note in particular the clause 'Limitation of our liability'. If you have any queries, please do telephone me.

Information Needed

Please let me have the following information:

- Name and address of your accountant.
- Your National Insurance number.
- The claim form for III insurers; I will complete this and return it to you for signature.
- As soon as possible, please let me have a list of your losses and expenses to date with receipts and estimates as appropriate. I will not need this immediately, but it will be easier for you to keep track if you start making the list now.
- Please keep a record as you go along of any problems you suffer as a result of your injury and any expenses you incur. Please also keep receipts, and other documentary proof of your losses.

Advice

You told me that you had a lymph node biopsy to the left side of your neck on 01.01.06 at Pleasantown District General Hospital. This was carried out as day surgery. You were under the care of Mr G Surgeon, but you are not sure if he carried out the operation. Your friend Anna is a nurse on the day ward and she told you that Mr Surgeon was supervising junior staff in two different theatres. You were sent home with no advice except to rest and take paracetamol as required. You were given a follow-up appointment for 16.02.06.

Almost as soon as you got home, you began to experience pain in your left shoulder and neck area with limited movement in your arm and shoulder. You assumed this was to be expected but as the pain was worse rather than better after a week, you consulted your GP, Dr Practitioner. He diagnosed 'post operative pain', told you to continue with the paracetamol but gave you no other advice.

Your symptoms did not improve and in fact got worse. On 24.01.06 you rang NHS Direct who advised you to go back to your GP. You saw Dr Practitioner 25.01.06; he prescribed Diclofenac tablets but gave you no further advice.

At your follow-up appointment at hospital on 16.02.06 you saw a junior doctor; she told you that the biopsy on your lymph node confirmed it was benign. You told her about your shoulder pain but she did not examine you, saying it was unrelated and you should ask your GP to send you to an orthopaedic surgeon. On 23.02.06 you received a telephone call from Mr Surgeon's secretary telling you there was a problem and asking you to go in and see Mr Surgeon that day, which you did. Mr Surgeon told you that a nerve in your shoulder had had 'a little bruising' in theatre. He referred you to Mr Plastic at the National Plastic Centre in London, saying he was 'good with shoulders'. You saw Mr Plastic on 29.02.06; he told you the nerve was damaged and that you needed surgery. Mr Plastic operated on 5.03.06.

Unfortunately, although you have a little more movement in your arm, you still cannot lift it above shoulder level, and you have persisting pain, which is particularly bad at night. Mr Plastic has said it is early days but you feel he doesn't expect more than slight improvement.

You told me that you are single and that you have depended on your mother to come in and help you on a daily basis, with housework and shopping and so on. You can't drive, or play golf. Your social life mainly centred on your golf club and you were a team member playing in tournaments on a regular basis.

You said you had had a bit of neck pain in the past but this was several years ago and you had not needed treatment.

You are understandably concerned about your financial position, as you are self-employed as a sole trader and have been unable to work since the surgery in January. You are a seamstress specialising in 'window treatments'; through your business 'Client Windows' you made curtains and blinds for show houses and department stores; you explained you were optimistic about securing a large contract with a television company just before your surgery. You have been living off your savings, which are now nearly exhausted. Fortunately, you own your own home and there is no mortgage.

I explained that, that in my opinion it would be reasonable to investigate a possible claim for damages against Pleasantown NHS Trust. We discussed the fact that your GP should possibly have referred you back to hospital sooner; my advice was that we should investigate the claim against the Trust in the first instance; I will ask our expert to advise about whether the GP delay made any difference to your recovery.

The issues that we will need to investigate are:

• Was the injury avoidable?
• Should your GP have referred you back to hospital sooner?
• Was the hospital follow-up care below a standard you were entitled to expect?
• Did any of the delays adversely affect your recovery?
• What are your prospects of further recovery and is there any further treatment available that might help, whether NHS or private?

As we discussed, in due course I will need your business and tax returns over quite a long period to calculate your loss of earnings; for the time being, I would be grateful if you would send me copies of your accounts and tax returns back to 2003.

It is early days in your recovery, but as I explained, you do have a duty to keep your losses to a minimum and you will need to consider what alternative work you might be able to do once you have made the best recovery you can. We can discuss this at a later date; I may be able to put you in touch with someone who could advise on this.

I will arrange a driving assessment for once you are ready for this; it is important to establish how soon you will be able to drive and whether you need automatic transmission.

Future Action

I reviewed with you all your alternative courses of action. Your instructions were that you wished to bring a claim for damages, as you do not feel that you would be satisfied by any explanation the Trust might give (even if they would consider a complaint out of time) and you are particularly concerned about recovering your financial losses.

As explained on the clinical negligence information sheet, it is necessary not only to prove liability or fault on the part of those treating you, but also that as a direct result of the treatment, you have been left worse off than you might otherwise have been. In order to investigate this, it is essential to see copies of your medical notes and records from the hospital where you were treated, and from your general practitioner. The form of authority you are to return to me will enable me to obtain copies of these records. £50 is the maximum fee payable for each different set of copy records.

I will let you know when the records have been received and organised so that you can have an opportunity to go through them. I will also take steps to identify an appropriately qualified medical expert in general surgery, who practises well outside the area where you received treatment. I will inform you of the likely costs of instructing that expert, and will formally instruct him once I have gone through the medical records with you.

Once I receive the expert's medical report, I will be able to advise you more fully about whether your injury should have been avoided, but then I will need to instruct an orthopaedic expert specialising in upper limb surgery and nerve repair to comment on whether you were adversely affected by any substandard care identified.

Once these reports are to hand, I will be able to advise you more fully about future progress of the case.

Costs

We have discussed the funding of your claim and I have considered with you legal costs insurance, community funding, conditional fee agreements, and private client funding. You have a policy with III Insurers that provides cover for legal costs, including clinical negligence claims. Fortunately, you notified them promptly of a possible claim. The limit of your indemnity is £50,000. I am reasonably confident that this will be sufficient cover to bring your claim to a conclusion but that cannot be certain at this stage. If you reach the limits of your cover before the end of your case, I would hope to be able to offer you a Conditional Fee Agreement, if the merits of your case at that time allow. I will discuss the implications of that with you, including the need for after-the-event insurance, when and if the need arises.

Our current hourly rates are as follows:

Solicitor (with more than 8 yrs experience)	£000.00
Solicitor or Legal Executive (with more than 4 yrs experience)	£000.00
Solicitor or Legal Executive	£000.00
Trainee Solicitor or equivalent	£000.00

Our charging rates are revised annually, usually in January. I will let you know in advance if the rate applicable to your case is to change.

You are primarily responsible for your legal costs but your legal insurance policy will indemnify you up to the policy limit of £50,000. I will enter into a separate agreement with your insurer.

I am required by the Law Society to give you an estimate of the likely final costs in your case. This is very difficult at this stage. Clinical negligence claims are expensive to investigate and to pursue, not least because of the need to instruct the medical experts, and if the matter proceeds to trial, the experts will have to attend to give evidence, and to hear the evidence given by the other side's experts. Consequently, clinical negligence cases that go to trial are likely to last at least 3 days, and the cost will be in the region of £30,000 to £45,000 for each side, but more if the trial is longer. Costs vary depending, for example, on how many experts have to give evidence, and how much time is spent preparing the case. I will try to settle your claim once we have all the information needed. If the issues are clear enough, it may well be possible to reach an agreement with the Trust in negotiation or by mediation.

In your case I estimate our total costs are likely to be in the region of £00000.00 for profit costs plus VAT, £00000.00 for disbursements including experts' fees, and £00000.00 for Counsel's fees. I will report to you every 6 months setting out the costs to date on your case. The other side's costs are likely to be similar, so this will give you an idea of how costs are accruing. Please also refer to the enclosed Costs Information Sheet.

I am only able to provide you with a provisional estimate of the value of your claim at this stage. I would hope that if your claim were successful your damages would be in the region of £000000.00. This is based on the information you have given to me at our initial meeting and I will need to revise this figure as your claim progresses.

As set out above, the costs of pursuing your claim are considerable but I consider that the potential benefit to you merits taking the matter further. I will be reviewing the position regularly and I will let you know if there is any change.

Case Handling

I confirm that I am the solicitor who will be primarily responsible for the conduct of your case. I may be assisted from time to time by S .... B .... a solicitor who also specialises in clinical negligence. If, at any time, I am not available when you call, please ask S ..., or for my secretary, J ...... D .... who will be able to deal with many of your questions and who will be pleased to take any message from you.

As part of our quality procedures all files without exception are supervised by a senior solicitor in the Department. In your case the supervisor is I .... K ...., partner.

We aim to offer all clients a friendly and efficient service. If, however, for any reason a problem should arise, you should first raise the matter with me. If any problems remain, please then do feel free to raise the matter with L .... M ...., Managing Partner.

I will report regularly to you on the case, but if at any time you have any queries, or wish to know what is happening, please do not hesitate to telephone me. I look forward to hearing from you.

Yours sincerely

3. LETTER OF INVITATION TO EXPERT

Dear ....

Claimant:

Date of birth:

Address:

Telephone no:

Name of case:

I am instructed by ...., to investigate a potential claim for damages for negligence in respect of the treatment afforded to .... by .... at the .... Hospital on ....

The potential defendant is ....; the consultant concerned is ....;

In brief the allegation is that ....

I write to ask whether you would be able to assist as an expert witness. In the first instance this would involve the preparation of a written advice based on the medical records and my client's account of events, dealing with issues of breach of duty and causation.

My client has the benefit of a legal aid certificate/legal expenses insurance/is funding the investigation from her own resources. I will need to obtain specific authority to incur your fee and I would be grateful if you could give me an estimate of your likely charges. I sometimes need to ask supplementary questions arising out of your report. Please take this into account when quoting your fee.

It would be of considerable assistance if you could give me a prompt decision on whether or not you can accept instructions from me in this matter.

If you are able to assist, please give an indication of the likely time scale within which I can expect to receive your report.

Please confirm that you have no reason to believe you will have a conflict of interest if you agree to advise.

Please confirm that you will not delegate any work associated with your report, without my prior agreement.

I will then provide you with a formal letter of instruction, the medical and other records disclosed to me, and my client's statement.

I look forward to hearing from you.

Yours sincerely

4. Letter of Instruction to Expert

Dear ....

Claimant:

Date of birth:

Address:

Telephone no:

Name of case:

Thank you for agreeing to act as an expert witness in this case.

My client has instructed me to investigate a potential claim for damages against ....
NHS Trust who administer .... Hospital.

The allegations of negligence arise in the following circumstances:

I should be grateful if you could prepare an advice commenting on issues of breach of duty and causation. Firstly, please could you provide your opinion on whether the standard of care afforded to .... fell below that of a reasonably competent ....? Please then advise whether, on the balance of probabilities,....................... has been adversely affected by any substandard care you have identified.

Documentation

I enclose copies of:

1. My client's medical records as follows:
   a. General Practitioner
   b. .... Hospital
   c. ....Centre

The records have been sorted, paginated and indexed; please use the number in the bottom right hand corner for reference–it has no other significance.

I have identical sets of records in my possession and you may retain the copies I am sending you. If you find there are records missing which may have some importance for my client's case, please let me know so I can obtain full discovery.

2. I am sending X-rays under separate cover. These are copies that belong to my client and not to the Trust. Please return them to me when you have finalised your report and dealt with supplementary questions that may arise.
3. Chronology of treatment.
4. My client's statement.
5. Complaint correspondence.

Please note that the limit of my financial authority for your report is £000.00; if you believe you will exceed that figure please telephone me to discuss. I may not be able to meet any higher fee incurred without authority.

Progress of Litigation

I am in the early stages of investigating the merits of this claim. Once I have your advice, I intend to instruct a .... expert to advise on .... Other experts may be instructed in due course.

Your Advice

Please prepare an advice on the basis of the disclosed documents. As you will be aware, in your report you should:

• Set out your qualifications and expertise.
• Comment upon the completeness and legibility of the medical records.
• Summarise the medical history and comment on the relevant medical events.
• Provide your opinion on the treatment provided and whether it fell below the standard my client was reasonably entitled to expect.
• State whether you consider that my client's condition was affected by any lapse in care identified.
• Review all the published material that relates to the treatment in question and provide a list of the literature you have reviewed, with copies of those you have relied on.
• If you prefer one text above another in arriving at your opinion, your reasons for so doing should be given.

In order to comply with Court Rules, I should be grateful if you would insert a statement that complies with CPR 35.10 and 2.2 of the related Practice Direction and also the following wording to go above your signature:

'I confirm that insofar as the facts stated in my report are within my own knowledge I have made clear which they are and I believe them to be true, and that the opinions I have expressed represent my true and complete professional opinion.'

You will be familiar with CPR Part 35, the associated Practice Direction, and the protocol for the instruction of experts but please let me know if you would like an up-to-date hard copy. Full details can be found on the CPR website www.justice.gov.uk.

I also draw your attention to the Civil Justice Council's Protocol for the Instruction of Experts to give Evidence in Civil Claims June 2005; we will aim at all times to observe the protocol and you are instructed on the basis that you are familiar with the protocol and will act in accordance with its provisions. Full details can be found on the Civil Justice Council's website www.civiljustice.council.gov.uk.

Please feel free to refer to all the enclosed documentation in the body of your advice.

I look forward to hearing from you.

If you would find it helpful to discuss any aspects of your instructions, you should not hesitate to telephone me or e-mail me on ....

Yours sincerely

5. LETTER OF CLAIM

Letter of Claim under the Pre-Action Protocol for Resolution of Clinical Disputes

Dear Sirs

Our client Mr Alfred Client DOB 02.02.62

We are instructed by Mr Client to bring a claim for damages for clinical negligence arising out of Mr Client's treatment at the Pleasantown District Hospital following his admission on 5 April 2006.

Mr Client was admitted to the Pleasantown District Hospital on 5 April 2006, following a fall from a horse. In the fall he sustained a fracture of the pelvis with associated neurological damage and soft tissue injuries to his left shoulder and elbow. A later (post-operative) CT scan also showed a subdural haematoma over the left frontal region of the brain.

Mr Client had a history of angina and was assessed by Dr Cardiologist and an anaesthetist before being taken to theatre on 7 April to have his pelvis stabilised. The anaesthetist in theatre was Dr Ether. As anaesthesia was induced, Mr Client suffered an electro-mechanical disassociation, indicating that his heart had ceased beating. The medical records show that the cardiac arrest lasted for 9 minutes before spontaneous cardiac output was restored.

Subsequently Mr Client has been shown to have suffered significant brain damage.

It is our case that Mr Client's cardiac arrest occurred as a result of sympathetic nerve blockade caused by the injection of a substantial dose of bupivacaine into the epidural space.

We allege this occurred as a result of negligent acts and omissions as follows:

1. Omitting carefully to monitor Mr Client's blood pressure after the initial 4ml of bupivacaine was administered at c14.15 hrs.
2. Immediately administering two further doses, making a total of 14ml of bupivacaine 0.5%, to Mr Client when he was anaesthetised with a systolic blood pressure of about 100mmHg (significantly lower than before anaesthesia).
3. Immediately transferring him to the operating theatre, during which time (including time for positioning) it would not be possible to monitor his blood pressure.
4. Consequently omitting to detect Mr Client's decreased blood pressure after the first dose of bupivicaine and omitting to prevent further decrease by rapid infusion of intravenous fluid, or alternatively by intravenous injection of a cardiovascular stimulant drug.
5. As a result of the above negligent acts and omissions, Mr Client sustained hypoxic brain damage, the effects of which are set out below.
6. We reserve our position as to the failure to perform a pre-operative CT scan or otherwise detect Mr Client's subdural haematoma and thereafter transfer him to a neurosurgical unit, and to the extent to which these omissions caused or contributed to his subsequent brain damage.
7. On the balance of probabilities, but for the above negligence, Mr Client would have recovered from his accident without brain damage.

After his accident but before surgery, Mr Client was lucid and orientated. Post-operatively, he was in a deep coma, as a consequence of his brain injury. He was manic and deluded for 3 days or so. Thereafter, he was disorientated, confused, hallucinating, and agitated for several days.

Despite rehabilitation he has persisting and permanent deficits. He shows a significant blunting of intelligence, impairment of memory and poor performance on tests designed to elicit frontal lobe abnormalities. He has significantly blunted cognitive abilities. He lacks drive and motivation, is emotionally flat and indifferent to his personal circumstances. These deficits impact upon his social and family relationships and render it unlikely that he will return to gainful employment as an Estate Manager. He is currently being cared for by his sister but is likely to need full time residential care in the longer term.

Mr Client's orthopaedic injuries have left him with left buttock pain, pelvis pain, and low back pain which are also likely to be permanent but which in themselves would not have prevented him returning to work.

We have obtained an advice from Professor X on the issue of anaesthetic negligence.

We have obtained reports from an orthopaedic surgeon, a neurologist and a neuropsychologist, dealing with Mr Client's injuries and his current condition and prognosis. We enclose copies with this letter.

We have not yet obtained quantum reports and we are not in a position to fully quantify the case, as Mr Client has only recently been advised he can expect no further recovery. We enclose a draft schedule of loss, setting out the heads of damage and providing as much information as we are able to do at present. We reserve the right to amend this as we obtain further expert advice. Our preliminary view is that the claim can be valued at in excess of £mmm.

We enclose a chronology of treatment. We have the medical records disclosed by your client; we also have the GP records; please advise if you wish to have copies of the GP records alone or would prefer us to provide a copy of our paginated bundle. Our copying charge is 00p per page.

We look forward to hearing from you with your client's response, within 3 months as provided for under the pre-action protocol.

Yours faithfully

6. CASE PLAN

CASE PLAN

Ms AB Client: case ref C1234

Accessory nerve injury – left side – Ms Client right-handed

Limitation expires: 01.01.09.
Defendant: Pleasantville NHS Trust (Mr G Surgeon = consultant in charge). Allegations may also involve Dr G. Practitioner - ?delay in referring back post-op

Ms Client had a left lymph node biopsy on 01.01.06 – day case ward – Pleasantville DGH. Op note indicates SHO operated with Mr Surgeon supervising. Ms Client thinks Mr S had two theatres to supervise. (Her friend is a nurse on the ward – won't say anything on record.) Sent home with follow up appointment in 6 weeks; Ms Client noticed pain in left shoulder/neck, assumed normal post-op, after 1 week saw GP, diagnosed post-op pain, analgesia, no advice. Pain persisted + limitation of movement. 24.01.06 rang NHS Direct: ref to GP. Saw GP 25.01.06 – analgesia increased, no advice. At follow-up appointment at hospital on 16.02.06 saw SHO who said lymph node benign, shoulder problem unrelated to surgery, see GP re possible orthopaedic referral. On 23.02.06 tel call from Mr Surgeon's sec – please could she come into clinic that day; saw Mr Surgeon who told her problems resulted from 'a little bruising' to the nerve in her shoulder, ref to Mr Plastic at NPC who is 'good with shoulders'. Appt with Mr P on 29.02.06, nerve damaged, repair surgery (Mr P himself) on 5.03.06. since then very little recovery, can't lift arm above shoulder level, pain persists, v bad at night. Doesn't expect more than slight improvement now.

Ms Client lives alone, mother has been coming in to help with housework; can't drive or play golf (more than a hobby – 'my life'). Ms Client was self-employed t/a 'Windows Galore' made curtains, blinds etc for show houses, department stores – was just about to secure TV work – hasn't worked since op; living off savings, now nearly gone.

Funding: has LEI, cover confirmed £50,000 indemnity, six monthly reports and usual authorities – diarised/noted

Issues:

1. Breach of duty
   - Was injury avoidable? (should get prompt admission)
   - Should GP have referred back to hospital ? When?
   - Was it appropriate for SHO to do follow up?
   - Substandard for SHO not to recognise accessory nerve injury?

2. Causation
   - Did any of the delays impair prospects of recovery?
   - Any pre-existing neck/shoulder problems (golf)?
   - Prospects of further recovery?
   - Any further treatment available eg privately – surgery, physio etc?

3. Loss of earnings:
   - Need accounts & tax returns back to 2003 at least for preliminary view on quantum
   - Client needs to consider other work–?offer referral to adviser
   - Needs driving assessment asap

Medical records received:

- GP–received
- Pleasantville DGH received, but minus the internal docs re adverse incident – chased
- National Plastics Centre – received, radiology on disk

Records collated

Mr DE. Cons Gen Surgeon instructed re breach of duty/initial delay. Due end June

Mr FG Cons Orthopaedic (Upper Limb + peripheral surgery) invited re causation & current condition/prognosis 3.5.07– Instruct by 01.07.07, receive report by 01.10.07

Consider if need GP liability report if delay affected prospects of recovery

Forensic accountant – Mrs G invited, agreed, needs prognosis report, instruct by 14.10.07, receive report by 14.12.07

Draft schedule of loss by 28.01.08

Conference with counsel: advise on quantum required before offers, arrange for 02.08, with a view to serving letter of claim with draft particulars and schedule by 28.02.08 + ? Part 36 offer

Def's Response due end May 08

Review next steps when response received

05.05.07

7. Agenda Template

CASE HEADING

AGENDA FOR EXPERTS' DISCUSSION BETWEEN

DR & DR At .... am/pm On 2003

At .... *Venue*

The solicitors for both parties have agreed the agenda for this discussion between the .... experts. The solicitors will not be present.

The purpose of the discussion is to assist the parties, their lawyers, and the Court by clarifying those issues of expert opinion that are agreed, identifying those issues which are not agreed and providing a brief explanation of the reasons for disagreement, referring to any published research or other published materials relied upon.

The experts are reminded:

- Their primary duty is to the Court.
- It is not intended the experts should arrive at a compromise view or otherwise attempt to "settle" the case.
- Where there is a factual dispute it is for the Court to decide upon the facts and for the experts to give their opinion on the basis of the alternative factual scenarios set out in the agenda.
- When considering the standard of care, the relevant standard to be applied, and expressed in the expert's answer, is whether the care provided accorded with the practice of a responsible body of professional opinion which existed in the UK in ....
- When considering the standard of care, the experts are reminded to consider the circumstances, as they were known at the time, and to avoid judging with hindsight.
- When considering causation, the experts must apply the legal test for causation, which is the *balance of probabilities* and not a higher scientific test.
- Experts should indicate if a question falls outside their area of expertise.
- At the conclusion of their discussion each expert should sign and date the agenda, which should be copied and sent to the Claimant's solicitors.
- If it is felt further action, information or research is required before the final view can be reached on any issue, this should be stated; **the remainder of the agenda should be completed and signed off in any event.**

BACKGROUND

QUESTIONS

CURRENT CONDITION

PROGNOSIS

CAUSATION

ANY FURTHER COMMENTS

Signed   ....

Date   ....

Signed   ....

Date   ....

8. Case List Template

Client Name	Matter No	Funding	Limitation	Other Key Dates	Quantum Band	Quarterly Review	Current Status

APPENDIX 6

Applications and Orders

1. APPLICATION FOR PRE-ACTION DISCLOSURE

Application Notice – third party disclosure

In the High Court of Justice, Queen's Bench Division Pleasantown District Registry	
Claim No.	HQ ....
Warrant No. (if applicable)	
Claimant(s) (including ref.)	Mr Alan Smith (By his mother and litigation friend Mrs B Smith)
Defendant(s) (including ref).	Pleasantown NHS Trust
Date	

You should provide this information for listing the application

1. How do you wish to have your application dealt with

a) at a hearing?
b) at a telephone conference   yes
c) without a hearing?

2. Give a time estimate for the hearing.conference
_____(hours) ____30____(mins)

3. Is this agreed by all parties?   No
4. Give dates of any trial period or fixed trial date
5. Level of judge Master
6. Parties to be served: Defendant

Note You must complete Parts A **and** B, **and** C if applicable. Send any relevant fee and the completed application to the court with any draft order, witness statements or other evidence; and sufficient copies for service on each respondent.

Part A (1)

1. Enter your full name, or name of solicitor

I (We) Solicitor's name   (on behalf of)(the claimant) (the defendant)

2. State clearly what order you are seeking and if possible attach a draft

intend to apply for an order (a draft of which is attached) that (2) (1) the respondent do disclose to the applicant's representative the applicant's healthcare records held by them pursuant to section 7 of the Data Protection Act 1998 and under Part 31.17.3 (a) and (b) of the Civil Civil Procedure Rules. (2) The respondent do pay the applicant's costs of, and incidental to this application pursuant to Part 48.1 (2) and (3) of the Civil Procedure Rules.

3. Briefly set out why you are seeking the order. Include the material facts on which you rely, identifying any rule or statutory provision

because (3) (1) The healthcare records for which disclosure is sought are likely to support the proposed claim of the applicant. (2) Disclosure is necessary in order to dispose fairly of the anticipated proceedings or to assist the dispute to be resolved without proceedings and save costs. (3) The applicant is entitled to his costs because the respondent has failed to disclose these healthcare records pursuant to the applicant's request under the Data Protection Act 1998 and made in accordance with the Clinical Negligence Pre-action Protocol.

Part B

I (We)   wish to rely on:

the attached (witness statement)(affidavit)   Yes

my statement of case

evidence in Part C in support of my application

4. If you are not already a party to the proceedings, you must provide an address for service of documents

Signed [_____]   **Position of office held** [_____]

(Applicant)('s solicitor)   (if signing on behalf
('s litigation friend)   of firm or company)

430

2. SOLICITOR'S WITNESS STATEMENT IN SUPPORT OF APPLICATION FOR PRE-ACTION DISCLOSURE

Filed on behalf of: Claimant
Name of witness: Anne Advocate
Witness Statement number: 1
Exhibit Refs; AA1
Date made:

IN THE HIGH COURT OF JUSTICE
QUEEN'S BENCH DIVISION   CLAIM NO:
PLEASANTOWN DISTRICT REGISTRY

BETWEEN:

Alan SMITH   Applicant
(A child by his mother and
Litigation Friend Mrs Brenda Smith)

-and-

Pleasantown NHS TRUST   Respondent

WITNESS STATEMENT OF ANNE ADVOCATE

I, Anne Advocate, of will say as .... follows:

1. I am a Partner in Solicitors LLP of 10 High Street Pleasantown PV1 1HA.

2. I am instructed on behalf of the applicant in this matter.

3. Save where it otherwise appears, the contents of this witness statement are based on my own knowledge.

4. My instructions are to investigate a potential claim for clinical negligence arising from the circumstances of the applicant's delivery.

5. On my present instructions, the respondent is not the defendant in the applicant's clinical negligence claim, but treated the applicant during the period 1997 to 2000.

6. Alan Smith was born on 27th November 1997 at A Hospital, London.

7. Alan Smith suffers from cerebral palsy as a result of hypoxic ischaemic damage. He is severely mentally and physically disabled. I am instructed by his mother and litigation friend to investigate whether those injuries were caused by the care provided to him and his mother at the time of his delivery.

8. At the age of six months, Alan Smith was referred to Pleasantown District General Hospital for assessment and treatment. He was under the care of a consultant and was seen both as an inpatient and in follow up clinics. A number of investigations into Alan

431

Smith's health were carried out including an EEG, MRI scans and a lumbar puncture. These records are fundamental to the investigation of the applicant's case on causation.

9. My original request for disclosure of the applicant's healthcare records was made under the provisions of the Data Protection Act 1998, by a letter dated 30th May 2007, enclosing a completed pre-action protocol form.

10. The respondents indicated in a letter of 15th June 2007, that they were unable to locate the records but that they would continue to do a thorough search and notify me when they had been found.

11. On 29th June 2007, my secretary telephoned the respondents and was told that they had yet to find the records but would continue looking.

12. No notification or further information as to the nature of the searches that were being undertaken was received. I therefore sent a further letter on 3rd July 2007 repeating my request for disclosure of the applicant's healthcare records.

13. On 6th July 2007 my secretary took a telephone call from the respondents' Medical Records Officer who informed us that they still could not find the applicant's medical records, that they could be anywhere in their storage rooms and that it would take a long time to find them.

14. As the records were not disclosed and no further correspondence was received from the respondent, I wrote on 21st July to say that I would have no alternative but to make an application to the court for disclosure of the records unless we heard from them, although I hope this step could be avoided.

15. My assistant followed up with telephone calls on 3rd and 4th August 2007, but the respondents' officer gave no further indication of when the records would be provided, saying that the applicant's records were in off-site storage but that they were still unable to locate them and did not have time to do so at the moment.

16. I wrote to the respondents on 12th August 2007, informing them that I would now issue an application for disclosure.

17. My secretary took a telephone message from the respondents, saying that the applicant's healthcare records could still not be located.

18. I refer to the bundle of correspondence marked "AA1" annexed to this statement that contains copies of the correspondence and attendance notes referred to in the paragraphs above.

19. In order to be able to advise my client's litigation friend whether or not Alan Smith suffered brain damage as a consequence of negligent obstetric care, it is essential for all of his healthcare records to be disclosed. These records will be fundamental in allowing the applicant's medical experts to provide their views to the court on issues of causation.

20. For the reasons set out above, my client is likely to be the claimant in a claim for compensation for personal injury and loss resulting from negligent medical care against the London NHS Trust.

21. Under the Data Protection Act 1998 and under paragraph 3.13 of Appendix 1 to the Pre-action Protocol for the Resolution of Clinical Disputes, the respondent is required to

disclose the applicant's healthcare records for the purpose of full investigation of the claim against the London NHS Trust for injuries and loss.

22. As the Trust responsible for Alan Smith's care during the period 1997 to 2000, the respondents are likely to have control of his healthcare records.

23. The healthcare records are documents that would be required to be disclosed under section 7 of the Data Protection Act 1998. This application is brought under section 34 (2) of the Supreme Court Act 1981 and complies with Part 31.17 of the Civil Procedure Rules.

24. The disclosure of these records is necessary in order to enable the claim to be effectively investigated and thereafter to enable me to advise my client's litigation friend whether his claim should be pursued or discontinued.

25. As the Trust responsible for Alan Smith's care during the period 1997 to 2000, the respondents are likely to have control of his healthcare records.

26. The healthcare records are documents which would be required to be disclosed under section 7 of the Data Protection Act 1998. This application is brought under section 34 (2) of the Supreme Court Act 1981 and complies with Part 31.17 of the Civil Procedure Rules.

27. The disclosure of these records is necessary in order to enable the claim to be effectively investigated and thereafter to enable me to advise my client's litigation friend whether his claim should be pursued or discontinued.

28. The application is necessitated by the respondent's unreasonable delay in disclosing these healthcare records. The respondents have failed to comply with the pre-action protocol and have failed to take all reasonable steps to comply with this obligation.

I believe that the facts stated in this witness statement are true.

Signed ....   Date ....

REF/00000001

3. Suggested Wordings for NI Claim Forms

(a) County Court claim

Brief details of claim

The claimant claims damages for personal injuries sustained and losses and expenses incurred (together with interest) as a result of negligent medical treatment by the defendant, its servants or agents, on the defendant's premises, A Hospital on or about 15 December 2006 and 23 December 2006.

Value

The claimant expects to recover less than £50,000 and more than £15,000.

(b) Fatal injury—including claimants' claim for personal injuries

Claimant

A Smith (widow and executrix of the estate of B Smith)
Address:
C Smith (a child by his mother and litigation friend A Smith)
Address:
D Smith (a child by his mother and litigation friend A Smith)
Address:

Brief details of claim

The claimants claim damages for their own personal injuries and losses (together with interest) in addition to a claim for personal injuries and losses (together with interest) pursuant to the Law Reform (Miscellaneous Provisions) Act 1934 and the Fatal Accidents Act 1976 as a result of negligent medical treatment by the defendant, their servants or agents, during the period commencing on or about 1 November 2000 until about 2005, resulting in the death of B Smith on 12 December 2005.

(c) Fatal injury—personal injury only

Brief details of claim

The claimant claims damages for his personal injuries and losses (together with interest) caused by the death of his wife, Mrs Sally Client on 3 January 2006 at Pleasantown General Hospital, as a result of acts and omissions for which the defendant has admitted liability.

(d) Birth injury claim

Brief details of claim

The claimant claims damages for personal injuries sustained and losses and expenses incurred (together with interest) as a result of negligent treatment by the defendant, its servants or agents, on the defendant's premises, A Hospital, on or about the time of his birth on 23 November 1994.

434

4. APPLICATION FOR EXTENSION OF TIME TO SERVE PROCEEDINGS

Application Notice – extension of time **You should provide this information for listing the application** 1. How do you wish to have your application dealt with a) at a hearing? b) at a telephone conference c) without a hearing? yes *complete Qs 5 and 6* 2. Give a time estimate for the hearing/conference _____(hours) _____(mins) 3. Is this agreed by all parties? Yes 4. Give dates of any trial period or fixed trial date 5. Level of judge: District Judge 6. Parties to be served: Defendant	**In the High Court of Justice, Queen's Bench Division Pleasantown District Registry**

In the High Court of Justice, Queen's Bench Division Pleasantown District Registry	
Claim No.	HQ ....
Warrant No. (if applicable)	
Claimant(s) (including ref.)	Mrs A Client
Defendant(s) (including ref.)	Pleasantown NHS Trust
Date	

Note You must complete Parts A and B, and C if applicable. Send any relevant fee and the completed application to the court with any draft order, witness statements or other evidence; and sufficient copies for service on each respondent.

Part A (1)

1. Enter your full name, or name of solicitor

I (We) Anne Advocate (on behalf of)(the claimant)

2. State clearly what order you are seeking and if possible attach a draft

intend to apply for an order (a draft of which is attached) that (2) the time for service of the Claim Form, Particulars of Claim, Schedule of Special Damages and medical evidence be extended to 1st May 2007. The court has the power to make this order under CPR Part 7.6.

<table>
<tr><td>

3. Briefly set
out why you
are seeking the
order. Include
the material
facts on which
you rely,
identifying any
rule or statutory
provision

</td><td>

because (3) the defendant has delayed in disclosing the medical records leaving insufficient time to investigate the claim and to advise as to whether it should be pursued. The defendant has consented to this application and a Consent Order is attached.

Part B
I (We)   wish to rely on:
the attached (witness statement)(affidavit)   my statement of case)

</td></tr>
<tr><td>

4. If you are
not already a
party to the
proceedings,
you must
provide an address
for service of
documents.

</td><td>

evidence in Part C in support of my application   **Yes**

</td></tr>
</table>

Signed [   ]   **Position or office held** [Solicitor]

(Applicant)('s solicitor)   (if signing on behalf
(~~'s litigation friend~~)   of firm or company)   [OX]

Part C

I (We) wish to rely on the following evidence in support of this application:

Please find attached to this application the following:

1. Relevant correspondence
2. Signed Consent Order in triplicate

This is a clinical negligence claim arising out of treatment afforded to Mrs A Client on 12th November 2003. In summary, Mrs Client attended A Hospital on 12th November 2003 after suffering a fall. It is alleged that her treating doctors at A Hospital were negligent in failing to diagnose a fracture to her tibia. She was diagnosed with a sprain. The extent of Mrs Client's injury was not recognised until she was referred back to A Hospital by her GP 7 weeks later. As a result in the delay in diagnosis the claimant has required surgery and suffered personal injuries and losses.

I was instructed by Mrs A Client in July 2006 but unfortunately difficulties were encountered in obtaining disclosure of the medical records. As a result of the defendant's failure to disclose all medical records relating to the claimant it has not been possible for our expert to complete her report on breach of duty and causation. We are not in a position to evaluate the merits of the claim. If the report is supportive we will require a report on our client's condition and prognosis before proceedings can be served. We therefore request an extension of time for service of the Claim Form, Particulars of Claim, Schedule of Special Damages and medical evidence to 1 May 2007. The defendant has agreed to this and a signed Consent Order is attached.

I have set out below the chronology of events concerning the disclosure of the medical records and attach relevant correspondence.

25.8.06	Letter requesting disclosure of medical records sent to defendant
Sept 06	Medical records received from non-defendant providers
13.10.06	Defendant chased for medical records
21.10.06	Defendant chased for medical records
01.11.06	Protective proceedings issued
20.11.06	Application issued for disclosure of medical records
12.12.06	Order for disclosure of records from defendant
20.12.06	Records received
07.01.07	Medical expert instructed
	Report expected mid February 2007

I request that the court makes an order in the terms sought.

Statement of Truth

(I believe) (xxxxxxxxxxxx) that the facts stated in Part C are true

Signed

Position or Office held

Date

Solicitor

5. CONSENT ORDER EXTENDING TIME FOR SERVICE OF PROCEEDINGS

IN THE HIGH COURT OF JUSTICE
QUEEN'S BENCH DIVISION
PLEASANTOWN DISTRICT REGISTRY   CLAIM NO: PT

BETWEEN:

MRS A Client

Claimant

-and-

PLEASANTOWN NHS TRUST

Defendant

CONSENT ORDER

Before District Judge ....sitting at Pleasantown District Registry, 2 Petersgate PLX1 1TL on ....

Upon considering the court file:

It is ordered by consent that:

1. The time for service of the claim form, particulars of claim, schedule of special damages and medical evidence be extended to 1st May 2007.

2. The defendant do pay the claimant's cost of and occasioned by this application

6. CONSENT ORDER FOR JUDGMENT ON LIABILITY AND INTERIM PAYMENT

IN THE HIGH COURT OF JUSTICE   **CLAIM NO:**
QUEEN'S BENCH DIVISION
ROYAL COURTS OF JUSTICE

BETWEEN:

> ALAN SMITH (a child by his mother and litigation friend
> Mrs B Smith)
>
> and
>
> AN NHS TRUST   Defendant

CONSENT ORDER

Before   sitting at the Royal Courts of Justice, Strand, London, WC2A 2LL on

Upon hearing Counsel for the Claimant and Counsel for the Defendant.

By Consent it is ordered:

1. Judgment is entered for the claimant for 85% of the damages, to be assessed.

2. The claimant may accept the sum of £300,000 (three hundred thousand pounds) by way of interim payment from the defendant.

3. The sum of £300,000 (three hundred thousand pounds) interim payment be paid to the claimant's solicitors by the defendant within 28 days of the date of this Order, thereafter to be transferred to the Court of Protection.

4. The defendant do pay the claimant's costs on liability on a standard basis to be assessed if not agreed, to be paid forthwith. Payment to be made within 28 days of assessment or agreement.

5. There be detailed assessment of the claimant's legal aid costs, to be paid forthwith.

6. The parties to file allocation questionnaires with proposed directions within 14 days of the date of this Order.

7. Costs in relation to quantum issues to be costs in the case.

Dated this   day of

....

Solicitor's details   Solicitor's details
Address   Address

Solicitors for the Claimant   Solicitors for the Defendant

APPENDIX 7

Website List

The sites listed below are considered to be useful or interesting to clinical negligence practitioners. The list is in no way exhaustive nor is it intended as a recommendation of these sites over and above others that provide similar information. It should be seen as a starting point for an exploration of the information available on the internet.

A. General Medical Information

Medical Conditions and Anatomy

<http://www.patient.co.uk/> (accessed 2 April 2007)

<http://www.innerbody.com/htm/body.html> (accessed 2 April 2007)

<http://www.intute.ac.uk/healthandlifesciences/medicine/> (accessed 2 April 2007)

<http://www.instantanatomy.net/> (accessed 2 April 2007)

<http://www.nhsdirect.nhs.uk/> (accessed 2 April 2007)

<http://www.brainnet.org/> (accessed 2 April 2007)

<http://www.nlm.nih.gov/medlineplus/> (accessed 2 April 2007)

<http://www.equip.nhs.uk/>(accessed 2 April 2007)

<http://www.bbc.co.uk/health/conditions/> (accessed 2 April 2007)

<http://www.netdoctor.co.uk/> (accessed 2 April 2007)

<http://www.ahaf.org/alzdis/about/AnatomyBrain.htm> (accessed 2 April 2007)

<http://www.ama-assn.org/ama/pub/category/7140.html> (accessed 2 April 2007)

<http://www.library.nhs.uk/SpecialistLibraries/> (accessed 2 April 2007)

<http://www.bnf.org/bnf/> (accessed 2 April 2007) (British National Formulary)

<http://www.pharmweb.net/> (accessed 2 April 2007)

<http://www.medinfo.co.uk/> (accessed 2 April 2007)

Medical Dictionaries

<http://www.medic8.com/MedicalDictionary.htm> (accessed 2 April 2007)

<http://www.nlm.nih.gov/medlineplus/mplusdictionary.html> (accessed 2 April 2007)

<http://www.medterms.com/script/main/hp.asp> (accessed 2 April 2007)

<http://cancerweb.ncl.ac.uk/omd/> (accessed 2 April 2007)

<http://www.medilexicon.com/> (accessed 2 April 2007)

Glossary of Medical Abbreviations

<http://www.medev.ac.uk/search/pharma_lexicon> (accessed 2 April 2007)

<http://www.rcgp.org.uk/default.aspx?page=4134> (accessed 2 April 2007)

<http://www.medilexicon.com/> (accessed 2 April 2007)

Organisations

<http://www.rcog.org.uk/> (accessed 2 April 2007) – Royal College of Obstetricians and Gynaecologists

<http://www.rcseng.ac.uk/> (accessed 2 April 2007) – Royal College of Surgeons

<http://www.rcn.org.uk/> (accessed 2 April 2007) – Royal College of Nurses

<http://www.rcm.org.uk/> (accessed 2 April 2007) – Royal College of Midwives

<http://www.rcpsych.ac.uk> (accessed 2 April 2007) – Royal College of Psychiatrists

B. SPECIFIC CONDITIONS

Strokes

<http://www.stroke.org.uk/> (accessed 2 April 2007)

<http://hcd2.bupa.co.uk/fact_sheets/html/Stroke.html> (accessed 2 April 2007)

<http://www.sol.co.uk/r/rsmacwalter/sites.html> (accessed 2 April 2007)

<http://www.equip.nhs.uk/topics/neuro/stroke.html> (accessed 2 April 2007)

<http://www.bbc.co.uk/health/conditions/stroke/> (accessed 2 April 2007)

Cancer

<http://www.cancersupport.org.uk/> (accessed 2 April 2007)

<http://www.cancerbackup.org.uk/Home> (accessed 2 April 2007)

<http://www.macmillan.org.uk/Home.aspx> (accessed 2 April 2007)

<http://www.ovacome.org.uk/Home> (accessed 2 April 2007)

<http://www.aicr.org.uk/?source=Adwords> (accessed 2 April 2007)

<http://www.cancerhelp.org.uk/> (accessed 2 April 2007)

<http://www.bbc.co.uk/health/conditions/cancer/index.shtml> (accessed 2 April 2007)

<http://www.dh.gov.uk/en/Policyandguidance/Healthandsocialcaretopics/Cancer/index.htm> (accessed 2 April 2007)

<http://www.cancerindex.org/> (accessed 2 April 2007)

<http://www.nhsdirect.nhs.uk/articles/article.aspx?articleId=72> (accessed 2 April 2007)

<http://www.breastcancercare.org.uk/> (accessed 2 April 2007)

<http://cancerweb.ncl.ac.uk/> (accessed 2 April 2007)

<http://www.breastcancer.org/> (accessed 2 April 2007)

<http://www.cancerscreening.nhs.uk/breastscreen/index.html> (accessed 2 April 2007)

<http://www.bco.org/> (accessed 2 April 2007)

<http://www.bowelcanceruk.org.uk/> (accessed 2 April 2007)

<http://www.bbc.co.uk/health/conditions/bowelcancer1.shtml> (accessed 2 April 2007)

<http://www.braintumor.org> (accessed 2 April 2007)

<http://www.braintumouraction.org.uk/info.htm> (accessed 2 April 2007)

Head and Spinal Injuries

<http://www.brainandspine.org.uk/> (accessed 2 April 2007)

<http://www.spinal.co.uk/> (accessed 2 April 2007)

<http://www.headway.org.uk/> (accessed 2 April 2007)

Cerebral Palsy

<http://www.scope.org.uk/index.shtml> (accessed 2 April 2007)

<http://www.bbc.co.uk/health/conditions/cerebralpalsy1.shtml> (accessed 2 April 2007)

<http://www.nhsdirect.nhs.uk/articles/article.aspx?articleid=93> (accessed 2 April 2007)

<http://www.mynchen.demon.co.uk/Cerebral_palsy/index.htm> (accessed 2 April 2007)

<http://www.brainwave.org.uk/general/cerebral_palsy.html> (accessed 2 April 2007)

Bladder and Bowel Conditions

<http://www.incontact.org/> (accessed 2 April 2007)

Learning Difficulties

<http://www.mencap.org.uk/> (accessed 2 April 2007)

Mental Health

<http://www.sane.org.uk/public_html/index.shtml> (accessed 2 April 2007)

<http://www.mind.org.uk/ > (accessed 2 April 2007)

Fertility

<http://www.infertilitynetworkuk.com/> (accessed 2 April 2007)

C. Freedom of Information

<http://www.nhsla.com/> (accessed 2 April 2007) – NHS Litigation Authority

<http://www.foi.gov.uk/> (accessed 2 April 2007) – Department for Constitutional Affairs

D. Complaints

<http://www.gmc-uk.org/concerns> (accessed 2 April 2007) – Against a Specific Doctor

<http://www.healthcarecommission.org.uk/homepage.cfm> (accessed 2 April 2007)

<http://www.avma.org.uk/index.asp> (accessed 2 April 2007) – Action Against Medical Accidents

<http://www.npsa.nhs.uk/> (accessed 2 April 2007) – National Patient Safety Agency

<http://www.dh.gov.uk/en/PolicyAndGuidance/OrganisationPolicy/ComplaintsPolicy/
NHSComplaintsProcedure/DH_4087428> (accessed 2 April 2007) – ICAS

<http://www.hcsu.org.uk/> (accessed 2 April 2007) – Healthcare Standards Unit

<http://www.adviceguide.org.uk/index/family_parent/health/nhs_complaints.htm>
(accessed 2 April 2007) – CAB details on NHS complaints

E. Funding

<http://www.legalservices.gov.uk/> (accessed 2 April 2007) – Community Funding

F. General and Procedural

<http://www.clinical-disputes-forum.org.uk/> (accessed 2 April 2007)

<http://www.apil.com/pdf/publicdocs/SuggestedModelDirsClinNeg-UngleyAndYoxall.
pdf> (accessed 2 April 2007) – Model Directions for Clinical Negligence cases

<http://www.dca.gov.uk/civil/procrules_fin/contents/protocols/prot_rcd.htm> (accessed 2 April
2007) – CPR Clinical Negligence Protocol

<http://www.newsquarechambers.co.uk/calculators/daycalculator.htm> (accessed 2 April
2007) – day calculator for use when drafting schedules of loss

<http://www.nhs.uk/england/aboutTheNHS/nsf/default.cmsx> (accessed 2 April 2007) –
National Standards Framework

<http://www.nice.org.uk/> (accessed 2 April 2007) – National Institute for Clinical Excellence

<http://www.nhsla.com/Publications/> (accessed 2 April 2007) – NHSLA journals and
publications

<http://www.dwp.gov.uk/lifeevent/benefits/> (accessed 2 April 2007) – Benefits Information

<http://www.the-mdu.com/> (accessed 2 April 2007)

G. Medical Experts

<http://www.jspubs.com/> (accessed 2 April 2007) – UK register of Expert Witnesses

<http://www.expertsearch.co.uk/> (accessed 2 April 2007)

<http://www.medneg.com/> (accessed 2 April 2007) – Subscription needed

<http://www.xproexperts.co.uk/> (accessed 2 April 2007)

<http://www.specialistinfo.com/> (accessed 2 April 2007) – Subscription needed

H. Alternative Dispute Resolution

<http://www.cedr.co.uk/news/resolutions/resolutions33> (accessed 2 April 2007)

<http://www.mediate.co.uk/> (accessed 11 April 2007)

I. Inquests

<http://www.inquest.gn.apc.org/> (accessed 2 April 2007)

<http://www.yourrights.org.uk/your-rights/chapters/rights-of-the-bereaved/investigations-
into-deaths/inquests.shtml> (accessed 2 April 2007)

APPENDIX 8

Further Reading in Clinical Negligence

Dow, D, and Lill, J, *Personal Injury and Clinical Negligence Litigation* (The College of Law, 2007)

Jones, M, *Medical Negligence* (3rd edn, Sweet & Maxwell, 2004)

Lewis, CJ, *Clinical Negligence* (6th edn, Tottel Publishing, 2006)

Powers, M, and Harris, N, *Clinical Negligence* (3rd edn, Tottel Publishing, 1999)

INDEX